UNSPEAKABLE

Junius Wilson

UNSPEAKABLE

The Story of
Junius Wilson

Susan Burch and Hannah Joyner

The University of
North Carolina Press
Chapel Hill

Designed by Nicole Hayward

Set in Minion by Keystone Typesetting, Inc.

Manufactured in the United States of America

This book was published with the assistance of the Z. Smith
Reynolds Fund of the University of North Carolina Press.

The paper in this book meets the guidelines for permanence
and durability of the Committee on Production Guidelines for
Book Longevity of the Council on Library Resources.

Library of Congress Cataloging-in-Publication Data
Burch, Susan.
Unspeakable : the story of Junius Wilson / Susan Burch and
Hannah Joyner.
p. cm.
Includes bibliographical references and index.
ISBN 978-0-8078-3155-7 (cloth : alk. paper)
1. Wilson, Junius, 1908–2001. 2. Deaf—North Carolina—
Greensboro—Biography. 3. African Americans—North
Carolina—Greensboro—Biography. 4. Greensboro (N.C.)—
Biography. 5. Greensboro (N.C.)—Race relations—History—
20th century. 6. Racism—Southern States—Case studies.
7. Southern States—Race relations—History—20th century.
8. People with disabilities—Abuse of—United States—Case
studies. 9. Mentally ill—Abuse of—United States—Case studies.
10. Diagnostic errors—United States—Case studies.
I. Joyner, Hannah. II. Title.
HV2534.W54B87   2007
362.4'2092—dc22
[B]   2007019400

cloth   11 10 09 08 07   5 4 3 2 1

Contents

Illustrations

UNSPEAKABLE

I am the Hope of the poor crazed beings who pine in the cells, and stalls, and cages, and waste rooms of your poor-houses. I am the Revelation of hundreds of wailing, suffering creatures, hidden in your private dwellings, and in pens and cabins—shut out, cut off from all healing influences, from all mind-restoring cares.... Could their melancholy histories be spread before you as revealed ... how promptly, how earnestly would you search out the most approved means of relief ... by ... the construction of a suitable hospital in which the restoring cares of skillfully applied physical and moral treatment should be received and in which humane and healing influences should take the place of abuse and neglect and of galling chains and loathsome dungeons.

DOROTHEA L. DIX, MEMORIAL SOLICITING A STATE HOSPITAL FOR THE PROTECTION AND CURE OF THE INSANE, SUBMITTED TO THE GENERAL ASSEMBLY OF NORTH CAROLINA, 18 NOVEMBER 1848

Introduction

IN 1990 JOHN WASSON of North Carolina's New Hanover County Department of Social Services was appointed guardian of Junius Wilson, an elderly African American patient at a mental institution in the town of Goldsboro. The patient's records revealed the story of a deaf man accused in 1925 of the attempted rape of a relative, found insane at a lunacy hearing, committed to the criminal ward of the State Hospital for the Colored Insane, and surgically castrated. Sixty-five years later, Wilson was still an inmate of the same hospital. Wasson was shocked when he discovered after reading the file and talking to staff that Junius Wilson was not insane.

J. Field Montgomery, director of Cherry Hospital in the 1990s, admitted that the institution had known at least since the early 1960s that the deaf man was not mentally ill. As Montgomery said, "You didn't have to be insane to be committed back then." The hospital also had evidence that the charges against Wilson had been dropped by 1970, which meant that he was no longer required to be incarcerated at Cherry Hospital. In spite of these revelations, the Goldsboro institution held Wilson for more than twenty additional years on the grounds that it was the most benevolent course of action. Junius Wilson had been incarcerated in an insane asylum merely because he was deaf and black; bureaucratic inertia and staff paternalism helped keep him there for sixty-five years.

What John Wasson saw as he sifted through Junius Wilson's hospital records was certainly not a typical account. But Wilson's story has much to tell historians trying to understand eugenics, deaf cultural identity, state institutions, racism, and the Jim Crow South. During his ninety-two years, Wilson experienced the effects of the racism endemic to the South. But communication difficulties evolving from his deafness isolated the young Wilson from the broader African American community and the protection (albeit limited) that this community might have afforded him.

FOR A SHORT TIME, Wilson had been a member of a different sort of community—the black deaf community. In 1916 the young boy entered the North Carolina School for the Colored Blind and Deaf in Raleigh, a state residential school and the first southern school for black deaf children. Life at a deaf school initiated Wilson into a distinctive deaf cultural identity. Interacting with deaf peers, deaf students learned to communicate primarily in sign language, shared in storytelling and deaf folklore, and created social connections.[1] But Wilson was separated from this community in 1924, when a minor infraction led to his expulsion.

At home in Castle Hayne, Wilson was no longer fully part of the local community or even his family. His misunderstood behavior was probably what prompted the apparently false rape charge against him. His inability to communicate was all that was necessary for a court to declare him legally insane and to force his incarceration at a mental institution.

Wilson's entrance into North Carolina's State Hospital for the Colored Insane in 1925 was his introduction into a community and culture that did not generally accommodate or even acknowledge his physical or cultural deafness. But as scholars of mental hospitals have demonstrated, such institutions did provide their inmates with a sense of place and identity.[2] Indeed, Wilson's integration into this environment caused his later caretakers to conclude that he could not leave it because it was his true home. Although Wilson seemed at times to suggest that he agreed, legal challenges to his incarceration were initiated on his behalf in the 1990s.

According to Marshall Smith, policies sparked by Wilson's legal challenges and other disability class action suits promised greater protection for current and future disabled inmates across the nation. As the histories of institutions such as Cherry Hospital are brought to light, various states are acknowledging forced sterilization campaigns. Efforts by psychiatric survivors and others who were the subjects of forced sterilizations represent a new wave of civil rights activism. They also point to evolving relationships between the state and society. Campaigns to acknowledge and compensate victims of eugenic programs raise thorny issues of justice that mirror other government reparations initiatives. How should a society—indeed, how can a society—make amends for past misdeeds?

TO DATE, NO SIGNIFICANT WORK—in film or in print—has examined African American deaf people's heritage and culture. Similarly "muted" from our common understanding of American history are people with mental illness and those perceived as such. Intentionally isolated, this vast population rarely receives public notice or historical study.

This book is a personal history of one man, a man first buffeted by the attitudes, prejudices, and policies of the early twentieth century and then insulated from self-determination even as these attitudes and policies evolved. It interprets twentieth-century culture, policy, and institutions both directly and through their effects on individuals, in particular Junius Wilson. It also provides evidence of attitudes and policies that are a shameful part of not only a single hospital's history but also a nation's history.

This approach has its challenges, one of which is finding information about individual lives. Wilson's personal history offers a rare opportunity to explore the history of eugenics and institutionalization from the bottom up, from the perspective of their effects on patients and inmates. Most academic studies of mental hospitals do not (one could argue that they almost *cannot*) capture the experiences of the people who work and reside in the wards and on the grounds. Nevertheless, several works provide a frame of reference to better understand Wilson's life at the Goldsboro institution. For example, Steven Noll and Peter McCandless map the evolution of southern institutions and the distinct role race played in state mental health systems.[3] Erving Goffman's pioneering sociological studies reveal the power dynamics within institutions and the potent impact of stigma on institutionalized people.[4] And Gerald Grob discusses the rise of professional psychiatric treatment against the backdrop of policy and structural changes.[5] These works, among others, have strongly influenced our understanding of the institutional context of this story.

Equally important to the development of this book are the fields of deaf history and disability history. Deaf and disability historians have long recognized the unique cultural experience of deaf people in America. These scholars point out that the meaning of disability and deafness at any given time is based more on a social construction of identity and contextual factors than on any biological reality.[6] We cautiously use terms such as "deaf culture" to describe Wilson's background and identity. His time at the deaf school clearly taught him the language of the black deaf community, evidenced by his continued use of Raleigh signs. But being part of a community means more than just sharing a language. Wilson's eight years at the school would have surrounded him with not just language but culture—a rich heritage of folklore, humor, community heroes, social opportunities, and even a strong tradition of intermarriage.[7] Unfortunately, we know relatively little about Wilson's actual identification with that cultural background, or about how he dealt with the deprivation of that cultural atmosphere for the six decades he spent at Cherry Hospital before individuals sought to provide him with some community affiliation as well as accommodation for his physical deafness.

Physical and cultural deafness were only some of the complicating aspects of Junius Wilson's life. A plethora of histories lay bare the cultural intricacies of race relations in North Carolina during Wilson's lifetime. Fitzhugh Brundage offers a portrait of the violence of race relations in the early twentieth century.[8] Glenda Gilmore, Jacquelyn Dowd Hall, and Jennifer Ritterhouse outline the complexities of racial conflict, gender, and activism in the early twentieth century.[9] Others, like Melton McLaurin and Suzanne Lebsock, offer helpful models for examining shadowed lives.[10]

Scholars often refer to Jim Crow to describe the racial caste system that pervaded the South before laws and attitudes began to correct the insidious residue of slavery and white domination. Unfettered racism charted much of Wilson's youth, from his attendance at a segregated deaf school and his family's vulnerable situation when he returned to them to his placement at a segregated mental hospital. Although many of the features of Jim Crow were dismantled by the 1970s, latent racism still permeated Wilson's treatment.

All of these scholarly studies enable us to place Wilson in a broader context and inspect more closely the ways in which race, geography, class, and policy collided to shape one deaf man's personal journey. A few other scholars have explored factors that also intersected with Wilson's life. Kathy Castle's work on cognitively disabled people in North Carolina maps both policy and lived experiences of institutionalized people.[11] Johanna Schoen studies forced and voluntary sterilization, particularly in North Carolina, illuminating the qualities that separated that state from others in the South while cogently describing the national and international forces that enabled forced sterilization, wrongful institutionalization—and, ultimately, disability civil rights activism—to thrive.[12]

Timing and place also matter. As many observers have claimed, what happened to Wilson in the 1920s would be unthinkable today. The evolution of civil rights activism, the understanding of mental illness and deafness, and the changing role of media coverage directly affected the options available to Wilson and to those who controlled many of those options.

Scholars beginning with Ulrich Phillips and W. J. Cash have argued that the

South possesses a distinct culture and history. Geography, economics, politics, religion, and race relations have contributed to a particular regional history. Location certainly mattered for Junius Wilson, who grew up near Wilmington, North Carolina, the site of a race massacre in 1898 and a region with an active Ku Klux Klan presence. Unlike his peers in the North, Wilson attended a racially segregated deaf school and later lived in a segregated mental hospital.

The Tar Heel State also had its own specific qualities. Had Wilson lived in any number of other southern states, he likely would not have attended school at all: North Carolina established the first school for black deaf and blind children in the South, while Louisiana, for example, offered no in-state educational options for such citizens until the 1930s. And the mental health system and economic-political character of North Carolina differed in important ways from its neighbors, as well.[13]

Although certain features of the state and region clearly contributed to the trajectory of Junius Wilson's life, this story uncomfortably represents larger national and even international trends. The historic racial and disability oppression detailed in this work was not isolated and, as exposés continue to reveal, has not yet been erased completely.

THE METAPHOR OF INTERSECTIONS has become a popular way for scholars to examine and discuss social and cultural history. Showing the ways that race, gender, and geographic location, for example, strongly color experiences in the South, the idea of historical intersections avoids some of the pitfalls that result from isolating singular identity factors from the mosaic that comprises the human experience.

In this story, language consistently intersects with and amplifies these factors. That the horrific events of Junius Wilson's life stemmed in large part from language barriers makes clear the power of language and our perceptions of language. Acknowledging both the individuals' experience and perception—to the extent that we can imagine or know it—and the ways that others perceived our subjects, we have intentionally chosen various terms to describe populations in this story. Inevitably these terms are fraught with political and social meaning. For example, for most of the twentieth century men and women who lived in the wards of Cherry Hospital were referred to as "insane," "mentally ill," and "patients." Many advocacy groups today might offer different labels: "psychiatric survivor," "consumer," "inmate." We employ many of these terms throughout as a way of both complicating and honoring the many experiences of people "on the inside."

Current scholars, activists, and others have engaged in rich and heated debates over significant issues such as whether *anyone* should be institutionalized, sterilized, categorized by his or her genetic composition, and educated in inclusion classrooms or in specialized segregated facilities. While it is hoped that this biography may contribute to these important dialogues, we intentionally chose not to advocate a specific perspective in these complicated matters. It is hoped that our own language choices provoke thought and perhaps reinterpretations rather than create new barriers.

ATTITUDES AND POLICIES about race, disability, and mental illness—specific to North Carolina or permeating national and international politics—are only a few of the aspects providing context for Junius Wilson's story. These and many other issues are lenses through which to view the life examined within the following pages, but they cannot answer all of the questions this story raises. Against this complex historical backdrop, Wilson more closely resembles a silhouette than a portrait. As with multitudes of institutionalized people, Wilson has remained frustratingly elusive.

The persistence of social stigma about disability and institutionalization reaches into current disability research. Many individuals like Wilson were out of sight, out of mind—and out of the traditional interpretation of history. Former and current patients, their family members, and hospital staff are often reluctant to speak about life inside the asylum. And privacy rights policies discourage research into myriad disability topics.

In order to protect inmates and patients, institutions will not release patients' records without the permission of their guardians. According to some hospital workers, staff during the first half of the twentieth century generally neglected paperwork, failing to document cases. Even when such documentation was produced initially, hospitals often did not preserve that information in a belief that such information was not important or relevant. When such source material survives at institutions, it does not always transfer to easily accessible locations. Efforts by archivists and historians to preserve historical materials often overlook institutions serving disabled people. Considerable data from previous decades and centuries has already been lost to historians, and more recent documents continue to be destroyed as institutions make room for the ever-increasing files of patients.

Even when historians can access information about institutions and their residents, limitations abound. Extant medical logs generally show a narrow, impersonal view of patients' experiences. When contemplating a biographical project, historians long for personal artifacts like diaries, letters, or drawings—items that reveal patients' own interpretations of their experiences. When these artifacts do exist, they are often the property of the institution, not of an individual or archive. Institutions have little motivation to release these artifacts to historians, especially if they shine light on policies or practices now considered shameful.

For all of these many reasons, it has been very difficult to discover Junius Wilson's own interpretations of the events, people, and circumstances of his life. The guardian of Wilson's estate, Helen Hinn, has authorized us to access his hospital records—boxes of medical and court files (dating mostly from the 1970s and after) that documented such intimate details as not only his surgical castration and psychological profiles but also his bank account status, his daily outings, and even his eating and sleeping habits.

But Wilson himself has left precious few clues—like diaries or letters—that show how he saw his life and the world around him. His life was filled with many faces, most of whom we cannot see clearly: men and women who lived on the Goldsboro campus, who greeted Wilson in the morning, who argued with him over chairs and food, who perhaps watched him as much as he gazed at them.

In order to address some of the gaps in Wilson's story, we relied heavily on oral history interviews. Many generous people shared their memories, offering detail and humanity that rarely filters through institutional reports. But even these rich sources are problematic. Familial relations presented unexpected complications. Many individuals received family titles such as "cousin" or "uncle" even though they did not share direct blood ties. We nevertheless chose to honor family definitions out of respect for cultural kinship.

Even Wilson's closest contacts could not tell us a great deal about his understanding of his world. Because of his educational background and physical deafness, Wilson had tremendous difficulty communicating with staff and fellow inmates, and they with him. During his time at the Raleigh school, Wilson was taught North Carolina's black sign language. But the interpreters and evaluators who worked with Wilson—both native speakers and scholars of this particular sign language—admitted that they usually could not fully understand him. Staff records suggest that the vast majority of employees knew no sign language at all. Although one doctor called Wilson's signs "elegant hand language," many staff referred to them as "crude gestures." Some claimed to understand Wilson completely, but when pressed they admitted that they never had full conversations with him; simple smiles and gestures (such as a thumbs-up, or rubbing the stomach to indicate hunger or a good meal) represented "complete understanding." Wilson never gave a formal interview on camera, and no one with whom we spoke could replicate with great detail any conversation shared with him. Although the men and women we interviewed generously shared real stories about Wilson's life and daily social experiences, they often revealed more about the perceptions of those around him than about Wilson's own understandings.

Others refused to discuss Wilson at all. His story is painful and embarrassing for many people. To some degree, both the hospital and his family feel responsible, or are seen by others as having been responsible, for his wrongful incarceration, isolation, and castration. Although we made efforts to contact any and all individuals familiar with Wilson's life story, some declined to participate in this project.

THIS WORK CANNOT BE a traditional biography. While any work of history can be seen as a projection of the author's perceptions and interpretations, this history is especially complicated for the authors. Although we hypothesize about Wilson's reactions and perceptions in certain cases, we note when we have done so. Out of a deep respect for Junius Wilson, and for the fact that we can never truly know him, we did not attempt a re-creation of Wilson's style of dialogue, either in general or relating to a specific event.

We are mindful that many issues separate us from our subject: racial, sexual, educational, geographical, political, and social identities make us outsiders. We are often painfully reminded that our lived experiences differ fundamentally from those of Junius Wilson. At the same time, we are equally painfully reminded that his story is our story—as both activist-researchers and as people living in America at this time. Just as John Wasson was appalled when he read Wilson's file in 1990, we felt heartbroken and angry while researching this story. The kinds of oppression, invasion, and injustice that Wilson experienced simply defy words.

Trying to narrate this story, described as a "southern Gothic" tale, has stretched our abilities as well as our own concepts of what biography can and should be. In spite of the limitations inherent in this work, we hope that there is much to learn and remember about Junius Wilson and the countless others who have lived unspeakable histories. It would be comforting to assume that the injustices perpetrated against Wilson were unique, unprecedented, and ultimately resolved. But that is not the case. Nor are those injustices completely insurmountable.

1

One Misstep (1908–1924)

> Being a minority in both caste and class, we moved about anyway on the
> hem of life, struggling to consolidate our weaknesses and hang on, or to
> creep singly up the folds of the garment.
>
> **TONI MORRISON, *THE BLUEST EYE***

IN 1910 MARY AND SIDNEY WILSON lived in a house facing a dirt road in the predominantly African American community of Castle Hayne, a rural area on the outskirts of Wilmington, North Carolina. Neighbors' homes dotted the lane. Their houses, many of which had dirt floors, were heated by fireplaces and woodstoves. Electricity and running water would not come to the community for many more years. Yards in the community were swept clean by brooms made from native grasses. Almost all of the homes were surrounded by vegetable gardens, where residents grew food for themselves and to trade with neighbors. Dirt roads connected Castle Hayne to nearby Wilmington. There were a few wagons and buggies. Most people walked wherever they needed to go. Children and adults fished and relaxed along the Cape Fear River that snaked around the town.[1]

In 1905, at the age of seventeen, Mary Wilson gave birth to her first child, a daughter whom she named Asynia.[2] Soon after, Mary apparently had another child who died shortly after birth. In 1908 she delivered her third child, this time a boy, Junius. Daughter Carrie followed in 1911. Her husband Sidney worked for the railroads as a woodcutter while Mary reared the children and tended the home. Junius's mother had grown up in Harnett County, North Carolina, the daughter of Nathaniel and Joanne Nixon Foy.[3] Before Mary was born, her father worked as a farm laborer in Pender County. Migrant work as a carpenter required Nathaniel to live apart from the family for extended periods, leaving them to manage on their own.[4] In her husband's absence, Joanne worked as a farm laborer to support Mary and her five siblings. Sidney Wilson also grew up in North Carolina. His parents likely were James and Annie, who, like the Foys and many other African Americans in the Tar Heel State, farmed the countryside.[5]

A few doors down from Mary and Sidney lived their older neighbors Arthur Smith Sr. and his wife Annie with their four sons: George, Arthur Jr., Jim, and King. In 1880 Arthur Sr. had worked with Mary's father on the farm in Pender County.[6] By 1910 Arthur Sr. and his adult sons worked alongside Sidney Wilson as woodcutters. Mary turned to Annie for advice about raising children. The families frequently gardened, collected firewood, and enjoyed free time together. Their bonds of affection and support strengthened over the years.[7]

Although the Wilsons' resources were meager, their lives must have seemed much more promising than the lives of their grandparents, who were almost certainly born into slavery. In just fifty years, their neighborhood of Castle Hayne had witnessed the enormous change from slavery to freedom. Progress in race relations was less linear; it included both profound opportunities for African Americans seen in very few areas of the South but also times of racial terror and brutal violence. Living in eastern North Carolina at the dawn of the twentieth century, Junius Wilson, his parents, and his community were the inheritors of a complicated legacy of freedom and horror.

FOR MUCH OF THE LATTER PART of the nineteenth century, Wilmington was a city of promise for African Americans. It did not start out that way. During the late antebellum period, the Cape Fear region in eastern North Carolina was one of the state's plantation districts, growing rice with the labor of enslaved African Americans. The sale of products made from pine trees—such as turpentine, tar, and rosin—served as the other main source of income for the region. Wilmington, the state's largest city at that time, was filled with commerce and industry. Although North Carolina as a whole seemed modest and middling compared to its wealthy neighbors Virginia and South Carolina, many of Wilmington's gentry laid claim to the polish and affluence of elite plantation culture.[8]

The Civil War facilitated the emancipation of more than half the population of the city of Wilmington. At the war's end, the economy came to a standstill: in addition to the loss of slave labor forces, railroad and shipping lines were badly damaged by war. At the same time, Wilmington filled with war refugees, both black and white, from around the South. Food was scarce and sanitation was inadequate. In spite of the chaos of daily living, members of the African American community began to celebrate their freedom and come together. Throughout the state, plans for economic survival and growth were charted. Political leaders began to emerge within the black community. Churches and schools were established.[9]

When the Union army began to withdraw authority from the Wilmington area, whites in the newly emerging Conservative Party (the name often used to describe southern Democrats of that era) attempted to reestablish their control over the county. In an effort to map out how planters and their former slaves would interact, they created the Black Code. The code effectively removed many of the rights that emancipation had promised African Americans. Both police and militias made sure that black citizens followed these rules. The Ku Klux Klan emerged to enforce racial subjugation. White-owned newspapers publicized the Klan, which rapidly grew in strength.[10]

In 1867, when the federal government required each southern state to adopt universal male suffrage, Conservative white elites lost not only their tenuous grip on their plantation labor force but also much of their political power. The voting population of the Lower Cape Fear region doubled as African Americans joined the rolls. Despite intimidation by the militias and the Klan, Wilmington's blacks were determined to claim their rights. In the April 1868 election, Republicans garnered more votes than the Conservatives in four of the seven Cape Fear counties. In the city of Wilmington, the large number of black citizens allowed the Republicans to receive twice as many votes as the Conservatives. Throughout the state, new opportunities arose for North Carolina's black community, sometimes created by blacks themselves and sometimes promoted by supportive whites. The Peabody Fund of Boston helped communities establish educational facilities for free schools for both white and black North Carolinians. The American Missionary Association opened a school for the state's deaf and blind African American children, and the state soon oversaw its operation. The future was awash with possibilities for African Americans and new fears for many in the white community.[11]

Wilmington's first Republican ticket did not include the name of a single African American. Soon, though, blacks not only represented the community in city government but also made up almost half of the officers of the police force. In 1869 New Hanover County elected its first African American representative to the North Carolina House. Members of the black community became barbers, restaurateurs, artisans, educators, preachers, lawyers, and physicians. Wilmington had an African American daily newspaper, the *Daily Record*. The city continued to send black legislators to represent the district in the North Carolina Assembly for decades. Many blacks regarded Wilmington as "one of the South's most successfully reconstructed cities."[12]

As the years passed by, it became clear to North Carolina's African Americans that significant change in the racial dynamics of the region would be a long battle with many setbacks and disappointments. Conservatives used techniques such as gerrymandering to dampen significantly the political voice of the states' African Americans. But in Wilmington, with its black majority, Conservative Democratic rule was never solid or stable. More than in other parts of North Carolina, Wilmington's African Americans retained some political voice. In addition, they continued to build a strong social infrastructure based on black churches, schools, and professional achievements.[13]

There were renewed hopes in the African American population of Wilmington when interracial alliances began to develop in the late 1880s. During this period, both Junius Wilson's mother's family and the Smiths moved closer to Wilmington. Black and nonelite white farmers emphasized their common concerns in order to gain more political power. In 1894 this coalition of Republicans and Populists, called the Fusion Party, was able to end twenty years of Democratic rule. By 1896 the Fusionists gained every statewide office. Interracial democracy seemed to be the way of the future.[14]

IN 1898 THE CONSERVATIVE DEMOCRATS struck back. Angered that white Populists had abandoned racial solidarity to unite with Republicans, Democratic leadership conducted a massive statewide white supremacy campaign in order to end what they called "Negro rule" and "Negro domination." The Democrats claimed the Fusion government was full of corruption and scandal.

Strategies to split the Fusion alliance were not all based on allegations of misdeeds, however. The Democrats' most successful tactic was the drawing of a fierce line between black and white citizens. Democrats suggested that Wilmington's African Americans were publicly disrespectful of whites. Extensive discussion of interracial mixing and black men's supposed interest in white women ignited flames of suspicion. From white racial fears emerged the image of the predatory and sinister black man threatening the purity of the defenseless women of the white South. Rebecca Felton of Georgia called on the white men of the South to "lynch a thousand times a week if necessary" in order to protect white women from black rapists. Her call fanned the flames of racial hatred and fear among Wilmington's whites.[15]

Alexander Manly, the editor of Wilmington's black newspaper, wrote a column in August 1898 responding to Felton and her supporters. He argued that, although true rape should not be condoned by anyone, the truth was that many accused rapists were innocent. Sexual relations between black men and white women were not by definition rape. African American men, as Manly wrote, could be "sufficiently attractive for white girls of culture and refinement to fall in love with them, as is well known to all." He continued that it was "no worse for a black man to be intimate with a white woman than for a white man to be intimate with a colored woman." The white community exploded in anger. Under headlines such as "Negro Defamer of White Women" and "A Horrid Slander of White Women," Manly's editorial was widely condemned in the white press for attacking southern white womanhood.[16]

The Democrats exploited racial tensions in order to dismantle the fragile Fusion alliance and end its progress toward interracial democracy. Alfred Waddell, a white supremacist who sought to oust the Fusion government, claimed that African Americans were inherently criminal and that white men who had betrayed their race by voting for the Fusionists were "responsible for the evils of Negro rule." He promised to protect his version of the South, even if he and his supporters had to clog the Cape Fear River with the corpses of Wilmington's blacks in order to end Fusionist rule.

The Red Shirts, a militant wing of the Democratic Party, backed up Waddell's threats by terrorizing both blacks and pro-Fusionist whites throughout the state. The Democrats, with their warning of impending race war, succeeded in almost silencing the Republicans in Wilmington and surrounding areas. By November 1898 white voters, persuaded of the dangers of black political participation, were galvanized to vote the party of white supremacy back into office. African Americans, on the other hand, avoided the polls in large numbers in order to evade bloodshed. In a city with a Republican majority of 5,000 in 1896, the Democrats won the 1898 election by 6,000 votes—a turnaround of 11,000 votes in two years.[17]

Although the Democrats had regained political power, many positions in the city government were not open for election and were still held by Republicans. The Democrats were unwilling to allow any vestiges of interracial democracy. The day after the election, a mass meeting of the city's white men approved the "Wilmington Declaration of Independence," a document that promised that blacks would no longer have any political power in the region. One of the document's resolutions explicitly condemned Manly's column and demanded that the editor leave Wilmington and cease publication of his newspaper. A committee of white citizens, appointed to carry out the declaration, called thirty-two prominent black community leaders to meet with the white committee. Waddell, head of the committee, told them they had been chosen to deliver the message to the black community and the ultimatum to Manly.

Although Manly had already closed the offices of the *Daily Record* and fled from Wilmington, a mob of as many as 2,000 heavily armed white men bent on violence gathered the next morning. The men marched to Manly's office, smashed his furniture, poured kerosene over the floors and walls, and lit it afire. This was just the beginning of a day of violence in the city. Although many

African American citizens fled to avoid bloodshed, others organized themselves for retaliation. When the white militia met the blacks, shots rang out. A white man fell. Then six black men fell during the heavy fire that followed. For the next hours, gunfire could be heard throughout the city. The white vigilantes moved into the poor black sections of town to "hunt niggers." Many African Americans left their homes to hide in the woods, where the mob could not find them. One witness reported the murder of an African American deaf man, shot by the mob when he did not hear and thus failed to respond to the white mob's order to halt.[18]

Newspapers varied tremendously in their reporting of the death toll. One paper estimated that nine people had been killed, while another guessed sixteen. Waddell himself suggested that about twenty blacks were shot to death. Some witnesses claimed that more than 100 of the city's African Americans were murdered. Many people told stories about the Cape Fear River being "choked" by black bodies.

Whatever the truth about the death toll, no one questioned the fact that black political power had ended in Wilmington. The mayor, city aldermen, and the entire police force resigned. Democrats took over their positions. Alfred Waddell was unanimously elected by the new board of aldermen to be Wilmington's mayor. The Democrats passed new regulations—such as the grandfather clause, poll taxes, and literacy tests—that severely curtailed black voting. Soon, following the Supreme Court's legalization of enforced racial separation in *Plessy v. Ferguson*, North Carolina passed extensive segregation ordinances that peppered the state with signs reading "For Colored" or "Whites Only."[19]

Many African American leaders and white Republicans were banished from the city, ordered by the Democrats to march to the train station along a route of jeers and bayonets. Hundreds of black citizens who were not expelled moved away as quickly as they could. The city lost its black majority. Wilmington was no longer a mecca for African Americans, but a place to be feared by them.

CASTLE HAYNE WAS SLIGHTLY out of sight of Wilmington, but never fully out of its reach. For years, residents of Castle Hayne looked to Wilmington as a place of possibility and opportunity. Now, however, their proximity to the city seemed dangerous. News of the riot surely spread like wildfire through the predominantly African American town and other local black communities. Although Mary and Sidney Wilson were still young when the riot occurred, their families as well as the Smith family must have heard accounts of the Cape Fear River clogged with dead bodies.[20] Perhaps people fleeing from the city shared their houses or camped in their fields. Perhaps they even knew people who were shot, or met their grieving families. Even after the violence had ended, the Wilmington Race Riot could not have been far from their thoughts. The lingering threat of destruction would have been palpable even for young Mary.

The aftermath of the Wilmington riot was devastating to the city's African Americans. Jim Crow regulations emerged, which put southern blacks in a new kind of shackles. Rather than feeling an expanding sense of power and pride, the residents of Castle Hayne must have felt besieged or even conquered. But the Wilmington area was not alone. Racial tensions were inflamed across the nation. Although Wilmington was one of the first race riots following Reconstruction, many cities followed. In 1900 violence erupted in New Orleans and New York. Springfield, Ohio, rioted in 1904 and Springfield, Illinois, in 1907. Georgia gubernatorial candidate Hoke Smith expressed his willingness to "imitate Wilmington" in his efforts to squelch African American advancement. Chicago's riot broke out in 1905. In 1906 Atlanta followed suit. Although each city's riot was unique, most followed a pattern of black achievements, white feelings of resentment, some catalyst such as an incident bringing up sexual fears, and then a brutal response by whites.[21] As the news of these other riots and their similarities to the Wilmington massacre reached the residents of the city and its environs, memories of the city's own revolution must have thundered in their hearts.

Massacres and riots were only one expression of violent racial tensions throughout the nation during the early twentieth century. Lynching was another. Earlier in 1898 there had been an incident in Lake City, South Carolina, just south of Wilmington. The home of the black postmaster had been set afire by angry whites. When the postmaster and his family tried to escape the flames, a mob opened fire with their guns, killing the postmaster and his infant child and severely wounding several other family members. Motivated by fears of black achievements and uncontrolled black sexuality, lynching expressed the white community's desire to right the social order. Although the number of white participants and the number of black deaths in any one incident were generally much lower than the numbers appearing in riot statistics, lynch law nevertheless terrorized African Americans. The uncertainty of who made up the mobs meant that anyone in the white community might be a lyncher. In addition, anyone accused of a crime was at risk. Since the mob would act without awaiting the results of a trial, anyone could become the victim of a lynch mob. As African American crusader Ida B. Wells laid bare in works like *Southern Horrors* and *A Red Record*, hundreds of black men and women died at the hands of vigilante mobs during the 1890s.[22] One historian estimates that a person was lynched every other day between 1889 and 1899.[23]

News of riots and lynchings reverberated for decades. For example, a few months before the Wilmington Race Riot, Emma Hartsell, a young white girl, was raped and murdered in Concord, North Carolina. The two men accused of the crime, Tom Johnson and Joe Kizer, were caught by a mob. A ballad about the lynching, sung for many generations after the deaths, gives an account of what happened next:

> They got to town by half past seven
> Their necks were broken before eleven.
> The people there were a sight to see
> They hung them to a dogwood tree.

The mob then riddled the men's bodies with bullets. Near the end of the song was a threat to all African American listeners:

> And one thing more my song does lack
> I forgot to say the men were black.[24]

For decades after the Wilmington riot, African Americans justifiably feared severe reprisals for anything perceived by whites to be a subversion of the racial hierarchy of Jim Crow society. Young black men were frequently the target of white fear and anger. One misstep could bring incarceration or even death to the individual and ruin to his or her family. Edgar Allen Hunt, a child at the time of the 1898 massacre, later recounted that his father repeatedly "told us what to expect, how to act, how to stay away from them [white people]. Don't trust them. I mean he gave us the whole ball of wax having been in the race riot seeing some things. So, coming up, we kind of knew what we were supposed to do." Parents' stories and lessons provided the next generation of Africans Americans with resources to survive Jim Crow.[25]

AFTER THE FIRST DECADE of the twentieth century drew to a close, both the Smiths and the Wilsons had reasons to feel hopeful. Although each had suffered the loss of infants, now their families were expanding. The couples had their own homes in a small but tight-knit community. The lumber industry provided Sidney, Arthur Sr., and eventually Arthur's sons with work. Focusing on the future but mindful of the past, the families on Blue Clay Road worked assiduously to eke out a living and to provide a better future for their children.[26]

Some time probably passed before Mary and Sidney realized that their young son Junius was deaf. It is not clear when or why he lost his hearing. Perhaps he was born deaf. His birth at home would not have been attended by a doctor, but even if it had been, a physician could not have made a diagnosis of deafness in a newborn. Junius possibly lost his hearing as a toddler. As a young child, he contracted several illnesses: measles, whooping cough, and scarlet fever.[27] All could result in deafness; scarlet fever was an especially common cause of deafness in children during this time. As a deaf youngster, Junius could not respond to calls, but unintended vibrations such as doors opening or pots hitting the floor could draw his attention, masking his inability to hear. Confusion might have escalated to frustration as Mary and Sidney tried to teach their child words and appropriate behavior. Without language, Junius might have misinterpreted his parents' expressions of anger, perhaps thinking they were amusing. Both child and parents likely felt helpless in the face of this invisible barrier to communication. Mary might have doubted her abilities as a mother or felt guilty about her son's disability. Perhaps she grieved, worrying that her son could never grow up to be independent, to marry and have a family, to be "a man." Many mothers of deaf children become especially protective of their deaf offspring, often leading to conflicts with other family members.[28]

Tensions within the Wilson household escalated. Eventually, Sidney left the family, ultimately moving to Georgia and remarrying.[29] Alone with three children, Mary leaned heavily on the Smiths. Now an independent young man, Arthur Smith Jr. tried to help his friend by counseling Mary and supporting her financially. Junius was especially difficult to manage since he was now able to walk and run but could not heed the warning calls of concerned adults. As the deaf boy matured, Junius's inability to convey his needs and questions—and his inability to understand the rules of Jim Crow society—might have raised several serious concerns for Mary and the Smith family: How do you teach a deaf child? What was he capable of becoming? How do you keep him safe? How do you keep the rest of the family safe?

THE ECHOES OF WILMINGTON resonated with a new voice during Junius's childhood. Thomas Dixon, a native of North Carolina, published *The Leopard's Spots* in 1902. The first book in a trilogy about race relations, *The Leopard's Spots* interpreted the events of Wilmington and Jim Crow ideology through a fictional lens. Dixon portrays a thinly veiled Wilmington as a community overwhelmed by the corrupt rule of African American legislators. Like preriot Wilmington, the fictional town has a newspaper owned and run by a black man. Dixon portrays a town where young blacks would no longer step aside to allow whites to pass on the sidewalks. Dixon's main character, Charles Gaston, fears "they could not be overthrown short of a political earthquake." The earthquake arrives soon enough. In a fictional mimicry of the Emma Hartsell rape and murder that preceded the actual Wilmington riot, Dixon tells of the rape and murder of young Flora Camp. After her body is found, a white mob lynches an African American. The man, protesting his innocence the whole time, is doused with oil and set afire. After Gaston is accused of causing the death of a black man, a mob of 500 African Americans threatens his life. As

Dixon writes, "This event was the last straw that broke the camel's back." And then: "The incendiary organ of the Negroes, a newspaper that had been noted for its virulent spirit of race hatred, had published an editorial defaming the virtue of the white women of the community." At this point in the novel, Gaston becomes Alfred Waddell, leading the whites of Wilmington into battle against the insolence and arrogance of the black community. After the office of the "Negro paper" was burned down and the editor put on a northbound train, shots rang out all over the city until all resisting blacks were driven into the surrounding woods.[30]

Dixon's second novel was even more inflammatory. *The Clansman*, published in 1905, tells the story of a white woman trying to escape a black rapist in the years immediately following the Civil War. As he did in his first novel, Dixon argued that the ultimate goal of any free African American was sexual intercourse with elite white women. Dixon believed that by attempting to have sexual relations with white women, African Americans were trying to convey two things: in addition to expressing the social equality of blacks and whites, sex with white women was symbolic rape of former slave masters. Any real-life efforts by African Americans to fight for racial justice brought white fears of social equality and the end of their privileged status. *The Clansman* intensified fears of "the black brute." Dixon's prose describes "the bestial figure of a negro —his huge black hand plainly defined—the upper part of the face is dim, as if obscured by a gray mist of dawn—but the massive jaws and lips are clear." The image is literally burned into the eyes of his victim, a "fire-etched record of the crime" on the "retina of these dead eyes the image of this devil." Only the Klan could respond to such terror.[31]

With such powerful visual imagery, it is no wonder that *The Clansman* was made into a movie. When the film was released in 1915 under the title *The Birth of a Nation,* it became by far the largest-grossing movie as well as one the most complex movies to date. Dixon's script combined with the filmmaking genius of D. W. Griffith to present a horrifying portrayal of Reconstruction to viewers. Dixon and Griffith sought to bolster their historical arguments by citing Woodrow Wilson's *A History of the American People.* Wilson had attended graduate school with Dixon at Johns Hopkins.[32]

AS WILMINGTON'S WHITE CITIZENS flocked to see the film that President Wilson called "history writ in lightning," Junius Wilson's family enrolled the boy at the residential North Carolina School for the Colored Blind and Deaf in Raleigh. Mary realized that her deaf son might gain opportunities there that his hearing peers in Castle Hayne might not enjoy.[33] Potentially, he could attend school longer than his hearing neighbors. He would receive vocational training as well as academic education. This training could enhance his chances of becoming independent—from family support as well as from state support—when he reached adulthood. The likelihood that Junius would become more literate than his mother seemed high. The school for African American deaf children also provided food, shelter, and clothing for enrolled students, easing the Wilson family's financial burden. Since the deaf boy was too young to help them support the family, the Smith men might have encouraged Mary to enroll Junius as soon as possible.

With few other options, Mary had to trust that sending Junius away to Raleigh was best for everyone. Given the family's complex and vulnerable situation in Castle Hayne, the boy's removal probably was a relief. Still, Mary, who had already lost one child, must have grieved the loss of Junius as he moved to the residential school. Having spent seven years nurturing and protecting him, Junius's mother now had to trust strangers to raise her child. Would they take good care of him? Because she could not communicate complex thoughts to her deaf son, Mary was unable to explain to Junius where he would be going or when he would be coming back to the family. Would he even understand that he was being sent to school and not being taken away permanently? Her sense of helplessness and loss were compounded by their lack of communication.

Since Junius had no clear way to communicate with strangers, sending the eight-year-old boy alone on the train to Raleigh seemed impractical. Annie Smith, who could read and write, accompanied him to the school. When they arrived, she filled out paperwork to admit Junius to the school. Although she listed Mary and Sidney as the boy's mother and father, she wrote that the person to contact for information or in the case of an emergency was herself. The postbox the school was to use belonged to her husband Arthur. Officially, the school considered Annie and Arthur Smith Sr. as Junius Wilson's guardians.

The first day at the school in January 1916 must have bewildered Junius. Lacking any formal language—written or signed—he could not understand why he was being taken away from his family. Nor could he appreciate the nature of his new setting. The boy had never attended school before. Classrooms and dormitories seemed alien and intimidating. The quick sign language flashing on his classmates' fingers might have fascinated him but, unable to comprehend, he might have misinterpreted their long gazes and touches, common features of deaf communication, as threatening advances. Months probably passed before Junius realized that his family would not be coming any day to get him and that the school was to be his home for the academic year.[34]

North Carolina School for the Colored Blind and Deaf
(Courtesy of Gallaudet University Archives)

Although the transition must have been difficult, Wilson eventually learned his way around, made friends, began to learn how to communicate more effectively, and settled in.

THE NORTH CAROLINA SCHOOL for the Colored Blind and Deaf, founded in 1868, was the first separate school for African American deaf children in the United States. The American Missionary Association provided the initial building on South Bloodworth Avenue, a street in the southern section of Raleigh. Several years later, North Carolina's state legislature provided new brick buildings. In 1907 the state mandated that all deaf children eight to twenty-one years of age attend school. In accordance with the law, Junius was sent to the residential program as soon as he was of age.[35]

In spite of the inherent limitations caused by Jim Crow's racial caste system, the Raleigh school enjoyed distinctive assets in its early decades. Its superintendent from 1896 to 1918 was John E. Ray, an experienced educator of the deaf. Beloved by the white deaf community, Ray earned praise as a "clear and forcible sign maker" and as an adept interpreter.[36] An advocate of deaf teachers and signed communication, Ray employed several deaf faculty members. The Tillinghast brothers, Thomas and David, master signers and leaders in the white deaf world, both taught at the North Carolina school. David left in the early 1890s, when the legislature established a new white deaf school in Morganton, but Thomas stayed on, working with black deaf students for another decade.[37]

Two black deaf faculty, both northerners, also joined the school. Blanche Wilkins graduated from the Minnesota School for the Deaf in 1893. She joined the literary department at the North Carolina school in 1895 and became the wife of the hearing African American principal, Charles N. Williams, in 1899.[38] Thomas Flowers graduated from the Pennsylvania School for the Deaf. Barred from Gallaudet College in Washington, D.C., because of his race, Flowers attended Howard University before accepting a position at the Raleigh school. Committed to the development of deaf education, particularly African American deaf education, Flowers actively participated in professional conferences for instructors of the deaf. In 1914 he presented a paper titled "The Colored Deaf," in which he underscored the parental role educators filled for deaf children. Emphasizing that deaf children looked to teachers for "kindness, gentleness, and sympathy," Flowers emphasized to his colleagues that a deaf student's "success in life depends entirely upon your encouragement and training during his school career."[39]

Highly educated deaf instructors of both races presented students at the Bloodworth Avenue school with cultural and racial role models unavailable elsewhere. Their contributions even provided some with the skills to challenge Jim Crow. One exceptional alumnus of the school, Roger Demosthenes O'Kelly, attended nearby Shaw University and in 1912 successfully received a degree from Yale Law School. O'Kelly was the only black deaf lawyer in America at the time.[40]

By the time of Junius Wilson's admission, the school had changed. Thomas Tillinghast retired from the school; Blanche Williams, widowed in 1907, eventually took her children north. By 1916 Flowers joined Williams in Chicago, where they married and participated in missionary work.[41] O'Kelly replaced Flowers for a year, then he, too, left.[42] National deaf pedagogical trends discouraged the hiring of new deaf faculty. By the turn of the century, the rise of oralism (the teaching of speech and lip-reading) motivated schools across the country to replace deaf teachers with hearing instructors who would speak to students rather than sign with them. By the end of the First World War, the percentage of deaf instructors employed throughout the nation dropped to roughly 20 percent. Deaf African Americans rarely graduated from deaf institutions and almost none found jobs as educators, either in the North or South. As oralism spread, the opportunities for exceptional black deaf teachers disappeared almost entirely.[43]

Ray died in 1918 and was replaced as superintendent by Gustavus Ernest Lineberry. Neither the new superintendent nor the principal knew sign language fluently. Lineberry steered the school towards oral policies, restricting the use of sign language inside the classroom. Few of the hearing teachers had facility in sign language. He firmly closed the door to deaf faculty.[44]

According to an alumnus of the school, Lineberry was a "Joseph with a coat of many colors." His letters to parents of students were condescending, and many people thought of Lineberry as hard and dictatorial.[45] He was also a product of the racial thinking of the time. Although he was an outspoken advocate for expanded provisions to his schools, Lineberry invested much more in the blind program for white students than he did in the deaf and blind program for black students. A teacher remarked that Lineberry believed "that blacks should be kept in their places and that vocational training took priority over developing academic excellence and scholarship. During his frequent visits to the campus, his demeanor toward the faculty and students was one of plantation owner to overseers and, if not slaves, the next small step up."[46]

Training offered at the school during Lineberry's tenure reflected his priorities and outlook. While state annual reports noted that North Carolina deaf and blind schools provided a rigorous curriculum "consisting of spelling, reading, writing, arithmetic, higher mathematics, geography, grammar, the sciences, kindergarten training, and vocal and instrumental music," it appears that in actuality, the colored departments lagged far behind their white counterparts.[47] The school emphasized vocational education. Racist expectations of African American pupils' low mental capacities and career potential led Lineberry, as well as administrators at other southern black schools, to emphasize the physical abilities of the pupils. In other words, they encouraged vocational work over traditional classroom work.[48]

In principle, vocational training promoted independence, allowing deaf adults to support themselves financially and relieving both their families and the state from long-term economic burdens. At the North Carolina school, black deaf boys were taught shoe repairing, carpentry, and cabinetmaking, along with dairy work.[49] These particular skills required little interaction among workers, solving the common communication problems for deaf adults seeking jobs. In practical terms, vocational training especially appealed to superintendents because it kept students busy. Without sports teams or other social outlets for students, schools needed to distract their wards during the long daytime hours. Also, vocational programs saved the school money as students produced furniture, food, and clothing as part of their training. A blind peer of Wilson's claimed that "all 'the Old Man' [Mr. Lineberry] wanted was to see us work." He continued, " 'The Old Man' campaigned for a new campus [in 1929] only because the [Raleigh] fire department was giving him trouble about the conditions of the building, and because the new site being considered had a farm—more work for us."[50]

Frustrated faculty and administrators complained about the academic structure of the school. Some lamented the lack of classroom differentiation. Thomas Flowers had already noted in 1914 that "the matter of poor classification and lack of grading according to mentality is a great drawback to the work." He continued, "The large and miscellaneous classes, poorly grouped, containing all sizes and ages, and oftentimes with no brain force" did not help matters.[51] Other faculty and staff complained that many students did not have the intellectual power to succeed in school. By 1914 school regulations allowed administrators to discharge "imbeciles" and those of "unsound" mind. Lineberry regularly invoked this clause, commonly judging students "feebleminded" in their expulsion papers.[52] As late as 1932, the North Carolina institution did not graduate a single student.

THE FACT THAT THE new generation of teachers did not understand much about deafness had significant linguistic and cultural consequences. Since the early 1800s, deaf residential schools represented the birthplace of deaf culture. In these environments, young deaf people and deaf adults, primarily white, shared a codified language of signs: American Sign Language, or ASL. From this intergenerational linguistic experience, a culture flourished. By the 1900s, black deaf children in the South rarely had such adult deaf role models or a consistent means to transmit a codified sign language. For many years, North Carolina had been the exception. But by the late 1910s, children at the Raleigh school, no longer exposed to signing deaf adults, crafted and transmitted their own signed language. In a reversal of roles, the students taught sign language to the hearing teachers at their schools. This dialect became known to many as "Black Signs," but the label does not capture the linguistic complexity of the situation. While ASL in white residential schools across the nation contained regional differences, Black Signs could vary dramatically between different states' segregated schools. As interpreters in the South have noted, without prior exposure to "Raleigh signs"—the name given the sign language developed by students at the North Carolina School for the Colored Blind and Deaf in Raleigh—or other Black Signs dialects, it is virtually impossible to understand the language, even if one is fluent in ASL.[53]

Jim Crow had specific linguistic ramifications. When the white deaf school relocated to Morganton, opportunities for black students to see white deaf children signing, or to have white deaf alumni as teachers, disappeared. Physical isolation, both from white schools and other black schools, meant that

Boy's dormitory, North Carolina School for the Colored Blind and Deaf
(Courtesy of Gallaudet University Archives)

Raleigh's black students created communication systems truly accessible only to their immediate community. The underfunded North Carolina school offered no public speaking or theatre performances, venues that traditionally promoted stylized and articulate signing. Even interpreted church services, popular during Ray's administration, seem to have ended when Lineberry took over. In contrast to the white experience, local black deaf communities also were denied close affiliation with the school. Consequently, Black Signs at the Raleigh school evolved independently, shaped more by students' creativity and immediate need to express basic ideas than by educated adults attuned to the rich and deep possibilities of visual language.

Junius, like his classmates, was unaware of the differences in sign languages. As Mary Wright, a student at the school a decade after Wilson, recalled, "I later learned that our signs were different, but at the time, I was not aware of the difference because we did not have any contact with the white deaf students" educated in the western part of the state.[54] As Junius gained language through Raleigh signs, his primary mode of communication was not readily understandable to deaf people outside his school, be they white or black. And of course, Raleigh signs were almost completely ineffective in communicating with hearing people.[55]

Raleigh signs did provide Wilson, who could not vocalize articulately, with a means of communication with his peers. The school gave Wilson both a community and a cultural identity—that of a black deaf North Carolinian. For roughly eight years, the school served as Junius's primary home and community. He matured from a child into a young man there. Junius learned that deafness was normal, at least within the school walls. He became aware that isolation and barriers reigned in the outside world but not in his own deaf community. Through Raleigh signs, Junius not only learned broad concepts but playful slang and visual humor. Merely by watching his peers, he could appreciate the value of close physical proximity and direct eye contact for easier communication. He came to understand the written and manual (signed) alphabet.

Junius Wilson also learned his name. Following deaf cultural traditions, his friends created a sign name for him. Something akin to nicknames, deaf name-signs usually embodied physical or personality traits within a regular sign.[56] Wilson's name sign was the initial *J* signed on the middle of the chest. The hand movement of his sign name mimicked the sign language word for "happiness," indicating that he might have been playful and enthusiastic in his new home. The placement on his body also mimicked the formal sign for "pride"; Junius likely puffed out his chest as he introduced himself.

While Junius Wilson's academic ability remains unknown, he apparently demonstrated enough skill and obedience to remain at the school for roughly eight years, despite the fact that many of his peers left sooner either because of academic dismissal or because of behavioral issues. Despite his schooling, documents suggest that Wilson was barely literate.[57]

Among deaf people, Wilson's restricted literacy mattered little. At the school, students learned the importance of easy signed communication. Along with his peers, Wilson embraced cultural deafness, including aspects of that culture that often made hearing people uneasy: gaining attention by touching each other, waving arms widely, and hollering to hard of hearing friends so they would turn heads and eyes to catch ensuing signs. Students at the North Carolina school spent most of their time together signing with one another, telling jokes and stories, informally educating one another.[58] Despite limited formal educational opportunities, the pupils galvanized a common identity and a sense of belonging, a sense of home.

JUNIUS'S STUDENT RECORDS offer conflicting information about his attendance over the years. A train ticket from Castle Hayne to the school in 1918 suggests that he returned to Raleigh for the fall term, but other forms announce that he was "out" during much of that academic year. It is unclear why Wilson was not enrolled in classes. The institution had not dismissed Wilson; nor had he finished his education. The ten-year-old boy had had only two years of schooling, enough to provide him with sign language skills but not much else.[59]

Various factors might have motivated Wilson's temporary removal from the school. Perhaps the Spanish flu pandemic worried Junius's mother. By October 1918, nearly 200,000 Americans had fallen victim to the disease. That same month, the city of Charlotte was quarantined, and many soldiers at Fort Greene fell ill. Millions around the world died from the flu by the beginning of 1919. Mary and her family almost certainly knew people who had perished from the deadly virus. Students in residential institutions were especially vulnerable to the spread of infectious diseases, and some students from the Raleigh school had already died.[60] Junius's mother might have preferred to keep her son at home under her own care.

Perhaps Mary, recently remarried, wanted her family together and felt that with her additional resources she would be able to parent Junius in her own home. Such an attempt at family life might have been more complex than she had imagined. Junius had to become accustomed to his new stepfather, Henry Clark, a man much older than his own father and totally unaccustomed to dealing with deaf people. No one in the little town knew Raleigh signs, the language that had enabled him to communicate freely for the first time in his life. Surely Junius became frustrated, unable to be fully himself even among his kin.[61]

Whenever he was home, Junius likely did small chores and followed his young sister Carrie around with the other little ones. Still too young to be of significant help, Junius would not be able to join the men cutting lumber for the railroad. World War I rationing and demobilization of troops created tensions in nearby cities. Many blacks felt concerned about another violent outburst. Focusing on home and security, Mary and her neighbors the Smiths might have wanted the children close to the household during this time. Young Junius was capable of antagonizing one of the white inhabitants of Castle Hayne and not even realizing his indiscretion. Such an act could endanger the entire family. Mary, realizing this threat, would have sought to avoid such a confrontation.

For Junius, the efforts to keep him safe might have felt especially restricting. Away at school, the young boy surely missed his family and the recreation he enjoyed along the river in Castle Hayne.[62] But when he left the Raleigh campus, his loneliness likely grew even deeper. Deaf children commonly feel ambivalent when they return to their biological families after extended time at residential schools. Junius missed his new friends, his new language, his new cultural community—in short, his new home.[63]

During the summer of 1919, before Junius returned to Raleigh as a pupil, a fresh series of race riots called the Red Summer spread like wildfire across the nation. Between April and October, more than two dozen towns and cities in both the North and South erupted in violence. Diverse factors fueled the outbreaks of Red Summer, including racism, xenophobia, a high unemployment rate, and widespread fears of communism and treason against the United States. The first major riot occurred in Charleston, South Carolina, a city just south of Wilmington and in many ways similar to it. Although Wilmington did not riot during that summer, concerns about racial violence were heightened both for the city's blacks and its white residents. In a time of such explicit danger, Junius's presence in the family could not have been comfortable. Perhaps his mother was relieved when her son returned to Raleigh in September 1920.[64]

WHEN WILSON RETURNED TO SCHOOL, his peers probably greeted him with hugs or pats and likely peppered him with questions, swapping stories about their time apart. It would be relatively easy for him to reenter the fold of this tight-knit deaf community. As the years passed, he became one of the older students in the school. New students probably looked up to the young man. Conceivably, he became one of the storytellers and informal mentors. As Junius watched peers and older classmates leave the school, he might have considered his own prospects for life after school.

In Raleigh, one annual event united the black deaf community with the hearing African American world: the Negro State Fair. Because of North Carolina's strong agricultural base, both county and state fairs were ubiquitous. Since the Negro State Fair's founding in 1879, African American communities flocked to the festival and celebrated the achievements of their race. As with other fairs, the Negro State Fair was filled with contests for the best livestock, produce, canning, and household exhibits. Young boys and girls displayed their wares from vocational programs. They also challenged their peers in athletic events. Couples and groups danced to folk music. Families wandered the exhibits and entertainment booths, taking in the mixed smells and sights. Young and old alike crowded around the fields to watch horse and buggy races.[65] Politicians stumped their party's line to whomever would listen. At night, the fair thrilled bystanders with firework displays. In the Jim Crow South, events such as the Negro State Fair were especially important to African Americans. The fair was an opportunity to celebrate on a large scale and to demonstrate their prowess as skilled farmers and laborers. Fundamentally, fairs promoted a sense of community pride.

For students at the black deaf school, the Negro State Fair represented one of the highly anticipated opportunities to leave campus as a group and intermingle with hearing African Americans in town. For some children, the fair was their first and only opportunity to see exotic circus animals and recent inventions, such as new plowing machines. Older students who had already attended one of the annual pageants likely told stories to newcomers at the school, spinning tales of adventure and games unimaginable to deaf youth from the rural South. Since the Negro State Fair in Raleigh occurred in late September or October, the deaf schoolchildren would wait with anticipation during the first month of school for their annual field trip.

The carnival atmosphere of the fair overwhelmed some students. Flashing hands asked for explanation or confirmation of the unusual visions before them. Probably, deaf students wandered the grounds in tight groups for fear of losing sight of, and thus all contact with, their friends. In the crush of people, it would be easy to become separated from one another. Unable to hear teachers call out, a deaf student could quickly become distracted and lost.

Junius likely attended the fair a few times as a student at the North Carolina School for the Colored Blind and Deaf. By 1924, when he was sixteen years old, he might have even been one of the students who spun stories about carnival food, agricultural contests, horse races, and parades to prepare younger pupils for the experience. But this year the fair would be different for Junius. Wilson remained at the fair long after his classmates returned to the institution. He had "slipped away while at the fair and stayed 2 nights and 1 day."[66]

It is unclear how Junius separated from his classmates during the field trip to the fair. Perhaps he considered his escapade for months. Knowing that the fair was coming to town, the deaf teenager might have calculated a way to extend his visit. Perhaps he just took advantage of a chance to slip away from his peers or became separated accidentally. But Junius could have easily rejoined his classmates that evening rather than two days later. Wilson likely had attended the fair often enough to know how to return to the school. Even if he had trouble finding his way, any adult in Raleigh would have assumed he belonged at the institution and helped steer him back there. Whether or not Junius intended to separate from his classmates, he intended to stay for a little while.[67]

The fair at night presented an exciting and exotic world to all its spectators. Fireworks lit up the night sky with unexpected brilliance, a visual display of flashing colorful explosions fully accessible to a deaf person. The pounding explosions vibrated and thundered in his body. For the young man raised in the sheltered environment of the residential deaf school, the fair was a feast for the senses. The flashing movements of the amusement rides, the odors of the stables, and the smells of carnival foods were exhilarating and liberating. Even decades later, Wilson grew animated describing the fair. As an old man, he mimicked the elephant's large swaying trunk and lumbering walk to all who

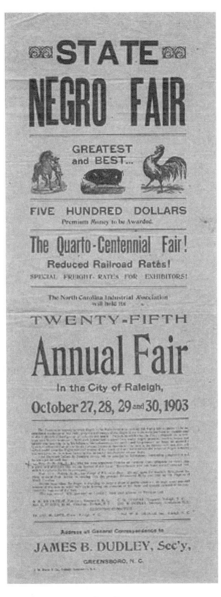

Negro State Fair advertisement

tried to communicate with him.[68] Wandering alone for hours among the throngs of people at the fair that first night away, the young Wilson might have felt simultaneously lost and free: his deafness would have gone unnoticed and his rebellion undetected. The sixteen-year-old young man possibly imagined that after finishing school, he would be able to visit fairs as often as he wished. Wilson's indiscretion appears to be less a deliberate rejection of the North Carolina school than a temporary escape to excitement and adventure.[69]

School administrators saw Wilson's act differently. Lineberry and others certainly believed that the escapade was deliberate and intentional. They interpreted Junius's disappearance as a blatant act of disobedience. The deaf boy demonstrated independence rather than submission. He challenged the white superintendent's authority and made the school look irresponsible. When Junius returned to the institution, the administration chose to expel him. Wilson's act caused particular consternation among the administration: of the roughly fifty dismissal files found in the school's records, his is the only one that contained an explicit reason for dismissal. It was made clear to the boy that he would be severely punished for his misbehavior, and the memory of that threat stayed with him into old age.[70]

The deaf boy's tenure at the North Carolina school had ended, and with it his ties to the black deaf community that had given him a cultural identity and a language. Wilson's brief escape to the carnival cost him his place at the school and sent him back to his family in Castle Hayne. He would soon find out that the community of his birth was no longer home.[71]

2

From One Institution to Another (1924–1931)

If a state is free of political corruption in the state hospital system and has
trustworthy superintendents as is true in North Carolina, the danger of
holding "the wrong person" in a state hospital is very remote.

STUDY OF MENTAL HEALTH IN NORTH CAROLINA (1937)

THE BIRTH OF A NATION, the film adaptation of Thomas Dixon's race novel *The Clansman*, opened nationally in 1915. Glorifying slavery as a needed system that kept otherwise violent African Americans under white control and protection, the film argued that emancipation and Reconstruction had fomented chaos. Black men released from bondage were portrayed as beasts that would destroy both white families and southern civilization as a whole. Across the silver screen, Republican politicians—the minions of black rule—brought about years of misery, corruption, and regression. Miscegenation, according to the film, was the ultimate goal of the black legislators. And when miscegenation could not be carried out by legal means, violence and rape could accomplish that same end. Film images of black brutes attempting to violate white women frightened and enraged white audiences throughout the nation. The savior of southern white women from rapists, and the white South in general from the "black menace," was the Ku Klux Klan. One black man who threatened a white woman in the film was found guilty at an extralegal trial held by the Klan. In the original version of the film, his punishment was castration. After the first few showings, the punishment was replaced: the man was lynched.[1]

D. W. Griffith's film was a powerful representation of widespread deepening class and racial tensions. Fueled by the message of *The Birth of a Nation*, crowds rioted in major urban areas such as Boston and Philadelphia. In Wilmington, racial tensions were exacerbated. The film served as a recruitment tool for the local Ku Klux Klan, which experienced a resurgence throughout the next decade. By the 1920s, crowds of as many as 2,000 hooded figures marched in the city and held rallies in the surrounding countryside. The Klan's membership encompassed a broad segment of the white population, including the so-called gentlemen of Wilmington. Most of their rallies were simply shows of force, but at least one demonstration was a response to the alleged rape of a local white woman by a black man.[2]

The Klan's power was buttressed by all-white police forces, all-white juries, Jim Crow judges, and a county jail full of African Americans accused of disrespecting the rules of segregation. As in other parts of the South, the Klan purported that its goal was the enforcement of local law, albeit by extralegal means. Although there was little mob violence in Wilmington during the 1920s, the presence of men in white robes carrying fiery crosses magnified the memory of the 1898 riot. Members of Wilmington's black community understood the consequences of any misstep.[3]

IN 1924, WHEN JUNIUS WILSON left the North Carolina School for the Colored Blind and Deaf and traveled back to his family in Castle Hayne, Wilmington was a far more dangerous home than the relatively protected Raleigh campus. The port city was alight with racial fury and the constant threat of violence. And the Wilson household was not a safe haven for the sixteen-year-old Junius. Not only had his father Sidney left, but Junius's elder sister Asynia had also moved away. Alone and unemployed, Mary Wilson in 1917 had married Henry Clark, a much older man.[4] The Clarks maintained close ties with the neighboring Smith family. Shortly after Junius had left for school, Arthur Jr. married eighteen-year-old Lizzie Sidberry.[5] This new Smith family grew with the arrival of son Deames in 1917.[6] Mary and Lizzie tended the house and gardens, watching over their children, Carrie and Deames, while the men were away at work. Junius returned to a family built on connections to people he barely knew.

When Henry Clark died in February 1925, Mary Wilson Clark strained to make ends meet. Junius, now seventeen years old and the sole male in his family, could not provide financial or emotional support. Mary relied heavily on the Smiths, especially Arthur Jr., to sustain them. Junius probably did not fully understand the new dynamics in his house. While Arthur and Lizzie considered Junius's mother and sister as extended family, they felt less kinship toward Junius. Having shouldered the burden of protecting the Wilson women in addition to his own family, Arthur felt responsible to solve the complicated issues Junius's arrival presented. Arthur's choices were limited. Because of communication barriers, Junius could not easily be sent to relatives elsewhere. Nor could Smith assume that other friends in Castle Hayne would help Wilson gain sustainable employment. Perhaps assuming that deaf people were less capable, Smith might have believed that Junius would never marry or live independently from his family.[7] The deaf boy's attendance at the state school had released the family from financial and communal obligations for many years. Now the prospect of permanent guardianship and responsibility likely seemed overwhelming.

Wilson's presence in Castle Hayne disrupted the rhythm of life that his family and community had carefully cultivated. The sixteen-year-old struggled to communicate with his kin. No longer part of the community of black deaf people with whom he could sign, Junius must have felt isolated. Certainly his family saw him that way. His great uncle summarized, "You couldn't tell him nothing because he couldn't hear what you say." At the same time, Junius's family could not understand him, either: as the uncle explained, "they couldn't tell what he was saying."[8] Writing was no answer for Junius's family (although it was for many white deaf southerners and their hearing families with access to schooling) since the degree of literacy taught by the North Carolina School for the Colored Blind and Deaf was limited. And the literacy of Junius's family, rural African Americans in the Jim Crow South, was also limited.[9] The family was at an impasse. As a cousin revealed later, "Most people kind of avoided him because they couldn't communicate. They didn't talk to him."[10]

In addition to the dangers to the family that any young teenage male might pose in such a situation, Junius seemed especially disruptive and uncontrollable. Even when playing with other neighborhood youth, he was often frustrated or angry and he acted inappropriately. As one recounted, "If he get a hold to you, you can't tell him to turn you loose because he can't hear. You just have to wait until he turn you loose." His deafness, in other words, made Junius less able to play by the rules established in the hearing community. Wilson's touching or holding people, stamping feet and waving arms (all common, acceptable, and meaningful interpersonal behaviors in the deaf world) were foreign and threatening to his hearing neighbors in Castle Hayne. "He played ball sometimes and he'd get mad sometimes so quick," recounted one playmate. "He missed the ball, then he'd throw the bat down and start at the man." The playmate remembered Junius many years later because, as he said, "he was so mean."[11]

Changing social and geographical boundaries would have added to any concern that Junius could not learn and was thus in no position to understand —much less accede to—the intricate and often demeaning rules of the Jim Crow South. Between 1900 and the 1920s, the slight buffer created by the physical separation of Castle Hayne from downtown Wilmington was shrinking. Immigrants from southern and western Europe moved into the community. Working as vegetable and flower farmers, these white newcomers quickly adopted southern etiquette and racial beliefs.[12] As long as Junius could live and work in an isolated community alongside his relatives and neighbors, his safety was fairly assured. But if he were to have regular contact with white supervisors, coworkers, and neighbors, they might easily misunderstand him. Bosses commonly became angered when workers did not respond to questions or calls. Wilson could unintentionally offend them. Unable to speak, Wilson might try to communicate by writing simple answers. Whites might view this as uppity, a disdainful show of his literacy. Wilson's deaf behavior—touching, yelling, staring—already concerned members of the black community. What if the young man touched a white man to get his attention, or stared him in the eye? What if he touched a white woman? Given the volatility of white anger, one misstep in racial etiquette could cost Junius his life.[13] It could also compromise the safety and stability of his family.

Given the frequency of visits between the neighboring adults, Junius would assume that he, too, was close to the Smiths. He wanted to communicate with them as he had with his peers at school. Needing friends and support of his own, Junius turned to those familiar faces for companionship, looking deeply into their eyes and touching them to get their attention. Later documents suggest that Junius watched "Aunt" Lizzie Smith especially closely, perhaps trying to read her lips.[14] Lizzie was one of the few people near him who was functionally literate; the deaf teenager might have sought out her company more than others, hoping that she could understand his limited written communication. Perhaps Wilson's seemingly invasive behavior concerned both Lizzie and her husband. From Arthur Smith Jr.'s point of view, Junius must have represented an impending if not immediate threat to both families.

IN LATE AUGUST 1925, almost one year after his dismissal from the school in Raleigh, Junius was arrested. Annie Mae Williams, Wilson's four-year-old niece, watched the police confront Junius and take him away. "It was out in the woods," recalled Williams. "We were all getting wood for firewood, and we were all out there. And, these two men came up and give my grandmother, his mother, a letter. I guess that was a warrant."[15] The police handcuffed him and removed him from the family. Arthur Smith Jr. had accused the seventeen-year-old young man of assaulting and attempting to rape Lizzie.[16]

It is unclear whether Arthur consulted with his family and neighbors before contacting the police.[17] It is also unclear how Junius's mother and the others felt about his action. Later testimony by younger relatives strongly suggests that Wilson was innocent of the charges and that Smith merely wanted to "get rid of" the young deaf man.[18] One must wonder what allowed such an extreme reaction. Several factors might have motivated him.

Junius was an economic liability. Families who owned farms could make use of a deaf man's labor. Farm life could keep Wilson isolated and protected at home with people who knew him well. But the Smiths earned a living as lumbermen and railroad workers. Working for bosses rather than themselves, the Smiths had fewer resources to find Junius employment. Commonly, deaf people were denied jobs like these because bosses and others assumed that hearing was necessary to maintain job safety. Rather than becoming the man of the household, providing for his family, Wilson would have likely been judged a drain on family resources.[19]

For eight years the state of North Carolina, which had demanded Wilson's attendance at the North Carolina school, had shouldered both the economic and social burdens of the boy's care. The state had provided not just an education and a language that separated him from his family; it also granted protection, housing, and sustenance for the boy. Arthur and Mary had grown accustomed to his absence and perhaps felt that the state should continue to bear the responsibility to support the boy. Now that Junius had been expelled from the institution for the deaf, it was impossible to send him back there. Perhaps Arthur considered other ways to ask the state to shoulder the burden of supporting and protecting him. Even though Wilson would face an uncertain fate in a racist judicial system, jail might have appeared the only option left for the family. Perhaps Arthur rationalized that in jail, Junius would be fed, clothed, and sheltered. Strong authority there would keep the boy in line, maybe even instill compliance that would enable him at a later date to return to the family. In jail, Arthur possibly reasoned, the deaf boy would be protected from vigilantes who might feel threatened by his "abnormal" behavior.

If Arthur Smith explicitly planned to try to have Junius jailed, he might have imagined that attempted rape of an African American woman would be the perfect charge.[20] If the boy was accused of a crime against a white person, he would be severely punished. If he was accused of a petty crime such as stealing a watermelon from a black farmer, the justice system might not get involved at all. Likewise a "mere" assault charge likely would not hold. An allegation of attempted rape of a black woman, on the other hand, might buffer the deaf boy from mob retaliation. Perhaps Arthur thought up the accusation when he noticed the close attention Junius was paying to Lizzie. Perhaps a minor incident caused him to realize how easily the boy's intense gaze could be misunderstood by others. Portraying Junius Wilson as a young man primed to become a rapist played on the fears and obsessions of the white community. Who would this out-of-control young man threaten next? The accusation of attempted rape would make the state intervene. This accusation could provide for Wilson's needs and at the same time "get rid of" him.

No evidence remains to detail what young Wilson understood about that August day. Since he was out with the two families gathering sticks and branches in the woods, Junius would not have suspected that Smith had accused him of a crime. No one present could explain to him in his own language why he was being taken away. Surely he would be frightened by the police taking him away in shackles. Handcuffs intimidate most people, but for a deaf person they present additional consternation because they greatly inhibit the ability to communicate in sign language. Unable to vocalize articulately, Wilson might have howled or yelled, flailed his arms in an effort to communicate in the only way he knew how. As he did so, the officers likely applied more force to quiet the rowdy boy who had been accused of an attempted violent crime. Junius was removed from Castle Hayne and taken off to jail in Wilmington.

JUNIUS STAYED AT THE New Hanover County jail from his arrest at the end of August until the November term of the Superior Court.[21] His family apparently did not tell the police that the young man was deaf. Although the court had no explicit knowledge of his deafness, Junius's inarticulate vocalizations and his lack of response to questions and commands made jailer Carl Cook consider the possibility that the young man could not hear. Cook, who claimed to know the language of the deaf well enough to carry on an intelligent conversation, tried to sign with Junius.[22] Getting no "coherent" or "intelligent" answers from the young black deaf man, the jailer assumed that Junius was unable to understand sign language. Almost certainly, Wilson *was* unable to understand fully the jailer's sign language, but not for the reasons that Cook assumed. Hearing people commonly overestimated their competency in sign language. Even if Carl Cook really knew signs, it was likely to be the American Sign Language used by the white deaf community. The Raleigh signs that Wilson used differed significantly from ASL. Racial differences further complicated any possible exchange. Accustomed only to black signers from his school, Junius might have been unsure how to respond appropriately to a white stranger who signed. Since the jailer and court did not apparently understand or believe that the boy was deaf and had attended the state school for the deaf, they were unable to classify him correctly.[23]

Cook must have expected a direct and deferential answer from Junius. He did not get it. When the jailer dismissed the possibility that Junius's inability to communicate was simply deafness, he began to assume that his deaf voice, inarticulate and perhaps quite loud, were howls of insanity. Knowing that Junius had been accused of attempted rape, Cook confidently stated that he thought Junius Wilson was "dangerous to himself or to others," a common classification for targets of incarceration.[24]

Carl Cook's suspicions, and perhaps his interpretation of the charges against the boy, led the county court to hold a lunacy hearing for Junius Wilson. In November 1925 Wilson appeared before a jury of white hearing men in order to determine his competency to stand trial. In addition to the jailer's statements about his ward's insanity, twenty-nine-year-old physician T. C. Britt argued that after thorough examination, he was also convinced that Wilson was in some way "defective."[25] At first he examined Junius physically: "I found no clinical evidence of disease at all." Apparently Junius attempted to explain that he was deaf. As Britt stated, "He believes he has some trouble." The doctor was confused by Wilson's attempts at communication. "He had me fooled at first," the physician confessed, "but I cannot find anything wrong with him [physically]."[26]

The medical examination of Junius consisted of "ask[ing] him questions about himself," to which Wilson would respond by "writ[ing] his mother's name and his own name." Wilson, the investigator explained, "would never answer the question, or write anything else." Rather than considering that Junius's inability to respond appropriately might be because of his deafness and low level of literacy, perhaps compounded by his fear and confusion, the physician speculated that he was "much below normal as far as I am able to determine." In other words, he concluded that Wilson was, in the parlance of the era, "feebleminded." With no evidence given by Junius's family that the boy had attended the school for black deaf students, nothing dissuaded the court from this diagnosis.

Britt did hesitate when Woodus Kellum, the state's attorney, asked him whether he thought Wilson was insane.[27] Although he initially said "Yes, sir," the doctor then deferred and stated, "He is one of those congenital cases, but it is hard to classify him." The lawyer pressed on: "Do you think he is dangerous to himself and others?" Britt again deferred: "I don't know that I feel that he is that or not; some of those cases will go through life and never do themselves or anyone else any harm; that is hard to say. It is hard to make a definitive statement." Only when Kellum reminded the physician of the charges did the doctor capitulate. Using the allegation rather than proven guilt, Kellum questioned him again: "But in this instance of an assault upon a female with intent to commit rape; with those facts and what you have found, what would you say?" Britt answered, "I would say he was dangerous after that, yes, sir." Now Wilson was deemed both insane and violent.

The same week the jury was called to decide Junius Wilson's fate, the film *The Birth of a Nation* reopened at the Royal Theater in Wilmington, yet again engraving in the minds of the jury the image of the black male rapist of white women. The *Wilmington Morning Star* made the story in the cinema seem all too immediate: just that week, several black men were accused of raping a white woman across the state in Asheville.[28]

The decision made by the lunacy jury was not a conviction. The members of the jury determined that the "defendant is insane and without sufficient mental capacity to undertake his defense, or to receive sentence after conviction." Junius Wilson was found neither guilty nor not guilty by reason of insanity. Instead, Judge Frank Daniels determined that whether or not he was guilty, Wilson's apparent insanity meant he should be institutionalized. Described by some as a "southerner of the old school," Judge Daniels disdained ambiguous decisions.[29] His pronouncement in Wilson's case was blunt: "The mental condition of the defendant is such as to render him dangerous to himself and to other persons, and that his confinement for cure, treatment, and security demands that he be committed to the hospital to be kept in custody therein for treatment and care." Officials sent Wilson directly to the criminal ward of North Carolina's State Hospital for the Colored Insane in Goldsboro.[30]

WILSON TRAVELED BY TRAIN to Goldsboro on 21 November 1925. In all likelihood, he enjoyed his temporary release from the jail cell, watching farmlands and small towns pass by as they rumbled toward their destination. He spied the Little River, which supplied water to Goldsboro's hospital and town and abounded with fishing holes.[31] Wilson might have hoped he could join the calmness there.

Crossing the threshold of the hospital doors marked a passage into a new world for Junius. Transferred from escort to nurses and aides, Wilson would not have known what these new brick buildings portended. Perhaps he believed it was an institution similar to the school for the deaf in Raleigh. His name and then patient identification was entered into the admissions book—number 8229. Following procedure, he was vaccinated and given a patient's uniform.[32]

Most documents from Wilson's early days and years at the hospital are now lost, but the entry book, yellowing and thick, remains. It describes the patients admitted the same week that Junius was admitted. Many were farmers and laborers. Wilson's occupation was listed only as "criminal." A startling lack of information distinguishes the rest of his admittance record. Virtually all of the other entries from that week list patients' supposed causes of insanity, age, nativity, birthplace, and the like. Wilson's solitary line shows nothing more than a diagnosis, inscribed at a later date: "constitutional psychopathic inferiority." This ambiguous label described people who demonstrated volitional and emotional control that grievously deviated from a prescribed norm. It also implied that such transgressive behavior was rooted in a faulty body, marking

State Hospital for the Colored Insane, Goldsboro (Courtesy of Cherry Hospital)

the individual as both physically and mentally defective. Unable to elicit responses that suggested the contrary, staff and doctors concluded from the available court documents that Wilson's alleged criminal behavior was the result of deviant biology—of a bad nature.

The State Hospital for the Colored Insane, founded in 1877, sprawled across 175 acres. Starting as an institution of 200 beds, the hospital had grown to over 1,000 beds by the time Wilson arrived.[33] By the early 1900s, in addition to housing African Americans deemed insane, the hospital also accepted epileptics, "idiots," and other "mental defectives."[34] Early hospital reports mention that the black "criminally insane, tuberculin patients, and all other patients judged insane, idiots and lunatics were housed together." The diverse population housed in Goldsboro's facility was symptomatic of a national expectation that asylums protect society from dangerous elements and "incapable" individuals from themselves. These twin responsibilities promoted the institutions as organs of control more than of healing.

Staff, widely outnumbered by patients, commonly used physical restraints. Cages placed outside on the grounds of the institutions held patients deemed especially hostile or unmanageable.[35] Rats infested many wards. By the 1920s many of the buildings had experienced severe flood damage. The seventeen-year-old Wilson probably saw little of the campus or its patients before he was hastily placed in the criminally insane (CI) ward, built only one year before his arrival.

The CI ward where Wilson initially lived was especially dangerous. Modeled on prisons, the two-story brick building was surrounded by barbed-wire fencing, and barbed wire encircled the top of the building. Bars covered the windows.[36] Built with poor sand, the cement floors already showed small holes.[37]

As Wilson entered, he would have walked past the "lock ups"—seclusion rooms that opened to the corridor of the main entrance in order to remind patients that the hospital would not tolerate disobedience.

The daily regimen at the hospital consisted of supervised trips for exercise with other inmates to a poorly ventilated "bull pen" behind the building.[38] The remainder of the day was spent in the bench-lined hall that served as a day room. Like other patients, Junius sat mutely on the benches for hours every day. As one superintendent later remarked, "Think for a moment of a person shut up in a room from one day's end to another with nothing whatsoever to interest or amuse him."[39]

At night, docile patients slept in simple iron bedsteads that were bolted to the floor, while more disruptive patients had only mattresses on the floor and bedding on which to rest.[40] Later hospital reports describe the building as "dank, dark, and fetorious," with "insufficient lavatories."[41] In the wards with noncriminal inmates, feebleminded children slept beside adult psychotic patients since patients were segregated neither by age nor by diagnosis. There were so many patients by the year Wilson arrived that they spilled over into the halls, sometimes creating not only chaos but also danger.[42]

Disease and illness spread quickly in the congested buildings. An influenza epidemic swelled at the time of Wilson's admission. Patients received vaccinations, but the medical officer admitted that this did not always help. Of the seventy-three men classified as criminally insane and admitted to Goldsboro between 1924 and 1926, eleven had already died.[43]

These conditions ensured that violence also erupted frequently. Patients attacked one another and the staff. Just before Wilson's arrival, two inmates died at the hands of other patients. An employee clubbed to death a third inmate. Wilson probably witnessed other acts of violence during his seven-year stay in this unit. As a superintendent blithely acknowledged, "These occurrences are much to be deplored but they do occur in institutions of this kind."[44]

This new institutional environment must have terribly confused and frightened the deaf teenager. Trapped in an unfamiliar space, surrounded by strangers, and without a means to communicate effectively, Junius must have felt lonely and isolated. Perhaps he felt guilty for some misbehavior at school or home and wondered whether this institutionalization was his punishment. Perhaps he wondered how long he would remain at the hospital. He likely felt insecure, unsure of his new identity and status.[45]

Wilson's deafness, both in its physical and cultural manifestations, made him especially vulnerable. He could not hear others approaching him or calling to him. Nor could he hear orders told to him by guards. Given that he was charged with attempted rape and placed in a unit of violent offenders, his inability to communicate with staff or patients might have made him appear particularly hostile and unpredictable. Communication barriers could lead to serious misunderstandings.

When unable to convey their ideas to people who do not share their language, deaf people have been known to act out their frustrations with loud outbursts and flailing arms.[46] Raised in a deaf cultural world, Junius would have typically grabbed and tapped other people to get their attention. Hearing people, then and now, often are startled and disturbed by these cultural behaviors. Staff in a CI unit might have been especially suspicious of Wilson. As reported in hospital reports, some feared such inmates were "crafty and vicious, always plotting to escape."[47] He probably tried to use sign language with the staff and the other patients, but his signing was just as futile here as it had been at home in Castle Hayne. It was likely viewed as even more threatening at the hospital.

Scant or nonexistent training contributed to the volatile situation in the wards. By the 1920s, the typical attendant at a mental hospital had little general education and no specific psychiatric training. Even with limited patient populations, attendants were forced to spend considerable time maintaining basic order and cleanliness. North Carolina's hospitals ranked far below average. Between 1926 and 1933, the national ratio was 6.5 patients to every one officer or employee, but in the state of North Carolina the ratio was 10.8 to 1.[48] In hospitals serving African Americas, the ratio was even worse. In addition, during the Depression years the government cut all state hospital employee salaries while increasing the patient census.[49] The absence of psychiatric social workers—or any professional support staff—at Goldsboro intensified the demands on attendants. Poor salaries, long days with difficult patients, and low status within the hospital hierarchy made it difficult for attendants to feel enthusiastic about their jobs. One director pointed out that someone had to make sure "the patients got up, got dressed and got something to eat and didn't kill one another."[50] Faced with the basic need to maintain order and survive dangerous encounters, many attendants relied heavily on threats, restraints, and, all too frequently, physical force.[51] As one historian succinctly explained, "Mental hospitals, after all, were coercive institutions."[52] Black employees, blocked from many jobs and limited in all positions, were in the ironic and unfair position of exacting a harsh control over other African Americans. Such was Jim Crow, insidiously present even in the most marginal corners of society.

ALTHOUGH ATTENDANTS AND NURSES often acted as overseers in the wards, the master of the domain was the superintendent. For most of its history, Goldsboro executives were relatively well educated, white, Protestant, native born, and socially established. Head administrators managed the physical operation of hospitals, lobbied the legislature for funds and support, and established personnel procedures. Invisible to mainstream society and separated from friends and family, patients could not command accommodation or reforms. The public showed little interest in the internal workings of such institutions, and state legislatures generally limited external oversight.[53] Lacking an organized central administration, hospitals relied almost exclusively on the advice and decisions of their superintendents. The board of directors for Goldsboro Hospital only visited the institution once annually, generally deferring to the director's written appraisals.[54] Medical autonomy and authority was the norm, and physician-superintendents, like the early administrators at Goldsboro, ruled with little oversight or challenge. Superintendents rarely if ever collaborated with their peers at other state institutions to compare patient care or administrative approaches. In addition to the general burden of administration, the rapidly expanding size of Goldsboro Hospital, with its diverse patient demographics as well as the abstract and ambiguous understanding of mental illness, made it difficult for superintendents there to focus meaningful attention on patients.[55]

When Junius Wilson arrived at Goldsboro, W. W. Faison headed the hospital. Faison's motto was "The utmost efficiency at a minimum cost."[56] He frequently proposed to his board of directors that inmates be classified so that all could do some kind of work "where they can produce a certain portion of what they consume." In the final years of Faison's administration, the daily cost was forty-seven cents per patient.[57] While this cost was roughly one-sixth the cost paid for white mentally ill patients, board members complained.[58] Faison claimed that the large numbers of criminally insane patients were a drain on the financial position of the institution. "These men and women of course do not work," stated Faison. "The institution has to furnish heat, lights, food, and cloth[e]s, and special guards for these criminal insane, and as they cannot go outside of the building they produce nothing, and this makes an additional expense for maintenance." As he pointed out, "But for this expense [the] cost per capita would come down."[59]

In 1926 the hospital entered a new era when W. C. Linville replaced Faison. Linville, a native of Forsyth County, North Carolina, had joined the staff at Goldsboro in 1905. Leaving in 1907 to pursue a private practice in Winston-Salem, he returned in 1915 to serve as assistant physician to Faison. An important member of the town, Linville was steward of his church, St. Paul Methodist, and enjoyed friendly relations with many prominent leaders in the state. Linville passionately advocated the expansion of the hospital facility. Included in the first permanent repair cost of the hospital for 1926–28, the director included over $5,000 to enlarge, alter, and furnish a new office for himself.[60] In addition, the hospital bought more land to extend the hospital's farmland.[61] At the same time, pressure mounted to keep maintenance costs low. Linville boasted that he succeeded in this endeavor: "Our per capita cost for the biennium is around forty cents per day," he claimed. "Our low maintenance cost we attribute to three things: competent organization, efficient administration, and intelligent farming."[62]

By 1928 Linville attempted to resolve the problem of criminal patient costs by requiring some of the ward's inmates to work. "We are giving useful employment to twenty or twenty-five of our criminal patients," he stated, "by hiring two extra attendants to watch over them."[63] His cost-saving techniques that year were undermined by floods that destroyed hay and corn crops. In 1929 floods again postponed work and wiped out the sweet potato crops and most of the feed crop.[64] Throughout his administration, Linville continued to search for ways to make the institution more cost-effective and self-sufficient.

Broader factors like demographics, regional characteristics, race, and science altered the development and nature of Goldsboro Hospital. Before the North Carolina institution was established, many local communities and states had erected small asylums for mentally ill citizens. Anticipating short-term care in a homelike environment, advocates for mental institutions in the early to mid-nineteenth century hoped to cure inmates and return them to their families.[65] By the latter part of the century, the patient population had exploded, including individuals with a greater variety of diseases and conditions as well as chronically ill people. Between 1880 and 1929, the national population had increased fourfold, totaling 272,527 patients.[66] Indeed, during the Progressive Era, the building of mental hospitals outpaced prisons, youth reformatories, and almshouses. By the early 1920s, more Americans were held in mental institutions than in all other kinds of custodial facilities combined.[67] In addition, by 1923 the majority of patients in mental hospitals in the United States had remained institutionalized for at least five years.[68] No longer small homes that sought to cure patients and created a close-knit community, mental hospitals increasingly served as custodial institutions.[69]

Psychiatry emerged as a recognized field by the early 1900s, and new professional opportunities often lured doctors away from institutional care. Commonly, psychiatrists viewed asylums as outmoded. As one historian of mental illness describes, "The role of caretaker for individuals who were socially marginal and who lacked either resources or families (or both) was frowned upon by a specialty that defined its mission in medical and scientific terms."[70] Consequently, mental hospitals increasingly relied on less-experienced specialists or on physicians outside the field of psychiatry.

Strapped for money, North Carolina's institutions scrambled to cut costs, often at the expense of patients. Local officials increasingly categorized senile poor people as insane in order to transfer the responsibility of their care from local poorhouses to the expanding state mental institutions.[71] Southern hospitals particularly languished under limited financial resources. Legislative boards, authorized to oversee public institutions, lacked funds and thus were unable to function.[72] Cost-saving efforts limited treatment for patients. Many Americans took for granted that criminal behavior or insanity among the poor was an incurable disorder.[73]

In the Jim Crow South, race especially mattered. Segregation practices demanded twice the number of hospitals in order to maintain racial segregation of patients. Per capita cost at institutions for African Americans were significantly lower than at white asylums. Treatment also was more limited. Administrators at Goldsboro and elsewhere consistently refused to hire African American doctors, allowing only white men to staff the hospitals. White domination prevailed within the walls of the institution, leaving both patients and black attendants generally silenced, disempowered, and with few options to navigate the hostile, desolate place in which they found themselves. The enduring history of slavery, a violence that had long cast people of color as predators, infiltrated the institution in other ways. Racial theories partly informed professional attitudes about mental illnesses: southern psychiatrists and other medical professionals generally believed that race determined individuals' susceptibility toward insanity.[74]

THE RISE OF EUGENICS changed the way doctors and society at large viewed inmates at mental institutions. Inspired by Charles Darwin's *Origin of Species* and Francis Galton's study of animal and plant breeding, eugenics promoted both scientific and political responses to improve the human race. Specifically, the eugenic movement sought to eliminate tainted or inferior stock. In the context of an extremely hierarchic and prejudiced society, the theories of genetics introduced by Mendel and other scientists were often applied unscientifically both to physical characteristics such as deafness and to social characteristics such as criminality. Intellectuals and reformers began to believe that inferior breeding inevitably created criminals, alcoholics, sexual deviants, and the impoverished. They considered deaf people—as well as feebleminded, insane, idiotic, and blind persons—to be defective genetic perpetrators if they chose to have families.[75] Eugenicists confidently proclaimed that people with epilepsy, mental illness, or mental retardation directly transferred their genetic impairments to their progeny.[76] Fueled by fears of social unrest, the influx of immigrants, the exodus of African Americans from the rural South to the urban North, and the darker side of industrialization and urbanization, reformers in the first decades of the twentieth century joined together to pass eugenics legislation.[77]

Many medical experts felt that sterilization could answer some of their deepest fears. Some suggested that forced sterilization could serve as a deterrent to crime or as a tool of punishment.[78] Walter Hidley, president of the State Society of Medicine in California in 1890, claimed that he did "not hesitate to advise that the following classes be required by law to submit to this procedure: idiots, those who commit or attempt to commit rape, wife-beaters, murderers, and some classes of the insane."[79] In the late nineteenth century, doctors castrated such patients, surgically removing the testicles, and thereby changing the patients' levels of testosterone. Because of castration's immediate impact on a patient's physical and psychological being, essentially feminizing both body and behavior, castration became the operation of choice for the criminally insane. As one early historian of sterilization in North Carolina wrote in 1950, "Castration was performed on men of vicious type, criminals guilty of attempted rape, and those who were problems in the hospital, since it was thought to quiet them down and make them easier to handle."[80] John Hurty succinctly described the attitude: "The knife only can reach them."[81]

The widespread practice of institutional and forced sterilization had its opponents. As one expert argued, sterilization "might become an instrument for the persecution of certain groups, particularly the negroes."[82] Citing the lack of good genetic knowledge, cultural and environmental factors in deviant behavior, and social bias toward racial minorities and the poor, the Committee of the American Neurological Association for the Investigation of Eugenic Sterilization recommended only voluntary and highly regulated procedures.[83]

By the late 1890s, male sterilization could be accomplished by vasectomy—making a small slit in the scrotum and severing the vas deferens, a procedure that did not affect the internal hormones of the testes. With the move from castration to vasectomy, many doctors, particularly those at state institutions, became leading advocates of sterilization.[84] These supporters focused on what they deemed to be the procedure's "eugenic" value: eliminating the spread of defective genes. By the 1920s, Ezra Seymour Gosney and the Human Betterment Foundation concluded that, according to a survey, "doctors were almost unanimous in their agreement that sterilization, especially in men, produced positive results."[85]

Eugenicists argued that "eugenic sterilization . . . is one of the many tested and dependable measures that will help reduce the burdens and increase the happiness and prosperity of the population in this and future generations. As such, it is one among many indispensable procedures in any modern program of social welfare."[86] Arguing that the procedure was not only good for the patient but also for society, nationally recognized eugenics proponents Paul Popenoe and Ellsworth Huntington advised others to "think of the economic loss to society and to themselves that all these socially inadequate classes represent." To these authors, sterilization was no longer about punishment.[87]

Politicians quickly attempted to propose legislation for sterilization. In 1905 Pennsylvania passed the first sterilization law, later vetoed by Governor Samuel Whitaker. Two years later, Indiana passed a law allowing that state to perform compulsory sterilization of rapists and other criminals in state institutions. Washington and California followed in 1909, although the former never applied the law. After World War I, the eugenics movement spread rapidly.[88] With supposedly scientific evidence to support them, southern policy makers passed additional miscegenation and racial integrity laws. Claiming that blacks had lower intelligence, scientists provided southern legislatures with compelling rationales for further restricting the citizenship rights of African Americans.

By the late 1920s, the main targets of sterilization shifted from criminals to inmates at state institutions for the mentally ill and feebleminded. In part, the change occurred as new intelligence testing and eugenic "research" revealed a staggering percentage of subaverage citizens. But class divisions and racism, among other dynamic factors, infused both the study of human subjects and the dehumanizing policies placed on them.[89] The "menace of the feebleminded," public figures proclaimed, could only be eradicated by fusing scientific management with social reform. Eugenics bills, explained a contemporary analyst in 1911, were ostensibly created for the "improvement of the human race by better breeding."[90] By preventing people seen as defective from procreating, the eugenics community hoped to create a society where all children had the genetic blueprint for a healthy body and mind. The 1927 Supreme Court ruling in *Buck v. Bell* served as a test case. Eighteen-year-old Carrie Buck, a white woman from Virginia, was labeled feebleminded (although she was never evaluated) and placed in the Virginia Colony for Epileptics and Feebleminded.[91] Her mother, described in the court documents as promiscuous and untruthful, had previously been committed to the same institution. Carrie had given birth to a daughter, also deemed feebleminded, although later evidence revealed that the child had no mental disability. Invoking Virginia's statue to forcibly sterilize feebleminded inmates, the superintendent of the Virginia Colony wanted to sterilize Buck by severing her fallopian tubes. Buck fought the decision. In the Supreme Court case that followed, the justices held that forced sterilization was indeed constitutional. Justice Oliver Wendell Holmes claimed, "The principle that sustains compulsory vaccination is broad enough to cover cutting the fallopian tubes. . . . Three generations of imbeciles are enough."[92]

In the wake of *Buck v. Bell*, politicians and regular citizens clamored for new eugenic laws. Sixteen states quickly passed mandates for sterilizing inmates of state institutions.[93] When tested again in 1931 in the *Eugenics v. Troutman* case, the Supreme Court upheld its previous ruling. By 1932 thirty states had passed eugenic laws.[94] "*Buck v. Bell* has now definitely committed the United States to a policy of human sterilization for good or for bad as a means of coping with the socially undesirable in our midst," wrote scholar J. H. Landman shortly afterward.[95] Between 1907 and 1940, 18,552 mentally ill people—or those labeled as such—were sterilized in the United States.[96]

AFTER SIX YEARS IN the CI ward, Junius Wilson was one of the first North Carolinians to be selected for sterilization. In 1929, four years after Wilson's incarceration, North Carolina passed "An Act to Provide for the Sterilization of the Mentally Defective and Feeble-Minded Inmates of Charitable and Penal Institutions of the State of North Carolina." The law gave the heads of institutions the power to authorize sterilizations on any patient deemed "mentally defective" or "feebleminded" as long as the sterilization "may be considered best in the interest of the mental, moral, or physical improvement of the patient or inmate, or for the public good." Between the law's passage in 1929 and the court's finding four years later that the law was unconstitutional (and its replacement with a new law), the state sterilized forty-nine people. Of these, twelve men in the state were not only sterilized but castrated. Junius Wilson, "asexualized" on 20 January 1932, was one of them.

When the State Hospital for the Colored Insane's superintendent W. C. Linville selected Wilson for castration, he provided on the state form a litany of reasons why sterilization was indicated for the young man. On one page he stated that Wilson was criminally insane, mentally deficient, sexually perverted, and deaf and dumb. On the next page he added that Wilson was feebleminded and sexually promiscuous. There is reason for historians to question all of the diagnoses with the exception of deafness.[97]

What did Linville mean when he labeled Wilson a sexual pervert? Almost certainly, institutional officials were aware of the charge of attempted rape, and perhaps the charge alone was enough to warrant the label. Or perhaps Wilson's behavior at the institution served to reinforce the charge. One of the forms completed to approve his sterilization suggests as much, discussing the patient's "sexual abuses" that would be cured by castration.[98] Wilson was a virile young man in his late teens and early twenties in a place that offered him no private place to express his sexual energy. Even when he thought he was masturbating in private, a guard could appear without the deaf man hearing his footsteps, or even his admonitions. Perhaps Wilson had made advances toward staff or patients, male or female. Given that the long list of justification for his sterilization does not include aggressiveness or violence, it seems unlikely that he attempted or committed sexual assault in the hospital. It is highly probable that Wilson expressed typical deaf cultural behaviors, tapping people on the arms and touching their hands, perhaps even their faces, to get their attention. Hearing staff members could misinterpret this as a sign of sexual interest.

Other reasons offered for Wilson's castration were feeblemindedness and mental deficiency. His school report stated that he showed no "signs of mental imbecility or idiocy," despite the fact that the school used those designations regularly with students they expelled.[99] However, lack of intellectual ability was mentioned in several places on the hospital's sterilization forms. When an evaluating physician only noted "criminal insane" on Wilson's sterilization form, superintendent Linville wrote next to it, "mental deficient."[100] Linville might have assumed Wilson's inability to communicate effectively was the result of retardation. Medical professionals unaccustomed to working with deaf people commonly confused this auditory disability with cognitive disabilities. Linville also declared on the state form that Wilson had no education, even though he had attended the state school for African American deaf pupils for eight years. Unfamiliar with deafness except for its medical meaning, the physician might not have realized that a black deaf North Carolinian could have attended school. But even if Linville did not believe Wilson was feebleminded, there was a reason why he felt compelled to include it: according to the law, criminal insanity alone did not warrant forced sterilization. Because the law's purpose was not control of institutional inmates, it stipulated sterilization for the mentally deficient. Whether or not he believed Wilson was feebleminded, Linville knew he had to write it down. To enhance his case, Linville added that Wilson was syphilitic because the law targeted this category as well.[101]

Linville wrote that he was "unable to get any history" from the deaf inmate and that he did not know the names of the patient's parents. Although the court records suggest that Wilson continually wrote the names of family members (and later hospital records state he still did even seventy years later), it is possible that Linville had no records of the man's background. On the other hand, Linville also knew that by not acknowledging Wilson's kin, he could expedite the process. While the 1929 eugenic law did not state that an individual's family must be consulted before sterilization, discussion had already started in the state about the constitutionality of such an act. Linville also concluded that Wilson "[came] from a family of mental defectives."[102] Although there is no evidence to support Linville's statement, it does show that Linville was willing to invoke family when it suited his purposes.

Superintendent Linville was especially involved with Junius Wilson's asexualization. He declared the diagnoses and the need for sterilization, petitioned the Eugenics Board, signed off on the surgery (in accordance with state law requiring the signature of the chief medical officer of a state institution), chose the type of surgery, and himself performed the castration.[103]

Although his institution carried out approximately one-third of the castrations performed in North Carolina during the 1930s, Linville was not alone.[104] The North Carolina Eugenics Board provided people like Wilson with very little protection. The state offered no free legal counsel in sterilization hearings and the deliberations occurred in isolation, apart from court proceedings.[105] In fact, the board was predisposed to agree with Linville's decisions. Their 1935 pamphlet claimed that "eugenical sterilization is a means adopted by organized Society to do for the human race in a humane manner what was done by Nature before modern civilization, human sympathy, and charity intervened in Nature's plans."[106] Two years later it recommended that the state's sterilization program be continued on a larger scale.[107] Nationally renowned eugenics advocate Harry Laughlin specifically praised the group, observing, "It is clear that your Eugenics Board of North Carolina is a very efficient body."[108]

After Wilson was castrated, he was removed from the criminal ward. The institution had used castration as a means of both punishment and therapy for him. His cure was in their interest. Before, he had been a drain on the meager resources of the institution. Once castrated, Wilson was considered less threatening, less in need of close supervision. He was likely to be calm and controlled. Additionally, his labor could be used to contribute to the institution. As Linville wrote on the sterilization follow-up form just a few months after Wilson's castration, the deaf inmate was "now on the farm doing manual work."[109]

Once castrated, Wilson behaved in a way more acceptable to the white hospital administrators and to white hearing southern society in general. He became a submissive black man. According to later hospital records, he withdrew into himself, rarely interacting with other inmates. Eyes downcast, silent, and reserved, Junius Wilson gained a reputation as a gentle childlike patient. Since physical contact, so common among deaf people, was misinterpreted by staff and patients, Wilson stopped tapping and touching people to get their attention. Instead, he set himself apart from other people in the hospital. Wilson repressed his own deaf identity in order to survive in the environment of the hospital.

ACROSS THE SOUTH, eugenic ideology melded with Jim Crow norms. Already legitimating racial segregation in order to preserve the purity of the Caucasian race, southern state governments saw eugenic policies as the obvious next step. National campaigns urging the sterilization of "unfit Americans" relied on stereotypes of poor people and people with disabilities as "animalistic," "oversexed," "naturally deviant," and "given to insanity." These were the same stereotypes that the white South applied to African Americans, especially African American men. Here, professional medical practices met broader social beliefs. Wilson's deafness complicated matters. Unable to articulate vocally and accustomed to deaf cultural behavior, Wilson seemed deviant to those who did not understand his auditory or cultural status. Superintendent Linville's action clearly demonstrates how the intertwined factors of eugenics, Jim Crow, disability, and institutionalization not only allowed but encouraged castration and sterilization of people like Junius Wilson.

Racist images like those projected in *The Birth of a Nation* combined with the latest medical thinking to provide new choices for eradicating "the black menace" that white southerners saw as threatening to their region. Extralegal violence such as lynching could be replaced with something more scientific and sterile: segregation from mainstream society through institutionalization and removal from the gene pool through surgical intervention.[110] Junius Wilson was only one of the casualties.

3

Walls (1930s–1950s)

He is still confused but gives us no trouble. His eating and sleeping habits
are good. He is cooperative and works on the farm. We continue
to give him the very best of care.

**SUPERINTENDENT MINTAUTS VITOLS, LETTER TO
MARY WILSON CLARK CONCERNING JUNIUS WILSON, 1958**

JUNIUS WILSON'S FIRST SIX YEARS at the State Hospital for the Colored Insane
swelled into seventy-six years. Following castration, the patient lived at the
hospital farm, where he worked to help pay for his institutionalization. Located
about a half mile from the main campus, the Farm Colony was out of sight
from the criminal insane ward, Wilson's first home at Goldsboro. The hospital
farm spread over nearly 1,000 acres and was surrounded by several hundred
more acres of woodland. Two rivers threaded across the property, providing
cool water to drink and in which to bathe. Cows milled around the pasture,
while chickens picked at corn and chased after each other.

The Farm Colony included a metal-covered brick dormitory that Wilson
shared with roughly 100 other men. Two other buildings nearby housed additional male and female patients. Erected in the 1920s and expanded in the 1930s,
the one-story Farm Colony dormitories had large dining halls and wood floors.
Sleeping rooms dominated the buildings, and woodstoves provided heat. The
smell of sweaty bodies, moist dirt, and farm animals likely pervaded the rooms,
but compared to the wards at the main campus, the colony facilities were
spacious and relatively calm.[1]

Even though the main institution housed everything from children to elderly patients, workers on the farm generally were young adults. Many had
families—wives or husbands, even children. How often they would see their kin

is unknown. Older hospital admission rolls reflect demographics common to North Carolina's black population.[2] Some individuals were farmers, others common laborers.

Inhabitants of the Farm Colony enjoyed certain benefits unavailable to the men and women at the main campus, including much less rigid supervision. Even administrators noted that "the patients in that building had more privileges getting in and out than anyone else in the . . . hospital."[3] Wilson would have quickly noticed the absence of fences around the Farm Colony facilities. In the criminal ward, bars and boundary markers—from hospital windows and secured yards to the cages that confined unruly inmates—had framed Wilson's daily life. On the farm, guards still directed much of his daily activities, but he had a kind of freedom unattainable at the main campus. Wilson could walk the grounds of the colony and could join other inmates and staff along the banks of the Little River. The comparative freedom must have been palpable for the young Wilson.

Food, one of the most valuable commodities at the hospital, was also more plentiful on the farm. In order to help colony patients work efficiently, attendants distributed rations of meat every day, milk every other day, and fresh seasonal vegetables when available. The patient-laborers ate their main meals in the middle of the day. At night, Wilson and his peers were fed a supper of light bread, coffee, and molasses. Well-behaved male workers, if they desired, received tobacco or snuff. Wilson developed a strong penchant for dipping.[4]

Wilson likely was pleased by the landscape of farms and forest. It might have reminded him of Castle Hayne. Nevertheless, his move from the main campus to the Farm Colony must have bewildered the young man. No one could explain to him why he had been transferred out of the criminal ward or what his purpose was in the colony. Staff members with whom he was unfamiliar directed him to follow the others. Wilson and other patients were loaded onto trucks in the early morning. Transported to the fields, they worked until 5:00 P.M. Perhaps Wilson wondered whether the work was punishment or reward.

Participating as a worker, Wilson became a more valuable patient, the kind that contributed to the financial welfare of the institution. Administrators considered the inmates at the colony mildly ill but not criminal. As one observer reported, "These men are selected because of their good behavior and good physical condition."[5] Ultimately, Wilson began to mute behaviors seen as normal at the deaf school. Subtle gestures, inarticulate speech, and occasional gazes replaced the close proximity to others, the direct touches and tapping, and the extended eye contact. This modified behavior diminished Wilson's difference from the other "good" patients.

The institution provided social events such as dances and film viewings for

Goldsboro Hospital farm (Courtesy of Don Edwards)

compliant patients. Allowed to participate in these events, Wilson hovered in the margins, watching his fellow inmates. At the dances, the vibrations from the music coincided with the swaying bodies. He shied away from joining others on the floor. Films might have been enticing for Wilson, and the old silent films, which accommodated his need for visual communication, were accessible to him. The newer "talkies," however, likely remained largely incomprehensible for the deaf man. In addition to recreational activities, the hospital offered church services. There is no record of Wilson attending any of these. Without an interpreter, it would have been difficult for him to comprehend what the preacher was saying.[6]

At the Farm Colony, patient outbursts were infrequent. When they did occur, staff and administration responded quickly. "When any of them becomes mentally or physically disturbed," reported one physician, "they are returned to the main buildings for care and treatment."[7] Perhaps Wilson guessed that patients forcibly removed from the farm were sent back to the criminal ward. Having witnessed the punishments meted out to violent offenders there, Wilson would have wanted to avoid being sent back. Or perhaps Wilson imagined other punishments for those who were expelled from the farm. Most of Wilson's fellow laborers seemed to comply with hospital rules. One observer explained, "The patients appear to be quite content and they look upon being in the farm colony as a definite promotion toward going home."[8]

IN THE DECADES AFTER Wilson's arrest, his family and the Smiths continued to live in Castle Hayne. The Depression hit the community hard, cutting into the families' already meager finances. Mary, now widowed, eventually took in laundry to earn extra money, but she did not have enough to make ends meet independently. By 1930, she moved in with Arthur's mother, Annie Smith, another woman who had lost her husband. Tying her future even more tightly to the Smiths, Junius Wilson's mother helped raise Annie's daughters and grandchildren with her own granddaughters. Arthur Smith Jr. and brother James lived down the street. Their children grew up knowing "Aunt Mary" as a quiet woman who wore a white bandana around her hair. One relative later described her as "graceful" and "sad."[9]

Junius Wilson surely thought about his family during his years in the hospital in Goldsboro. He might have supposed they did not know where he was and hoped they were searching for him. Wilson suggested in later years that the loss of his family wounded him deeply.[10] Certainly his absence left wounds in Castle Hayne. Whether or not Mary Wilson Clark had gone along with the initial decision to accuse Junius of attempted rape, there is abundant evidence that she struggled with her son's removal from the family.

In later years, relatives suggested that everyone knew the accusations against the young man were untrue. Arthur Smith's daughter Fannie Thomas stated that she had "heard that [Junius] was attacking my mother, and of course, that was why he was sent away." But she also suggested that there were more complicated dynamics involved in the charge: "I heard that it was a conflict between my mother and my father." Junius Wilson's niece, Jennie Bowman, agreed that the charge was "something concerning my uncle bothering with [Arthur's] wife." She was quick to point out, "But most people—what I've been told, he didn't do anything to her."[11]

The family agreed that Wilson's mother, Mary Clark, struggled with the charge. Annie Mae Williams reported that Mary "didn't believe it." Jennie Bowman stated that after the arrest, Mary avoided serious contact with Arthur Smith Jr.: "She would only speak to him. I noticed that she would give him the time of day and that is it." Only years later did Bowman understand "how much she disliked him for putting him [Junius] away." André Branch, Smith's grandson, said that Annie Williams told him that Wilson's mother "never was quite right after they took her baby."[12]

Various emotions—guilt, sadness, frustration, doubt, and despair—might have flooded over Mary when she remembered her son being taken away in handcuffs by the police. Unable to read or write and dependent on the Smiths for support, she felt helpless to contact her son or fight his incarceration. Instead, she kept whatever feelings she experienced inside. According to family members, for years following Wilson's arrest, neither Mary nor her neighbors ever referred to him, and there is no evidence that family members sought to visit or contact him.[13]

Meanwhile, conditions at the Hospital for the Colored Insane deteriorated in the 1930s. As the effects of the Great Depression hit the institution, it was forced to maintain an even tighter budget. All state and community facilities faced similar struggles. Goldsboro was especially hard hit. The institution's responsibility to pay for inmates' care put great demands on the paltry hospital fund. The vast majority of patients' families—poor and undereducated black North Carolinians—could not easily pay for psychiatric care for their committed family member. Patients admitted through the court system required full funding by the institution. As the superintendent reported, "Since . . . August 1938, I have not turned down a single application for a patient who was in jail, but urged the authorities to send them to the Institution here as soon as possible."[14]

As the Depression went on and more people faced desperate situations, the number of men and women admitted to the insane asylum skyrocketed. The economic collapse of the cotton and tobacco markets and state resistance to federal relief programs exacerbated poverty in North Carolina, and desperate families institutionalized elderly and ill relatives that they could no longer support.[15] Soon, the hospital was severely overcrowded. Between 1928 and 1930, the patient population at Goldsboro had jumped from 1,754 to 3,160.[16] The increasing number of inhabitants further increased the hospital's expenditures for housing, board, and medical care. Despite the need for extra doctors and staff to care for the growing inmate population, the hospital was forced to cut salaries and reduce the number of staff. It was impossible for staff to provide patients with proper care and treatment under such restricted circumstances.[17] Hospital trustee W. A. Dees defended the institution, claiming that "the Hospital, like all other institutions, is now laboring under unusual difficulties on account of shortages of labor and shortages of many materials, but I think it is doing an unusually good job under the circumstances."[18]

Despite the institution's defense of itself, it was commonly believed that the conditions at Goldsboro were worse than at any other state facility for the mentally ill.[19] The combination of racism, economic pressures, and general disinterest in institutionalized and mentally ill individuals contributed to Goldsboro's desperate situation. In 1933 North Carolina had the second-lowest budgetary allotment per inmate in the country. Only five other states had a higher patient-to-staff ratio.[20] The shortage of beds forced staff to improvise, creating bins of cornhusks and other materials for "excited" patients to use in order to spare coveted mattresses for more compliant individuals.[21]

WILSON'S PLACEMENT AT THE Farm Colony was part of another plan to curtail costs at the institution. From the beginning, the hospital tried to produce enough food to feed its inhabitants. Due to the changes that occurred as a result of the Great Depression, the wards could not hold all of the patients and the fields could no longer produce enough to feed them. One of the worst droughts in memory hit Goldsboro in the early 1930s, wiping out almost half of the crops. "The future . . . looks a little dark," L. M. Blue, chairman of the board of directors for Goldsboro Hospital, noted dryly. The amount and quality of food decreased, and the administration worried about making ends meet. Because mass-produced, cheap food was not yet available, agricultural production re-mained vital. Administrators were forced to purchase more land and to nearly double the number of patients working on the farm. The hospital constructed new dormitories at the Farm Colony to house the patient-workers.

In addition to providing food for the inmates of the Goldsboro Hospital, farmwork kept patients busy, so they required less staff supervision. "The farm is one of the outstanding features of the Hospital," the hospital assured the state legislature, "and since so many of the colored people are willing to do farm work there is an abundance of help for all farm activities. In fact, it would be possible to extend the farm and still have enough help."[22] Until his death in August 1938, Superintendent Linville advocated patient labor in the institution's fields. His successor and former first assistant, Frank Livingston Whelpley, built on his mentor's model.[23]

Starting after World War I, the Goldsboro Hospital not only required pa-tients to work on the farm but also rented patients out to local farmers during cotton season.[24] This practice earned thousands of dollars annually for the asylum. Farmwork, as well as leasing patients to work on private farms, was so lucrative that state inspectors questioned the policy's potential negative aspects. Physician James Watson said in the 1940s, "In talking with Mr. Purser [the farm manager] and Dr. Whelpley, I stressed the danger of putting the farm ahead of the hospital so that patients are kept in the institution for the sake of working on the farm. They both seemed aware of this danger and said they were seeking to avoid it."[25]

Isolated within the hospital grounds, Wilson only indirectly felt the impact of the Great Depression. As a farm laborer, Wilson's diet might have been less affected than that of his peers on the main campus. No one could explain the change in staff as the institution tightened its belt in the 1930s.

Farm labor performed by inmates was an integral part of hospital policy, just as it was at other institutions throughout the South.[26] Since the days of Reconstruction, the state of North Carolina commonly used institutionalized people for free labor. Throughout the late nineteenth and early twentieth century, various institutional reports noted the growth of farms. Particularly in the cash-strapped Depression era, state institutions increasingly turned to patient labor. Farms were common components of schools for the deaf, colonies for the feebleminded, prisons, and mental hospitals for both races. The fields provided food for residents and staff, kept maintenance costs low, and symbolized the goal of imitating—or assimilating into—the world outside the institution. Institutions for black North Carolinians, typically housing more concentrated populations of inmates than did white institutions, tended to have larger farms and workforces.

Farmwork was not the only kind of labor done by inmates of the state's institutions. North Carolina's prisoners, predominantly African American, built and fixed roads for the state, saving the government considerable money and producing noticeable transportation improvements. Chain-gang workers were shackled together as they worked. Unable to walk away from the gang to relieve themselves, prisoners were surrounded by the smell of urine and excrement. Insects and rodents surrounded the patients' cells and cages. Frequently underfed, they were vulnerable to the spread of disease. Cruelty could be even worse than disease: stories abounded of workers with skin peeling away from their bodies due to whippings and beatings.[27] As one North Carolina prisoner wrote in a petition to the governor, "We are beat up like dogs. . . . They work us hard and half feed us [and] beat us with shovel and stick." Said another, "They are whipping right on. We can't get water but one time a day. We can't live."[28] Prisoners—like mental patients—had little chance of challenging the brutality of such "free" labor programs since they were so often ignored or disdained by mainstream society.[29]

Administrators at state institutions often suggested that laboring on the farm was restorative for mentally ill patients. As Whelpley boasted in 1938, the hospital saw agricultural labor as "a very satisfactory and beneficial form of occupational therapy with our class of patients."[30] They believed in the notion that fit bodies promoted and represented fit minds. Being productive made patients feel more normal, believed administrators, and allowed them to maintain the kinds of skills that they could use to assimilate after release from the hospital.

The superintendent suggested that patients themselves wanted to labor on the farm. "Nearly all of them have at some time during their life lived and worked on a farm," said Whelpley. "We find most of them not only willing but anxious to get outdoors and do something of that kind as soon as they get a little adjusted here."[31] The ability to recruit willing workers for the farm highlights the complex and hierarchical power dynamics between patients and administrators. Although hospital administrators determined the outlines of inmates' lives, these men and women were not defenseless. By positioning themselves as valuable workers, patients could escape the drudgery of the locked wards. By working conscientiously, they gained special favors and privileges from guards. By pretending to be too ill to work, individuals occasionally were able to avoid hard toil. At the same time, farmwork fostered a tight community, as the laborers spent endless hours in the fields together. Friendships among patients and between inmates and staff provided protection and even stability—albeit transitory and limited—for some individuals at the hospital.

By providing free labor, select men and women could enjoy benefits that mattered to them. Some might have seen this option as a valuable choice, even as a subversion of the hospital system. Administrators, in turn, stated that work by patients was a tool of frugality as well as a therapeutic intervention meant for the benefit of patients. They earned political recognition and praise while exploiting the labor of their inmates.

SHORTLY AFTER WILSON was moved to the Farm Colony, another man with a startlingly similar background came to Goldsboro. James McNeil was admitted to the State Hospital for the Colored Insane in 1933. As in Wilson's case, McNeil's deafness played a significant role in his incarceration. Like Wilson, he had been accused of attempted rape, found insane by a jury, and admitted to the Goldsboro asylum. According to the trial records, McNeil had approached Pattie Alston in a town where no one knew him. Tapping Alston and waving his arms, the deaf man frightened the woman, who thought he was an aggressor. Police quickly removed him from the scene. Census materials suggest that Alston was an elderly black woman who lived in the same county as Winnie Graham. Graham, also African American, claimed that a "James Graham," who "cannot speak English," was her lodger. The man apparently worked as a laborer on her farm, and over the years she might have claimed him as kin.[32] When McNeil arrived at the courthouse in Halifax County, he was referred to as "Dummie Graham."[33] Neither McNeil's biological family nor his friends knew of his arrest: "It appears to the Court that the defendant has no relatives within the County, and the residence of such relatives as he may have is unknown, no notice was issued to such relatives."[34]

Like Wilson, McNeil was incapable of articulate speech. No one who could understand Raleigh signs was present at the trial. No counsel was provided for the defendant. McNeil probably attempted to explain himself through signs and gestures, which, coupled with his grunts, might have disturbed his interrogators and suggested to them that he was insane. The jury of white hearing men quickly concluded that "Dummie Graham" was incompetent to stand trial. The judge in the Halifax County Court during McNeil's trial was F. A. Daniels, the same judge who oversaw Wilson's trial in Wilmington nine years earlier.[35]

Because of the charges against him, "Dummie Graham" was placed in the criminal ward. Shortly after his arrival at the hospital, Superintendent Linville decided to do to McNeil what he had done to Wilson: Linville surgically castrated the deaf inmate on 13 April 1934.[36] McNeil also was sent to work, but not on the Farm Colony, where he would have met Wilson. Instead, McNeil worked in the dining hall on the main campus, returning to the criminal insane building at night. Like Wilson, "Dummie Graham" slowly gained the trust of staff and assisted them in exchange for favors and freedoms. Hospital workers found his ability to mimic others amusing. Hospital staff began to call him a new name, "Big Dummy."[37]

At twenty-seven years old, McNeil was significantly older than Wilson had been when he entered Goldsboro's insane asylum, but the two men were roughly the same age. Born in 1906 in Corinth, McNeil had attended the State School for the Colored Blind and Deaf in Raleigh at the same time Wilson had. They shared the same language and the same culture. Given the insular character of deaf residential schools, the two black deaf boys almost certainly knew one another. Perhaps they played together or lived in the same dormitory. The two might have even taken classes together.[38]

For years, the deaf men endured similar trials at the asylum and lived in close proximity. Apparently, each man remained unaware of the other's presence even though communication could spread rapidly through informal but astonishingly intense channels. Perhaps the hospital made a conscious choice to avoid putting the men together, thereby preventing them from communicating in a way the administration and the attendants could not understand. Or perhaps the asylum was not even aware that Wilson and McNeil shared the same language and background. Whatever the circumstances, the two deaf men, who could have sustained each other through lifetime incarcerations, continued in their linguistic isolation for many more years.

FOLLOWING THE LEGAL injunctions of the court, Junius Wilson should have remained in the criminal ward until he was considered sane enough to stand trial. At that point, the law required that he be returned to Wilmington to face the charges against him for the alleged attack of Lizzie Smith. The hospital did not follow such a prescription. Instead, he was castrated and swiftly sent to the

Farm Colony. According to its own reports, the farm only housed men and women who behaved well and were deemed at most mildly ill. Wilson's transfer indicates that the hospital saw him as moderately sane and nonthreatening.

In contrast to inhabitants in the criminal ward, Wilson seemed relatively calm and controllable. Even though staff members were conscious that Wilson was different from his peers, they were convinced that he could not, and should not, leave the hospital grounds. They assumed that he was somehow deficient even if they could not specify his deficiency. Conflating his deafness with mental illness or retardation, the hospital intended to continue his incarceration on the grounds that Wilson belonged at the hospital more than he belonged in society.

Had he been released, Wilson was guaranteed neither greater freedom nor greater opportunity. If he stood trial for the alleged crime, the all-white jury in Wilmington might have found him guilty. The deaf man would have to spend his years in a jail, a fate not dissimilar to his time in the criminal ward. If Wilson were found not guilty, he probably would have been unable to return to his family given that the Smiths had lodged the accusation against him. With no network of signing allies to parlay his vocational training into marketable skills, he would have had trouble supporting himself. Language barriers and misperceptions of deafness might have caused considerable challenges for him in mainstream society.

Perhaps Superintendent Linville saw himself as a responsible caretaker by removing Wilson from the criminal ward and "treating" his criminality by means of castration. Surely Linville was eager to put Wilson's healthy young body to work. The superintendent might have believed that farmwork was a way for Wilson to redeem himself through manual labor. Sustaining others by his labor, Wilson would symbolically repay society for any alleged or actual infraction. The fact that Wilson's efforts economically benefited the hospital must have entered his mind, as well.

Whatever his ultimate reasons, Linville violated judicial procedure by removing Wilson from the criminal wards but not sending him back to stand trial. Mintauts Vitols, a Goldsboro superintendent in the 1950s, was shocked when he read of Linville's decision: "I actually have to admit that after I got [Wilson's] charge with rape and so on . . . especially when you tell me that he is in Farm Building, how in the hell—excuse me, how did he get to the Farm Building being charged with a felony?"[39]

As with Wilson, McNeil was to return to the court system as soon as he was deemed sane enough to stand trial. Like Wilson, he was put to work after his castration rather than sent back. Linville knew that whatever actions he took were unlikely to be challenged. The men's families were not likely to intervene because, in contrast to patients admitted by relatives, both Wilson and McNeil entered the Goldsboro Hospital as wards of the state. Their similar experiences suggest that Linville systematically chose to castrate state-admitted patients labeled criminally insane and sexually deviant. By this measure, the hospital could alter their status and exploit them through labor.

Linville's actions reveal the unchecked power of institution administrators in a patriarchal, authoritarian, Jim Crow South. It would be easy to scapegoat him as a medical vigilante. Still, it is important to remember that Linville existed in an environment that fostered this kind of exploitation. The U.S. Supreme Court had already upheld the right to forcibly sterilize institutionalized people. North Carolina's Eugenics Board supported Wilson's castration and made no comment on his transfer to the farm, even though board members understood that he was an accused felon who had not yet stood trial. The state and the South in general vigorously supported patient labor. Politicians specifically praised Linville and his successors for the Farm Colony program. Linville's actions were born in a world that supported, if not explicitly encouraged, the exploitation of people like Wilson and McNeil.

BY THE 1930S, counter forces began to emerge. Reform efforts spearheaded by the federal government pressed on the walls of the State Hospital for the Colored Insane. The election of President Franklin D. Roosevelt and the implementation of his New Deal programs marked a rapid expansion of federal responsibilities and influence.

Rural regions like the South tried to avoid dependence on federal support. Southern resisters were concerned about more than their pride, however. They wanted to protect traditional agricultural systems, such as sharecropping. They believed that only with these discriminatory labor practices could agriculture remain profitable. With federal aid came pressure to reform, including pressure to improve social and working conditions for African Americans. Programs such as the Civilian Conservation Corps explicitly rejected racial discrimination. Other programs provided jobs, literacy training, and government-funded music projects for black North Carolinians.[40] Despite the White House's restrictions on some of its policies to accommodate allies in the "Solid South," and despite the fact that local administrators from federal relief agencies often wanted to preserve the caste system of Jim Crow by making more aid available to whites than to blacks, the pervasive presence of New Deal efforts seemed to threaten the ability of southern states to maintain economic and social control over its black constituents. Across the state of North Carolina, many local politicians and citizens resisted Depression relief initiatives.[41]

The South, with its agricultural base, generally received less funding from

Roosevelt's New Deal programs than did the rest of the country. North Carolina was not a primary recipient of targeted projects like the Tennessee Valley Authority. Still, programs like the Works Progress Administration (WPA) funneled tens of millions of dollars into the state for the improvement of roads, schools, military bases, libraries, and hospitals.[42] Goldsboro was one of the hospitals directly affected by the New Deal plan. Perhaps out of desperation, Superintendent Whelpley's administration accepted the extended hand of the government in order to expand the capacity of the hospital. Between 1938 and 1940, WPA projects supplied almost half the funding needed to build "a new administration building with separate offices for assistant physicians, an executive department, examining rooms, and offices for stenographers. Included were a new x ray room, laboratory and dentist's office, . . . male and female convalescing wards; additionally two new U-shaped buildings for male patients, accommodating 300 patients each; [a] new female insane building which holds 100 beds; [and a] new superintendent's residence."[43] Staff also received new housing. White employees "gained six new five-room cottages, complete with baths for each and nice shingled roofs." Six one-story duplex cottages with metal roofs were meant for "colored" employees.[44] An additional WPA project helped the hospital construct several other buildings by the summer of 1939. Whelpley wrote Governor Clyde R. Hoey, "We are hurrying arrangements to move into these buildings. Part of this project is replacement and part new buildings, and will give us an increased capacity of approximately 450 patients."[45]

Even as Goldsboro administrators accepted federal aid, they refused to alter internal procedures. Food rationing continued. Inspections consistently noted that the hospital needed more staff. Trying to keep the board of directors from knowing about the dire state of the hospital, administrators reduced the number of meetings with the board. One director resigned in protest.[46] Both Linville and Whelpley walked the fine line between emphasizing the positive services offered by the hospital and asking for relief from the acute situation there.

BETWEEN 1930 AND THE 1950S, Goldsboro changed superintendents four times. With only one exception, all of them were promoted from within the institution. Although a few physical modifications were apparent—new buildings, expanded farmlands, additional equipment, and the like—hospital policy remained static. The institution continued to emphasize custodial care rather than psychological treatment.

During this period, activists promoted efforts at societal improvement that swept the country. Physically segregated from mainstream society, many state institutions across the nation were slow to adopt reforms. After more than a decade of campaigns, advocates of prisoner rights eventually succeeded in forcing North Carolina to respond to their concerns. By the 1940s, the state eliminated the system of leasing out convict chain gangs. Despite the limited reform, North Carolina continued to require state work such as road repair to be done by prisoners.

Around the same time, the state experienced some pressure to reform its mental hospitals that housed white residents. A 1942 exposé of the Morganton Hospital sparked the call for improvements. Lawyer and journalist Tom P. Jimison spent a year as an inmate at the Morganton asylum. The appalling conditions he found there motivated him to write a series of articles on the state of the hospital and publish them in the *Charlotte News* and *Greensboro Daily News*. As Jimison detailed, illiterate and untrained staff depended on assistance from patients for daily tasks and received favors in turn.[47] As in Goldsboro, Morganton patients sewed clothing, maintained the grounds, and labored on the institution's farm. Although the work was arduous, men and women often actively sought such assignments, said Jimison, because "work was more than an avenue to special favor. Work details afforded momentary escape from the wards and provided the only opportunity for physical exercise in an otherwise unplanned daily regime of sleeping, eating, and aimless waiting. Patients who worked could at least escape the hours of dreary wandering on the ward."[48]

Jimison's shocking reports caused a public outcry. Ordinary citizens demanded that the state investigate and resolve the problems that he described. A hasty state inspection concluded that Jimison's claims were not credible. The momentum for reform temporarily stalled.[49] Although the public outrage abated, organizations such as the Charlotte Mental Health Society continued to demand enhanced state supervision of the mental health system. Significant reforms did not occur for another decade. Conspicuously absent from the flurry of responses to the Jimison series was concern over the status of the state mental hospitals for African Americans.[50]

In 1944 the state legislature established the North Carolina State Hospitals Board of Controls as a means of overseeing the entire mental health care system. One of the goals of the board was to reign in the unchecked authority of superintendents over their individual institutions. In 1945 a group was appointed by the governor to inspect all the state mental institutions: Morganton, Raleigh, Goldsboro, and the Caswell Training Center. As one scholar later reported, the tour "made [the leader] so physically ill that on several occasions during the tour he had to excuse himself from the group. The shock of recognizing conditions within the hospitals" motivated him to call for immediate and significant change.[51]

North Carolina's mental hospitals resembled institutions across the South and the nation. During the 1940s, numerous articles and books revealed appalling conditions of state mental institutions from New York and Ohio to Georgia.[52] Calls for action resulted in some reforms. Like leaders across America, North Carolina's new governor, Greg Cherry, espoused hospital reform. He specifically criticized the superintendents at Caswell and Goldsboro for "operating on a 'make-do' philosophy."[53] Despite his statements, the hospital at Goldsboro remained underfunded and understaffed. Until the hospital integrated in the 1960s, Goldsboro continued to use patient labor for profit.[54]

THROUGHOUT THE GREAT DEPRESSION, black doctors and activists added to the pressure already felt by Goldsboro and other segregated institutions, frequently referring to the stark conditions at black hospitals in their quest to gain access. Issues of economics and social uplift pervaded their solicitations. Activists argued that black physicians would provide better care since they had a vested interest—professionally and socially—to care for members of their race. Repeatedly, advocates pressed the governor and board at Goldsboro to allow the outside community in. They received a cold response.

Charles Clinton Spaulding, the leading advocate and voice of the African American community in the state in the 1930s, was particularly interested in Goldsboro Hospital. As head of the North Carolina Mutual Life Insurance Company, one of the largest black-run businesses in the world, Spaulding had close ties to the medical community and to the black middle class in Durham.[55] Like Booker T. Washington, Spaulding advocated racial uplift through educational and business success.[56] Acutely aware of the need for both improved medical services to black patients and greater professional opportunities for black physicians, Spaulding allied with Edson E. Blackman, the head of the Old North State Medical Society (the state's black physicians' association). Both men wanted black doctors to have opportunities to work in state hospitals. They even dreamed of African American leaders running the segregated institutions.

Efforts to integrate the workforce of hospitals like Goldsboro reflected important changes in the medical profession and in the Jim Crow South. During this time, as one historian has summarized it, "Public hospitals . . . were run by whites. . . . Most African Americans who worked in the region's public hospitals before the 1950s did so with a mop, not a scalpel."[57]

The professionalization of medicine promoted affluent white men and increasingly shunned minorities.[58] Opportunities for African Americans to enter medical school were slim. However, in the early part of the twentieth century, North Carolina was one of the few states in the South that offered medical training for blacks. Leonard Medical School in Raleigh, a division of Shaw University, had been established in 1880.[59] In its formative years, Leonard was considered the most successful medical school of its kind. The state had donated the site for the school's buildings. The Baptist Mission Society for Negroes, as well as individual philanthropists, helped fund the program.[60] The school's faculty included both white and black professors. By 1909, the school had 125 students and roughly 500 alumni.[61]

Racism undermined the long-term success of Leonard and other schools. Even with training, African American doctors would have been marginalized in the South. But black medical schools generally also were underfunded, had inadequate facilities, and offered shorter programs and lower requirements than white schools. They had no accreditation from the American Medical Association, the preeminent professional organization of physicians. Consequently, graduates of black medical schools were blocked from many medical societies, residency programs, and professional appointments.

In 1910 Abraham Flexner, an eminent educator and researcher, produced a report for the Carnegie Foundation for the Advancement of Teaching, eviscerating most of the medical programs for women and those with small endowments, including black southern medical programs such as Leonard in North Carolina. The Flexner report encouraged philanthropic and state sponsors to fund only two black medical schools: Meharry Medical College in Tennessee and Howard University in Washington, D.C. Many organizations complied with Flexner's recommendations, and by 1920 only Meharry and Howard were still open. Leonard held on for five years after the report was published but closed its doors in 1915.[62]

Spaulding and Blackman's campaign to place black doctors in Goldsboro began with a stream of letters to Governor J. C. B. Ehringhaus. Following a similar plea by Blackman in the spring of 1934, Spaulding challenged the white-only cadre of doctors at Goldsboro. He made his case to Ehringhaus: "As a Trustee of the Morrison Training school located at Hoffman, North Carolina, it has been my pleasure to witness the efficient management and continued progress of that institution. . . . It has been my experience that Negro physicians are in [a] better position to know the needs of this group in the execution of a rehabilitative program than others, because the Negro physician is better acquainted with the social background and the social factors contributing both to delinquency and insanity."[63]

As the only such institution of its kind in the state, and as a particularly neglected facility, Goldsboro represented an important battleground for Spaulding. As he wrote, "The object of this plan is purely in the interests of the inmates of the Insane Asylum for Negroes at Goldsboro with the hope that a Negro personnel, including an executive, be appointed for that institution. There are a number of physicians of my own acquaintance that are eminently fitted for responsibilities involved in the management of such an institution. I would be pleased to recommend such a person at such a time as proved satisfactory to you."[64]

GOVERNOR EHRINGHAUS FORWARDED the letters to Goldsboro, asking the board of directors to resolve the issue. By the end of the summer, the board had discussed and decided the matter. The board and the governor curtly informed the Old North Medical Society that Goldsboro "use[s] no internes [sic] at the Hospital and have no arrangements for such service, which would require additional outlay in housing facilities not now available." Board members also suggested that African American interns were inherently inferior to any white doctors: "The physicians used at this institution are those of special training in the treatment of mental and nervous diseases," they explained, alluding to the limited training that black doctors commonly received. Neither the board nor the governor acknowledged Spaulding's larger request for a black executive or board member.[65]

Blackman and his fellow doctors continued to press. Hoping to incite reform from above, they wrote again to the governor the following January: "Our Society wants to be of service to the State, and we are respectfully requesting Your Excellency to appoint two members of our Society on the Board of Directors of the Hospital for the Insane at Goldsboro when such vacancies occur. This gesture would encourage not only the members of our profession, but the entire Race. Our society stands ready at all times to be of service to you and the State whenever the opportunity presents itself."[66] They received no response.

The activists reached out to other allies, including Charlotte lawyer William F. Scholl. Seeking a middle path, Scholl suggested that black doctors could uplift the institution without undermining white power.

[The Old North State Medical Society's] view is that [Goldsboro] hospital is exclusively for negroes and that this would be an encouragement to the professional negro man of the state. Inasmuch as a large section of our colored population has made a splendid advancement, it seems to me that we ought to do all that we can, not inconsistent with the existing social order, to assist and encourage their continued progress. I hope very much that you will have the same view about the matter and to do something along this line to help them.[67]

Refusing to intervene, Ehringhaus immediately wrote back to Scholl and reminded him that the black association had already contacted him. The matter belonged with the board of trustees, said the governor, "who as you know [has] complete control of the situation."[68]

By the end of that summer, John B. Cranmer had resigned from the board and the superintendent only had four physician assistants. Despite the openings on the board, the hospital made no move to include black doctors or trustees. Eventually, white physicians filled the spots.[69]

The state's new governor, Clyde R. Hoey, surprised many by expressing interest in the cause of black doctors at Goldsboro. In a letter to W. A. Dees, head of Goldsboro Hospital's board of trustees, Hoey suggested that the board consider designating African American doctors to the visiting staff for the hospital. "Of course I understand that you will select a white man as the doctor in charge, but I believe it would be a very nice recognition to give to worthy negro physicians to place some of them on the staff of visiting physicians of the Hospital. This is done for both of the white hospitals, at Morganton and Raleigh."[70] The governor also pointed out that visiting black doctors would not cost any more money. As he stated, "The visiting [white] physicians are not paid anything, but they come to the Hospital at various times and perform services and operations and other things when called upon by the physician in charge."[71]

Dees responded to the governor, "There have been from time to time for quite a number of years suggestions and efforts from one source or another to connect up the Negro medical fraternity in the State with the operation and services of the State hospital here. Though frequently the suggestions have looked plausible upon the face, they have been determined as impracticable after careful consideration." He continued, "There seems to be some difficulty in the relationship between the White and Negro races and in the relationship perhaps especially between the White and Negro physicians which makes the operation of an enterprise by their joint participation impracticable." Not wanting to seem close-minded before the governor's request, Dees demurred: "Due consideration is being given to the matter by the Board and I am requested to state that you will be further advised as to the consideration advanced."[72] Hoey did not apparently press him further on the issue.

As Hoey's administration came to a close, Spaulding appealed to the governor's desire for a lasting legacy: "Before you leave office, I should like for you to have credit for doing just a few more outstanding things for the Negroes of North Carolina." He continued, "We would like to see you appoint a Negro physician as Superintendent of the Goldsboro Insane Asylum for Negroes. Our state institutions, which are operated for negroes, are the only places in the State wherein Negroes can demonstrate their ability to successfully lead others into worthwhile pursuits."[73]

There was significant pressure to resist. Many whites believed that black physicians, regardless of their credentials, were fundamentally inferior to white physicians. For them, no black doctor was worthy to serve in the asylum. Even as a marginal and underfunded institution, Goldsboro still represented a dominion of white control and power. Superintendents like Linville and Whelpley had little interest in sharing their facilities with black doctors. Administrators may also have been concerned that African American physicians, supported by an all-black staff, would question or challenge exploitative programs like patient leasing and the hospital farm. The hospital was completely dependent on patients' free labor to subsidize its budget and feed the hospital community. As an institution founded in large part on Jim Crow beliefs, the Goldsboro mental institution could not consider abandoning or reforming the practice. Perhaps the board also feared that black doctors or trustees might draw undue attention to other problems on Goldsboro's campus: poorly prepared food, lack of bedding, rat infestation, and the cages on the lawn still used for unruly patients. If black doctors were allowed to work at the hospital, they would be able to use their knowledge of the internal workings of the hospital to reveal the truth through black newspapers and other media that in turn would harm the reputation of the administration and state. The risks seemed too great. Jim Crow ruled the South, and it was inconceivable for a state hospital to challenge this. In the end, Goldsboro Hospital chose racist policies over the alternatives posed by black activists.

Throughout the 1930s and 1940s, hospital administrators and advocates contested all efforts to change the institution. W. A. Dees was especially adamant: "The State has no reason to feel in the least apologetic for what it is doing for this group of our unfortunate colored population."[74]

Conditions within the hospital remained relatively unchanged over the years. Although the institution isolated Wilson and the other individuals from some of the chaos occurring outside, it also created barriers to reforms that might have bettered the lives of the inmates: the efforts of the federal government, the investigations of public interest groups, and the campaigns by African American doctors to seek employment within the walls.[75]

ALTHOUGH JUNIUS WILSON might have experienced a slowed sense of the passage of time within the virtually unchanging world of the hospital, that was not the case for his family in Castle Hayne. By the 1940s, Mary Wilson Clark's life altered dramatically. In 1937 Annie Smith passed away after a battle with cancer. Arthur Smith Jr. died in November 1944 from heart and kidney failure.[76] Their deaths left Mary without necessary financial assistance, but at the same time she had a new kind of freedom.

Mary's need for financial support probably motivated her to locate her former husband, Sidney Wilson. After leaving the family decades earlier, Wilson's father had moved with the railroad to Waycross, Georgia, where he remarried.[77] Since Mary could not read or write, it would have been difficult for her and Sidney to maintain contact after their divorce. He likely did not even know about his son's arrest or institutionalization. No longer tethered to the Smiths, Mary and her literate daughter Carrie sent word to her father and he returned to North Carolina.

At Mary's request, Carrie and Sidney traveled to Goldsboro to seek Wilson's release. As they entered the town on 5 June 1947 and turned down the main road to the hospital, they passed by the banners and flags erected to celebrate Goldsboro's centennial anniversary. Sidney and Carrie arrived on the grounds of the State Hospital for the Negro Insane. Apparently, both father and daughter believed in Wilson's innocence and sanity. They hoped that by revealing his true condition, they could get him out of the institution. They also had a pressing need that, they believed, provided mitigating circumstances to the deaf man's incarceration: Mary wanted a home constructed in Castle Hayne. As her only son, Junius Wilson was expected to help provide for his mother in her old age. For the Wilson family, it was time for him to come home.

Walking onto the grounds of the hospital—with its fences, barred windows, and patients in cages—must have frightened Carrie and Sidney. They located the administration building to ask where they might find Wilson. Waiting while his files were located, they spoke with the social worker on duty. Staff member G. M. Johnson entered a brief account of the visit in Wilson's patient file: "Patient's sister Carrie Gill . . . visited today for first time in 22 years. She was going to build a house and wanted patient to help her. . . . Patient's father Sidney Wilson . . . also came."[78] Carrie implored the social worker for his assistance: "Carrie insisted the p[atient] be released to live with his mother. She also said he was to live with his aunt at Bolton. It was fairly obvious that she & her father wanted p[atient] to assist them with building a House near Castle Hayne N.C."[79]

After describing the nature of their visit, Carrie and Sidney followed a staff member out toward the farm where the deaf patient lived and worked. The distance between the main campus and farm would have offered them some time to reflect on Wilson's environment. His sister and father must have wondered if their relative would recognize them. He was only a young boy when his father had left and only a teenager when police had taken him away in front of Carrie. Decades had since passed, and all three had changed significantly. How would they communicate with each other? How could they make him understand what they wanted?

It is unknown what transpired during the meeting or how long the visit lasted. In order to read their lips, Wilson might have leaned in close to his sister and father. Unable to voice articulately, he might have gestured his life story at the hospital, pantomiming farmwork, the criminal ward, perhaps memories of Castle Hayne or the deaf school. Perhaps he felt confused, even frightened, by their presence and unsure what to do or say around them. Communication barriers, compounded by years of separation and misunderstandings, could have intensified emotions. Surely he was hopeful. Wilson must have wondered whether he would finally be going home.

Sister Carrie spelled out words she wanted to convey, including their mother's married name (Mary Clark) and her new address in Castle Hayne. Over the next five decades, Wilson repeatedly wrote this new information down for anyone who would look, pointing at names and addresses and nodding at them. He knew his family and he remembered his home. He wanted to be there with them.[80]

What happened at the end of the family's meeting? Did Carrie and Sidney believe that they would attain Wilson's release? How were such decisions made, and when would they be notified? Eventually Carrie and Sidney walked away from Wilson. Frustrated and unsure what their visit meant, he watched them go. Did he think he would see them again?

Wilson was not released from the asylum. Legally, the hospital could not simply discharge a man accused of a crime and found insane. If they said that Wilson was mentally competent, hospital administrators would have to send him back for trial in Wilmington. The hospital would lose a valuable worker who, from their perspective, had become closely integrated into the hospital community. Perhaps the racial discrimination of the era further reduced Wilson's chance of being released. The administrators at Goldsboro might have paid scant attention to undereducated, working-class blacks such as Sidney Wilson and his daughter. They might have had little respect or sympathy for the relatives' plea. Perhaps realizing that family efforts at intervention were futile, both his father and sister refrained from subsequent attempts to see Wilson. According to the hospital documents, he never saw his sister or father again. It would be almost five decades before Wilson would see any of his relatives.

Unable to get her son back and without a house of her own, Mary decided to leave her hometown in North Carolina. She moved with Carrie to live in New York. Depending on her literate daughter to dictate her letters, Mary continued to contact Goldsboro and ask about her son's welfare. Although the hospital did not save her letters, a copy of one reply from the superintendent in May 1958 remains in Wilson's file, acknowledging Mary's letters of concern. Because Wilson had received no formal diagnosis, superintendent Mintauts Vitols had little to say about his mental status. Nor did he mention Wilson's deafness. Vitols kept to a description primarily of Wilson's behavior: "He is still confused but gives us no trouble. His eating and sleeping habits are good." Emphasizing that Wilson was a "good" inmate, he continued, "he is cooperative and works on the farm." Vitols ended the note: "We continue to give him the very best of care."[81] Wilson apparently never saw his mother's letters or knew that she continued to write them.

JAMES MCNEIL, MEANWHILE, presented a similar quandary for the institution. By the 1940s, hospital employees working in the CI ward knew that the black deaf man was not a dangerous menace who needed to be locked up. Instead, McNeil's calm demeanor and friendly personality made some staff members treat him as more of a peer or a pet than as a patient. During his tenure, A. B. Howell, the supervisor of the CI ward, befriended the deaf inmate and became his de facto patron, bringing McNeil home with him for meals and vacations. In return, McNeil assisted Howell, watching patients and running errands during the 1940s. The white supervisor eventually discovered the circumstances leading to McNeil's admittance to the institution and helped him find his family. Sometime probably after the Second World War, Howell drove McNeil to the family homestead. The reunion did not go well. According to another staff member, McNeil's kin "didn't seem too interested in him."[82] Howell pressed Lizzie McNeil, the deaf man's mother, to come see her son at the hospital, which she agreed to do. No evidence remains of the visit. Howell told a colleague that the mother did not return after that. He later told other staff that the woman had passed away by the early 1950s. McNeil did not attend the funeral. Hospital employee H. Jack Allen met McNeil's sibling during his own tenure in the CI building. "He had a sister who came to visit in the 1950s," the thin white man remembered, "but then no one else came."[83] It is not fully known to what extent hospital policy, McNeil's legal status, and his family situation, among other factors, kept him at the hospital for more than half a century.

FOR THE DECADES THAT Junius Wilson lived at the Farm Colony, the deaf man learned to make do, assisting staff with extra jobs in order to gain favors from them. Ultimately, he was able to negotiate his own place in the institution, living in the margins and making himself useful.[84] Wilson was exposed to a level of freedom beyond anything he had experienced before at the hospital. Like Wilson, McNeil found a place for himself doing what he was supposed to, working for the hospital, and making friends with the staff. By improvising, these two men, like countless others, weathered the Depression years.

Goldsboro enforced the isolation of Wilson and McNeil. The deaf men saw no one who knew their language and culture. Within their own worlds, Wilson and McNeil spent years unaware of the presence of the other. While his supervisor sought improvements for McNeil, apparently his kin could not or would not seek his return home. In contrast, Wilson's immediate family sought to break that isolation, writing to the hospital and petitioning for his release. His family's efforts, like those of reformers, were unsuccessful. Walls, both real and symbolic, continued to confine the men.

Renaming, Remaining (1950s–1970s)

He has no workup here in the hospital and no diagnosis has
been made. Patient resides in the farm where he is described as
very co-operative, eating and sleeping well and causing no trouble.

JUNIUS WILSON MEDICAL FILE CLINICAL NOTES, 31 MAY 1963

He communicates with his own learned sign language but it is
difficult for the staff to interpret the signs and . . . he tends to withdraw
or isolate himself from people if he does not get response from
what he wants to say to people. In this situation his affect becomes
somewhat sad because he cannot be understood.

**HERNANE C. RESTAR, M.D., TREATMENT TEAM REVIEW
NOTES FOR JUNIUS WILSON, 17 OCTOBER 1975**

NORTH CAROLINA, ALONG WITH many other states, has a long history of
renaming its mental institutions to reflect current thinking about both the role
of such institutions and the position of inmates within. Originally called the
Asylum for Colored Insane, the institution became the Eastern North Carolina
Insane Asylum by the early 1900s. Despite the implications of its moniker, the
mental institution in Goldsboro housed black mental patients from across the
entire state. The geographical name referred to its location in the eastern part of
the state rather than the population it served. Fundamentally, the name change
represented only a shift in state-level categorization.

By the end of the nineteenth century, state institutions across the nation
sought to redefine their facilities in profound ways. New belief in the power of
treatment meant that asylums sought not to hold patients away from the demands of the world but provide therapies that would allow their return to
larger society. To symbolize their changing purposes, states and superintendents replaced the word "asylum" with "institution" or even "hospital." "Inmates" became "patients."[1] The institution in Goldsboro became known as the
State Hospital at Goldsboro. Similar changes occurred at other state mental
hospitals. In addition, institutions designed to provide education for students
with disabilities began to clarify their names to reflect their mission. Such
places as the school where Junius Wilson had been a student changed from its

original 1868 name, the North Carolina Institution for the Education of the Deaf and Dumb and the Blind, Colored Department, to the State School for the Deaf and Blind, Colored Department, by the First World War.

In June 1959 North Carolina's state legislators contemplated yet another name change. With a stroke of the pen, they ratified House Bill 1131, an uncontroversial law that changed the names of many state hospitals and training schools, including Goldsboro's mental institution.[2] Wilson's home since 1925 was now to be known as Cherry Hospital. The new title honored former governor Greg Cherry, a man who had advocated expanding state mental hospitals during his administration. State representatives gave new titles for other state mental institutions as well, naming the Raleigh hospital after famed reformer Dorothea Dix and others after other North Carolina governors. By affiliating mental hospitals with prominent state leaders, politicians hoped to invoke respectability for their facilities.

In many ways, House Bill 1131 and the renaming of the institution presented merely a superficial policy shift. The state did exert greater supervision over its health care providers, but changes in the treatment of patients happened very slowly. And although its new name nudged Cherry Hospital into closer rhetorical alignment with its white-only counterparts, actual parity and integration would take much longer to realize.

Jim Crow customs remained at Cherry Hospital into the 1960s and beyond. The institution's business office argued that "the lack of facilities is not due to racial biases but the fact Negro patients are willing to accept what is provided for them 'which is more than they have at home.' "[3] A nurse followed up: African American patients were at the institution "for refuge more than for treatment."[4] Others echoed the belief that black patients were fortunate to live at the hospital: "They have three hots, a roof and a warm bed so they have no reason to complain."[5] Another nurse added, "I know the Negroes well, I have lived with them all of my life. They just don't demand. They are conditioned that if the roof falls in, 'don't be concerned,' or if they are out of work, 'don't worry, food will be available somehow because the whites have always looked out for us.' " She was skeptical about offering additional privileges to African American patients like those offered to white patients at other state asylums: "[Blacks] are going to have to show they can be responsible for the same things the white people have earned."[6]

Ignorant of repeated efforts since the 1930s by Charles Spaulding and the Old North Medical Society to integrate hospital staff, one white hospital inspector reported in 1955: "I talked with some of the people about the fact that there were no colored physicians on the staff. One person brought up the fact that to his knowledge no colored physicians had ever applied. I would rather suspect that this is so, since the number of colored physicians trained in this country is relatively small and most of them find ready and lucrative employment in some of the larger northern cities where they feel better accepted." Inspector Robert Barnes, like most of the staff, concluded that Jim Crow power hierarchies would remain firmly in place: "I suspect that the day when there will be well trained colored physicians available for these positions is a long ways in the future."[7]

DESPITE THE PERVASIVE RACISM that surrounded Cherry Hospital, there were signs of imminent change. Both staff members and patients at the institution heard news of the emerging civil rights movement. Some might have seen 1955 television footage of Rosa Parks and the Montgomery boycott. Others knew of Martin Luther King Jr., or about the sit-ins that led to the desegregation of Woolworth's lunch counters in nearby Greensboro, North Carolina. Over the next decades, important steps would weaken the barriers built by Jim Crow. Freedom rides beginning in 1961 grew into Freedom Summer in 1964. Federal civil rights acts and voting rights acts answered countless beatings, lynchings, and acts of unnamed terror that had marginalized thousands of American citizens for generations. For many Americans, including many African American staff members at Cherry Hospital, this period represented a heady time of direct action and willing a dream to life. But for many institutionalized people like Junius Wilson and James McNeil, much of the rhetoric and experience of civil rights activism remained remote, if not utterly invisible. Instead, such patients remained inside the walls of the institution, segregated from the tangible promise developing in the world outside.

The push for civil rights against entrenched Jim Crow norms played out somewhat differently in Goldsboro than it did in other parts of the state. Eastern North Carolina historically represented the most conservative part of the state, and semirural areas like Goldsboro consistently supported staunch segregationists. After the *Brown v. Board of Education* Supreme Court decision in 1954, white supremacist organizations like the North Carolina Patriots, Inc., gained support in the area; its vice president, Robert E. Stevens, was a Goldsboro resident.[8] In 1968 voters from the region strongly supported presidential candidate George Wallace. One observer noted several years later that "on a highway billboard not twelve miles from Goldsboro [was] printed the message, 'Welcome to Ku Klux Klan country.' "[9] After the 1969 Supreme Court ruling against duel school districts, Goldsboro adopted desegregation policies much more rapidly and successfully than did other towns across the state and region.[10] In recognition of its progressive desegregation plans, Goldsboro's city schools won a Thom McCann award.[11]

But even as white and black schoolchildren began to study together, race relations outside the classrooms changed little. African Americans increasingly moved into the town, but Jim Crow boundary lines distinguished neighborhoods by racial composition.[12] The town leadership also remained monolithically white and affluent.[13] Unlike Atlanta or Durham, the semirural Goldsboro had no parallel African American power structure. For these reasons and more, few prominent white elders could even recall the names of important black citizens from Goldsboro.[14]

Goldsboro's psychiatric hospital also remained apart from broader national trends in mental health care. By the mid-1950s, psychiatric drugs such as thorazine, as well as antidepressants and tranquilizers, became popular treatments for patients in mental institutions. Organizations like the National Association of Mental Health increasingly demanded government reform for mental health services and promoted broad public awareness campaigns.[15] They specifically called for better funding, enhanced staff training, greater research on mental illness, and more service options for patients. Across the nation, a turn toward community psychiatry, which included new forms of treatment and rehabilitation programs, began to blossom at this time.[16] Sociological studies like Erving Goffman's 1963 classic work, *Stigma*, criticized the inherent oppressive character of asylums. Investigative reports called for an end to "warehousing" men and women inside hospitals.

JUNIUS WILSON CONTINUED to work on the hospital farm through the early 1960s. His main job was that of "the water boy," remembered one staff member. While other patients worked in the fields, he went to nearby houses and pumped big buckets full of water to take back to the work parties. "He'd keep it in the shade to keep it cool and that was his job," stated the employee, "to keep water for the patients working in the field." Norwood Davis, the child of hospital employees, remembered that when he was a little boy, he would try to communicate with Wilson when the deaf man came to their house on the grounds of the institution to get water.[17] Wilson went on his own unsupervised to fill the bucket. No one was worried that the patient would escape.

The woods surrounding the area offered more choices and more opportunities to Wilson and other patients than the farm did. Residents explored the river, caught fish as well as small land animals that they persuaded the kitchen staff to cook, built camps in the woods, and roamed relatively freely around the large expanse of hospital land.[18]

Many of Goldsboro's citizens fished in the Little River, a tributary that ran by Cherry Hospital and meandered through the region. Others took picnics to the Quaker Neck Power Plant pond and fished there. To get to either fishing spot,

Little River, Goldsboro (Photograph by Susan Burch)

city residents had to cross the bridge and pass the intersection of Old Smithfield Road and N.C. 581-West, the main drag near the hospital. Junius Wilson established himself on the east side of the intersection and joined other patients selling cans of worms to passersby.[19] They dug up the worms in the woods near the river. Wilson knew that Goldsboro residents on the way to the fishing holes would pay him for his labor. One man remembered paying twenty-five cents a can, or a penny a worm.[20] "But let me tell you," remembered one staff member, "he'd sell you a cup full of dirt if you didn't watch out." Just a few worms would be on the top. "If you weren't careful, he'd hustle you."[21]

The son of a hospital employee remembered joining the patients by the roadside. "Me and other children," he said, "we'd all go dig worms and stand on the corner near the oak trees and we'd all rush to sell them." The children, like the patients, made "some cents to buy a Pepsi Cola" or other treats. "We were in competition with them."[22]

With the money he earned selling worms, Wilson bought more than the usual amount of candy and other snacks from the small country store located on the grounds of the institution. He ate some himself, but the majority he sold at inflated prices to the residents of Goldsboro who stopped at his worm stand. He made as much as twenty cents profit on each item.[23] One staff member who knew Wilson well claimed that he also acquired his goods without paying for them. "If he didn't have any money, he'd just take it," said the employee. "He was like a professional pickpocket. They couldn't never catch him. He was good at it. The man at the store told me many times, 'I know he's getting my stuff but I just can't catch him.' "[24]

After a while, he acquired a bicycle. "I have no idea where he got that bicycle from," said one staff member. As the years passed by, Wilson bought other bicycles.[25] Owning a bicycle gave Wilson independence that other patients did not enjoy. On his various Schwinns, Wilson could speed past pedestrians and investigate the perimeters of campus quickly. He escaped the more congested areas of campus and found solitude in little-visited areas away from other patients and staff. Often he went to the local store. After filling his basket with pouches of tobacco, Coca-Cola, and candy, the deaf man sold the goods to people he passed on his journeys. In that way he earned additional money to buy what he liked or to save carefully. He guarded his wheeled treasure, locking it away when not in use. Cleaned carefully everyday, Wilson's bike was his first prized possession.

Sometimes when Wilson was working on the farm, perhaps as far as five miles from the main hospital and from town, he would ride off on the bicycle. "And then he'd come back with a jar of water with ice in it." Staff on the farm "had no idea where it came from but it was mighty good [and] cold."[26]

Generations of children knew Junius Wilson as an affable, approachable man with a bicycle and a smile. His interest in their games and his playful demeanor fascinated many of Goldsboro's youth. They believed that he was "safe" and understood that he would never attempt to enter their homes or harm them in any way. Wilson especially identified with the boys riding bicycles. Expressing their own sense of freedom from the gaze of watchful adults, the boys shared a common understanding with Wilson that required no language.

Goldsboro resident Tim Harvey first saw Junius Wilson when Harvey was about six years old. He and some of his young friends sometimes threw rocks his way and then ran away. Sometimes Wilson teased them back: he hid around corners and jumped out at the boys. Often he watched the boys ride their bicycles and do tricks. Wilson even helped them build a bike ramp at one of their houses. Once, Wilson mimed to one of Harvey's friends that the boy was unable to perform a bicycle jump properly because his weight was distributed incorrectly. With Wilson's guidance, the boy learned to jump the ditch. Harvey knew a bit of sign language because his cousin attended the North Carolina School for the Deaf in Wilson. Between his rudimentary sign language abilities

One of Wilson's bicycles (Photograph by Susan Burch)

and Wilson's talents at pantomime, the boy and his friends were able to forge a friendship of sorts with the institutionalized man.[27] His bicycle gave Wilson the opportunity to smudge the labels that separated institutionalized patients and regular Goldsboro residents.

Wilson "was a fixture" around Cherry Hospital and the community at large. "He was somebody you expected to see," riding around downtown on his bicycle.[28] "I think anybody who grew up in Goldsboro in the '50s and '60s would remember him," stated one community member. To everyone in the small town, claimed one man, Junius Wilson "was an institution."[29]

JAMES MCNEIL WAS AN INSTITUTION, as well. He continued to live in the CI building until the 1960s. McNeil, still called "Big Dummie" or "Dummie Graham" by most of the hospital staff, had an "outside privilege card" that gave him the autonomy to travel around the campus, just as Wilson did.[30] While he spent his nights as a patient in the locked CI ward, during the days McNeil had the opposite persona: that of police officer. Although the post was not an official one, it was one recognized by the administration and one that lasted for decades.

Every morning he donned an official police uniform complete with hat, stick, and whistle and solemnly patrolled the grounds of the institution, including the hallways of the CI ward.[31] "He loved his little uniform," remembered a hospital employee.[32] One staff member thought that the assistant superintendent provided McNeil with a new police uniform every year.[33] Another suggested that "Dummie Graham knew all the Deputy Sheriffs that came to the hospital to admit patients. Several of them provided him with their old uniforms." Sometimes they also offered him ties or old badges or handfuls of quarters.[34] For at least a decade in the 1970s, James Sasser, the sheriff of Wayne County, gave McNeil a personalized brass nameplate (with the name "Dummie Graham") just like the ones he provided for the county's police officers.[35]

As one staff member recalls, McNeil was very proud to carry a whistle. "You see policemen carried a whistle . . . and Dummie felt that he should, too." Being deaf, McNeil had difficulty understanding exactly how to make it work. Rather than blow air into the mouthpiece, the employee chuckled, "he'd go 'whooo' into the whistle." McNeil's uniform was not complete without a pen or pencil. "People were forever giving them to him," remembered an employee. The pen was simply part of the costume: "Dummie couldn't write at all." Similarly, although he could not tell time, "he liked to have a watch and had one on all the time. He always had a watch."[36] One person even suggested he carried two cap guns.[37] James McNeil was particular about his dress and firm in his commitment to appearing professional. He watched how the sheriffs acted when they brought new patients to the institution and he emulated their behavior carefully.

McNeil, called "Police Dummie" by some employees, assisted the staff in controlling other patients. If he spotted a patient "doing something he wasn't supposed to, he'd go to the staff and tell them," said one employee.[38] McNeil also policed staff members and reported any questionable actions to the administration. Hospital workers were aware of this edge to the patient-policeman: "He wanted to rule you, you know?" When "Dummie" saw staff members eating in the patient dining hall, which was against hospital rules, he quickly called in Jack Allen, Howell's successor as supervisor of the CI ward. "He'd go to Jack's doorway and when the technician comes by, he'd grab them and jerk them into the room," recounted one employee. Then McNeil would "start gabbing" by making noises and gesturing, mimicking the staff eating chicken and miming the chastising he felt they deserved.[39] Similarly, if he saw a staff member "with a bottle of whiskey or anything" (even in their off-hours in homes on the hospital grounds), "he'd come up immediately" and inform the worker's superior. As one of the superiors said, the employees often "didn't like it too much but they were afraid to mistreat him because he stood in with the boss." Jack Allen himself acknowledged, "Dummie" would "watch what was happening" and "tell everything."[40]

During these decades, McNeil directed traffic at the crossroads that ran

James McNeil

through the campus of the hospital.[41] When the institution held a big celebration and invited the governor, McNeil proudly directed the governor's car.[42] Sometimes people would assume that the patient was an actual employee. "People would come up to him, thinking he was a cop, and they'd ask for directions," explained Chris Lancaster, a former hospital employee. "He'd start gesturing and making noise, and they'd just drive away, shaking their heads, wondering, 'What kind of policeman did they hire in this place?'" Even new employees could be fooled by McNeil. One person remembers trying to impress the policeman on her first day of work at Cherry Hospital. After she parked her big '63 Ford, "I thought I'd done so good parking in front of the policeman, and only later I learned he was a patient. . . . I tried so hard to impress him!"[43] Chris Lancaster, like other staff members, loved watching their confused expressions after encountering "Police Dummie."[44]

Through his persona as a police officer, McNeil found a way to straddle the border between staff and inmate. One staff member looked back on McNeil's experiences at the hospital and speculated, "He probably thought he was a staff member."[45] Another seconded that belief: McNeil avoided entertainment designed for patients, he reasoned, because "that was 'for the patients' and he wasn't a patient. He was a boss."[46] Perhaps, but no matter what McNeil did during the day, he knew where he slept at night. His active policing of the campus embodied myriad and complicated meanings.[47]

McNeil's chosen uniform explicitly symbolized power—power certainly unavailable to most mental patients housed in the CI ward. He also expressed power over low-level staff by exploiting his connections with superintendents and other superiors. At the same time, staff saw McNeil as a naive child whose antics merely provided amusement. The patient's expression of authority was so removed from the reality of the experience of hospital inmates that it simply confirmed for many staff members a certain amount of mental illness.

BEFORE DESEGREGATION, all hospital employees were required to live on the campus of the institution. Living on the grounds of a mental institution sometimes made for an unusual life for staff members. Once, when a visitor came to spend the weekend with the family of institution physician Clyde Brown Sr., the man said after his first night that he couldn't sleep well "because of all that screaming and hollering all night long." But most of the children of hospital employees grew up hearing the noises and "were used to it," according to Clyde Brown Jr.[48]

The behavior of some of the patients made for good stories to tell outsiders. For example, an elderly African American gentleman named Seaman believed he was the son of Christopher Columbus. Another was sure he was the president. "The only time he'd get upset was when they had the presidential elections," remembered Brown. When the radio announced that Franklin D. Roosevelt had been elected, the usually calm and gentle patient burst out, "How can they say so and so was the president? *I'm* the president!"[49]

Another patient traveled along the paths of the institution on foot, acting as if he were driving a car and slamming on breaks and squealing when necessary. But Brown's favorite story was this one: "I know one time they had in the CI building, they had a fellow there, he had one arm," reminisced Brown. "He escaped and ran right across the street . . . to our front porch, and sat in daddy's chair. . . . Instead of trying to get away, he'd come across and jump in that chair. Naked as a jay bird."[50]

H. JACK ALLEN BELIEVED that McNeil, despite his designation and nightly confinement in the CI building, was harmless. Allen became close to McNeil. Their friendship, although clearly shaped by their hierarchical relationship, was a real one. McNeil tended the garden behind the white supervisor's house. He also sometimes babysat Allen's children. "He enjoyed being around them and he'd just laugh and he'd hand them their toys," recounted Allen. "He wouldn't play ball or throw one back to them. But he was good to watch after them." Although McNeil usually did not come inside his house, Allen insisted that he eat with the family on one occasion. McNeil enjoyed his dinner, but "looked like he was concerned he was in trouble, doing something wrong."[51]

On several occasions Allen even took McNeil to the beach for the weekend. By including McNeil in the family vacations, Allen was continuing a caretaking tradition set by A. B. Howell. Often Allen and "Dummie" would fish together— or rather, as Allen recalled, McNeil would "stand there and watch me fish." Sometimes he teased McNeil by asking him to hold his line for a minute while he walked away. "And a fish bit it once and instead of him winding it in," said Allen, "he started screaming. He'd scream and laugh and enjoy it when a fish was caught, but he didn't want to fish himself. He didn't do that."[52]

McNeil actively expanded his circle of patrons on campus. After walking out of the CI building in the morning, McNeil regularly walked across the street to Clyde Brown's cottage. The two men had likely met inside the CI building, where the doctor conducted rounds. Brown's son vividly remembered McNeil's reserved place at his parents' breakfast table: "Mama would fix him breakfast. And he'd hang around the house and he'd always have a newspaper but he couldn't read. And he couldn't speak English, just squeal."[53] Then the deaf patient helped clean up. "He'd wash the dishes . . . and then do a little sweep up."[54] Mrs. Brown and McNeil established their own relationship. "He'd motion with his hands and he'd [talk with] Mama. If she wanted to know where my Daddy was and she'd put her hand on her forehead and put the hair back, and that meant 'Where's my Daddy.' And Dummie could just about tell her where he was. He knew everything that went on in the hospital. . . . He was smart."[55] By assisting the Brown family, McNeil found a refuge where he could enjoy a fresh-cooked meal, a home environment, and normal activities away from the CI ward.

James McNeil was not the only patient who spent time in white employees' houses. Only patients that the staff trusted were allowed to leave their wards. Staff families were selective about who they invited into their homes, as well: "You know, [only the ones] who were not violent," stated one man who grew up at the hospital.[56]

Some of the patients held regular jobs in white staff members' homes. Although the hospital might have forced inmates to do domestic work for the white employees, Clyde Brown Jr. believed the common practice of hiring patients existed only because patients "wanted to get out" of the more oppressive areas of the institution. Women typically did domestic work. "We had . . . a couple of ladies, one named Josie. I don't know her last name," remembered Brown, and there was Gladys who helped his mother do the cooking and cleaning. "They were like members of the family. One of them about adopted me like her child. She thought a whole lot of me."[57] The patients probably appreciated the opportunity to spend part of their days in a noninstitutionalized setting. No matter what their real attitudes about their employers, likely they were pleased by the small amounts of money they earned by doing such labor.

Elderly male patients sometimes served as child-care workers for the white families. Captain, "a nice old gentleman," watched Clyde Brown Jr. for years.[58] "I thought a lot of him," he said. "I probably thought more of him than I did my father." Captain entertained the children with a billy goat and looked after the chickens that provided the family's morning eggs. When the hospital held a Christmas parade, Captain would "hook that goat up to a cart-wagon and he'd put [my sister and me] in the parade with the goat."[59]

Captain also introduced young Brown to chewing tobacco—at the age of three or four. "I had all the vices. He made me a pipe, a corn cob pipe, and we'd sit around and smoke," recalled Brown. "But back then they didn't fuss or nothing." Captain shared his tobacco ration not only with young Clyde but also with the billy goat.[60]

WHILE MOST WHITE STAFF lived in comfortable homes along Shady Lane, most black attendants were grouped into houses on "Happy Hill" along N.C. 581-West. Eugene Bell looked back fondly on his days growing up at Happy Hill.[61] The families who lived there regularly had dances and picnics. Often they sat outside socializing. "There were so many families, you couldn't get bored," recalled one neighborhood resident.[62] A white staff member who recognized both the closeness of the people who lived at Happy Hill and its segregation called the area "a community unto itself."[63]

Both black and white children of hospital employees enjoyed playing on the campus of the institution. "When I arrived, it looked like a castle," remembered Clyde Brown Jr. "Like a big old castle." The land spread out over a hill and was covered with oak trees. "The whole hospital was our playground," he reflected. "I couldn't have had a better place."[64]

Black and white children often played together, "getting into mischief and carrying on," as well as swimming in the Little River, playing baseball, and skating. Sometimes they built forts out of bales of hay from the hay barns. "We got along fine," recalled one white man reflecting on his years growing up at the institution.[65] Active outdoor play allowed relatively easy association across racial lines.

Quiet play, requiring contact that was physically closer, challenged racial ideology significantly more. But the isolated environment of the hospital and the children's limited social opportunities encouraged the youngsters to try to find ways to cross boundaries. Often, for example, the children read comic books and traded them when they were finished: "They'd have some and we looked at them," stated a white person who grew up on the grounds, "then we'd swap ours with them."[66] Although the groups of children remained clearly set apart from each other in many ways, their play allowed black and white children to interact and identify with each other at least to some degree.

Crossing the road to reach Happy Hill represented an important if unmarked threshold. The highway line symbolized both Jim Crow and the regulations of the hospital: it separated white from black housing, while also dividing inhabitants in the wards from their caretakers. Patients traveled along this border constantly, selling worms or crafts. Wilson stayed mostly on the perimeter, selling worms at the stoplight but not crossing the highway. McNeil, on the other hand, sometimes ran errands to the houses there and frequently policed the area. On special occasions like Christmas, "Dummie" knocked on the cottage doors "so that he could get his gift that each family had for him."[67] Although the families of white supervisors such as H. Jack Allen and Clyde Brown welcomed McNeil into their neighborhood, the residents of Happy Hill were sometimes suspicious of him. For them, McNeil represented ties to the white establishment. They tried to avoid his watchful gaze, concerned that he would tell on them.

McNeil was active in the life of the institution. On Sunday mornings, he attended Sunday school and church services with staff members and other patients. Sometimes he went on picnics with residents from Happy Hill, for which staff members made his favorite foods, such as lemon custard. "Often times I would make it for him just because it was his favorite dish and to reward him for his thoughtfulness," recalled Pandora Wooten. "The activity that he enjoyed the most of all," she remembered, was the Friday night dance.[68] Held near the institution, patients flocked to the outdoor square dance. "All the female patients that were not too mentally upset, they'd dress up in the finest dresses," recalled Clyde Brown Jr. "And the men would dress up in their clean overalls and ties, and they'd go out. . . . That was their social outlet." Hospital staff members watched, occasionally joining the twirling squares.[69] Pandora Wooten remembered James McNeil as "a very smooth dancer" who could do all the dances of that day—"the waltz—the tango—or the slow drag."[70] As he did when wearing his policeman's uniform while patrolling the institution or pretending to read the newspaper while visiting the Browns, McNeil carefully mimicked the behavior of hearing, "normal" people around him.

IN ADDITION TO HIS WORK as a police officer, McNeil assisted staff members as they parked their cars. When one employee drove to the parking lot on her first day in 1971, McNeil motioned for her to pull out of the parking spot where she had parked. When she told him she would be working in the Royster Building, he read her lips, then escorted her car to the Royster parking lot. There he assigned her a parking spot. "I used it for . . . years," remembered the employee. "And every day he pointed and showed me where to go." When she worked the evening shifts, McNeil gave her a more convenient spot that was usually occupied during the day. "He made sure I had that second row to park in." She realized that McNeil was looking after her.[71] He always carried a towel with him so he could wipe down the car of a favored staff member.[72]

Sometimes McNeil would go to the canteen to pick up something that individuals needed. At other times, he brought some of them newspapers.[73] He also ran errands for staff members and administrators. Although he was illiterate, he could recognize several written words. "He would go to the mail room," remembered one employee, "and they'd give him the mail for the carpenter shop and for the criminal department and he could look at it and tell [the names of the supervisors at those departments]."[74] Stated another employee, "When he was a policeman, they'd let him take little messages around, charts and stuff to the CI building. That's the place where he worked."[75] The building did not have a telephone at that point. Instead, messengers dropped notes through slots in the front door. McNeil's work as a messenger spared the labor of paid employees of the institution.[76] He was not the only patient to work as a messenger. "We had patients who were runners," remembered an employee. Her personal runner delivered not just information but packages around the campus. "It was a way to get off the ward and have a little freedom."[77]

Although it was against hospital policy to give patients money, it was clearly not an uncommon practice. Apparently, McNeil was given money by many people at the hospital: "He always had some money," said Chris Lancaster. "I don't know where all he got it from, but he always had some money in his pocket."[78] McNeil knew his labor was valuable. "Now he could make a '6' or '9' or other figures," said CI supervisor Jack Allen. "On pay day, he'd get a pencil and paper and write a few numbers he knew and put numbers underneath it and draw a line as if he was adding up, as if he were presenting you a bill." He continued, "You were supposed to pay him when payday came along. And mostly we did."[79]

Like McNeil, Junius Wilson acquired money through contacts with staff members. They paid him for favors and for running errands, and they paid him marked-up prices for goods he brought from the local store. Not only did the two men have pocket money, they also were given the responsibility to decide how to spend it. With the money Wilson earned, he bought bicycles and bicycle accessories as well as special foods and jigsaw puzzles. Eventually Wilson accrued more than $7,000.[80]

Money was sometimes offered not as direct payment or as bribery but out of gratitude and friendship, mixed perhaps with pity. One hospital employee appreciated the help James McNeil offered her. When she learned that "he was mute and read lips," she decided to "give him a little money." It was her way of acknowledging his help. "When you knew him, he would do anything for you," she remembered. "I saw him as a human being who needed love and showed love," the woman expressed. One way she offered her love to McNeil was by presenting him with a box of candy on Valentine's Day. Even when the weather was too cold for McNeil to be out in the parking lot, she knew how to get it to him. She left the box on the dashboard of her unlocked car. She knew that when he went out, "he'd go and pick it up. And then lock the car afterwards. And he knew my car and I'd leave that for him on the dashboard."[81]

BY THE LATE 1960s, Wilson and McNeil knew about one another and occasionally had an opportunity to meet face-to-face. One social worker remembered the two men crossing paths, aware of one another, but almost living in different worlds. Wilson "was outside a lot, that's how I remember him. He enjoyed being out. . . . His ride [on his bicycle] was from the river to the railroad track." He would watch Wilson come closer, on "that road [that] was the same one Dummie directed traffic on."[82]

Both seemed drawn to a place near the center of campus: the baseball diamond. One man who grew up on the grounds remembered Wilson in the 1960s: "He was the guy that loved ball games. If someone hit a home run, he'd get so excited and would holler. He didn't care what team won."[83]

Wilson might have been reminded of his childhood days when he played ball with neighbors in Castle Hayne. Older, and more wary of crossing boundaries, the deaf man chose not to join the men on the field.[84] It is unknown whether anyone invited him to try. McNeil, too, held back, but the two former classmates watched the players swing and slide into bases and enjoyed the communal celebration of the game.

In addition to enjoying the visual spectacle of baseball, the sporting event provided each man with financial opportunities. "He always rode his bicycle with his wagon behind it and sold different items," one of Wilson's customers noted. The same man remembered McNeil "because he pushed a food cart to the ci building. . . . He would go down in the woods and get fishing worms, and sell them to people going fishing. During the summer he'd take the money from the fall or spring and go to the store to buy sodas and snacks. Then, he would come back to the ball field and to sell the items."[85] No one knows whether each man learned to sell his products merely by watching various hearing patients, or whether they learned from one another. But each reached the same conclusion: the way to enjoy perks—tobacco, snacks, and the like—was to have some business initiative and a dependable clientele. They had both.

No one present at the time understood the cultural meaning of these exchanges. It had been decades since each man had left the North Carolina School for the Colored Blind and Deaf in Raleigh, and they might not have recognized each other immediately. But eye contact and signed communication marks a deaf person, and the men apparently struck up easy conversations. One witness claimed that "when they got together they used sign language." Returning to Raleigh signs might have felt awkward for the men at first, having been denied access to their native language for so long. Deaf people who are isolated from signing for extended periods commonly refer to such linguistic reunions as "a relief," "coming home," or even, more tellingly, "waking up." As others watched the game, the men chatted. "They seemed to have fun around each other," one man recalled. "They'd use their sign language to communicate to each other."[86]

It seems that the deaf men did not actually seek out each other, except for the baseball games. Importantly, Junius Wilson and James McNeil did not join forces selling worms and snacks or travel together around the campus. Each man protected his own property and guarded his domain. Employees and experts later suggested that McNeil had limited intelligence and more limited language ability. One or both men might have felt his sign language skills had atrophied since arriving at Cherry.

Wilson might have felt uncomfortable around the man usually dressed in a policeman's uniform. Memories of his arrest and time in jail could have frightened him away from all officers. Some later suggested that Wilson believed he had been sent to Cherry because of his escape from the deaf school back in 1924. Memories of the school—like classmate McNeil—might reasonably unsettle Wilson. And Wilson consistently downplayed his difference from others at the hospital in order to get by. Communicating in actual sign language with McNeil might expose this difference. McNeil sought similar ends, but his means were opposite. He clearly saw himself as distinguished from all patients and did not want to socialize with those he saw as beneath him. Communicating in signs with Wilson could expose his similarity with another patient, undermining McNeil's uniqueness.

Junius Wilson and James McNeil used two different tactics in their efforts to distinguish themselves from the other mental patients at Cherry Hospital. Wilson was able to create an independent place for himself by taking full advantage of the expansive grounds around the Farm Colony. The river and the woods provided respite from institutionalized life. There, he was far removed from locked wards and unseen by guards. The presence of people on their way to local fishing holes gave Wilson the opportunity to fill his pockets with change. Eventually, the money he earned allowed him to purchase his first bicycle, a way to put even more distance between himself and the demands of the institution.

Wilson did his work without resistance, followed rules, and did not try to escape. Although he distinguished himself as an unusual patient by virtue of his dependability and apparent sanity, Wilson actively did not call attention to himself. Because of his good behavior and unobtrusive ways, supervisors did not hesitate to let him move freely around the community of Goldsboro. Although there were certainly ultimate limits to his freedom at Cherry Hospital, Wilson himself seemed to determine on a daily basis what the border of his world would be.

McNeil found a very different way to create opportunities for himself within the institution. Unlike the shy man on the farm who avoided engagement with people in authority, McNeil had constant contact with staff members. Rather than trying to escape their watchful eyes, he actively cultivated friendships with them. He sought to become one of them rather than one of their charges. Unlike Wilson, he distinguished himself not by acting like a sane patient but by acting like he was not a patient at all. The staff humored McNeil's efforts to pass as an employee. Although his tactics gave McNeil increased freedoms, they were ultimately seen by employees as a source of amusement, a harmless joke. He was "Dummie" to the staff, even to those who loved him. The forces of institutionalization had reformed both of the deaf men in critical ways, suppressing their cultural and linguistic ties and thus reinforcing their isolation.

5

Classified (1970s–1981)

No otherwise qualified individual with a disability in the United States . . .
shall, solely by reason of her or his disability, be excluded from the
participation in, be denied the benefits of, or be subjected to discrimination
under any program or activity receiving Federal financial assistance.

REHABILITATION ACT OF 1973, SECTION 504

Unable to care for himself because of his handicapps [*sic*].

**PHYSICIAN QUESTIONNAIRE FOR
JUNIUS WILSON, 29 DECEMBER 1975**

Respondent is mentally ill, and is imminently dangerous to himself or
others, and is in need of continued hospitalization.

COURT ORDER FOR JUNIUS WILSON, 11 JANUARY 1979

NEARLY A DECADE AFTER the *Brown* decision, mental hospitals in North Carolina began to desegregate. The 1964 Civil Rights Act, coupled with antidiscrimination policies with the lawsuits brought by black doctors and other factors, pushed state hospitals to integrate.[1] Many staff and patients had listened to radio reports or even followed the news of civil rights campaigns since the 1950s, but Cherry Hospital still seemed separate from the wave of social unrest and change that washed over the nation. Attendants and nurses received little information about patient transfers and had no official outlet to express their own concerns about integration.[2] Cherry employees, in turn, did not generally prepare the men and women for the impending disruption of racial status quo. Staff later confirmed that the patients had been told at the last minute or not been told at all that the hospital was desegregating. One nurse said: "I'm sure most of the patients heard about it on the radio or TV or they heard the staff talking about it. It wouldn't have made any difference because they had to go one way or the other."[3]

Junius Wilson, like many other black inmates, still labored on the farm during this transition and thus remained relatively isolated from the arrival of white patients on the main campus. News must have spread quickly, although it is unclear how or whether Wilson understood the profound implications of Cherry's new policy.

Both black and white staff at Cherry described the process as difficult. "Staff had to work real hard. It was an adjustment for us as well. And this was turbulent times racially for staff," recalled nurse Lulu Jolliff. "Of course Cherry had been a black hospital with a predominantly black staff and through integration they had to bring in and share both ways and that took some real doing on both parts. As I look back, it was a growing experience for us and sometimes a painful experience." She noted that a new hospital director, who had emigrated from Europe and was thus unaccustomed to the cultural complexities of Jim Crow, exacerbated tensions. "It was a problem for black staff because he was not as sensitive to issues in the South—coming from England—so there was an uprising of the black staff and he wasn't allowed to come back on campus," she explained. "As a result, we had several months of a lot of unrest. That got better when he was gone."[4] Silvia Weaver, an occupational therapist who arrived in 1971, added, "There was general unrest at the hospital . . . there was a lot of stuff going on, the racial stuff, and we saw that at the hospital."[5]

Some patients were sent to hospitals closer to their homes. A staff member complained:

> So what we had to do was locate the counties where these patients came from, locate families to move them, and then [transfer] them into the hospitals that would serve the counties where they were from. This was very traumatic. And vice versa. I worked with white hospitals and moved patients from there to Cherry. This was a terrible time for many patients. It uprooted them from hospitals where they had been for many years. Especially for Cherry—this was the only place where some had ever been. I went with transport to carry the patients to their new homes, worked with families around accepting this, and if they had no families they went to totally unfamiliar places.[6]

The influx of white attendants and black social workers, nurses, and physicians further challenged the hospital's traditional racial hierarchy. By 1970 the hospital had hired African American doctors and a dentist, adding a new layer of black authority to the hospital staff. Some white nurses were unaccustomed to working with black superiors and submitting to their judgments. Disagreements over titles and terms of address reflected broader concerns about status. Previously, black attendants were called only by their first names. White employees expected to be treated with more respect. White doctors at Cherry had always enjoyed deference from patients and staff, but black doctors did not always receive similar treatment from white patients or resistant white staff.

Racial tensions also flared between patients and their caretakers. As one report noted, "For white patients going to Cherry Hospital, and their families who visited, the 'separate-but-equal' principle which has historically guided the operation of all public institutions was, so to speak, at the door to haunt them."[7] Occasionally, white patients hurled insults at their African American nurses and health care technicians, who sometimes felt uncomfortable subduing or correcting white patients. They feared white staff and administrators would accuse them of "picking on the whites."[8] White employees had never expressed similar experiences or concerns when dealing with black men and women on the wards. White patients and their families, shocked by the conditions they faced at Cherry, commonly voiced their concerns and demands to administrators and to politicians. They, unlike black peers previously, generally received some response to their grievances.

Although many men and women praised the material improvements at Cherry that came with integration, the unequal distribution of resources became a central point of conflict. Black staff and patients were acutely aware of the material privileges afforded only to white patients. With the influx of whites came "cold water coolers on each of the floors, chairs replacing benches in the dining halls, knives and forks provided in addition to the traditional table spoons to eat with, patients allowed to wear personal clothes, a better grade of soap and toilet paper (a factor mentioned by most of the ward staff, both Negro and white), and larger issues of towels, washcloths, and other linens though still not near the needed level."[9] But at the beginning, only one building offered all these amenities, and most white patients were housed there.[10] As one disgruntled employee quipped, "I can't say the business office didn't plan to give the patients all these things before the whites came, but it's strange we never had any of these comforts for the many years before the transfers began."[11]

The arrival of white patients also disrupted broader labor practices. Earlier, staff commonly relied on patient labor to maintain the wards, run errands, and perform other menial tasks. "Before, no matter how the patients were 'coaxed' into working they were kept busy cleaning the floors, walls, windows, and ceilings," recounted a staff member. "It was part of the daily routine for the patients to do their assigned chores just as much as it was for them to eat and make their beds."[12] White patients, accustomed to limited chores at their previous institutions, refused to serve black staff. Although some men and women still provided voluntary service in order to curry favors, the practice of patient labor decreased significantly.

One of the most noticeable labor changes occurred on the farm. For decades, Cherry had used patients' unpaid labor to till the land and feed the campus. By the 1960s, hospital administrators hired more staff and encouraged fuller mechanization to supply food to its community. Rather than attempt integration of the farm, the hospital chose to transfer Wilson and his peers to wards on the main campus. It formally ended its use of patient labor on the farm.

Integration also altered the grounds of the campus. As the hospital began to integrate its wards, administrators had to consider ways of addressing the desegregation of employee housing. Although patients had little choice about the changes, staff members voiced their opposition. To avoid controversy, the hospital changed its housing policy: staff members were no longer required to reside in the institution's cottages. By 1970 most employees no longer lived on campus.[13] In the next several years, the hospital demolished some of its general dormitories for patients and some of the old staff housing. Only a few remained, including the house that Clyde Brown Sr. and his family had inhabited across the street from the CI building.[14]

WILSON'S TRANSFER TO THE main campus was not a completely positive move. Although life at the farm colony was often hard, requiring long hours in the hot sun, Wilson had managed to avoid much of the backbreaking work by serving as the water boy. He had grown accustomed to the daily rituals of farm life, rising early and heading out to the fields, sitting under shady trees during lunch, and returning to his dormitory in the late afternoon. He liked the animals on the farm, too. Sometimes employees noticed Wilson petting the mules, running his hands along their manes and patting their stocky sides.[15]

Wilson's file does not describe his response to the move. As with all other patients on the main campus, Wilson now lived in a locked ward. Apparently the hospital kept almost no records of Wilson or other patients at this time and thus were faced with the challenge of guessing his age. Assuming he was ten years older than his actual age, staff soon pressed to have him placed in a geriatric ward.[16]

By the mid-1950s, Goldsboro's hospital began medicating certain patients with tranquilizers and psychotropic drugs. Doctors apparently did not prescribe such pharmaceuticals for Wilson, but some of his peers on his ward were almost certainly heavily medicated.[17] Thorazine, a common antipsychotic drug, produced spasms and made it difficult for some of the men to eat. Many likely paced the halls, shuffling through the daze that tranquilizers and other medications manifest.

Other elderly men likely spent their days playing checkers or watching TV. Anecdotes from mental hospitals around the United States suggest that patients commonly passed the time by sitting or sleeping on chairs, gazing out the windows, or talking with others around them. Surrounded by less active patients, Wilson might have been frustrated. In addition, he had to instruct his new staff how to communicate with him. He would need to establish his own territory and rituals in this new space. Learning and teaching took time.

On the farm, Wilson had gained not only respect for his abilities but also the trust of staff members. After the move, he needed to prove again that he was unlike the mental patients on his ward, that he deserved special privileges and treatment. At the farm colony, he had easy access to open spaces and life away from the eyes of staff. In the geriatric ward, he found a life constrained by walls.

AT ROUGHLY THE SAME TIME that Wilson moved to the main campus, McNeil also changed wards, although not to the same one where Wilson lived. Since the Second World War, North Carolina had sent teams of inspectors to assess various state hospitals and mental institutions. During the 1960s, several groups came to Cherry Hospital, partly to inspect the campus in general and partly to examine the progress of integration. During one such visit, health officials questioned the status quo at Goldsboro's facility for the criminally insane. "The first thing [one inspector] saw here," remembered an institution employee, "was this fellow and we had another one, going in and out—we just had two." The investigator was shocked. He asked about McNeil, only to learn that the "policeman" was actually a patient assigned to the CI building. The inspector was uninterested in the rationale for breaking common hospital policies. He immediately set down the law: "You don't have any traffic in and out except in handcuffs or supervised," he told one employee. Rather than shackle the police-man, McNeil was transferred to another ward.[18]

In some ways, McNeil's move out of the CI building represented progress. The new ward presented calmer patients and fewer incidents of brutal violence. But it had its disadvantages. Like Wilson, McNeil had to establish a form of gestural communication with the staff at the new ward. He also lost contact with his friend, H. Jack Allen, who no longer could let McNeil assist him at the CI building. To a new crop of attendants, he had to prove that he and his job were important to the working of the institution. McNeil was still allowed to don his uniform and serve as a police officer, but as the years passed by, this treasured activity slowly came to an end. McNeil's paperwork, if there had been any, did not transfer with him. Staff who knew the deaf man starting in the 1960s only referred to him as "Dummie Graham," or "Policeman Dummie." A. B. Howell had tracked down McNeil's true identity decades earlier, but now no one knew his real name.

SIMILAR TO AFRICAN AMERICANS, people with disabilities and their allies had long fought for greater inclusion in society. For years disability activists had argued that physical, emotional, and mental difference caused fewer barriers for individuals than did society's discriminatory response to that difference.[19] They, like other civil rights advocates, rallied for equal opportunities and access. By the 1960s the political and social climate had changed, promoting more liberal interpretations of citizenship and culture and sparking widespread consciousness-raising campaigns.[20] As black and white students pressed schools and universities across the South to integrate, Ed Roberts entered the University of California at Berkeley. Roberts, who was quadriplegic, had convinced the state university in 1962 that severely disabled individuals could and should be able to live on campus and attend classes. Within a decade, a dozen more paraplegic and quadriplegic men and women were enrolled at Berkeley, prompting new measures to empower and assist disabled students. Centers for Independent Living appeared at Berkeley, as well as Boston, Houston, and Los Angeles.[21] Federal support for independent living centers appeared in the following decade.[22]

PRESIDENT JOHN F. KENNEDY, whose sister Rosemary had a cognitive disability, called for community centers and other alternatives to large residential institutions to serve people with development and psychiatric disabilities.[23] In 1963 Congress approved the measure known as the Mental Retardation Facilities and Community Mental Health Center Construction Act.[24] With this act, the government legitimized community-based programs, countering state mental hospitals and the historic practice of institutionalization. Specifically, it sought to reduce "warehousing," or the abandonment of patients in facilities. Kennedy's brother Robert, along with Burton Blatt and Fred Kaplan, continued the cause, exposing the appalling condition in various institutions in their 1966 photodocumentary book, *Christmas in Purgatory*. Increasingly, mainstream society came to understand state mental hospitals as inherently flawed at best and likely to be oppressive and utterly degrading to the men and women they were supposed to serve.[25]

The confluence of the civil rights, antipoverty, and antiwar movements sharpened the call for more direct federal action. Previous state and federal policies increasingly came under attack, as activists demanded a significant overhaul of "the system." Facing thousands of disabled veterans from the Second World War, Congress had passed measures to construct more hospitals, promote medical research and rehabilitation, and find ways to make health insurance available to all citizens. As early as 1956, congressional representatives expanded Social Security benefits to include disability benefits for eligible persons over the age of fifty.[26] By the 1960s, amendments to the Social Security Act went much further. The creation of Medicare (Title XVIII) in 1965 provided universal health coverage to most citizens aged sixty-five or older. Taxes on employees and employers were intended to defray the costs of this program.[27] Title XIX, or Medicaid, also drew its funding from the Social Security tax but served a different population—poor people of all ages.[28] Described by some as an afterthought or last minute addition, Medicaid's passage in 1965 had a profound effect on economically marginalized individuals. This state-administered public assistance program employed means testing for eligibility. Individuals who sought Medicaid support had to demonstrate that they lived at or below the poverty level. But individual states determined the official poverty line for their constituents, and southern states, which adopted Medicaid in 1969 and 1970, commonly set that amount significantly lower than did the federal government or northern states.[29]

Inextricably tied to the broader civil rights movement, disability rights provided a new critique of America's health and medical system. While court challenges like *Brown v. Board of Education* forced the opening of classroom doors to citizens of all races, legislation like the 1968 Architectural Barriers Act required that new federally funded buildings remove physical barriers for people with disabilities. By the early 1970s, disability rights activists had achieved other victories: federal policies that provided counseling, special education and training, entitlement to food stamps, medical assistance, and day care for individuals with disabilities. Section 504 of the 1973 Rehabilitation Act, modeled closely on the Civil Rights Act of 1964, prohibited any federally funded institution or activity from discriminating against individuals with disabilities.[30] This act became a vital tool for disability rights activists to challenge systemic barriers.

IN THE LATE 1960S, Wilson lived in the Richardson Building at Cherry Hospital.[31] His new assignment kept him indoors, assisting in the dining hall.[32] Long tables and benches lined the beige-colored room. Observers noted the strong smell of coffee, but the smell of unwashed men and women likely also pervaded the dining hall.[33] Wilson helped clean up Richardson's cafeteria area, mop floors, and clean off the metal trays.[34] Because he was still active and had experience working with the farm, Wilson also started to help out with grounds work. His supervisors regularly logged in notes to his file that complimented his dependability and labor. Wilson did odd jobs on the side to supplement his tobacco habit and purchase other goods he enjoyed.

Patients commonly performed small jobs around campus, often earning money off the books for their labor. Wilson and others washed cars in the 1960s. One man who passed by Cherry regularly recalled seeing Wilson: "I saw him washing cars as we passed through the grounds. . . . He had two small metal buckets, and a pile of rags and he washed cars. He washed with plain water, wiping the cars."[35] Another man also remembered Wilson in the parking lot: "He would walk around with a bucket and would wash staff's cars. And that was my first knowledge of him."[36]

In the early 1970s, when Wilson was transferred to the geriatric ward, an administrator at Cherry had just learned about industrial therapy. The program allowed the hospital to pay federal wages for working "handicapped" patients. The hospital applied for and received the necessary certification. As one person involved explained, "We opened up a car wash at Cherry. Later on we opened up a pallet (to put products on). . . . As a result . . . we had to run time and motion studies to see how much they could produce as it related to a 'normal' individual and that was the rate of pay."[37] Wilson was one of the first patients placed in this program.[38] He "became an employee in the car wash. . . . He worked in that car wash until he became disabled. . . . He worked in it for years," an employee noted. "[H]e'd vacuum the cars out. For years and years he did that," remembered Chris Lancaster, who worked at Cherry at the time.[39] "He would do everything—vacuum, wash tires and cars, wipe the dash, . . . anything that a car wash would do."[40]

Wilson's good service defined his relationship to the hospital through the 1970s. In the 1990s William Eugene Howe, the supervisor, remembered Wilson as "a fantastic worker," and that "performance wise, he was excellent." According to Howe, "he was very conscientious, very thorough. We had no problem with him whatsoever."[41] In work reviews from the 1980s, however, both Wilson's supervisor and Howe consistently noted that the patient-worker's attendance and punctuality was poor. On average, Wilson only attended his work therapy about 10 percent of the time expected of him. In one review, his supervisor complained that Wilson was "late every day." The supervisor thus docked his pay. Federal minimum hourly wage during the mid-1980s was $3.35. Wilson earned $2.51 an hour.[42] If reduced pay had been intended to spur Wilson to greater action, the plan clearly failed. Practical matters might have undermined administrators' efforts. Staff members who knew Wilson assumed that he could not tell time or fully comprehend monetary matters. It is possible that he did not understand the rules of industrial therapy, or the outcome of his work other than as a task he was allowed to perform or which he could choose to do whenever he felt like it.

In finite amounts, time at the car wash clearly pleased Wilson. Outside of the locked wards, Wilson felt more at liberty. He took pride in his work, pointing and gesturing at the cars he vacuumed. He also made a new friend, Chris Lancaster. Lancaster, who drove vehicles for the hospital, had met Wilson in the 1960s when the deaf man still worked on the farm. Now the two greeted each other regularly and began to mime and gesture extensively with one another.

The white employee especially loved these interactions with Wilson. "I used to play with him all the time," he remembered. After Wilson bought a new bike, Lancaster teased that he would "take it away from him." Eventually, when Wilson gave in and told him he could ride it around the campus, Lancaster backed off and mimed that he was too old.[43]

Because Wilson could not hear, he was an easy target for some kinds of pranks. When Wilson made noise to get his attention, sometimes Lancaster did not respond immediately, but then he would turn around very suddenly and act as if the noise had startled him. Lancaster pulled his favorite prank regularly at the car wash: "I'd come up behind him and unplug the vacuum cleaner and he would be vacuuming and it wouldn't be doing anything." When Wilson touched his hand to the end of the vacuum to see whether it was vibrating, Lancaster would quickly plug it back in so it was working. When Wilson caught on, said Lancaster, "he'd act like he was real mad and then he'd laugh and laugh . . . he looked forward to it."[44]

Sometimes Wilson teased back. When Lancaster picked him up to go out driving, he sometimes mimed that the elderly gentleman should ride in the trunk of the car. Wilson would laugh and indicate that Lancaster should get in the trunk and that he himself would drive. Then they got in their usual places and Wilson was entranced with the outside world going past his windows as Lancaster drove the car to appointments or shopping.[45]

Lancaster intended his teasing as a way of showing that he liked and cared about Wilson. Wilson seemed to know that and appreciate the employee's efforts to communicate with him. Lancaster was sure that Wilson "liked me to pick on him like that." The teasing also revealed a relationship not based on pity. Lancaster accepted Wilson as he was and established a way of communicating across the chasm that separated the two men.[46]

Teasing was a way to interact without using language. Playing little jokes on Wilson was a way to further the depth of the friendship. At the same time, it was clearly a statement of the hierarchical nature of relationships between staff members and the patient.

CHERRY'S POLICY REFORMS now emphasized patient therapy and social outlets. The "Therapeutic Center," which opened in 1971, "had bowling, weight lifting equipment, music rooms." An enthusiastic nurse added, "They had an activity building that was beyond anything they would have experienced anywhere. First-class movies, bowling alley, recreation building that had everything you could imagine in it . . . wonderful recreations, trips, picnics. They went and did things they would never have done at home. And Junius was one of them."[47] Another employee later commented, "I only saw [Wilson] as he was involved with the other therapists playing cards."[48] He continued, "Best I can remember . . . his favorite game was some kind of card game that he played with other aides in the building. He came to the center every day."[49] More comfortable dealing with individuals in small groups or one-on-one, Wilson chose activities that minimized his deafness and allowed him to watch others around him.

Other men and women from the wards eagerly anticipated festive events. A technician reported, "We had a Christmas party every year, and Thanksgiving . . . [there] was a dance in a chapel. . . . And that's where all the patients and staff went to socialize. Sometimes they gave you some snacks, cakes, and sodas for refreshments."[50] Wilson attended the dances but focused more on the food than the swirling bodies. If the music was loud enough, he could feel the vibrations, but he was reluctant to approach women to ask them to dance.[51]

Movies, however, fascinated the deaf man. The hospital showed all kinds of films—Westerns, nature documentaries, and classics. None had subtitles, so Wilson would have to guess what the characters were saying. But he eagerly attended, delighted to see worlds outside his own flashing on the screen.[52] For the remainder of his life, Wilson would ask staff to take him to movies and gesture animatedly, reenacting the stories he had seen.

THERE WAS OTHER ENTERTAINMENT as well. The hospital looked to local events outside the institution in order to expose patients to the outside world. One of the most popular excursions was the North Carolina State Fair. Shortly after Junius Wilson's ill-fated visit to the fair in 1924 with his classmates at the school for the deaf, state administrators moved the festivities to a permanent arena west of the State Capitol. The new Spanish Mission Revival style exhibit halls steadily grew in size and popularity after their opening in 1928. The midway expanded, providing flashy and enticing rides and booths. Crowds poured into Dorton Arena (completed in 1953), their numbers climbing every year.[53]

Despite its new location, the fair maintained its character. Booths exhibited regional cuisine, prize livestock, and arts and crafts. Churches put up booths. Politicians gave speeches, shook hands, and kissed babies. Funnel cakes, cotton candy, and carnival rides laced the grounds. The Ferris wheel soared and lights twinkled. Carnies waved and beckoned passersby into tents. Prizes were handed out to winners at the shooting gallery and other games. For children and adults alike, trips to the state fair were exhilarating, if sometimes overwhelming.

For Cherry Hospital staff members, the annual trip was an enjoyable event. They especially liked sharing moments of freedom with patients who were constrained to live within the circumscribed boundaries of the hospital. They watched the patients closely, smiling at their expressions of surprise and glee, easing the anxiety of others who were intimidated by the shrieks and exotic sights.

As the bus pulled into the parking lot on Wilson's first trip with the hospital group, he looked at the new buildings. They held no special meaning for him. But upon entering the carnival, both past and present collided. None of the staff knew about his previous trips to the fair. None even knew that he had attended school nearby in Raleigh. A confluence of questions probably crossed Wilson's mind: Is this a test to see if I will run away again? Or is this a reward for good behavior at Cherry? How long can I stay? When can I come back?

Entranced by the melee of rides, rodeos, and cook-offs, the deaf man took in all that he could. "He looked all around," explained a hospital staff member, but "I never known him to ride on any rides." Wilson especially liked to observe. "He did a lot of looking. It was a different world, different from Cherry," said the attendant. "The fair was about all they had."[54]

Wilson loved to pet the farm animals displayed in the booths. And, as for many North Carolinians, Wilson's first experience with exotic animals occurred at the fair. The arrival of an elephant to the carnival particularly impressed him. Even in his advanced years, Wilson gestured excitedly, miming the rides and describing the animals he had seen. He swayed an arm back and forth, imitating the long trunk, and beamed.[55]

Supervisors carried money to share with the patients and encouraged the men and women to play games, try the sweet and rich foods, and watch the races.[56] Staff were assigned to patients and made sure they did not wander off. Some patients even helped monitor the behavior of the visitors. "Police Dummie wanted to look after everybody, make sure they got back on the bus," one employee recalled.[57] Wilson was cautious, making sure to return promptly to the bus at the end of the visit. This time there would be no indiscretions. He had already learned his lesson. Following the rules paid off.

As the fall season came again and buses lined up to bring patients to the fair, it eventually became apparent to Wilson that this special reward would be available to him and the other "good" patients every year. As in his school days, he waited for the leaves to change color, looking forward to his autumn reunion with the carnival.

WHILE JUNIUS WILSON WAITED for events like the fair, much larger changes were looming. The 1960s and 1970s witnessed innovative approaches to mental illness and its treatment. Many of these measures emphasized community and collaboration; they commonly rejected traditional hierarchies within hospitals. Instead of allowing individual doctors to assess and dictate a patient's treatment,

teams of health care technicians, including social workers and other professionals, partnered to address patients' particular situations. Suspicion of state
institutions as oppressive forces fed the drive to deinstitutionalize patients and
inmates and integrate them into mainstream society. Day hospitals were created
to allow men and women to live at home and attend therapy seasons during the
day.[58] The deinstitutionalization movement gained rapid momentum.

Since the Settlement House movement and other progressive social uplift
programs had taken root in the late nineteenth century, modern social work
had begun to evolve into a specialized and professionalized field. During the
Kennedy and Johnson administrations, civil rights ideology and expectations
motivated a new generation of social work students. Particularly, "War on
Poverty" initiatives drew individuals committed to social justice and community action into the field. Many in this cohort understood the rhetoric of civil
rights as a central component of their profession. They demonstrated their
liberal ideology in their work with men, women, and children of diverse economic and racial backgrounds. Dee Gamble, a professor of social work at the
University of North Carolina at Chapel Hill, remembered teaching during the
late civil rights era: "All of that kind of sense about social justice was certainly
percolating into the curriculum of the schools of social work at the time." Race
especially mattered. "It just was part of the social justice issue," she explained.
"Why should people be treated differently because of their skin? Why should
the expectations for their development, aspirations, opportunities, be diminished because they are darker skinned than I am? . . . It was yet another piece of
the 'what's fair in society' question that I think social workers should be asking
all the time. What's fair or unfair and for whom and why is it happening?"
Gamble challenged her students to consider these fundamental issues.[59] John
Wasson, one of Gamble's graduate students in the late 1960s, remembered that
"community organization was the theme that permeated . . . at that time. . . .
The whole movement . . . was being incorporated in university curriculum."
Social work in the 1960s, Wasson explained, "took a different approach. A lot of
it was 'the community is your client.' . . . Those [kinds of] values a lot of us took
into our respective jobs."[60] These activist–social workers infiltrated previously
neglected arenas, including mental hospitals. Their own integration into institutions like Cherry Hospital noticeably altered internal dynamics.

Teams of professionals collaborated to assess individual patient needs at
Cherry, producing detailed files for the first time since the creation of the
institution. Imbued with civil rights ideology as well as new theories of social
work and psychology, these individuals rejected the traditional custodial treatment of patients in favor of active medical and social rehabilitation. As in
mental hospitals across the nation, Cherry established a community center in

order to train select patients in independent living skills and prepare them for possible return to mainstream society. Deinstitutionalization—the effort to remove patients from hospitals and place them within the community—had taken root by the 1970s. Over the next decades, upwards of 95 percent of men and women previously institutionalized in state mental hospitals left the locked wards. Many factors fueled this movement: a belief in the salutatory effects of less-restricted environments, an emphasis on community involvement and activism, a general suspicion of hospitals and "the establishment," federal programs like Medicaid that paid for elderly men and women to live in nursing homes rather than hospitals, and the new use of psychotropic drugs and other therapies that suppressed some of the antisocial or disturbing behavior of many individuals with mental illness.[61] The treatment teams at Cherry Hospital were committed to removing as many eligible patients as possible from the wards and prepare them for life "on the outside." One social worker later explained that staff focused especially on residents who had been institutionalized for long periods and assessed ways of enabling them to leave the institution.[62]

IN 1970 A TREATMENT TEAM looked closely at Junius Wilson. Wilson's slim medical file shed little light on his situation, but staff had long recognized Wilson as exceptional and treated him as an independent resident, an unpaid aide, and friend rather than as a typical inmate. Physician Nelson Macatangay later stated that Wilson was assessed in 1965 and "diagnosed as a deaf-mute . . . [and as having] social maladjustment without manifest psychiatric disorder."[63] Their conclusion was clear: Wilson did not appear to have any psychiatric disorder; he was not mentally ill. This analysis supported the decision to deinstitutionalize the deaf man. But team members were concerned that the legal charges against Wilson that helped land him in the institution were still pending. Social worker Garde Parson, who also tried to find out more about Wilson's past, questioned the original charges. "They said he raped a white woman back in 1920-something," Parson noted, "but we think he approached a woman and because he couldn't speak it scared her. . . . We think that's what happened. . . . That was the reason for his admission. . . . Different doctors looked at his records etc. . . . They came up with the conclusion that it didn't happen like that."[64]

In September, social worker James F. Burnette contacted the clerk of superior court at the New Hanover County Courthouse to confirm Wilson's criminal status. Burnette explained that a doctor recommended that Wilson be released on a trial visit, "if relatives could be contacted and if there are no charges pending against him at this time."[65] The original admission had included a Criminal Court Observation Commitment, or COC. "Evidently at one point during his hospitalization the patient's commitment was changed from coc to Mental Legal Commitment. At this time we are unable to find in the patient's folder any evidence that the charges have been dropped against him. What we would like from your office if possible is the patient's legal status at this time."[66] In November, Deputy Clerk Elizabeth M. George responded, claiming that the charges had been "Nolle Prossed with Leave."[67] This meant the charges that Arthur Smith Jr. had initiated in 1925 had been dropped.

BURNETTE TRIED TO REACH Wilson's family in the hope of expediting the man's release from Cherry. After finding her letters to the hospital from the 1950s, Burnette wrote to Mary Clark, Wilson's mother, at a New York City address. He informed her that, "Your son, Junius, was reviewed on 09-09-70 by the Unit I Staff. It was the recommendation of the staff that your son be released on Trial Visit. You may come for him at your convenience. It is very important for Junius to continue with his medication and also visit the mental health clinic in your area. If we may be of further assistance, please do not hesitate to contact us."[68] The letter came back unopened. Burnette and others did not realize that Mary Wilson Clark had returned to Castle Hayne. Neither had he learned that she had died from a heart attack the previous year, on 18 May 1969.[69]

Burnette also attempted to reach Wilson's sister, Carrie Gill. With only the report of her long-ago visit to Wilson for reference, Burnette sent a letter to the Castle Hayne address she had listed in 1947. As with the letter to Mary Clark, Burnette urged Gill to come for Wilson as part of a trial family visit.[70] There was no response to Burnette's solicitation. Several days later, Clinical Director E. C. Fowler sent another letter to Carrie Gill, also using the North Carolina address. The invitation to see her relative at the hospital for "Christmas visits" came back to the hospital on 11 December 1970, marked "addressee unknown."[71]

Social worker Lulu Jolliff tried again in the summer of 1972, contacting county social services. Jolliff informed the department that Wilson had been recommended for release since September 1970 "to go and live with a sister, a Mrs. Carrie Gill" in Castle Hayne.[72] The request added, "A letter was received from the Clerk of Superior Court, New Hanover County, stating that there are now no pending charges on Mr. Wilson. He is taking care of all needs well and has been working at the car wash at the hospital for a number of years. He is a deaf mute but does communicate well by writing. If your agency can help us find any information concerning Mr. Wilson's family, it would be most helpful for he is still able to be released on Trial Visit."

In August, the department responded that it was unable to locate any of Wilson's relatives.[73] Olivia Whichard, another social worker on the team, looked for Wilson's father Sidney. She called the Seaboard Coastline Railroad in Georgia, his last known employer. "The railroad has no information on this man," her report dryly explained.[74] Sidney Wilson and his wife Avery had remained in Ware, Georgia, but the hospital would not have been able to speak with him. Sidney Wilson had died in March 1963 from kidney failure; Avery passed away the following month.[75] Jolliff later recalled the frustration: "I remember the file on the 1947 family visit. I had to locate lost families. And that was one of them. Until [decades later] . . . nothing was heard from his family." Jolliff insisted that, "We made an effort in Castle Hayne with different addresses and people we knew. Some mail went out and never came back (which made us think people got it to Junius's family)."[76] Jolliff and others imagined that Wilson's family was unable or unwilling to take him back. They abandoned the hope of reintegrating him into his original community.

AT THE SAME TIME SOME team members searched for Wilson's relatives, others pursued internal procedures to rehabilitate the deaf man. In order to help men and women return to the community, Cherry Hospital had established a Community House. In this setting, staff trained patients in basic life skills and exposed them to life outside the institutions, taking trips downtown. For hospital staff and outsiders, the move to deinstitutionalize symbolized a new approach to mental illness, one that empowered individuals and emphasized their humanity.

Over the decades at Cherry, Wilson had become adroit at watching and mimicking others around him. Wilson could follow a group, clear his dinner setting, dress himself, and keep his room clean. Staff called him "industrious" and "pleasant." They commonly believed that Wilson did not really belong in the hospital. The rising popularity of deinstitutionalization provided an opportunity to resolve this. His treatment team selected Wilson for training in the Community House.

Staff in the Community House welcomed Wilson and attempted to include him in their activities. It took time for them—and Wilson—to become accustomed to one another. And ignorance of the broader ramifications of deafness ultimately isolated Wilson and undermined his chances to leave the hospital. Music therapy, a popular program for men and women at Cherry, had little appeal for, or application to, Wilson. He sat with the others, watching them listen to music or play instruments that he could not hear. One social worker offered him a balloon to hold, hoping he would feel the vibrations better. Usually Wilson complied, but no one could explain the purpose of music therapy. One employee who saw Wilson head to these sessions recalled, "I'd see him follow the group but he'd look up at me and look at me like, 'Not interested.' "[77]

LANGUAGE BARRIERS HAMPERED the experiment more broadly. Social interaction, a vital indicator of a "successful" candidate, eluded Wilson. Staff members who knew him claimed that they communicated facilely with the deaf man, yet none could explain complex ideas or instructions in sign language. He struggled to articulate his desires or questions to strangers, gesturing and grunting, sometimes staring, unsure what the mouth movements or returned hand signals fully meant.

Staff doctors like Nelson Macatangay could not assess Wilson because of the language barrier. He and others relied on staff to interpret Wilson's gestures during his monthly assessments with the physicians.[78] Some of these staff members felt they had "no communication problem" with Wilson but also admitted that they did not know any actual sign language and never engaged in deep conversations with the deaf man. Although notes in Wilson's medical file occasionally suggested that staff develop better communication with their client, there is no evidence that anyone actively sought tutoring in American Sign Language for technicians and nurses, or for Wilson. Perhaps because Wilson served as a "good" and generally compliant inmate, staff felt there was no need to alter his treatment or his interactions with them.

Unable to share in a full dialogue, the deaf man resorted to his successful survival techniques: follow, mimic, submit, assist. Although staff consistently praised Wilson for these attributes, they felt he demonstrated total dependence rather than "industry."

When his usual efforts to express himself failed, Wilson occasionally resorted to anger, shoving people or yelling loudly. Patient outbursts always received immediate attention. In Wilson's case, staff entered notes whenever the deaf man acted out. Several referred to Wilson's lack of social skills, his stubbornness and irritability, and his unwillingness to follow instructions. "Is very moody," determined a technician on Wilson's ward.[79] One team member wrote, "He gets irritated easily when people do not give him attention or [are] unable to comprehend what he wants." The notation added, "He still has some problems in socialization and probably because of his physical handicaps."[80] Reports increasingly described problems with Wilson, clearly marking his difference, specifically his deafness, as an insurmountable handicap to his independence. While they surely allowed others, including themselves, to get "irritated easily" without their capacity for independence being questioned, team members applied a higher standard to Wilson's independent living prospects. They became convinced that outside the safe confines of the hospital, Wilson would flounder and suffer.

AS EVIDENCE OF WILSON'S inability to assimilate outside the hospital, several caretakers noted that Wilson refused to get on the bus that took men and women on their regular institution outings. These trips allowed staff to observe the patients in mainstream settings and evaluate their skills and comfort with experiences "on the outside." One caretaker who knew Wilson well remembered, "We would take trips and he would be so scared. He stayed right with me [because he felt more secure being around people he knew]."[81] Another concurred: "We had an activity bus to visit the park, beach, whatever. He didn't want to go to any of those places. . . . We had a day program and [would] go visit facilities. . . . He just wouldn't get on the bus. . . . I thought I was doing a favor, trying to get him out. I thought he could benefit by leaving."[82] Another was more firm: "Junius was a person who could not adjust outside the institution, he was petrified. . . . It took a long time to get him to go to the cars. And he'd be absolutely scared to death. And people were very kind and gentle with him."[83] Because Wilson would not join the group, his treatment team concluded that he would never adapt to the vicissitudes of mainstream life. "Our goal was to get them out of Cherry Hospital and into the community. . . . Mr. Wilson would have no part of it," a treatment team member lamented.

One must wonder how much language barriers and Wilson's prior experiences informed his reluctance to take trips with the others. Was he frightened that staff members would leave him in an unfamiliar place, where his deafness made him more vulnerable? A team member later noted that Wilson was suspicious of trips "because the community house was new and they drew from staff from other parts of the hospital."[84]

Many men and women who have lived for extended periods in mental hospitals find change threatening and disconcerting. While Wilson's peers might also have felt anxiety when confronting new environments, staff could better calm them with soothing words. Even those who had constructed primitive gestures with Wilson could not explain the meaning of the bus, just as they could not explain the meaning of music therapy. Other patients might not have fully grasped the goals of this program, either, but they did recognize the final aim: to leave the hospital. Wilson might have thought their departure was a punishment for their misbehavior.

Left behind and left out, Wilson rejected the continued efforts by the staff to include him in Community House activities. When asked whether he would like to move from his ward to the house, he fervently shook his head: "No." Over the next decade, staff frequently referred to Wilson's response. "He indicated that he did *not* want to move to this [building]."[85]

One report revealed much more: "Communicated by signs that he wanted to stay in Woodard [his current residence] or *go home to Castle Hayne*" (emphasis added).[86] Staff did not have the language skills to explain why he could not return to his original home. For decades, Wilson continued to write the same few phrases, likely hoping that the words on paper held more meaning than his gestures or facial expressions. "Mary Clark." "Carrie Wilson." "Castle Hayne." It did not help.

BOTH CONSPICUOUSLY AND SUBTLY, Wilson's deafness framed much of the treatment team's diagnosis. One report claimed: "Although the patient appears to be able to adjust to some extent in the hospital setting, it is doubtful in view of his being a deaf-mute whether he would be able to adjust to a community setting."[87] A doctor added, "He is extremely well adjusted in this environment but seems to need some elements of it and has helped create some of the environment around him and its safeguards." The report continued, "Placement does not seem feasible at this time due to his hearing constraints, his age constraints, and his special adaptation here."[88] His treatment team concluded: "He has difficulty of being deaf-mute and he has already learned his way around and the way to communicate with different staff members and employees and seems very happy."[89] Perhaps newer team members questioned this assessment —some entries seem to suggest defensiveness. Several years later, another doctor's report claimed that Wilson was "admired for his compensation for his deafness and for his skills in doing jigsaw puzzles."[90] Their misunderstanding of deafness sometimes caused them to overestimate his abilities, assuming that the deaf man could read lips perfectly. At the same time, they underestimated him, expressing amazement that he could complete puzzles.

As both an outsider and insider at the hospital, Wilson could navigate dynamics on campus well enough to gain status and some influence, but not enough to be considered truly normal and qualified to leave. No one drew attention to the ways that Wilson or McNeil had displayed both skill and creativity in the ways they assimilated into Cherry, and no one considered those abilities relevant for adapting to a new environment.

AS SUPPORT FOR REHABILITATING Wilson waned, members rationalized their decision to keep him at Cherry. Even though social worker James Burnette had asserted that Wilson was no longer charged with attempted assault on his aunt, others began to question again Wilson's right to be free. "Placement not practical because of old legal constraints" dots Wilson's file throughout the early 1980s. Silvia Weaver, one of the treatment team members, later explained, "I think it was the legality of the situation: I think it was the nature of the charges. . . . I think it had to do with the charges along those lines. And for him to be placed, he would have had to have the charges dropped. There were quite a few patients in that category. Back then they were 'life-timers.' "[91]

"Financial considerations" also complicated matters. Wilson did not meet the criteria for Medicare because he was considered unemployed and did not pay taxes into the system. He, like the other men and laborers, had received no real salary for "work therapy" at the hospital farm. Staff consequently tried to qualify individual patients in the state institution (like Wilson) for Medicaid. But ironically, Wilson was not eligible for Medicaid. His outside work, including his worm-selling business and domestic support for staff members, ultimately earned him upwards of $7,000, an amount that exceeded North Carolina's Medicaid guidelines.[92] Wilson's entrepreneurial abilities—selling fishing worms, running errands, and selling snacks to staff and patients—earned him status and praise on campus.[93] But the same activities, according to health care policies and bureaucrats, disqualified Wilson from other care options. Efforts to achieve a more "normal" life—by Wilson and by the medical system—ultimately justified keeping Wilson in Cherry Hospital.

Others blamed the absence of family for complications to any plan to deinstitutionalize Wilson. "There were many efforts to contact Junius's family," said Lulu Jolliff. "I do not recall ever having a response from them. And I certainly don't recall a visit. During the years I never saw a visit from relatives." A peer added, "Some time ago there was a contact with a sister, but later on correspondence has been returned to us. She is not in that place. There is no family with whom communication is maintained."[94] A staff geropsychiatrist felt Wilson was unsuited for placement outside the hospital in 1976, in part because "he [had] no interested family."[95]

Again and again, staff insisted that Wilson simply belonged at Cherry. A treatment team member in the 1970s recorded: "This patient has been in this institution for 52 years. There is no way that this patient can adapt back in the community in a different environment. . . . Staff communicates with him by signs and actions and he has been able to function in this environment." One member was especially adamant: "I don't think attempts should be made to get him in the community because for sure it would disrupt his whole life."[96] Another later rationalized: "Then of course by the time he was older and there were procedures to deal with it, then it was felt [Cherry Hospital] was his home and he wouldn't survive on the outside and he seemed like this was all he had known; he was comfortable there."[97] One wrote: "This is his home and I do not think he should be sent away from his home."[98] In an interview decades after, the social worker recalled that "someone from Raleigh thought people should be placed in the community. I told them, 'No. This man is 80 years old. This is his home.' He didn't know sign language. We understood him. I was not going to send this poor soul out into the world."[99]

Often, treatment team notes referred to prior judgments by staff as evidence of Wilson's inability to leave. "Regarding this patient's community placement in light of his institutionalization here since 1925, it is felt that this patient would not be a candidate for community placement because of his inability to adapt to new surroundings." But in the suggested treatment, the author added, "Continue efforts to place the patient in the community."[100] Another doctor countered in an entry a few months later: "Placement is not possible."[101]

Despite these conclusions, between the 1970s and early 1980s, Wilson's manifest "normalcy" bothered staff. "He was just so different" from the others, recalled one of Wilson's caretakers. "What I remember is that he was so 'unpatient like.' He was almost like a staff member."[102] Regularly, staff reiterated the idea that community placement for Wilson should be pursued. For various and complicated reasons, this call remained muted.

The fact that Wilson caused little difficulty for staff members actually buttressed claims to keep him at the hospital. Regularly, Wilson's file describes the deaf man as being "no trouble," "not management problem," and "very cooperative."[103] The many individuals who wrote in Wilson's medical files—health care technicians, psychologists, social workers, and nurses—emphasized that Wilson seemed happy at Cherry. References to the hospital as his home, and how frequently Wilson smiled and assisted others, were ubiquitous. "Mr. Wilson smiled today and help [sic] me get the elevator. He enjoys assisting others," wrote one health care technician.

At the same time, many of the staff believed that Cherry was not merely Wilson's de facto home, but a true sanctuary for him. Donald Davis, one of Wilson's psychiatrists, claimed that "he seems to be in good harmony with his environment. He is now 87 years old and seems to be ideally adjusted to this environment and appreciated by it, reinforced by it, in symbiosis with it and cherished by the Director."[104] Reported another staff doctor, "He continues to be friendly and helpful on the unit, smiling at most times."[105] One social worker was more emphatic: "We made every effort to help prepare people to live in a different environment. And in 90% of the cases it *was a lesser environment* [emphasis added]. We were never able to prepare him (and not for lack of trying). His friends were at Cherry, it was home. And he was loved."[106] Individuals and occasionally small teams voiced concern that Wilson did not belong at the hospital. But their expressions remained trapped on paper as those with more authority—sometimes caseworkers, sometimes doctors or administrators—overlooked or ignored them.[107]

A longtime employee believed that Wilson and McNeil "weren't mental patients. They were 'out of the system.'" The two deaf men stood out "because they weren't psychotic, . . . they just had their own rooms, they didn't give anybody any trouble. I know it sounds like they shouldn't have been there but by the time we came on . . . all they did was house them. And when they realized that a mistake was made, it was too late. It [was] almost too cruel to put them out."[108] Others suggested that McNeil and Wilson exploited hospital staff: "People just catered to him [McNeil]."[109]

Although many Cherry employees felt that racism and ignorance likely motivated Wilson's and McNeil's original placement at the hospital, they felt that the men's continued institutionalization was based on benevolence. This position enabled staff members to acknowledge past misdeeds but avoided the stigma of complicity with unknown perpetrators. Moreover, this interpretation acknowledged their sincere affection for the men while maintaining a position of power over them.

EXPANDED LAWS AND POLICIES regarding patient treatment and hospital commitment demanded that Cherry Hospital formally justify Wilson's continued care. Beginning in 1972, legal representatives or custodial guardians asked the New Hanover County judge to commit Wilson as an involuntary patient. Considered a danger to himself because he was "unable to care for himself because of his handicapps [sic]," doctors diagnosed Wilson as a "deaf-mute" with "social maladjustment, without psychiatric disorder." The conclusion might have seemed too certain for some of the medical experts. "At present it is difficult to determine his mental status because he is unable to talk. He communicates with his own sign language, but it is difficult to interpretee [sic]. He usually withdraws when he can not get responses from what he wants to say to people," the doctor demurred. Seeking to bolster the diagnosis of maladjustment, he added, "He is an accomplished pick-pocket."[110] Diagnoses later in the decade labeled Wilson with "inadequate personality," suggested that he was "unable to care for self," and that he perhaps suffered from "organic brain syndrome." An undated "Medical Questionnaire for Physician" that apparently supplemented the first affidavit to involuntarily commit Wilson is peppered with blanks and question marks. "Deaf-mute" was listed as Wilson's physical condition as well as his tentative mental diagnosis. Under "first symptoms noted" was written "social maladjustment." His conduct was "not known," and the author put question marks in answer to whether Wilson had demonstrated "violent behavior, [was] suicidal, threatened suicide, attempted homicide, threatened homicide, used alcohol, or drugs." The form asked whether the person was mentally deficient. The author wrote "No." Has the patient been treated in a mental institution previously? "NO." Smaller letters followed: "In Cherry hsp. Since 1925."

The hospital later admitted that between 1970 and 1972, Wilson was held without any "official or unofficial status" and "without the benefit of legal advice."[111] Between 1973 and the late 1980s, Wilson's legal and mental health status vacillated, partly as the Tar Heel State altered its policies. In 1973 North

Carolina's legislature promulgated a new mental health code. The revised policies emphasized patients' rights and altered hospital admission options. Written notice justified immediate release for patients who entered the hospital under "voluntary commitment." Involuntarily committed patients subsequently had the right to hearings to determine when or whether they could be released. Legal guardians or advocates were required to help protect the rights of institutionalized people.

Concerned about the legality of Junius Wilson's position, administrators wanted Wilson to sign documents that he could not read. The form presented to him in September 1973 attested that Wilson had "voluntarily" committed himself indefinitely to Cherry Hospital.[112] By November, the hospital moved for Wilson's involuntary commitment. His deafness, and specifically his inability to communicate effectively with others, was the primary justification in the series of involuntary commitment forms that followed.

A new chance to deinstitutionalize Wilson arose in 1980, when Nelson Macatangay concluded that Wilson was mentally ill but not a danger to himself or others. The physician recommended that Wilson be discharged from the hospital. Moving swiftly, treatment team members had Wilson again sign voluntary admission papers allowing him to remain at Cherry. It is unclear whether Wilson knew what he was signing. Both the doctor's assessment and the voluntary commitment papers were dated 10 January 1980.[113]

JUST AS THE CHANGE IN the name of Cherry Hospital was not reflected by immediate shifts in the reality of life at the institution, changes in the classification of Junius Wilson did not immediately alter his experiences. Throughout the decades of the fifties, sixties, and seventies, Wilson's status was considered, reconsidered, and relabeled. His condition—mental, physical, linguistic, and geographical—remained relatively static. Ironically, Wilson's ability to integrate into hospital life—a clear sign of his intelligence and ingenuity if not his sanity—caused him problems when the institution reconsidered its relationship with him. By the 1950s, everyone who interacted with Wilson believed that he was sane. Yet as time passed and options for reform and rehabilitation increased, most considered Wilson so perfectly adapted to the hospital that they could imagine no other environment for him. People who knew the deaf man later remarked that he had become "an institution" at Goldsboro. More accurately, he became fully institutionalized.

6

Vital Signs (1980s–1991)

I'm sure that you realize how difficult it is to obtain a guardian for a person
who has no family, or has family who will not consent to assume
guardianship. Your assistance in this matter will be greatly appreciated.

LINDA TAYLOR TO JOHN WASSON, 11 DECEMBER 1990

You are an effective advocate for him. I have heard of situations like Mr.
Wilson's where years ago convicted sex offenders had been castrated in
state hospitals, yet I never knew of one until now.

JOHN WASSON TO LINDA TAYLOR, 18 DECEMBER 1990

IN JANUARY 1981 vocational rehabilitation evaluator Rachel Wright trailed behind a nurse in the Woodard Building. The nurse unlocked one of the ward
doors, allowing her to pass through on her way to the day room. Wright had
been sent to the geriatric ward to conduct an interview with Junius Wilson. Her
task was to assess his communication and educational ability in order to gauge
his vocational rehabilitation options. New policies linked to industrial therapy
and other rehabilitation work required institutions like Cherry Hospital to
evaluate regularly individuals in vocational rehabilitation programs. The older
man, whom she saw as "small, dainty, not tall, a little bit stooped," was dili-
gently working on a complex jigsaw puzzle.[1] She recognized Wilson immediately; she had seen him bicycling around the campus and working at the car
wash. Wright got his attention, then began to ask him questions. This exchange
differed significantly from all his previous interactions with staff.

The granddaughter of a deaf couple who had graduated from North Carolina's white school for the deaf when it was located in Raleigh, Wright had
grown up communicating with signs and was comfortable around deaf people.
Although Wilson was suspicious of Wright at the outset—she sensed he was "a
loner, intelligent, quiet"—he responded quickly to her signed queries, informing her that he had attended a deaf school and finger spelling his name. While
he answered in the black deaf school's Raleigh signs, his style of communication

was similar enough to her grandparents' white Raleigh signs that she could understand him.[2] For the first time in nearly sixty years, Wilson talked with a staff member who could communicate in a language he understood.

Each Wednesday afternoon for the next three months, Wright spent an hour with the deaf man: "I wanted to see if he could converse, if he had communication skills, if he had academic skills." Over time, Wilson shared more information with Wright. Wilson explained that he had "plenty of money" and boasted about the TV he had bought and his bicycle. He noted that he had owned two other bicycles but that "someone stole the first one."[3] He showed Wright the key to lock his bike. Working at the car wash pleased him, Wright learned, and he took great pride in his accomplishments there. When Wright found that he liked fruit, she began to bring him bananas.

Wright pressed for more personal information. "Where are you from?" her hands flashed.

"Castle Hayne," his fingers spelled back.

"Near Wilmington?" she questioned.

He nodded: "Yes." He remembered streets in Wilmington.

Wright continued: "Where is your family?"

At the question, Wilson broke eye contact. He signed dismissively that he had not seen any family members "in a long time." She pressed him. "They're all dead. All dead," his simple signs conveyed. His fingers spread out and down, adding the word GONE.[4]

In a later meeting, Wilson shared his relatives' names and then wrote them down. His large, scrawling cursive showed "Miss Carrie Wilson" and "Mrs. Mary Clark."

It was not only Wilson's language that she recognized. To Wright's eyes, Wilson was fundamentally a deaf person demonstrating standard deaf behavior. Even when he dismissed her and became disinterested in their conversations, he acted in a traditionally deaf manner: he turned away, breaking eye contact, and resumed work on his puzzles. She, in turn, used deaf cultural communicative features in her conversations with him: to get his attention, Wright tapped his shoulder rather than shouting at him.

The evaluator surveyed the world in which Wilson existed. The hospital's absence of sensitivity toward deaf people and deaf culture struck her. With surprise and frustration, Wright witnessed the extent of his language isolation and realized that the long years of limited communication had taken its toll on Wilson's language skills. As she reported, his "education has suffered loss due to lack of persons to communicate appropriately in his language."[5] When staff signed at Wilson, "all I witnessed were homemade signs. And they were not accurate." She wrote angrily in her evaluation, "Staff members use crude or inappropriate signs to communicate."

One event especially stood out to her: "A male attendant came over to where we were and made the deaf sign for 'can't, can't, can't' several times in front of his face. I asked the attendant what he was trying to sign." She continued, "The attendant replied that it meant, 'go to work.' This indicated staff members should have learned true basic sign language to have communicated intelligently with Junius all these years rather than make up gestures which mean something other than the message they intended to convey."[6] Previously, staff had called Wilson's gestures "crude" and "primitive." Wright offered a different perspective: "He has learned to compensate to Cherry Hospital *staff's* crude signs and gestures" (emphasis added).

Wright believed that Wilson had long been mistreated at Cherry. He had become "one of the forgotten deaf people," left in a place where he did not belong for the great majority of his life. But she was uncertain what to do at this point. To her knowledge, there were no group homes in North Carolina open to deaf people. Ultimately, Wright conceded that, lacking family and home on the outside, Wilson should remain at the hospital. Still, Cherry Hospital owed Wilson for the wrongs it had committed. "Cherry Hospital might desire to make special arrangement for Junius to make him as comfortable as possible to compensate for his long term hospitalization," she argued, "when he could have possibly been community oriented at age 35." One suggestion was that staff and administrators who worked with Wilson and other deaf people at the hospital be required to take sign language classes. Seeking immediate implementation of the idea, she even instructed some of the classes. Wright was very disappointed when none of Wilson's caretakers learned sign language. Wilson remained "a forgotten deaf person." Wright finally recommended that the deaf man be allowed to participate in the community during the day and return to Cherry at night.

Although Rachel Wright enjoyed more facile communication with Wilson than did other staff members, Wilson generally did not seek her out or become close to her. According to Wright, Wilson treated her "like I was a bad obstacle to what he wanted to do." She imagined that he was thinking, "I'll answer you but get out of the way. I want to get back to my puzzle." Wright empathized: "He didn't care to be bothered with such baby questions. . . . He'd [respond] in a hurry, to get me out of the way."[7] She assumed that he was bored with the endless questions she would ask and, seeing no purpose to them, he frequently turned his back to end conversations. Clearly he preferred to focus on the activities that brought him pleasure. Perhaps he resented her assessments, her obvious supervision of his language and academic skills. Also, Rachel Wright was white and female and not a regular member of Cherry's community. She might have made Wilson ill at ease. Even though they shared a communication style, the two came from starkly different worlds. After nearly three months of working with him, Wright completed her evaluation, and her interaction with Wilson ended.

WRIGHT'S RECOGNITION OF Junius Wilson as a culturally deaf person with access to language reflected more than her own personal relationship with the deaf world. Although many people outside academia still considered American Sign Language as merely a gestural system akin to pantomime or another inferior mode of communication, linguists during this period developed numerous studies that showed the language's fullness and complexity. By the 1980s, even mainstream society was more aware of deaf people and their language through television programs like *Sesame Street*, where Linda Bove signed stories with children, as well as through the proliferation of sign language classes in community colleges and some universities. Actors from the National Theater for the Deaf, created in 1967, traveled across the nation bringing signed and interpreted performances to numerous stages. State governments began to establish departments to address the needs of deaf and hard of hearing citizens. Since the founding of the Registry of Interpreters for the Deaf in 1964, professional sign language interpreters increasingly appeared in courtrooms, doctors' offices, and on television news programs. As understanding of ASL increased in mainstream society, some of the barriers between deaf and hearing people began to decrease. Even individuals less acquainted with sign language started to absorb society's models of deaf people as capable and competent human beings.

IN 1983 FRANKIE JORDAN, a secretary at vocational rehabilitation and also a sign language instructor, evaluated Wilson's sign language. It appears that hospital officials tacitly acknowledged his deafness and thus sought evaluators who might conceivably be better able to reach him. Following deaf cultural customs, Jordan likely asked him early in their conversation where he had attended school. Apparently, he told her about his time at the Raleigh school. Jordan understood that Wilson had spent considerable time there and had benefited from his schooling, but that "he had forgotten most of his former education from lack of use."[8] Jordan, like Wright two years earlier, was struck by Wilson's interaction with nurses and health care technicians: "There is no one on the staff working with him knowledgeable of sign language skills. For that reason Mr. Wilson gestures to make his desires and concerns known."[9] The evaluator understood the limited communicative efficacy of gestures. She also empathized with the frustration and unfairness that a deaf person would feel if unable to convey his thoughts in his natural language of signs. Jordan's assessment chided Wilson's caretakers for their negligence of Wilson's language needs.

IN SPITE OF THE FACT that invited evaluators provided clear guidelines for accommodating Wilson, Cherry Hospital did not take significant action to promote signed communication with Wilson and other deaf patients at the hospital. Because of Cherry's limited resources, sign language classes, tutors, manuals, videos, and other instructional supplements must have seemed extravagant. Given the small number of patients who could use sign language, administrators apparently concluded, such an investment was unreasonable. Sign language training took time, and overworked staff likely did not seek the added work and responsibility, especially if there was little or no compensation offered. Moreover, to require staff to learn a foreign language in order to accommodate deaf patients disrupted traditional hierarchies of authority. Assuming that Wilson had facility in a language that others should accommodate undermined the hospital's long-held view of the deaf man as a dependent member of the community. If the hospital accommodated Wilson, perhaps they would have to accommodate James McNeil, as well, even though he was widely considered even less capable of independence than was Wilson. Placing deaf persons' needs above the needs of the staff would not have been easy for the hospital. The evaluations of Wilson's language abilities, accompanied by copies of pages from sign dictionaries and pictures, remained in his files and soon were buried under mounds of paperwork stating only that the patient ate his meals well, took care of his own needs in the bathroom, and continued to work successfully at the car wash.

THE EVALUATIONS OF JUNIUS WILSON's language abilities by Wright and Jordan confronted the hospital with difficult issues concerning its actions toward their patient. If Cherry staff members accepted that Wilson was educated and fluent in sign language, the idea that he could not survive outside the walls of the institution no longer resonated. The external evaluators suggested that by denying Wilson access to true language, Cherry staff members were perpetrators of an injustice against him. The idea that the hospital might be guilty of mistreatment conflicted with the kindness that Wilson's attendants believed they lovingly provided for him. Until the new evaluations emerged, no one had seriously considered Wilson's language competency, assuming that he lacked language. They had always assumed that the patient was happy at the hospital, that no significant problems existed for him there, and even that his true home was within the walls of the institution. Now, when outsiders questioned Wilson's treatment, the hospital had to face the radical disconnect that existed between its long-standing vision of Wilson and a new, more complicated picture of the man. Previously, staff saw Wilson as unique, capable of many functions that his peers at the hospital could not achieve. This gave him certain privilege and status. Fundamentally, though, staff had seen the deaf man as incapable of living outside the institution. Now, he was presented to them as an individual systematically denied his rights for almost sixty years. Two separate evaluations in a five-year period had drawn the same conclusion about Wilson, suggesting that this interpretation was gaining ground and would not disappear even if hospital officials chose to dismiss it at this time.

In many ways, the evaluations of Junius Wilson in the early 1980s embodied two conflicting cultural perspectives infused with medical, social, and linguistic meaning. Cherry staff, who felt a keen personal and emotional attachment to the man, saw Wilson through their "hearing" eyes. When advocates considered deinstitutionalizing Wilson, they looked for settings in which a hearing man of Wilson's age and intelligence might prosper. Finding his deafness too complicating to enable that option to be effected, they sought to make his current environment as homelike as possible. But not knowing sign language or deaf culture, the hospital made this "homelike" environment a hearing home. Outsiders—people who knew sign language and deaf culture but not Wilson himself—saw the man as a member of a community that did not exist at Cherry. Rather, to their way of thinking, Wilson represented a culturally deaf individual, competent linguistically and intellectually, who should be removed from this hearing environment and placed in a welcoming deaf cultural atmosphere. At a minimum, if Wilson were to stay at the hospital, he needed additional access to language. White, hearing administrators at Cherry proved only nominally committed to resolving these two disparate interpretations and ultimately discarded the options and perspectives provided by the outside evaluators who had observed Wilson and the institution.

IN AN IRONIC AND TRAGIC TWIST, just as these outsiders proclaimed Wilson's language abilities and needs and pushed for the hospital to address these issues, an unexpected event thwarted them. In July 1986 Wilson's treatment team noticed that he had begun to have some new symptoms. "P[atien]t noted to have weakness of right side," wrote one attendant in their regular progress notes, "right arm limp with weak grip, dragging right leg."[10] Three weeks later, Wilson was found in an unresponsive state, "mouth drawn to one side, mouth full of food, eyes focus to one side, no response to touch." After a few minutes, he slowly began to respond. The treatment team decided to report this incident to Wilson's physician at the hospital and to observe the patient to see whether he had any further episodes.[11] One of Wilson's physicians detailed his symptoms: "He moves his fingers but the fingers of the right hand don't move as fast. The grip in his left hand is 4 times as strong as that in his right hand, but neither one of them are exerted with great force." The doctor thought it was likely that Wilson had sustained a small or transient stroke.[12]

Although in the medical file staff noted physical and behavioral changes in Wilson, none raised questions about what the stroke might have meant emotionally and personally to the deaf man. The complex cognitive and physical changes that occur during a stroke can be devastating for patients. Unable to learn from staff what had happened to him, Wilson might have felt especially afraid. Being unaware of what his prognosis was, or what he might expect to regain or permanently lose after this trauma, Wilson might have had amplified feelings of fear, agitation, or depression.

Some of Wilson's basic skills were severely affected by the stroke: feeding himself was problematic due to his weakened right hand, and staff complained in his medical log that he now frequently spilled food on himself. Occasional problems with incontinence required that staff help him clean himself and dress again. Not only could Wilson no longer care for himself as he had before, but now there also seemed to be attendants around him all the time, monitoring his every move. Nurses insisted that he take medications. Concerned staff hovered around, making sure that he was all right.

THROUGH A CONTACT AT Dorothea Dix Hospital in Raleigh, Wilson was referred to Sharon Moore for language evaluation in the fall of 1986. As per procedure, Moore would have read a report on Wilson that noted his communication problems. Staff might have selected Moore specifically because she had some knowledge of sign language.[13] Her report noted Wilson's knowledge of signs: "When shown various pictures or items (i.e. Pepsi, milk, coffee, bathroom, cookies etc), [the patient] was able to make some signs pertaining to those items but not all of them. He would imitate signs he could not spontaneously produce. He did fingerspell his name upon request." Like the previous reviewers, Moore found that the long period without accessible communication had been an injustice to Wilson.

Moore saw an opportunity for the hospital to address the inadequacies of Wilson's care. "It is felt that [the patient] is capable of learning a core vocabulary utilizing sign language," she stated, and hospital technicians should learn the same. "I will provide the unit staff with handouts," she offered, "containing pictures and instructions for various signs." She also planned to "develop a picture/sign booklet for Mr. Wilson and train him to use the pictures."[14]

Typically, speech pathologists maintained ongoing assessments of their clients. Annual reevaluations would allow a therapist to confirm or to adjust an individual's therapy goals.[15] Wilson's medical file suggests that neither Moore nor any other speech pathologist had an opportunity to test his communication style or skills in the several years following his stroke. Perhaps she, as a novice signer, missed the effect of Wilson's stroke on his signing. And not having previous interaction with him, Moore would have had no evidence with which to compare his current signing capacity.

WILSON'S MOST SIGNIFICANT SYMPTOM, the weakening of his dominant signing arm, had profound consequences. Unable to gesture, sign, or finger spell facilely circumscribed his already limited communication options with those around him. An observer who knew signs recalled later that Wilson "repeatedly said he signed better but not now, [and] was apologetic about his signing."[16] Wilson tried to compensate by relying more heavily on his left hand to finger spell, but this always seemed awkward. Not only was his signing ability diminished, but holding a pencil to write also became impossible. A social worker several years later noted that "he tried to sign his name for me to show me his handwriting, but could only manage a shaky signature & indicated that his arm doesn't work as well as it used to."[17]

Wilson's stroke limited his ability to move independently around the grounds of the institution. The patient therefore lost contact with friendly staff members who did not work on the geriatric ward. He could no longer maintain his job at the car wash. Previous symbols of his comparative affluence and status—extra candy, tobacco, and sausages—disappeared because he no longer earned the extra pocket money. Wilson could not even personally contact his friend from the car wash, Chris Lancaster, or other staff members to let him know what had happened to him.

Wilson also grieved the loss of his ability to ride his bike. Although he had long ridden his yellow Schwinn "with the greatest of ease and confidence,"[18] the stroke caused Wilson to lean to his left, making it difficult to balance. The deaf man tried to communicate this sense of loss to others. One person who listened explained that "what most distressed him was about the stroke—it really bothered him. . . . He regretted the things that he couldn't do—noticeably biking. So we talked [about] bicycles. The bicycle was freedom and independence. And he missed not riding."[19]

Staff members noted some of the changes they saw in Wilson's behavior. "In the past it has been his interest to work on jigsaw puzzles," wrote one, "but since having had a stroke, the patient's interest seems to have no patience. He is rather easily getting frustrated."[20] Another reported that Wilson became possessive of property on the ward: "He is sometimes seen to express anger at peers whenever they move [furniture] in the dayroom."[21] Sometimes, he shoved other patients away from his favorite chair. Now that he was confined to the geriatric ward day in and day out, this seemed one of the few available ways Wilson could express some control over his surroundings.[22]

Surely Wilson recognized that his status at the hospital had been compromised. An evaluator later explained: "The stroke had reduced Wilson's level of function. Previously, his level of function and independence at the hospital had been one of the highest functions."[23] Staff psychiatrist Donald Davis was one of the hospital employees who formally acknowledged that Wilson's life had changed significantly because of the stroke. Treatment team members had documented, stated Davis, that Wilson was no longer going outside or "even putting puzzles together lately." Reading through Wilson's file and noting the patient now needed assistance with so many facets of basic personal care, he recommended immediate physical therapy to allow Wilson to regain some of his prestroke abilities.[24]

When Wilson was seen by the physical therapy department five months after his stroke, evaluator Derek Lewis did not seem to consider any intervention necessary. He accepted the information on the hospital chart, which incorrectly reported Wilson's age as eighty-four—a full six years older than he actually was.[25] It did not seem reasonable to him that the hospital would offer its scant resources to such an elderly man with what seemed to him relatively mild physical infirmities. He also thought, perhaps correctly, that Wilson would be unlikely, at least at the outset, to comply with any physical therapy regimen.[26]

In his next treatment note, psychiatrist Davis commented that Wilson's symptoms had not abated in the few months since his last evaluation. This time he noted Wilson's subdued behavior and depressed demeanor: "He doesn't say anything." He recognized that Wilson was concerned about the changes in his abilities. "He makes signs indicating distress about clumsiness of his hand." The change in Wilson's emotional state due to the effect of the stroke on his hand was significant and of concern to Davis. Although he was unsure if Wilson would "cooperate with therapeutic efforts" designed to improve the functioning of his right hand, the physician felt that it was imperative that they be offered.[27]

Over the years that followed, the same physical therapy coordinator evaluated the many requests by staff to consider therapy for Wilson. He continued to recommend that Wilson receive no rehabilitation: "Considering client's age and physical abilities I do not recommend any form of physical therapy intervention at this time."[28]

One of Wilson's attendants on the geriatric ward suspected that Wilson's mental status might have been affected as well as his body: Wilson "indicated that he might do some fishing which he used to do before and riding his bike this coming summer. With his impediment this patient has continued to require supervision."[29] Although Wilson possibly dreamed of his old days of relative liberty on the campus, in reality he now spent his time watching a television that he could not hear and which had no captions. His other enjoyment was "watching other people walk by."[30]

The men who had lived with Wilson undoubtedly noticed the change in their hall mate. Some might have tried to assist their friend, while others perhaps tested territorial claims to his favorite chair. Apparently Wilson responded aggressively to overtures, shoving individuals and occasionally swinging his arm at them.[31] Medical notes do not explain the motivation or outcome of these confrontations from the perspective of the other patients, but dramatic physical or mental changes directly affected the dynamic in the isolated setting of the ward.

IN NOVEMBER 1988, Junius Wilson was called into a meeting with several staff members involved in his care. Donald Davis had been on Wilson's treatment team for several years. For years he had seen Wilson as "pleasant and cooperative" as well as "expressive." Davis was also concerned that Wilson "could be assaultive yet."[32] On this late autumn day, Wilson seemed to him to be more withdrawn than usual. "He sits rather quietly," Davis wrote. "He seemed a bit disgusted when asked to come and talk to us and he had to give up his chewing gum." Davis then stated in his brief note something that the whole treatment team had surely noticed immediately: Wilson wore a baseball cap with the caption, "High Voltage Lover."[33]

Staff members knew that Wilson loved to wear hats. They occasionally gave him new ones for his collection. "I must have brought him twenty-five or thirty caps," remembered Chris Lancaster, the healthcare technician and transport driver who knew Wilson from his work at the car wash. When they could not exchange words easily, exchanging gifts and favors was a way to establish a relationship.[34]

Why did staff members give Wilson this particular hat with "High Voltage Lover" written on it? Perhaps the hat was his favorite color. Perhaps Wilson even picked it out himself on his jaunts to local stores with staff members (although he would not have understood the caption). The employees thought of the gentle patient as "shy with women." All of them seemed aware that he had been castrated years earlier. They apparently concluded that the procedure had not only sterilized Wilson but had erased his sexual identity and ability to experience any sexual pleasure. Asexualized—both surgically and socially—

Wilson presumably could not live up to the suggestive title on his hat. Staff members were amused by the irony of the caption and knew that other staff members would find it entertaining as well. This joke was not one that he could have shared with them. Wilson wore the punch line without being aware that he was the butt of their joke.

AS WILSON'S DAILY LIFE slowly changed, bigger changes took place on the outside. Important disability rights actions appeared in the early 1980s that had significant implications for Wilson and McNeil. A year before Rachel Wright sat with Wilson, Congress had enacted the Civil Rights of Institutionalized Persons Act. This act empowered the U.S. Justice Department to file civil suits on behalf of residents of institutions—including hospitals, jails, and juvenile detention centers—whose rights were being violated. Within two years, the National Council on the Handicapped fused disability rights with traditional minority rights, calling for political leaders to expand the Civil Rights Act of 1964 to include persons with disabilities. Concurrently, in another expression of racial and community solidarity, members of America's deaf community established the National Black Deaf Advocates organization.

During the mid-1980s, disability activism gained momentum. Radical theatre groups like Wry Crips began performing in California. Pressure to improve employment options for people with disabilities resulted in new Rehabilitation Acts. The mental health movement witnessed significant change as more former patients took leading roles in the campaigns. The newly founded National Association of Psychiatric Survivors, for example, challenged oppressive treatment and stereotypes of mental illness. In 1986 legislators passed the Protection and Advocacy for Mentally Ill Individuals Act, which legally recognized supported employment as a viable goal for rehabilitation.[35]

In 1988 new legal mandates opened doors for some institutionalized people when Judge James McMillan of the U.S. District Court for the Western District of North Carolina ruled in favor of the plaintiffs in the *Thomas S. v. Flaherty* lawsuit. The suit brought to light the misplacement of people with intellectual disabilities into institutions for the mentally ill. The case, which had begun six years earlier in 1982, started as a federal case involving a North Carolina resident who had lived in forty different foster homes and institutions before the age of nineteen. In the early 1980s, an order of relief was entered on his behalf because he was, or was perceived as, cognitively disabled rather than mentally ill. This effort blossomed into a class action suit representing men and women with mental retardation, or those treated as such, held in violation of their constitutional rights in North Carolina's mental hospitals since March 1984.[36] Unlike other cases brought on behalf of patients in mental hospitals, *Thomas S.*, as the case became known, did not attack institutionalization directly. As one lawyer familiar with the case later noted, "It wasn't a deinstitutionalized case per se. It was to get people into appropriate services. For many of them—community services, for some—institutions. But individualized."[37]

Carolina Legal Assistance (CLA), a group of attorneys in Raleigh who advocated for individuals with mental illness across the state, became centrally involved in the case. The lawyers combed through files and interviewed potential members of the *Thomas S.* class. They found scores of African American men and women who had been dumped in hospitals, abandoned by communities, and otherwise mislabeled as feebleminded.[38] Junius Wilson, a patient whom evaluators had proclaimed as clearly not mentally retarded, did not qualify for *Thomas S.* protection. But James McNeil did.

It is unclear exactly what factors encouraged the lawyers to deem "Dummie Graham" mentally retarded or perceived and treated as such. Many people suggested that, at least by the 1990s, McNeil exhibited starkly limited language ability. Some also noted his unusual behavior (such as acting as a policeman) to be an indication that he lacked either intelligence or normal social skills. His obvious difference from others, differences that he did not attempt to disguise, might have also motivated his new classification as a *Thomas S.* member. Because of his new affiliation with the class action suit, McNeil was set to leave Cherry Hospital.

The examination of McNeil's hospital record held immediate ramifications. Staff members in the geriatric ward learned how little they knew about the man. When McNeil had transferred from the CI building decades earlier, he had lost touch with people like Jack Allen, who not only knew him well but understood his history relatively accurately. Perhaps most important, Allen had known McNeil's real name. Now, staff in Woodard and elsewhere consistently referred to the Halifax deaf man as "Dummie Graham," reverting to the name he had been assigned when he was an unknown admitted in the 1930s. After he became part of the *Thomas S.* proceedings, McNeil received closer attention and evaluation. He got his real name back, at least for staff members who cared for him directly. Hospital employees who did not work with him or have access to his medical file continued to call him "Police Dummie."

Deinstitutionalization for *Thomas S.* patients was slow. Paul Pooley, a member of CLA in the 1990s, recalled that after the judgment in 1988, "They [the state] kept appealing, so they didn't have to do anything. Then, when they ran out of appeals, . . . they brought in a consulting firm to design a process by which the service delivery system would be [conducted] and that took forever."[39] The lawyer analyzed, "There are four teams . . . so there was nothing to come out for a long time. Or there would be a pilot project that only took 90 people. That would go for about a year. So it just took a while to roll out services." Hospitals and legislators faced significant challenges: "It was a big headache for people. . . . They had to start providing the services . . . [and] all the clients now had a right to expect that we'll get them adequate services," noted Pooley. "That's just hard to do."[40] Bureaucratic inertia set in. The case demanded stronger state involvement and closer collaboration between local and county governments. Such changes did not come quickly. Consequently, Pooley lamented, "Many people didn't get helped."[41]

James McNeil was one who received minimal assistance from *Thomas S.* His treatment team likely focused more on his deafness and other apparent special needs, but sign language evaluators later noted that his communication skills remained impenetrably limited.[42] Some staff began to take classes in sign language, but how much or whether their exchanges with McNeil deepened is questionable.[43] And the deaf man still resided in a locked ward in the early 1990s. His lawyer explained that "McNeil, because of the class [action suit,] got on a 'good conveyor belt' but 'not a great one.' "[44] There was simply no clear answer to the question: Where should James McNeil go?

IN EARLY DECEMBER 1989, social worker Linda Taylor joined the staff of Cherry Hospital. Meeting her new clients in the geriatric wards of the Woodard Building, Taylor introduced herself and struck up conversations with the patients.[45] As a new employee, she had not yet read through all the charts. She hoped that the men and women living there would be able to share some of their history and experiences with her. Taylor approached Junius Wilson and introduced herself. "I started talking to Junius and the technicians explained that he couldn't talk, he was deaf," she recalled. The staff members quickly assured her that "there were some things that he seemed to be able to understand, like did he have enough clothing, was he warm enough, things like that."[46]

Unaccustomed to working with deaf people, Taylor struggled to communicate with Wilson. Through gesture and speech, she invited him to walk with her and to pick out snacks from the vending machine. Wilson complied. "He liked to go outside," Taylor remembered. No longer able to leave the ward and wander the campus unaccompanied, Wilson might have particularly appreciated Taylor's invitations.[47]

The initial meetings troubled the social worker. "I wondered why he was there," she said. "I didn't see much wrong with him. He seemed to be behaving. He seemed to go to his programs." Accustomed to working with patients with clear signs of mental illness, Taylor was perplexed. Communication barriers posed the greatest obstacle for her: "The hard part about it was you just didn't know what he was thinking."[48]

She also worried about Wilson's social environment. While other patients at Cherry engaged in various activities, Wilson seemed isolated. Taylor motivated Wilson's treatment team to encourage him to attend crafts workshops and other occupational therapy and social sessions. After that, his medical charts showed increased attendance at hospital workshops. The impact on Wilson remained unclear. Given that many activities relied on voiced communication, the deaf man had limited access to the activities and demonstrated his frustration. As his language skills declined in the years after his stroke, this frustration mounted, occasionally flaring into loud or violent outbursts.[49]

During this time the social worker also met James McNeil. She watched as Wilson and McNeil conversed, concluding that "neither of them knew sign" but "they could kind of get through to each other."[50] Technicians, claiming that Wilson and McNeil were sign illiterate, assured Taylor that they had no difficulty understanding the men.[51] Given the comparative ease with which they seemed to communicate basic ideas to the deaf men, Taylor had little reason to question her colleagues at Cherry. Still, her own inability to speak directly with Wilson bothered Taylor. How could she be sure he had all that he needed?

She and her treatment team members agreed to a professional language assessment. They brought in Camille Costa, a speech-language pathologist at the hospital. Costa met with Wilson in the fall of 1990. She determined that she could not conduct a standardized test on Wilson because of communication difficulties. Although Wilson could "respond by using gestures that were clearly recognizable," Costa could not engage him with more formal signed communication. The deaf man did not "finger spell, spontaneously use appropriate manual signs, point to picture/word cards on a communication board, or understand most manually signed instructions and questions," she concluded.[52]

Ten years earlier, Wilson had clearly communicated using sign language when Rachel Wright assessed him. His stroke in 1986, causing weakness in his dominant signing hand, might have limited his cognitive language function. Perhaps this change accounts for Costa's interpretation. But Wilson might have seemed language deficient to Costa because of her definitions of what signed communication should be. Her report did not state what type or types of sign language she used with Wilson. Costa referred only to her instructions given in "manual sign language."[53] Depending on how much it differed from his own language, he might not have understood her. Likewise, when Wilson used Raleigh signs, she might not have understood his motions as anything other than "gross gestures."

Costa's response to the deaf man fit with how many at Cherry were beginning to see him. Staff increasingly portrayed Wilson as stubborn and willful. The man seemed dismissive when they tried to compel him to do something he preferred not to do. Frequently, he refused to submit to assessments because, as some believed, he felt they wasted his time and prevented him from enjoying his puzzles or other hobbies. Wilson clearly preferred staff whom he knew well, and the unfamiliar Costa might have been unwelcome, difficult for the deaf man to understand or trust.

In her evaluation, Costa stated that Wilson "possesses ample gestures to functionally indicate basic needs and desires in his immediate environment." Costa counseled staff to create a communication board with pictures, words, and signs to facilitate broader exchanges with Wilson.[54] Since Costa felt that Wilson did not communicate with formal language, she made no recommendation to provide sign language training for the deaf man or his caretakers. Linda Taylor later described the report as "a general summing up of [Wilson]" and was disappointed that it did not offer more specific advice to help her serve her client. "It didn't kind of leave us anyplace to go," concluded the social worker.[55] And Wilson rejected some of the accommodations offered as a result of Costa's recommendations: Taylor remembered that "he didn't like to use the communication boards."[56]

TAYLOR'S COMMITMENT TO reach her client through language reveals a starkly different perception of Wilson by a social worker. Unlike her predecessors, Taylor actively adopted what advice she received from the speech pathologist and continued to seek alternative means to communicate with her client. She used her combined positions of new evaluator and integral Cherry Hospital staff member to try to reconcile the competing understandings of Wilson's identity. Still, Taylor lacked authority to fundamentally alter Wilson's situation.[57]

Concerned by Wilson's "communication isolation" and his declining health, treatment team members had begun exploring guardianship options for him. They were especially anxious "because of possible need for somebody to assist him at making an informed consent for any medical problem that may arise."[58] Although he was still called a "voluntary" patient at the hospital, Costa's report challenged whether allowing him to make decisions about his care was reasonable: "Currently this patient is unable to give informed consent." Staff moved swiftly. Within two weeks, a judge deemed Wilson incompetent and ordered a guardian ad litem appointed to the deaf man.

Linda Taylor contacted John Wasson for help. Wasson was the assistant director for social services in New Hanover County, the county where Wilson originally lived. Taylor asked him to serve as guardian and informed him of the basic outline of Wilson's case. He was immediately intrigued by the story: "I have heard of situations like Mr. Wilson's where years ago convicted sex offenders had been castrated in state hospitals, yet I never knew of one until now."[59]

John Wasson (Courtesy of John Wasson)

Still, he was concerned that "the assumption on the part of the hospital was that 'we just sort of rubber stamp a preordained order of treatment'—whatever that might be." Instead, Wasson believed that guardians should be "very much advocates for our wards."[60] He wanted to know more about Wilson before agreeing to serve as guardian.

When the first documents arrived from Cherry, Wasson was disappointed. "At first they just sent basic information: who he was—that he was deaf, and black, and his age," recalled Wasson. Perplexed, he looked for Wilson's diagnosis. "I expected to see something like 'paranoid schizophrenic' or something like that." Instead, he found "the diagnosis was something like 'phase of life adjustment disorder' or something to that affect." He knew "that could be, like, me moving to [a new county]. That could happen to anyone." But Wasson also knew why it had to be written in the file: not because it was relevant to therapy but because "in order to get Medicaid, you have to have a diagnosis."[61]

Wasson sent more questions to Cherry. Donald Davis, the psychiatrist who evaluated Wilson during this time, fielded some of his queries. The doctor described Wilson's "treatment" since he entered the hospital. After being incarcerated, Wilson "worked in the farm building with a kind of practical occupational therapy."[62] Had he undergone any surgical procedures? Davis began with a narrowly medical response: "He had a bilateral orchidectomy." The psychiatrist noted that castration "was customary in those quaint and past days for the kind of crime that he is alleged to have committed."[63] A phone call with Linda

Taylor also "raised the term 'castration procedure'" but apparently could not clarify other aspects of Wilson's historic status.[64]

Wasson also had asked about Wilson's prognosis. Davis was not optimistic. Wilson likely had "only a few more years probably to live" but he "is well adjusted to" Cherry Hospital. The county assistant director wanted to know who previously gave consent on Wilson's behalf. No direct answer could be provided. "I'm unable to determined [*sic*] from chart review," the doctor demurred.[65] Then he shifted tone, pressing Wasson to serve as guardian in case Wilson faced any medical emergencies.

Wasson leafed through the files carefully. He found what staff had long known: that Wilson was neither insane nor feebleminded. He also discovered that hospital administrators knew that the criminal charges against Wilson had been dismissed. The true story of Junius Wilson's life slowly emerged: he had been incarcerated in an insane asylum merely because he was deaf, black, and poor, and bureaucratic inertia and staff paternalism helped keep him there for sixty-five years.

Wasson's anger swelled: "I saw the names of many social workers who had been involved with him—and I often wonder why someone didn't do more at that time." Wasson knew firsthand the challenges facing his colleagues—the lack of resources, heavy case loads, bureaucratic red tape. Still, he had trouble rationalizing their inaction. Some people, the bespectacled social worker knew, had had the authority to act, but did not: "I was really angry at the hospital."[66] Wasson decided to accept the case.

AN UNEXPECTED CONFLICT erupted between the social worker and the assistant director. When Wasson informed Taylor that he would bring a reporter with him on his initial visit to meet Wilson, she balked. Fearful that a journalist would only exploit Wilson's story and humiliate the deaf man, Taylor quickly petitioned the court not to appoint Wasson as guardian after all. In her letter to the clerk of court in January 1991, Taylor argued that Wilson's right to confidentiality, as well as his right to protection concerns, disqualified Wasson as an appropriate guardian. Her correspondence suggested her sincere concern that the New Hanover assistant director was seeking personal fame rather than responsible guardianship of her ward.[67] Perhaps she also worried about the potential damage to Cherry Hospital and the entire state hospital system that such an exposé might create. Wasson rejected her concerns. In a letter to the social worker, he clarified his position: "I plan to play a strong advocacy role for Mr. Wilson. One way to exercise that advocacy role is, I believe, to publicize the facts of Mr. Wilson's incarceration, historical maltreatment, and to focus on the current treatment he is receiving, if any, and your plans for him." He expressed

his own dismay at Wilson's treatment by the hospital and held them account-
able: "It is difficult for me to understand how your client could be any more
exploited that he already has been. His incarceration, his subsequent castration,
and the many years at Cherry cry out for public scrutiny." For Wasson, there
was no choice but to bring Wilson's story to the public in order to enact change.
"If anything, [this] would improve his situation and perhaps similar situations
for other patients."[68] Eventually realizing that they shared the same commitment to Wilson, Taylor withdrew her opposition to Wasson's guardianship. The
outside world was coming in.

7

Reinterpreting (1991–1992)

He must have gotten lost through the cracks. He's the last vestige of what formerly was a very unfortunate and often inhumane system of care.

TERRY STELLE, CHIEF OF NORTH CAROLINA'S MENTAL HEALTH SERVICES, QUOTED IN GARY WRIGHT, "PRISONER OF THE STATE," *CHARLOTTE OBSERVER*, **20 JUNE 1993**

The state really failed to understand that Mr. Wilson's deafness wasn't a sentence for him and that in fact, he could live a normal life in the community the way deaf people did then and do now.

PAUL POOLEY, WILSON'S LAWYER, ON NATIONAL PUBLIC RADIO'S *ALL THINGS CONSIDERED*, **4 DECEMBER 1993**

ON 12 MARCH 1991, the New Hanover County Court formally appointed John Wasson as Wilson's guardian.[1] Shortly thereafter, the social worker drove to Cherry Hospital to meet with his new client. It was a brief visit. An aid brought the deaf man into a meeting room. Wilson "had what we call a flat affect," Wasson remembered. "He was just sort of *there*."[2] Soon Wilson started waving his arms and shifting in his chair. Staff explained to Wasson that this meant Wilson was agitated "and so they took him out" of the room.[3] Wilson, not understanding the impact this relationship would have on his future, had no interest in humoring yet another nonsigning white man he had never seen before. Meanwhile, Wasson was frustrated by his own lack of proficiency in sign language and his inability to understand his ward effectively.

The troubling story that Wasson found in Wilson's file motivated him to seek legal support from experts acquainted with disability issues. Even before he met Junius Wilson, Wasson contacted legal services attorney Jim Wall in Wilmington to help him decide what to do about the patient's situation. Wall recommended that Wasson contact CLA, the organization that had been centrally involved in the *Thomas S.* case and other prominent disability advocacy suits.

When Wasson called that day, attorney Paul Pooley answered the phone. "I think he wanted confirmation that [Wilson's situation] was as outrageous as he thought it was," said Pooley, "and I think he wanted to talk to somebody who was every bit as appalled." He continued, "Quickly establishing that we shared that, we moved quickly to, 'What do we do now?' "[4] The men exchanged questions and started to explore options. "This was just too awful, and it was close enough to what we [CLA] do. And at that point I think we still thought he might have mental illness," Pooley explained.[5]

The CLA lawyer and Wasson strategized that they should first focus on Wilson's language issues. They needed to learn what, how, and with whom Wilson communicated. Pooley, who had some experience with deaf people and sign language, was familiar with various services for the deaf.[6] He first turned to Denise Parks, an employee at the Caswell Center (a nearby institution for individuals with cognitive disabilities), to interview Wilson. Parks had taught deaf children and was familiar with sign language.

In late April 1991, Parks, Wasson, and Pooley "met in a large room," as Parks remembered. "It was filled with all these people in suits and ties."[7] Although the number of people present at the meeting puzzled her, she asked no questions before she was ushered into an adjoining room. Before her were "staff members sitting there with an older gentleman, an older black man, and he was just smiling, and seemed to be quite delightful."[8] She thought he "was just a sweet little grandfatherly fellow . . . a little black farmer, a cutie. He was very well dressed, looked real nice. Seemed to be well adjusted. He looked very healthy." Junius Wilson "had a hat on and he took it off and then he watched me and was very aware what I was doing."[9]

Parks smiled at Wilson and tried to size up the situation. "I had no idea why I was there, other than to interpret on a job." She waited, then "someone asked me very calmly to please meet Mr. Wilson and to just assess his signing skills. And so that's exactly what I did." This was an unusual request for Parks, who freely admitted that she was "not a certified interpreter" and that her "signing skills [were] limited to that of a teacher of the deaf." Nevertheless, she began signing with the deaf man.[10]

"He had exceptional eye contact," Parks noticed. "It was like he could communicate with his eyes." It also was apparent to her that Wilson had "been provided manual sign language instruction in the past."[11] Still, she had trouble following him: "It seems like he had some really strange homemade signs." Parks concluded that they "were some really important home signs, signs that had been made up while he was at Cherry." Home signs, she later explained to Pooley, were "signs that are not necessarily official, according to standardized sign language manuals, but are nonetheless developed by the individual and his friends or family for survival communication."[12]

She shifted her own signing from American Sign Language toward a pigeon form that more closely resembled written English. "I sat there with him and I started using straight English signs with him." The two conversed through a mix of gestures, formal ASL signs, and pigeon signs for a brief period. Parks asked Wilson casual questions, avoiding invasive questions like his educational background, family situation, or other personal information. Wilson shared his sign name with Parks, an indication that he felt comfortable communicating with her. Sign names, visual monikers unique to individuals, are often not shared with hearing strangers. For the first time in his long hospital file, the name he had been given as a child at the deaf school, a "*J* on the chest," was written into his chart.[13]

Wilson enjoyed the attention. "He appeared to be happy," Parks remembered. Staff that he knew and trusted encouraged Wilson to tell the woman additional information and laughed with him when he recounted jokes they shared. Parks was quick to notice their close rapport: "There was a wonderful relationship between him and the staff . . . and they very much understood one another. There was a good camaraderie between them." She added, "The staff seemed really to love him."[14] Parks watched as they gestured and pointed to one another, impressed by Wilson's ability to express himself to those who knew no formal sign language.

The meeting did not last long, remembered Parks: "I was in there with him ten minutes, max." Then staff escorted her back to the large adjoining room. The social workers, lawyers, and treatment team waited expectantly for her assessment. "Can he sign?" they wanted to know. "Did he have any sign language skills?" Parks resolutely answered them: "Yes, yes, he had sign skills." She qualified her assessment slightly: "Quite a number of them are homemade signs, but he is quite capable of understanding signs." She looked around the room. Later, she described the impact of her answers. "They were like, 'Ah-ha.' And they started talking amongst themselves."

Wilson's guardian, lawyer, and treatment team began to discuss the implications of this revelation. Questions began to pour forth. One member present asked Parks whether the people working with the man should learn American Sign Language. Parks answered, "I told them that I thought he should have signers around him."[15]

Like Wright a decade earlier, Parks had no more contact with Wilson after the assessment. After she left the building, Parks typed up a formal report for Pooley. As he read the report, he knew that *Thomas S.* mandates had enabled the CLA lawyer and others to provide James McNeil with the promise of specialized accommodation. Now the attorney and the other advocates could build a case for similar support for Junius Wilson.

WILSON'S GUARDIAN AND LEGAL representatives wanted to assess his mental status in addition to just his language abilities. Over the next month, they looked for experts nearby who could perform such an assessment and suggest resources that might benefit him. At their request, Rose Verhoeven, a clinical social worker proficient in sign language from the town of Cary, came to meet with Wilson.[16]

The June visit proved to be complicated. Inside the Woodard Building, staff "were not happy that [the psychologist] was coming in there," remembered one observer. "They wanted [her] to sit in the main hallway and do the evaluation [there]." Verhoeven resisted, telling them, "This will not do. . . . I [need] to have a private place." A technician told her she had to have staff members with her during the assessment "because [Wilson] might be violent with [her]." She was observed disagreeing with the technician. The evaluator "had worked in mental institutions" previously and "just didn't feel that notion that he'd be violent."[17] Despite Verhoeven's protests, a male staff member remained with her as the social worker began her assessment.

As with Wasson, Wilson was not particularly interested in another conversation with a white hearing stranger. Meeting in a conference room with staff present, "Mr. Wilson seemed agitated, appeared anxious, and was generally uncooperative during the first part of the assessment," recalled the evaluator. Later reports suggested that "Mr. Wilson was so distracted by" the staff member who came in to "protect" Verhoeven that she "finally asked him to leave and [told him that she would] take responsibility."[18] But Wilson already was upset. After roughly twenty minutes with the social worker, the deaf man "closed his eyes" to definitively end all conversation. Verhoeven did not tap him to get his attention as Wright had tried to do during her sessions with Wilson. Instead, she walked down the hallways with him and allowed him to return to his room to rest. Several hours later, they met again, now in a private room without interruption.

"The second interview proceeded smoothly," wrote the clinical social worker in her report, "with Mr. Wilson becoming more willing to cooperate and seemingly more relaxed." She began to question him, covering territory that Rachel Wright had traveled a decade earlier. "Mr. Wilson can fingerspell and write his name." Where had he learned these skills? Wilson "affirmed he had gone to school a long time ago." She also discovered abilities previously missed, such as the fact that Wilson could "recall and repeat three digit numbers."[19]

She asked Wilson about his life at Cherry. His arthritic fingers stumbled when spelling out names and numbers, but Wilson was able to describe his previous work. She asked whether he had driven a car. NEVER, he answered, but he informed her that he traveled by bicycle. Walking over to the windows, he pointed, sweeping a line across the campus to show where he had previously ridden.

Their conversation relied heavily on "minimal language: gestures, looking at pictures, smiling, shaking head, pointing." The evaluator demonstrated correct ASL signs for objects Wilson had described with homemade gestures. He reacted positively. "He'd respond to me when I showed him the sign. He did it back," Verhoeven later stated. It seemed clear to her that Wilson was a man who could still learn some things.

She tested his emotional responses. Placing pictures of facial expressions on the table, the social worker observed Wilson smiling and frowning, mimicking the images before him. She did not ask him directly about his family or how he arrived at Cherry, but Wilson's responses to certain images were suggestive. Sad and tearful faces upset him. He "put up his hand, shook his head no, and refused to look at [them]." More images were shown. One depicted a boy learning to ride a bicycle. To this "he indicated pleasure and laughed . . . shaking his head 'yes' and pointing at himself." Another picture drew an especially complicated response: "He smiled, then his affect became pensive, and he looked away when shown a picture of a man and child in an embrace."[20]

Verhoeven prepared a report of the interview and an assessment. "Mr. Wilson appears to be of average intelligence, oriented to his environment, and able to communicate on a basic level in sign language." His environment, she felt, was a primary concern. Although she, like staff, found the deaf man to be "sometimes friendly and cooperative, other times frustrated and hostile," she qualified this conclusion: "Considering the circumstances, this seemed appropriate and consistent."[21] She continued: "He appears frustrated, angry, and hostile at times when he is unable to convey his message and to emotionally withdraw as a result of this." Wilson's inability to "accurately convey his thoughts, feelings, and needs" led to "long-term frustrations."

Staff affection for Wilson aside, the evaluator found that the hospital had failed him. She likely had carefully read the three previous language assessments, as well as Wilson's broader medical reports. "His records . . . indicate sporadic attempts at evaluation with little follow-up or consistent, long-term efforts to enhance his communication abilities."[22] She found copies of sections of a sign language book in his file, but she also observed that hospital employees did not typically use appropriate signs with him. Although she knew the staff believed they were "able to communicate adequately with him by gestures" and saw "no other communication needs for him," the clinical social worker disagreed. Revealing the paucity of language shared between Wilson and Cherry staff, she reported how simple their interactions were: "When asked if he is OK, Mr. Wilson nods his head 'yes' and if asked if he needs anything, he nods his head, no."

Verhoeven laid bare the problem: "Mr. Wilson's emotional and mental needs have been inadequately addressed as there have been no consistent attempts at communicating with Mr. Wilson, except on a rudimentary, concrete level (pointing, physically directing him, facial expressions)." She stated what needed to happen: Wilson "has a need for dependable, structured environment and adequate social support systems."[23] She provided specific changes to address these needs. Since sign language use was the priority, she recommended that both the staff and Wilson receive sign language training, allowing them to develop consistent and accurate signed communication. Such a program would take careful and extended work. "For Mr. Wilson to derive adequate benefit from efforts made on his behalf," the evaluator wrote, "I strongly recommend daily exposure to accurate communications and a patient rebuilding of his skills."[24]

In addition to language enrichment within the hospital, Verhoeven suggested that in order to enrich Wilson's social and linguistic opportunities, the hospital locate a volunteer, fluent in ASL, to meet regularly with the deaf man. Community outings, especially with other deaf people, would benefit him, too. She explained the need for Wilson's social worker to have a sign language interpreter present during all counseling sessions with Wilson. She also pointed out the need for a closed-captioned device for his television.

JOHN WASSON AND PAUL POOLEY considered the options available. Given that at the time they thought that Wilson was ninety-six years old,[25] both advocates felt that they should use techniques that would be effective as quickly as possible. They were concerned that their client might die before the state could redress its mistreatment of him. Although the most obvious course of action was to bring a lawsuit, both Wasson and Pooley knew that legal wrangling with the hospital and state could actually delay help for Wilson. Eventually, reported one, "We made a pretty critical 'fork in the road' decision that we would not pursue litigation if we felt we could get services faster and better by . . . taking a nontraditional path." According to Pooley, "[We] didn't feel like we had the luxury of time to pursue this in a sort of usual pace of 'moving it down a conveyor belt a little at a time'—like in civil suits."[26]

Instead, they pursued a different path. First, they would focus on a direct appeal to the state government, hoping that the attorney general in Raleigh would intervene on Wilson's behalf. If that failed, they would pursue the other track: "to litigate if we had to."[27] Wasson enlisted Jim Wall from Wilmington's Legal Aid Office and Roger Manus from CLA as he and Pooley assessed the details of their plans.

Wasson and the lawyers started writing letters to state officials. During the summer of 1992, Wasson outlined Wilson's story, then his demands, to the state: "Mr. Wilson is very elderly and may not live much longer," he began. "Nevertheless, I insist that in the time he has left, that his unique need to communicate be accommodated. It seems to me that given Cherry Hospital's unwillingness to meet any of those needs for 67 years, that you and your staff would feel some moral obligation to make the time he has left as productive and as pleasant as possible."[28] At first, no response came.

A few months later, the lawyers sent letters to North Carolina's secretary of human resources, David Flaherty. Wall and Manus knew that "Flaherty had cosponsored legislation in 1971 that required the state's mental hospitals to check patients to make certain no one was being held who should not be."[29] As they expected, Flaherty was receptive to their pleas: "This was tragic. Mr. Wilson was the type of patient that we were trying to find," he later explained.[30] The state official forwarded the letters to North Carolina's Justice Department lawyers.

When Michelle McPherson, a lawyer with the attorney general's office, read Wilson's story, she responded quickly. McPherson had been involved in the *Thomas S.* case for the attorney general's office, and the class action suit made her intimately familiar with the stories of individuals wrongly warehoused in psychiatric wards. Pooley credited McPherson with expediting the process to reach a settlement from the state. Years later he described her vital role: "When she saw the Wilson case, she was a good enough person to say, 'We need to do the right thing right now.'" Unlike some bureaucrats faced with similar challenges, McPherson "immediately leapt over all the stalling . . . and she jumped to, 'We gotta figure this out right now.'"[31]

While negotiating with the state, Wilson's representatives also tried to enlist the hospital's help. The men hoped that conclusive evidence of Wilson's abilities and needs would pressure the hospital voluntarily to accommodate him. With a little prompting, the team had advocated for and eventually purchased a television with closed-captioning. But Wasson and the lawyers wanted a richer language environment than that. Relying again on the language experts' reports, Wasson made "a lot of recommendations" for accommodating Wilson's communication and social needs. Staff needed to learn sign language, he reminded them. Wilson needed nonstaff companions who could sign, as well.

More than a year passed before the hospital hired interpreter Cathy Sweet from the nearby town of Wilson to teach staff some American Sign Language and sensitize them to aspects of deaf culture.[32] In her initial visit to Cherry, Sweet assessed Wilson without the benefit of any staff preparation. "The purpose of my visit was to evaluate, to see what kind of interpreter services would benefit him. Language was of course an issue. I needed to know: Can he communicate in a signed language?"[33] In her brief conversation with Wilson, she recognized the Raleigh signs that other African American deaf people had used around her when she lived in Winston-Salem. To Sweet's eyes, Wilson presented a culturally deaf man deprived of his natural community and language. After her first visit with Wilson, she walked back to her car. "I cried all the way home," she remembered.[34]

The ASL interpreter soon returned to Cherry to begin working with the deaf man and the staff. Like the psychologist who had assessed Wilson, Sweet considered a language-rich environment crucial for Wilson. Her training sessions for staff emphasized basic but authentic ASL. The instructor understood that Cherry required certain staff to attend and that some of them resented the pressure. There was "not a lot of enthusiasm" for the classes, explained Sweet. "Linda [Taylor] was positive about it, but clearly everyone was forced to be there. It was forced on them."[35] Although she knew the classes were necessary for Wilson, she empathized with the staff's predicament. Having to care for numerous patients took time and energy. Learning sign language simply added new burdens. Having outsiders insist that staff change their basic interaction with Wilson perhaps also created resentment and might have undermined the effectiveness of the sign classes.

The hospital tried to make other adjustments. During the second half of 1992, treatment team notes describe repeated efforts to coax Wilson into group sessions where staff studied ASL. Hiram Grantham, a deaf janitor at the hospital, stepped forward. Although Grantham signed, he had attended the deaf school for white pupils in Morganton and his language therefore differed significantly from Wilson's. Still, treatment team members concluded, he could communicate better in sign language than other hospital employees. Grantham was assigned to begin visiting Wilson.[36]

Wasson and Pooley acknowledged Cherry Hospital's progress, but they expected more. "I thought he was treated humanely at Cherry but he did not get the kinds of services that would let him keep up his skills," reasoned Wasson. For decades, hospital staff had underestimated Wilson's abilities and needs, perhaps because of paternalistic and racial attitudes that prevented them from thinking about his relative existential state. Describing the language assessments and research on deafness, Wasson noted, "We realized he could sign and do a lot of things people thought he couldn't do."[37] For numerous reasons, it was extremely unlikely that staff would become proficient in sign language. Wilson would be unable to regain his deaf identity and communication skills if he remained isolated on Cherry's campus. To correct this, the deaf man needed interpreters, frequent tutoring, and opportunities to meet with members of the African American deaf community. This kind of support could become expensive. Wasson knew from long experience that institutions were unlikely to provide such accommodations voluntarily.

Other factors seemed to compound Cherry's unwillingness to comply. Staff members resented outsiders suggesting that they had mistreated Wilson. Some thought the provisions requested were inherently flawed and unrealistic. At one point Cherry's director, J. Field Montgomery, lashed out at Wasson. Maybe, Montgomery suggested, Junius Wilson "just might not want to learn a new language at 95. Isn't that a little harsh, a little cruel, to spring all this on him at this age? Maybe he just wants to lie around and watch TV."[38]

EIGHTEEN MONTHS PASSED and little had changed. When Wasson saw the "woefully inadequate" response by the hospital to his recommendations, he understood that he must escalate his efforts. After much discussion, he, Pooley, and the other advocates for Wilson warned governmental leaders in Raleigh that they would sue the state for discrimination and damages.

Weeks later, on 26 October 1992, the state of North Carolina and Wilson's representatives reached a settlement. In addition to training staff in sign language, the state agreed to pay for a qualified interpreter, counseling for Wilson, and additional language and psychological assessments, as well as certain medical, rehabilitation, and recreational services. The settlement also provided Wilson with tailored instruction in sign language and "designated items"—like a reclining chair—for his sole use. Wilson's advocates knew that having objects of his own rather than sharing items with dozens of others made Wilson feel both independent and respected.

Wilson's attorney and guardian were empowered to hire a consultant to monitor the implementation of the new policies, with the state paying part of this cost.[39] The settlement also stipulated that if Wilson did not receive treatment "in a timely manner," his guardian could alert the director of the Division of Mental Health, Developmental Disabilities, and Substance Abuse Services. This director could then "take immediate corrective action." Leaving the door open to changes in Wilson's living arrangement, the state also agreed that "the guardian may ask him to be placed in the community." It continued, "If requested, placement must be ready within 60 days of the guardian's decision." After paying CLA attorney fees and costs—roughly $13,000—North Carolina had one requirement for Wasson and the legal team: the settlement was binding and final. Wilson's advocates had to promise not to file a new lawsuit.[40]

WHILE PLEASED WITH THE legal settlement, Wasson and Pooley knew that it held value only if those with influence enforced it. In previous work with activist organizations, Pooley had closely studied ways of using the media and public support to assert pressure on those with authority. Immediately after the state signed its contract with Wilson's guardian and lawyers, the team of advocates contacted the press. Over the next several months, Wasson and Pooley kept Wilson's name and plight in the news. The legal guardian later explained, "We were doing a lot of publicity, hoping to motivate the state, that the state would do the right thing."[41]

Readers in North Carolina were riveted by Wilson's story. Splashed across the front pages of several state newspapers, Pooley and Wasson's careful outline of Wilson's history inspired readers to demand justice. Select reporters had the opportunity to see transcripts from Wilson's 1925 trial, a critical state evaluation of Cherry Hospital from 1948, a 1970s treatment team description of Wilson that showed that the hospital did not believe that Wilson was insane, and Wilson's financial earnings during the 1970s and 1980s. Advocates familiar with the case pointed accusing fingers first at the hospital then at the state.

Wilson's lawyers spoke dramatically about the injustices done to the deaf man. Jim Wall was moved by "the sheer horror of someone being committed to a mental hospital since 1925 without any diagnosis of mental illness." He emphasized that what happened was "obviously a horrible crime."[42] One advocate charged that "it was patently a lie to say he was of imminent danger to himself or others," as the hospital had stated in order to justify Wilson's continued institutionalization. "No one could read what his doctors wrote and believe that."[43] When the hospital tried a different tack and pointed out Wilson's voluntary status there, the attorneys attacked that point as well: "No one there could communicate with him. They admit they couldn't. Yet they say they asked him and he volunteered," Wall exclaimed.[44]

CLA attorney Roger Manus told one reporter that "Mr. Wilson has been warehoused for most of his life. Hospital records offer no legitimate explanation for his never having received treatment."[45] His colleague Pooley told another reporter that he thought Wilson was "pretty much lost from the day he went in."[46] He emphasized the personal cost: "He lost his life. He lost the chance to live in his home and do what he wanted to do."[47] Perhaps Wall put it most succinctly: "They locked him up and threw away the keys. There was no effort to do anything more than warehouse him. He was written off as a human being."[48]

Picked up by the national media, the story of what happened to Wilson ignited outrage across the country for the injustices that had shaped Wilson's life.[49] It resonated with reporters and readers around the world. Many readers, touched by Wilson's vulnerability, sent letters and gifts to the elderly man. Wasson later recalled, "Someone from the Charlotte Hornets sent him a baseball hat; some anonymous person from California sent him a catcher's mitt." Wasson claimed that Wilson "had more hats than he knew what to do with . . . which I thought was a cool thing."[50]

Although the attorneys were vocal in the newspapers, it was Wasson, Wilson's guardian, who became the primary voice demanding action. First, he intentionally emphasized Wilson's mettle and heart, humanizing and valorizing the man the readers had never known: "He's a survivor, or he wouldn't have lasted this long. . . . I can't imagine what strength of spirit it would take to persevere under those conditions."[51] Wasson pulled at the public's heartstrings: "I don't think anyone can make up for the fact that he spent most of his life at Cherry Hospital with little or no services, but in the time he has remaining, we're going to see he gets whatever he needs."[52] He reminded readers that "the man's life has been taken away from him. I think all of us in North Carolina owe this man something."[53]

Wasson's call for state responsibility convinced many readers. Josie Douglas from Knightdale, North Carolina, wrote the editor of the *Raleigh News and Observer*: "When a deaf person is in a mental hospital, he needs someone available at all times who can communicate with him. Can you imagine anything any more inhumane than being institutionalized over a long period of time and having no one to communicate with you?"[54] She continued, "It is sad that Wilson has suffered this treatment. It is equally sad that deaf citizens who are mentally ill and who are in need of treatment do not receive appropriate services." Echoing the call from Wilson's advocates, she asked plaintively, "How can mental health professionals evaluate the patients and prescribe the proper treatment of medications without being able to communicate with them?"[55]

With calls streaming in, state officials tried to control the public relations damage. Walter "Terry" Stelle, deputy director of mental health services for the state, admitted that he thought "it shameful that this would have occurred in one of our institutions. It's an embarrassment to all of us."[56] When reporters pressed him to explain Wilson's case, he demurred: "How it would have occurred, I unfortunately don't have a good answer for that." Rationalizing Cherry's later actions, he added, "He had been there for so many years, people just assumed that he was an old, mentally ill man."[57]

Stelle's constituents were outraged by Wilson's tragic story and by the state's slow and inadequate response. They demanded action. Stelle tried to assuage them by pointing out that as soon as he learned of the story, he "asked [Cherry Hospital's director J.] Field Montgomery to search out every single person in the hospital who is deaf and assure me in writing that they were receiving appropriate treatment, evaluation and services."[58] He not only asked Cherry to investigate its patients; the deputy director also called on all state mental hospitals to conduct similar searches.

The search found about twenty-four deaf patients among the 2,300 people in North Carolina's mental institutions. Two additional deaf patients resided at Cherry. Although the deputy director did not name them, reporters tried to track down their stories. Stan Swofford of the *Greensboro News and Record* discovered that one of the deaf patients was James McNeil. According to Swofford's article, McNeil, like Wilson, was classified as a voluntary patient at Cherry from 1979 until 1990.[59] But Stelle insisted that none of the other patients found during the search resembled Wilson's case. The official promised that from that moment on, deaf patients in psychiatric hospitals would receive all necessary accommodations, including interpreters and other communication services.[60]

Paul Pooley considered the new policy changes "small, but remarkable steps forward for deaf services." Wilson's case began to serve a larger purpose: "Because we were able to make Mr. Wilson's case front and center, we were able to get some faster responses in other areas. . . . There was a clear sense in the department that they didn't want more of 'these cases' popping up."[61] He continued, however, to see problems in the state system everywhere he looked: "I had other clients who were deaf and mentally ill in other hospitals and they weren't getting served or getting any tests done because they didn't have any staff people who could sign, or any interpreters." Pooley's commitment to these patients and to reform merely intensified.[62]

NEITHER CHERRY HOSPITAL administrators nor North Carolina government officials appreciated their portrayal in the media. The hospital staff especially resented their vilification in the press. Director J. Field Montgomery found the rebuke of his staff and institution highly inappropriate and inaccurate: "We are very compassionate people here," he insisted. Answering the accusatory questions about Wilson's commitment at Cherry, he exclaimed: "Nobody here is going to kick a 75- or 80-year-old man out on the street." Although Montgomery admitted, "I know damn well I wouldn't want to spend my life here," he also contended that "as old as [Wilson] was, we knew he couldn't make it" outside the walls of the institution.[63] The administrator wanted readers to know the human side of the hospital, not merely Wilson's story. He chided reporters, claiming that their depiction "has been an affront to a lot of good people here. We have treated him with compassion. We're his family, his home, and he considers us just that."[64]

Chris Lancaster, Wilson's friend from the hospital car wash, later echoed Montgomery's sentiment: "Believe it or not, whatever you heard, he was happy there, content. There is no doubt in my mind." The employee shook his head sadly. "The general public had the impression that he was locked up in a cage, with only a mattress on the floor. Junius went where he wanted to go. He was just as free as he would have been at his home."[65] Lancaster acknowledged that Wilson's early incarceration and castration were a terrible misfortune, but he distinguished Wilson's early treatment from his life at Cherry since the 1960s. "I can't say that what they did to him was right," he said, but in the time that Lancaster worked at the hospital, he knew that "Junius Wilson never was mistreated." Like many staff, Lancaster saw Cherry ultimately as a positive factor in Wilson's life. There Wilson "had a decent place to live, it was clean, which he might not have had at home." Without Cherry's protection, Lancaster continued, Wilson would have been more likely to suffer. "He wouldn't have lasted as long on the streets," he said, then repeated, "He got better care than on the street." The greater wrong seemed to Lancaster to be unfair public opinion. "It was a raw deal for the people to think that he was put in a cage or something, against his will," he lamented.[66] Other staff members agreed. When asked about issues of mistreatment, one scoffed, "Malarkey." Wilson, she stated, was not an "abused patient and he certainly was not restricted." She went on: "He had the best of both lives and both worlds and loved every minute of it."[67]

WILSON'S GUARDIAN AND LAWYERS knew that the media blitz in late 1992 could force Cherry Hospital and the state of North Carolina to address the injustices they saw in the institutionalization of Junius Wilson and other patients in the system. They did not predict the other crucial outcome that resulted from the media coverage. Although several articles described Wilson's known relatives, such as his parents and sister, the hospital and the reporters both assumed that Wilson had no surviving family members. When members of Arthur Smith Jr.'s extended family read the newspaper reports about Wilson's story, they were startled by the possibility that the patient might be their kin. Willie Sidberry, Arthur and Lizzie Smith's grandson, remembered the newspaper articles: "We were surprised to find that Carrie [Wilson Gill] even had a brother," Sidberry, a resident in Castle Hayne, explained. "And my mother didn't know."[68] André Branch, another grandchild of Arthur and Lizzie, was baffled, as well. He had grown up knowing Carrie Gill but "was shocked to learn that she had a brother. I never knew she had a brother."[69] He began to ask his older aunts and uncles to share what they knew about Wilson. Few could tell much about him. Nor were they certain that they should immediately contact the Cherry inmate. They were reluctant to become embroiled in this complicated story and unsure what the consequences would be.

Friends of the family eventually decided to contact John Wasson.[70] Discussions began to reunite the extended Wilson clan. The Sidberrys and Linda Taylor began their own cautious but excited conversations. Questions abounded on both sides: What was Junius Wilson like? What was the family like? What had happened to both over the many decades? When could they meet?

8

New Places, New Faces (1993–1994)

ON THE FIRST DAY OF April 1993, Junius Wilson and a small team of Cherry Hospital staff loaded into a van and headed east.[1] As they turned off the highway toward Castle Hayne, what Wilson's advocates and family were watching for happened: he lit up with excitement. A treatment team member later recalled that Wilson "pointed to a general area of Castle Hayne and gestured, ME, ME to signify, 'That's my home.'"[2] Another team member remembered, "They drove him past a place where his old home used to be and then he got real excited and pointed at the bushes." His interpreter concluded that Wilson "thought that was where home had been."[3] The group passed by an old school and church. Cherry staff pointed to the buildings, their faces asking whether Wilson remembered them. He nodded quickly, eyes darting back to the view outside the van. His reaction touched his caretakers: "It was a very poignant moment in the van when he definitely recognized what seemed to be the road that went to his house. He became very animated," explained John Wasson.[4]

Their vehicle continued down the road. A staff member noted that the deaf man "was then taken to the small development [where] his mother last lived. [Wilson] seemed to recognize the area."[5] As they moved past Mary Clark's previous home, Wilson "made a moving motion, appeared very sad and almost tearful."[6] Another person in the car added, "He looked really forlorn, maybe from a sad memory. He might have remembered what happened that summer when he was arrested and sent away. It was tragic but he seemed to just want to move on."[7] The driver took them to the Sidberry's house. Wilson "smiled and shook hands but did not seem to recognize [Willie Sidberry]."

Wilson was then taken back to the area where he had lived prior to his hospitalization. The group wandered into a forested area because the house "no longer exist[ed] and the area [was] complete woodland. The cousin recalled a path that led to the house but was unable to locate it." The van moved slowly along while Sidberry searched for the old path. Suddenly, Wilson "pushed [the] therapist's arm making incomprehensible sounds and pointing to a wooded area." Willie Sidberry followed Wilson's pointed finger: "This was the path that led to the house [the patient] once lived in."[8] Wilson's hands fluttered. He recognized the area.

The group eventually turned back to Goldsboro. Passing by the school and church, Wilson smiled and gestured, affirming that he remembered them. When they returned to Cherry's campus, Wilson spotted Hiram Grantham, the deaf employee who worked with him. An observer noted in Wilson's daily logbook that the patient "began signing and gesturing in an elated manner to employee about his home visit."[9]

The visit clearly changed Wilson. His social worker noted that he was "somewhat more cheerful in his attitude." The treatment team psychiatrist wrote, "From what we could tell, he appears to be interested in any follow-up visit."[10] John Wasson agreed: "He looks like a different person. He looks happy. He has more character in his face. There's more life in his eyes."[11]

THE DISCOVERY OF WILSON's existence had surprised his family. Not everyone welcomed his presence as quickly or fully as did the Sidberrys. The public attention to their incarcerated relative perhaps had embarrassed some of Wilson's kin. They simply avoided conversations about the deaf man.

Although the Sidberrys and other relatives believed in the value of caring for the extended clan, they were unable to bring Wilson into their home. It might have been hard for them and the others to reconcile their strong commitment to family and Christian hospitality with the complex challenges posed by their newfound relative. The Sidberrys felt that Wilson was well looked after at Cherry, perhaps because there he had care from people who, unlike themselves, had known him for years. His deafness was a major factor, since no one in the family knew sign language nor had they had time to establish less formal ways of communicating with their relative.

André Branch, living on the West Coast, apparently heard about Wilson later than did the Sidberrys and others living in North Carolina. He peppered his elders with questions about Wilson during a family get-together. Some, like

Sarah Peoples, claimed that she did not know anything. Others apparently did not disclose much.[12] But Branch persisted, hoping to reunite Wilson with family.

In January 1993 Branch reached out to Carrie Gill, Junius Wilson's younger sister, who was living in New York.[13] He wanted to determine how he might help reunite the siblings. Branch later remembered that when he called Gill, she told him, "I want my brother out of that place. If there is anything you can do to get him out of that place, I will love you forever."[14]

Wasson received a late-night phone call from Branch. He "called me at midnight. He was very complimentary. He identified himself. Told me who he was. Told me that people in Castle Hayne were relatives, but were afraid to come forward."[15] Branch also offered to facilitate a meeting with Wilson's sister.

Wasson asked attorney Paul Pooley to arrange a meeting with Carrie Gill and André Branch in New York. The lawyer hoped that Wilson's sibling could raise the veil that covered much of Wilson's life. "I was trying to get family history," Pooley later explained. "John's department had concluded that there were no [immediate] relatives, so when he found out that there *were* . . . we reopened the thing and I went up there on John's behalf to hopefully draw them in and learn more. We at that time had a very inexact intake form and didn't know the full family history."[16]

Pooley and Branch went to Gill's brownstone in Harlem, but she refused to meet with the white lawyer or with Branch. The attorney never spoke directly with Wilson's sister but tried to be empathetic to her difficult situation. "I think she just felt, 'I need to pull back,'" he surmised. Instead, Pooley spent time getting to know the Seattle relative. "André and I kind of hung out," recalled the lawyer. They got along well: "We were simpatico. I think he liked me because I was progressive enough and 'got it.' I got the race part of it and the southern part of this. . . . We didn't accomplish much but talk . . . and drink coffee."[17] The two men did come up with some ideas about using more African American nursing personnel and interpreters for Wilson.[18]

After the two men flew home, Branch began writing to Wasson. Assuming the role of family representative, Branch again praised Wasson, noting that he and his relatives were "greateful [*sic*] for the care and concern you have demonstrated as guardian for their brother and uncle." Realizing that Wasson had served as Wilson's legal protector because no relatives had been discovered, Branch moved quickly to assure Wasson that his role as social worker was still needed: "In light of your willingness to cooperate with the family, they desire that you continue in your role as guardian."[19]

The letters suggest that Wilson's relatives respected Wasson's sincere commitment to his ward and to a just resolution. Branch wrote him that the family appreciated "all that you have been able to accomplish for our loved one. Given your involvement with Junius Wilson's case over the last two years, having learned of the hospital's horrific treatment of him, we know you can appreciate our desire for our relative to be free of the dehumanizing and demeaning environment of Cherry Hospital."[20] Like Wasson and Pooley, Branch and his relatives wanted to "move swiftly and sensitively to restore some semblance of normalcy to his life's remaining years."[21]

André Branch suggested in one of his missives to the guardian that Wilson be taken to New York to see his sister. "Ms. Gill is adamant that 'the lawyers, guardian, and men at that hospital bring my brother to see me,' " he wrote.[22] A summer reunion would allow other relatives to attend as well. He ended the letter, "As a concerned family member, I am at your disposal."[23]

TWO MONTHS PASSED before Wasson responded to Branch's letter. The social worker outlined the recent efforts to move Wilson out of the locked wards. After consulting Wilson's caretakers and lawyer, Wasson decided not to send Wilson to New York. He explained his position to Branch, stating his concern about Wilson's health status. He suggested a reunion at the hospital or in Castle Hayne as an alternative.[24]

The long delay in Wasson's correspondence, his disappointing response to the request for a reunion, and Wilson's continued residence behind locked doors began to infuriate Branch. The family representative wondered whether paternalism and racism were at the root of the problem. Branch's written retort stung: "Apparently, though times have changed, the attitudes of some people have not."[25]

Holding his ground as guardian but attempting to maintain ties to the family, Wasson replied. He detailed the negotiations with the hospital: requests for a cottage to house Wilson and demands to the North Carolina Division of Mental Health. During this period, Wilson had experienced fainting spells serious enough to have him sent to Dorothea Dix Hospital for tests. During one episode, his heart apparently stopped. Wasson did not share this information with Branch previously, although certainly it was a factor in Wilson's inability to travel. Wasson tried to articulate the institution's unwillingness to move the deaf man.[26] He added, "Please understand, I also am frustrated that Mr. Wilson continues to reside on the locked geriatric ward at Cherry Hospital."[27] André Branch was not persuaded.

DURING THE LATE 1980s and early 1990s, the position of deaf people and deaf issues became more visible in American society. Deaf advocates like Jack Gannon and Leo Jacobs published significant community histories that clearly celebrated a separate deaf cultural identity.[28] Scholars, too, began to investigate the development of deaf culture in America.[29] Schools increasingly recognized and used American Sign Language as a vital form of communication for deaf students. Popular entertainment mirrored these changes. Linda Bove continued to model sign language on *Sesame Street*. Marc Medoff's 1980 dramatic work *Children of a Lesser God* appeared on Broadway to rave reviews. That year the play garnered Tony Awards for best play, best actress (Phyllis Frelich), and best actor (Jon Rubinstein). Over the next five years, deaf characters would appear on numerous television programs, from *Little House on the Prairie* to *Barney Miller* and *Magnum PI*. As millions watched on television in 1986, deaf actress Marlee Matlin received an Academy Award for her leading role in the successful Hollywood version of *Children of a Lesser God*.

In 1988 hundreds marched in Deaf President Now actions, cheering and signing "We Have a Dream, Too," as they demanded that Gallaudet University in Washington, D.C., the only liberal arts college in the world serving primarily deaf and hard of hearing people, consider a deaf person as they searched for a new university president. Two years later, Congress passed the Americans with Disabilities Act (ADA). Echoing the rhetoric of African American civil rights leaders, deaf and disability activists insisted that all people, regardless of physical or cognitive differences, enjoy equal access to work, politics, and mainstream social affairs. For the first time, their arguments reached a very large audience. Specifically protecting individuals with disabilities from discrimination, the ADA sought to ensure equal opportunities for persons with disabilities in not only government services but also in the work environment, transportation systems, public accommodations, and commercial facilities.[30]

AS JOHN WASSON STRUGGLED to connect Wilson with his family members and with Castle Hayne, Paul Pooley tried to implement policies from the state's settlement, such as sign language training for Wilson. "I did a lot of the follow-up work on this part," he explained, because "in this kind of thing you have to win, then you have to win the implementation."

Because communication remained a central feature of Wilson's case, his representatives asked for yet another language assessment. Rather than rely on Cherry staff or state employees, the advocates decided to use an independent evaluator. By now, the Raleigh lawyer distrusted Cherry: "We knew we would have to go outside the hospital . . . because John [Wasson] had already run into, 'This is just really a hospice procedure.' Maybe they just wanted forms signed." Feeling that the hospital merely sought to provide basic daily care, Wilson's advocates looked elsewhere for cultural, social, and linguistic support. In the end he realized, "We didn't go that far outside [the hospital and the state system] because we used Brenda Aron, whose husband was second or third in the division of Services for the Deaf and Hard of Hearing." Pooley knew that Aron, who was deaf, could potentially best comprehend what Wilson needed specifically. With Aron's help, Pooley and Wasson finally "got people who could provide full services to deaf people, which," the lawyer dryly added, "had not apparently occurred to the state to do for some sixty or seventy years."[31]

Aron's participation in Wilson's treatment forced the hospital to consider more than just his language status. As a deaf person, Aron understood cultural and social factors better than those who previously assessed Wilson. She also recognized some of the more subtle forms of discrimination that Wilson faced as a deaf person at Cherry.

The hospital received its first culture shock when Aron appeared for a meeting with administrators. The hospital had asked staff member Hiram Grantham, the deaf janitor who was accustomed to communicating with hearing employees at the hospital, to serve as her interpreter. Even though Grantham had attended a deaf school, he had neither the ASL vocabulary nor the training to translate successfully the complex concepts the language-psychological specialist needed to convey. Aron insisted on a professional sign interpreter, and eventually the hospital relented and hired one. She used the interpreter for all subsequent interactions with the treatment team and administrators, teaching them appropriate etiquette in communicating with deaf people. Her professionalism reinforced to them the fact that ASL was a real language.[32]

After Aron entered the room in which Wilson was sitting, the deaf man likely perked up when he discovered that she was deaf. His expressions would show what many signers call a "deaf face." Aron began with small talk, asking him about the people around him and the things he did at Cherry. His homemade signs referred mostly to life and factors in the hospital environment.

She asked his name. He finger spelled it back: J-U-N-S W-I-L-S-O-N. Aron considered this important: "This shows a strong sense of self," she reported. She wondered if he knew how to read his name. "When I showed him his name typed on paper," she reported, "he recognized it." She pointed to other men in the room, such as James McNeil, questioning whether he was "Junius Wilson." The deaf man "laughed hard and shook his head 'no.' "[33]

She watched him interact with staff. "He has displayed a very common method of getting hearing people's attention by yelling and mimicking hearing speech behavior (speaking and gesturing) as if he thought this is the way people should act even though his speech was not understandable." In her report, she also noted that Wilson "knew the difference between a deaf and a hearing person." Seeing Wilson in person enabled Aron to challenge certain remarks in his medical logs. "He stopped using his voice when I told him I was deaf," she stated, but then he "yelled to gain attention at a hearing member of the team when her back was turned."[34]

Wilson seemed to feel at ease sharing visual language with another deaf person. Gesturing and signing, the two talked more about Wilson's hobbies. Aron was impressed with Wilson's ability to use and adopt certain grammatical features from American Sign Language, thereby demonstrating that he had some training in formal sign.

She tested his understanding of time. His hands flitted responses, suggesting he could use the concepts of past, present, and future, but not always specifics. She then analyzed his understanding of place. She asked in ASL, WHERE YOU LIVE? Wilson "signed LONG-AGO and FAR-AWAY in response to the question."[35] She asked more about his past. What about his family? He "responded with shoulder shrugs until asked about his sister." Then, "he signed FAR-AWAY" while shrugging and shaking his head.[36] Knowing some of the details from Wilson's file made his response less cryptic to the deaf evaluator.

FOR PAUL POOLEY, the hospital had been negligent to the point of conspiracy: "To me that's sort of the great moments when they've been lying to us and saying 'How sad it is—this man has lost all ability to communicate.' And we're sitting in Linda Taylor's office and . . . [the interpreter] voicing for Brenda [is] telling us to come in there [to Wilson's room] and she's telling us, 'Hey, this man can talk! He can sign!'" But individuals expressed widely different perspectives on who was at fault. For some, simple bureaucratic inertia had imprisoned the deaf man. Paternalism further enforced his place within the walls of Goldsboro's institution.

Over the next months, the red-haired Aron visited Wilson every few weeks, monitoring his language training and offering ways to promote his socialization with other deaf people. Soon she was joined by Paul Schreyer, another deaf evaluator. The man worked with both Wilson and staff to promote signed communication. In the beginning, he was skeptical. "I tried to understand him and assess how to help him, showing him pictures, etc., to start," stated Schreyer. He felt, "We didn't understand each other at the outset. He had a limited attention span, quite limited."[37]

Both deaf evaluators were adamant that Wilson should receive appropriate sign language communication. In her report to Wilson's treatment team and guardian, Aron described his need for an interpreter. Aron wanted to ensure that a professional interpreter was used instead of a series of volunteers: "It is imperative that this interpreter knows and uses ASL. Often educational interpreters use an English-based sign system which would not help Mr. Wilson at all."[38] Aron contrasted the way Wilson generally interacted with staff with her own experiences. Addressing individuals who shared his identity as deaf, especially those who were from outside the hospital system, seemed to create a special connection for the black man. "Wilson smiled and laughed whenever he sees me signing or others signing to each other. As if this was a long time since he has seen that and it delighted him," Aron remembered.[39] She and others felt that previously, hearing staff members controlled language in Junius Wilson's world. Now Wilson's advocates had the authority to monitor who communicated with him and how.

Working with hospital staff was complicated. As Paul Pooley lamented, "The people at Cherry did not realize how they had mistreated Wilson."[40] Pooley insisted that Wilson attend some of his treatment team meetings, requiring that Pam King, a certified interpreter, accompany him. Brenda Aron eventually attended meetings as well. Having two deaf people in the room altered the language and power dynamics among staff. Wilson and Aron sat where they could watch the interpreter. Staff members were discouraged from interrupting one another or talking at once in order to let King accurately convey what they had said. Rather than talk about Wilson, the treatment team now had to figure out ways to talk with Wilson.

Some team members wholeheartedly committed themselves to the process. Wilson's primary social worker especially impressed Schreyer: "Linda Taylor was really wonderful. She wanted to make sure Wilson had regular services. . . . She was really patient. She worked with Wilson, and she's a white woman! She was really patient and regularly visited him and he eventually accepted her."[41] Brenda Aron agreed. Wilson, she said, "lighted up when talking about or seeing the social worker."[42] Both deaf evaluators also recognized that Carnell "Willie" Mewborn, the health care technician who had worked with Wilson for many years, enjoyed a close connection to the deaf man. As Aron later explained, even though neither Taylor nor Mewborn had "good sign skills," they nevertheless "showed concern and took an interest in Wilson. It is reciprocated. It is believed that . . . activities with Carnell and the social worker's visits really benefit Wilson."[43]

Perhaps the strongest evidence of Wilson's affection for Linda Taylor and Carnell Mewborn were his own words. In deaf culture, sign names convey personal attributes but also individuals' place among deaf peers. As Wilson chatted with Aron and Schreyer, he shared the sign name he had created for Taylor. He smiled as his hands went to his eyes, mimicking glasses, then traveled near the side of his head, where open fingers squeezed air slightly downward. Aron recognized who he meant at once because Taylor wore eyeglasses and had loose, almost fluffy blond hair. Mewborn's sign name also reflected his physical appearance: RUB-BALD HEAD, Wilson signed, pointing to his friend. Although

Junius Wilson and others, Cherry Hospital (Courtesy of Everett Parker)

Wilson might have created nicknames for other employees, he shared only these two. Wilson's sign names for Taylor and Mewborn suggest an expression of deaf cultural behavior. They also demonstrate a type of claiming. Deaf people create sign names and slang signs for people and places that they refer to frequently. By naming these two individuals with specific signs, Wilson showed that he wanted to talk about them as people central in his life. Signature sign names provided the deaf man with a way to refer to them facilely. It also enabled him to incorporate them more fully into his understanding of the world. Perhaps Wilson chose to give names to the social worker and health care technician because these two distinguished themselves from other staff by attempting to communicate with him in his own language.

BRENDA ARON MIGHT HAVE been the first deaf woman to interact with Wilson since he left his school in 1924. She might have been the first deaf white woman he ever encountered. Paul Schreyer was aware of the ways in which race complicated language and culture issues: Wilson "was very passive, and he had spent so many years trying to pass and just get along." The evaluator knew that this had been common among deaf people of color in North Carolina. Schreyer explained further: "I'm white. . . . It seemed that Wilson should have a black worker with him, not a white one, and preferably use black deaf communication."[44]

Using some of the same ideas that Paul Pooley and André Branch had discussed over coffee in New York, Paul Schreyer wanted to find someone more like Wilson to add to the team. From his work at East Carolina University, he had met Doris Bowden, the daughter of a black deaf man who had attended North Carolina's segregated deaf school in Raleigh roughly a decade later than Wilson. Schreyer and Wasson asked whether Bowden's father Everett Parker would visit Wilson at Cherry Hospital. The sprightly sixty-six-year-old deaf man, now living in nearby Farmville, agreed.

Parker and Wilson quickly became friends. "The first time I met him, we spent all afternoon socializing," Parker's long fingers flashed as he smiled. They talked about everyday matters, "food, clothes, different things."[45] Wilson immediately understood that Parker was deaf and that they shared other commonalities. Shifting from ASL to Raleigh signs, Parker watched for recognition in Wilson's face. Wilson beamed. Parker was unsure how much his new friend recalled Raleigh signs, but it was clear to Parker and others that Wilson clearly enjoyed watching the Raleigh graduate communicate with him and "lit up" whenever Parker visited him.

Paul Schreyer believed that, because Parker "was more like Junius," he was the best companion to foster language and socializing.[46] After seeing how much Wilson opened up when in Parker's presence, Schreyer asserted that "Wilson didn't work as successfully with a white deaf person or white people generally." He recognized that Parker's presence had the potential to assist the team in their efforts to understand Wilson. "I asked [him] questions but conceptual questions he couldn't answer. Everett [Parker] could tease out some information." He added: "Wilson opened up to Everett a lot more, but even he said Wilson wasn't verbose. He nodded, went along in conversations, but was more passive."[47] Schreyer and others convinced the hospital that paying Parker to visit Wilson regularly fulfilled some of their duty under the settlement. Parker quickly agreed to come for regular visits.

During his subsequent meetings with Wilson, Parker returned with a yearbook. SCHOOL? he signed. For most deaf people, this question brims with cultural meaning. More than simply asking "Where did you attend school?" the simple sign also asks, "What language do you know?" and even "What is your cultural identity?" Parker already knew where Wilson had studied since there were no other options for black deaf students in North Carolina at the time and because of Wilson's use of Raleigh signs.

The Farmville man had attended the same school Wilson had and, although the institution had changed in some ways by the time he matriculated, many aspects of the school remained the same. "The school was pretty strict," he remembered, and the old superintendent from Wilson's days was still there. "Lineberry would punish by hitting students on the hands," Parker recalled.

Junius Wilson and Everett Parker
(Courtesy of Everett Parker)

The curriculum also continued to emphasize vocational training. Young Everett worked in the dairy.[48] When Parker asked Wilson about his own classes in Raleigh, the Cherry inmate simply shook his head, "No." Parker showed his new friend pictures of the Bloodworth Avenue school.[49] Wilson had not seen his alma mater for nearly seventy years. No one reported how he first responded to the images.

Parker explained to the deaf and hearing members of the treatment team about the history of their school, including its original place in Raleigh and its later removal to Garner Road. Reading his explanations, the others could see even more clearly Wilson's background and experience. In Parker, they also had a stark reminder of what Wilson could have been. Over their many visits, Parker and Wilson returned to the photos frequently. One observer recalled that Wilson "would look at Parker's school pictures then smile, then became very quiet."[50]

The visits clearly delighted the Cherry resident. One observer noted that "he became more animated and picked up language most from Everett Parker, using an old black sign language."[51] His communication improved but only in limited ways. "Parker knew old black signs and would sign these with Wilson," Brenda Aron later recalled, "but Wilson would just smile and nod. He enjoyed watching signs from Raleigh but he didn't seem to truly understand them." Parker agreed. "Visiting Cherry Hospital," he said, "I thought he would know signs, but his signs were awkward and slow and I had to help teach him signs again." Still, "he improved and could spell his name [accurately] eventually. I was the one who showed him that," stated Parker.[52]

WILSON SOON BEGAN TO express an interest in leaving the grounds of the hospital himself. By the summer of 1993, he repeatedly told his caseworker Linda Taylor that he wanted "to go home."[53] Another member of Wilson's treatment team also felt that Wilson wanted to leave the hospital. This individual described an experience with him during a brief walk: "Junius pointed to different cars. Asked if I have a car. I said, 'Yes.'" They eventually turned to head back to the locked ward. "Suddenly, Junius turned to me, winked and said YOU, ME, DRIVE AWAY. I said, 'No, I can't do that.' He winked again, and nodded his head. YOU, ME, DRIVE AWAY." At the time, the employee had tried to let him down gently, saying, "No, I am sorry, I cannot do that or the hospital will not let me see you again." The person remembered that "he pouted then nodded his head and we walked back. It was sad really."[54]

CHERRY HOSPITAL HAD BEEN Wilson's home for almost seven decades, but it was unclear where home should be for his remaining time. Although some members of the team harbored hopes that Wilson might return to his original homestead, the possibility seemed unlikely. Wilson's medical log for this period is silent, offering no evidence of family members stepping forward to move him to Castle Hayne. Had they offered, Wilson's advocates would almost certainly have encouraged them to take Wilson into their home. But the prospect of long-term care for this virtual stranger with whom they could not communicate easily must have been daunting.

The staff psychiatrist felt Wilson should stay at Cherry: "The humanitarian thing would seem to be to permit him to go ahead and live out his life in the hospital setting."[55] Brenda Aron disagreed and advocated for a sign-rich and culturally deaf-centered environment away from the hospital. Earlier, she had written to his guardian that "the situation would be improved if Wilson could live in a home with other deaf clients similar to the Day Hospital setting on grounds with personnel who take an interest in working with this group and learning American Sign Language." She continued, "Bringing together deaf clients with some diversity such as some age difference and abilities would still be a benefit rather than a problem as Deaf people think of themselves as Deaf first."[56] She argued that her plan was feasible: "Actually this is not a new idea. It has been adopted in many parts of the country and is beneficial to the Deaf clients' development as well as to meeting their civil rights."[57]

Another participant in Wilson's care suggested a complete removal from Cherry with more independence than a deaf community house could offer. She suggested that Wilson live in an apartment in the town of Wilson "because that's where there was a deaf community he could tap into."[58] But Schreyer pointed out that access to interpreters as well as medical care made relatively rural places like Castle Hayne and the town of Wilson less viable. And most people acknowledged that his need for regular care and supervision undermined the idea of Wilson living independently in a space like an apartment in town.

Those who cared for Junius Wilson disagreed about what was the most beneficial for him. Linda Taylor summarized it: "It is hard to tell what is best for him. People are kind of on the fence, like, well, he has got people here he knows, he has got Mr. Parker, his very best friend, things like that." She questioned whether another environment really would best serve Wilson. There seemed to be no perfect answer. "If someone could show them a program that they thought Junius would like and benefit from," she said, "I think everybody would be 100 percent." She emphasized, "We haven't found that yet."[59] Schreyer claimed that he, too, "struggled with the questions: Where to place him? . . . Who would be responsible, etc.?" Most people were agreed on one point: Wilson should not be kept in the locked wards. But where else could he have familiarity and support?

BY EARLY 1993 a new option started to take shape. At the urging of a staff member who worked with Wilson, Paul Pooley and John Wasson investigated a small cottage on the grounds of the hospital.[60] It had previously belonged to hospital physician Clyde Brown. Unbeknownst to Pooley or the others, it was the home James McNeil had visited regularly decades earlier. The small one-story house sat near the intersection of N.C. 581 and Goldsboro Road, its front window looking out toward the original building for the criminal insane. Medical students now resided in the family dwelling and the hospital still owned and maintained it. Wasson soon visited this and similar cottages along a row on the campus and felt the buildings "looked really nice and thought that would be good for [Wilson]."[61] Pooley petitioned the hospital to provide one of the cottages on the grounds for Wilson. For some time, the institution ignored the request.

During the continuing discussions among treatment team members, someone suggested that Wilson and McNeil live together at the cottage. Although this seemed like an acceptable answer to both men's situations, bureaucratic policies thwarted them. One observer familiar with Wilson's care found Cherry's rules counterproductive: "Hospital policies often were silly," she explained, shaking her head. "For example, some didn't want to put the two deaf men together. Why? There was a concern that it was a 'fire hazard,' that they would not be able to wake one another up if there was a fire alarm." She challenged this thinking: "But some patients who were hearing were not capable of functioning at a high level. So why keep deaf people—who could communicate *best* with each other—apart?"[62]

State laws proved even harder to overcome. *Thomas S.* mandates precluded McNeil from living in the cottage. "The hang-up was . . . their settlement with the state. . . . All [*Thomas S.* members] had to leave the grounds. So he couldn't stay there."[63] Instead, McNeil was to remain on the locked ward until his case might finally be dealt with. Wilson's guardian tried to exert media pressure to convince the state government to make an exception to the *Thomas S.* rules. In one article about Wilson, a reporter wrote that "Mr. Wasson thinks it might be best for Mr. Wilson and the longtime friend—perhaps the mentally retarded man he rooms with—to move into a cottage on the hospital grounds."[64] But Halifax County's Department of Social Services, which oversaw McNeil's case, did not seem to be interested in intervening.

In July treatment team members formally demanded that the hospital transfer Wilson to the cottage. Wasson and Pooley refused to commit to whether such a move would be permanent or simply part of a process to integrate Wilson into mainstream society.[65] A Cherry representative formally rejected the request.[66] Wilson's guardian explicitly reminded the hospital that the deaf man was able to transition to a new home and that the hospital was expected to accommodate the relocation. Hoping to reinforce his demand, Wasson invoked a protective clause from the state settlement, authorizing Pooley to contact the state's Division of Mental Health, which supervised the hospital, to demand action. The hospital eventually agreed to renovate Brown's old cottage. The team began to prepare both Wilson and themselves for the changes to come.

ONCE AGAIN, BUREAUCRATIC policies delayed Wilson's transfer. When workers began renovating the cottage in anticipation of Wilson's arrival, they discovered lead paint. Initially, Cherry informed Wasson and Pooley that Wilson could not enter the contaminated home until it was cleaned up. State guidelines required bids for work on state properties, including the little home across from the CI building. Removing the lead paint made the renovation costs skyrocket, and the process stalled. Cherry had set an expected move-in date of the first of December, but that date was clearly not going to be honored. Wilson stayed in the locked ward.

Pooley scoffed: "It seems a little absurd to worry about his lifelong exposure to lead paint at this point in his career."[67] All of Wilson's advocates fumed. In the winter of 1993, Pooley and Wasson decided that the only way to move things along was through their own activism. "We just went on the offensive," Wasson explained.[68] Returning to the tactic that had served them well previously, Pooley contacted local newspapers. On 1 December, the day Wilson was supposed to move into the cottage, front-page headlines of the *Wilmington Morning Star* proclaimed "Deaf Man Still Held at State Psychiatric Hospital." A close-up portrait of Wilson in a baseball cap stared out at readers. Reporter Kirsten Mitchell had provided considerable coverage of Wilson's case months earlier. Her new exposé attacked government red tape and Raleigh's continued miscarriage of justice.

Money, according to state officials, was the root of the problem. Steve Johnson, the assistant chief of Mental Health Services, pleaded for understanding. Renovation of the cottage would cost $62,000, a sum for which no one took responsibility. He told the reporter plaintively, "We have to identify a particular funding source."[69]

Pooley fired off a letter to the state, berating the government's "business-as-usual" pace to resolve the matter. Mitchell reported that the attorney nearly hissed, "It is simply unconscionable to force a 97-year-old man, held for 68 years in psychiatric hospital principally because he is deaf, to wait any longer for a decent place to live and staff and companions who can understand and communicate with him."[70] She also reported that a modular home could be built for less than the renovation price tag, further undermining the government's weak position.[71]

Mitchell's exposé sent a warning shot to Raleigh: Wilson's guardians would consider going to court to force a solution if the state mechanisms failed to resolve the matter quickly. To build further momentum and demonstrate their commitment, Wasson and Pooley spoke with reporters again over the next week. Repeatedly, Wilson's allies painted the state as unresponsive. One news headline announced, "Deaf Man Caught Up in Red Tape." Another wagged, "State Still Lagging on Home for Wrongly Confined Man."[72]

Wasson and Pooley hoped that the governor would set aside the ban against lead paint and simply let the elderly deaf man move into his new home. The CLA lawyer told reporters, "We have talked about it for months now. Instead of acting on that, they chose to spend their time discussing cost efficiencies and the risk of lead-based paint. It's pretty ridiculous when you consider the man is 95 years old and everyone agrees he shouldn't be there [in the locked wards of the institution]."[73]

And once again, editorials and letters from North Carolinians abounded, supporting Wilson's cause. The *Wilmington Morning Star*, 2 December 1993, ran an editorial titled "Victim of the State Deserves Action Today," and the *Raleigh News and Observer* the next day featured the powerful headline, "An Innocent Man Suffers."[74]

Just days after the first article, a national audience heard the news as National Public Radio spotlighted the story on its program *All Things Considered*. Wasson and Pooley offered a cogent message: "What is so outrageous about this," Wasson said as his clear southern voice punctuated each word, "is that Mr. Wilson was never mentally ill and yet he is housed with mentally ill people. And basically, he is an old, deaf, black man that people forgot about up there. And it appears to me that this has been treated as a public relations issue and not as a human being issue."[75] Pooley followed. Speaking crisply and full of passion, he said, "It's unconscionable that the state has agreed to provide for Mr. Wilson what he deserves in the time he has remaining and then acts as if they don't have enough money to perform the services that they've agreed to do."[76]

In response to the rising tide of negative press, Raleigh officials offered to move Wilson temporarily into an apartment in Goldsboro and give him full-time, live-in care. The treatment team considered the offer but ultimately decided that such a move would be too traumatic for Wilson. They would wait for the cottage to be readied. The next day, state officials announced that a lower bid had been approved to renovate the cottage.[77] Wilson would finally move to his new home at the beginning of the coming year.

AS THE WINTER HOLIDAYS approached, staff members were keenly aware of Wilson's ambiguous status. Returning permanently to Castle Hayne was not possible, yet keeping him isolated in the wards seemed increasingly depraved. The long wait to transfer Wilson to the cottage cooled relations between Wasson and Wilson's extended family. Both parties were frustrated, desiring to see Wilson receive some justice.

With the hope of fostering closer ties between Wilson and his family, Linda Taylor arranged for Annie Sidberry and André Branch to visit Wilson at Cherry during the Christmas season. After arriving on campus, the pair entered the Woodard Building. "To me it felt like a prison," she remembered. "I have never been to a prison, I don't want to go, but you knew you were in a restricted area." Visitors were required to sign in. "We had to stop in the lobby and there was this big, big door that they had to open." Sidberry understood that "whoever was behind that locked door wasn't getting out easily." Her eyes took in the interior of the building. "I remember thinking that this setting was like something out of World War One or Two." She had to stop in front of several more large doors. Each time, "you had to go through the door and someone had to unlock it to let you in, and every room you went in, there was a lock and key somewhere." Shaking her head slightly, she recalled that "they had to open this heavy steel door to let us in" to the ward where Wilson lived.[78]

The cousins wound their way through the wards until they reached Wilson's. "André and I went together," explained Sidberry. Images of prison again echoed as they approached Wilson. "He was still locked up," she recalled. "He was still behind locked doors in the hospital." Sidberry looked around: "He was like in a dormitory. . . . I think many people lived together. . . . There were many beds in a row and he had one in the corner." She looked at the other men who lived with him and realized how different Wilson was from those around him: "You could tell all these people were in different states, . . . some just sitting there."[79]

Taylor led them over to Wilson. A "tall brown thin guy with a leather cap on" stood near him, serving as the interpreter. They were signing to one another as Branch and Sidberry approached. The relatives introduced themselves. Sidberry thought to herself, "He was quiet. He didn't really know who he was looking at." Branch wanted to know Wilson's history and to understand the family story better: "We were trying to ask him questions, and he seemed like he would nod his head." But the deaf man didn't offer any real answers. Sidberry eyed the interpreter: "I guess he had just enough language to get his job done, not enough to respond to the questions."[80]

The two stayed for less than an hour. Unable to converse freely with the deaf man, Sidberry and Branch said their goodbyes and followed staff out of the wards. Waiting for locked doors to open, slowly winding their way back outside, perhaps Annie Sidberry thought of her conversation with Linda Taylor before she arrived. Taylor had stated "that there was nothing wrong with this man, he just couldn't speak." Now she witnessed it for herself. Describing the visit later, she repeatedly stated, "We weren't sure why he's behind locked doors."[81] Branch expressed dismay at Wilson's situation. "No one is listening to what Mr. Wilson wants," a staff member recalled Branch saying. Branch and Sidberry left feeling hurt and angry.

JUNIUS WILSON HIMSELF expressed frustration regularly now. "Usually, at least once a day, he signs that he wants to go home," states his medical file. "Sometimes he will make a fist when he signs this; at others he just shakes his head, spreads his hands & looks at the floor."[82] But as the year turned from 1993 to 1994, both Junius Wilson and James McNeil continued to live in locked wards.

9

Almost Home (1994)

Free at Last

HEADLINE, *MONTREAL*
***GAZETTE*, 5 FEBRUARY 1994**

It's pretty much like home living.

J. FIELD MONTGOMERY,
DIRECTOR OF CHERRY HOSPITAL

AFTER MORE THAN SIXTY-EIGHT years of life as an inmate at Cherry Hospital, Junius Wilson started his life as a free man on 4 February 1994. The eighty-five-year-old man moved from the locked ward to a newly renovated, three-bedroom brick cottage located on the grounds of the institution. White awnings and white-trimmed windows looked out onto manicured shrubs that ran alongside the bungalow.

At the cottage, Wilson had regular access to a car and driver to take him places he wanted to go. The number of personal belongings he owned had greatly increased, and he took pride in the ownership of them. For the first time in his life, he had myriad choices, from what bedspread he could have to what the attendants cooked for dinner. But even as progressive advocates pushed for unprecedented measures on Wilson's behalf, the long history of racism, bureaucratic inertia, and disability discrimination undercut their achievements. The problem of creating a home, like much of Wilson's story, defied simple solutions.

STAFF MEMBERS INVOLVED in Wilson's care, as well as the team of activists who worked on his case, were full of suggestions for making the elderly man's transition to freedom successful. They planned to fill the cottage with "flower baskets, figurines, touch lamps, [and] pictures with animals." The housekeep-

The Wilson cottage (Photograph by Susan Burch)

ing department brought over linens and planned to refresh them regularly. In addition to items designed to make the house into a home, the team came up with a list of people to meet and field trips to take. They planned a visit to a church attended by many deaf people. Someone suggested that Wilson visit the new location of his old school in Wilson, North Carolina. His main social worker continued to take sign language classes so she could communicate with him better about his needs and wants in his new home. All those involved in the case were excited about the opportunities to help Wilson enjoy what was in essence a new life.[1]

Before Wilson moved to the cottage, Cherry staff members prepared him for the upcoming transition. Attendants reported that the elderly man visited the house on 11 January and "seemed pleased [with] what he saw." A week later, he visited the house again, this time in the company of his friend Everett Parker and favorite staff member Willie Mewborn. He stayed for about fifteen minutes, especially admiring the view from the front windows.[2]

Wilson's team from Cherry supported the idea of continuing the elderly man's gradual transition to the cottage. They considered regular visits over a period of time and perhaps considered scheduling overnight visits. The legal mandate, however, required that as soon as the cottage was ready, Wilson would be allowed to move in immediately.[3]

One way to prepare Wilson for the transition was to purchase a new outfit for him to wear on moving-in day. Staff members took him shopping for a dark suit and a tie. While they were at the store, they bought him some more casual trousers and shirts as well.[4]

Although Wilson apparently understood that the efforts to renovate and furnish the cottage were for him—and surely he recognized that he was being offered more material goods than ever before—he continued to doubt that a change would actually occur. As Linda Taylor wrote in his daily log, until the night he actually slept in the cottage, Wilson's misgivings remained: "[he acts] as though he really doesn't believe it when [she, his social worker] tells him that he will move into the cottage soon."[5]

THE DAY DID ARRIVE, despite Wilson's doubts. The last line of the treatment team's note in his log before the move to the cottage stated excitedly, "The 4th is occupancy day!" The plan was to take Wilson from the wards to his new house at 2:00 P.M. But as attorney Paul Pooley stated, "The moving plan was made by a group of people that didn't include Mr. Wilson." When the morning of 4 February arrived and the team informed the deaf man that it was moving day, he insisted that the transfer happen sooner.[6]

Staff members helped him put on his new dressy clothes. Wilson topped his outfit with a Washington Redskins hat that someone had given him.[7] A car and driver picked him up at the hospital ward and drove him the hundred yards to his new cottage.[8] He was then transferred from the car to a wheelchair and pushed up a ramp to the front door.[9] The wheelchair became a necessary support as Wilson's health had declined. The model of his chair required someone to push it, as well as someone to assist with safe transfers into and out of cars.

At 11:30 A.M. Wilson, newly relocated, was sitting in his new home with Pooley and John Wasson, as well as Everett Parker. "He was smiling big time," reported Pooley. "He [was] ready to be over here." To celebrate the beginning of his new life, Wilson shared a lunch of fried chicken, mashed potatoes, and sweet iced tea with Parker.[10]

Wasson was pleased as he looked around the cottage. "It's a nice, nice place," he reported. "The hospital went all out to furnish it."[11] The house, furnished in the Early American style, looked to some like a furniture showroom.[12] Cherry Hospital director J. Field Montgomery noted that the cottage was also equipped with a washer and dryer, a refrigerator and freezer, and a microwave oven. "It's pretty much like home living," he stated.[13]

Wilson on moving-in day (Courtesy of John Wasson)

"PRETTY MUCH" WAS an appropriate qualification. In a few significant ways, Wilson's new residence still resembled his former hospital ward. Health care technicians were assigned to monitor Wilson twenty-four hours a day, seven days a week. Nurses stopped by the cottage three times a day to take his vital signs. His bodily functions were charted by the same people who charted them when he was living in the Woodard Building.[14] Hospital employees were charged with cooking for Wilson, driving him around wherever he would like to go, and taking him back to visit friends still living in the locked wards. While Wilson benefited in tangible ways from many of these services, they belied the celebratory claims that the deaf man had finally and fully achieved "freedom." He continued in their minds to be a patient rather than an independent man.

Increasingly concerned for his health, and aware of outside observers monitoring the level of care they provided to the elderly man, attendants refused to let Wilson drink coffee or purchase tobacco. They noted in his daily medical log that he "got a little agitated when he could not [keep] it," but then added that his "agitation didn't last long."[15] Although almost everyone who worked at the bungalow called it "the Wilson House," it took almost a year before Wilson received a set of keys to his own front door.[16] To top things off, the site of the house was directly across a narrow street from the site of Wilson's earliest incarceration, the old ward for the criminally insane.

WHEN JUNIUS WILSON MOVED into the cottage on the Cherry Hospital grounds, newspapers around the nation published stories, often on their front pages, about his transition. "Free at Last," announced some headlines.[17] John Wasson was pleased that his ward had finally achieved some measure of liberty. "I've got an immense feeling of relief," Wilson's guardian told the press. "My biggest fear was that he was going to die before getting into that cottage." Wasson did not want his hard work on behalf of Wilson to prove fruitless. Now, at least to a degree, his work was nearing its conclusion. The soft-spoken guardian smiled as he looked back on Wilson's new environment: "I thought the hospital did a really great job, not only with the home but putting Mr. Parker on the payroll. . . . I don't know if anything will make up for his treatment so many years ago but in his last few years I think everybody did right by him."[18]

In addition to facilitating Wilson's removal from the wards of the institution, Wasson had forced both Cherry Hospital and the state of North Carolina to acknowledge not only their past policies but also the ramifications that history had on the current experiences of patients.[19] Not all agreed with the negative interpretation that the activists and the media had heaped on the hospital. Cherry administrators frequently pointed out how much the hospital had done to allow for Wilson's transition. J. Field Montgomery defended the institution: "We don't think he got lost. I feel like he was cared for. We don't know whether he knew whether he could or couldn't leave. He never tried to escape." Clearly enunciating the limits of Wilson's new status, he added, "Now Wilson is a voluntary patient."[20]

Although their acceptance of responsibility was not as complete as many of Wilson's advocates would like, people from both the institution and the state attempted to apologize to the newly released man. As Kim Parker, spokesperson for the North Carolina Department of Human Resources, told reporters, "We can't repay those years Mr. Wilson has been locked up. Nobody can. We're very sorry. Our goal now is to ensure he is happy and in a good environment and that he is where he wants to be and needs to be."[21]

Others involved in the case recognized how much remained to do before Wilson was truly free. Although attorney Paul Pooley recognized that the move to the cottage was a "big event," he pointed out that "in a funny way, it's a beginning point, not an end point." He continued, "It's taken a long time for him to leave the locked ward, but this is now the beginning of his transition into the community beyond the hospital."[22] There was still work to be done.

POOLEY'S SENTIMENT COULD easily have referred to another deaf man of color who left a state institution two months after Wilson's celebrated transfer. After four decades of imprisonment in Arizona's state mental hospital, Artie Martinez was set free from the Cholla Ward, a notorious wing of the hospital that housed dangerous and chronically mentally ill patients. The prior year, a doctor had found Martinez sane and concluded that he had been lost in the system "because he didn't have an opportunity . . . to make his case, to be understood, and to talk his way out of it." Denied signed communication during his incarceration, the deaf man had violent outbursts and was known as a loner. Although he showed signs of mild mental illness, Martinez did not receive a complete diagnosis when he entered the facility in 1955 because no one on staff knew American Sign Language. Staff considered Martinez for deinstitutionalization in the 1980s. At the time, a psychologist diagnosed him as sane. Still, social workers and hospital staff ignored his case. During his long incarceration, the graduate of the Arizona School for the Deaf and Blind lost touch with siblings as well as his parents, who passed away during his incarceration.[23] In 1991, when the Arizona Center for Law in the Public Interest assumed a supervisory role at the hospital, patient advocates lobbied for deaf services and fought to remove Martinez from the locked wards. His move into a senior group home marked significant progress, just as Wilson's move to the cottage signified a shift toward independence. Like Wilson, however, Martinez was deprived of the capacity to function independently by years of institutionalization.[24]

JUNIUS WILSON SEEMED to most people to be pleased with his new living arrangements. Wasson noted that he "just took such great pride in showing people around. . . . He was really proud of the facility, of his home." Hospital officials agreed. Linda Taylor explained that Wilson enjoyed taking visitors around the cottage, showing them "his bed, his fixtures, his TV, pointing to himself and nodding his head and indicating that he is saying, 'This is mine.' "[25] Staff supplied a monogrammed blue, faux-leather photo album filled with pictures of Wilson's hospital treatment team members in it. Near the scrapbook sat stacks of magazines to which the hospital had subscribed on his behalf: *Field and Stream, Ebony Man, Jet,* and *Black Enterprise.*[26] The personal items and amenities contrasted sharply with his previous dwelling at the hospital, which "resembl[ed] an army barracks, very neat and sparsely furnished."[27] In gestures and signs, Wilson told guests that his house and his things were "very nice, . . . very expensive."[28] After a lifetime of limited ownership, Wilson pointed out these new belongings to person after person. Repeatedly he showed "the hats he has collected, the bed, pictures on the walls, and essentially indicating that it is his," wrote a health care technician in Wilson's file. "This appears to make the pt. rather happy."[29]

Wilson showing off his home (Jamie Moncrief, *Wilmington Star-News*)

NOT EVERYONE FELT THAT Wilson was adjusting perfectly to the move. Soon after Wilson began living in the cottage, social worker Linda Taylor stated in a progress note that "Mr. Wilson just sat looking out of the windows . . . as if he felt a little 'left out.'"[30] One observer who was familiar with the men had hoped that James McNeil would live with Wilson in order to prevent loneliness. "I thought it would be good to have those two together," the employee said. When this plan did not work out because of legal restrictions,[31] the hospital employee worried that Wilson would "be more isolated in the house" since he would be "without exposure to other deaf people" and away from "where many people knew him." At least in the locked ward, he was not without peers.[32]

Although Wilson often expressed both contentment and pride in his living arrangements, sometimes he seemed frustrated. "The patient will be vehement and will point with his right hand, and vocalize in a loud voice," Taylor noted. "He indicates at times that he wants to move 'home' but as Mr. Wilson does not communicate a great deal in American Sign Language, it is difficult to assess his thoughts or wishes." She continued, "It seems at that time that he may be indicating that he wants to take his furniture, etc. and move far, far away."[33]

The physical separation from his peers and the ward intensified his isolation.

As an expert on deafness explained, a "hearing person . . . can pick up the phone and call another hearing person even if they move to another place." But for Wilson, "this [was] not possible."[34] Modern technology like telecommunication devices for the deaf (TTYs) that enabled deaf people to call others independently would not alleviate the situation because Wilson did not "know any of the deaf" with TTY machines.[35] Although Everett Parker owned such a device, Wilson was unable to utilize it because of both his limited literacy and his limited social experience.[36]

The home lacked cultural and practical amenities for an elderly deaf inhabitant as well. In spite of ADA regulations, no visual alarm rang when a visitor pressed the doorbell, leaving Wilson unaware and generally unable to welcome guests himself.[37] The front porch, a specially prized aspect of Wilson's new property, had no handrails, making it difficult for the elderly man to climb the stairs.[38] Although he was known to love music and would move to the vibrations, years would pass before stereo equipment with ample speakers arrived at the house.

CONCERNED ADVOCATES ATTEMPTED to add touches to Wilson's daily regimen that they felt would promote a more personalized and cozy atmosphere. Acknowledging his love of fishing and catching worms, Brenda Aron suggested the purchase of an aquarium. When escorted to the pet store, Wilson rejected the offer of pet fish. Such symbols of domestic caretaking probably seemed quite foreign to him. Staff could not convey effectively why this should appeal to him.

Later, John Wasson recommended a canine companion. Laughing about it afterward, he remembered, "Well, I thought he should have a dog—a black lab or a retriever or something." During a visit to Wasson's Wilmington home, Wilson had taken a shine to the family dachshund, Megan. Wasson's daughter carried the dog over to the guest. Wasson remembered, "I never saw Mr. Wilson show a lot of expression, but he lit up—like a Christmas tree . . . so we thought it'd be good for him to have a dog."[39] But concerns over maintenance and housekeeping motivated hospital administrators and staff to resist the proposal.

Employees and friends regularly showered Wilson with gifts. His hat collection covered the wood rack in his bedroom. He frequently showed off the many outfits that filled his drawers and closets.[40] What he seemed to care for most were smaller gifts of food. During outings to local stores in Goldsboro, Wilson tried to negotiate with his escorts, cajoling them with wagging fingers and winks to compel them to give him cookies or tobacco. Sometimes they relented.

Various guests visited Wilson in his new house. Although the Sidberrys and others had met him in the wards previously, these gatherings always occurred with many hall mates wandering around. At the cottage, even with its coterie of staff members, Wilson could enjoy comparatively more privacy with his guests.

Time with Everett Parker might have seemed different to Wilson now, too. As a resident of his own home, Wilson now had more in common with his deaf companion. Regularly, the Farmville friend came to join Wilson for lunches, TV watching, and quiet time on the front porch. Going to see Parker and his wife in Farmville necessitated the use of a chauffeur and unplanned visits might have been discouraged, but the pleasure of the drive and the chance to see Parker regularly clearly delighted Wilson.

In addition to the regular visits with Parker, staff sought to broaden Wilson's social experiences, driving him to local baseball and bingo games or sightseeing around eastern North Carolina. As one technician explained, Wilson's favorite activity was to ride in a car. "He doesn't care where he goes," the man told his colleagues, "he just likes looking out the window and just seeing things. He would constantly point out things he saw."[41]

Both Parker and staff encouraged him to go to Sunday church services, although Wilson's responses varied. Observers noted that he seemed to enjoy the movements of gospel singers, often clapping his hands with them and waving. Other times he would sit quietly for a while, then stand abruptly and leave, requiring his escorts to follow him back to the car.[42] It is unclear whether church members other than the Parkers offered to visit Wilson or provide him with any material supports, such as a church might do for other older persons attending regularly. His medical files do not suggest that the congregation pursued membership for him. Eventually, the team gave up trying to take Wilson to church.

FOR THE FIRST TIME, Wilson was granted the right to turn down recommended experiences as well as gifts. Although many of his negative responses were probably borne out of weariness, boredom, or simple distaste, perhaps he also enjoyed this newfound power to control more of his destiny. Advocates often did not understand why he refused certain things. Nor did they always understand why he sometimes responded positively. Anecdotes from caretakers suggest that Wilson occasionally expressed desires that baffled them. A wall clock and watches, for instance, were prized possessions for Wilson even though staff and evaluators concluded that he could not accurately tell time.[43] These hospital employees apparently failed to learn about Wilson's long-standing love for watches and clocks. Wilson's medical files from as early as the 1970s show that he owned several, including a Bulova wristwatch.

At times, staff could not understand what he was trying to request. After several months of meetings with Wilson at the cottage, Linda Taylor expressed concern. Every time she visited him, he indicated that "he would like to go (far, far he signs, home). It is difficult to tell if he just wants to visit or if he wants to go there to live." His expressions had become more emphatic: "Occasionally he is very angry and agitated." Taylor added in her report, "Usually [I] can calm the pt. but sometimes it takes several minutes. This never happened on the ward in [her] experience."[44] She interpreted the outbursts and emphatic signs "to be requesting to visit home," but she could not, nor could Parker or his interpreter, say with certainty what Wilson actually intended with his signs. In June she called Wasson to gain permission to bring Wilson to Castle Hayne to visit his relatives. The guardian granted the request, but arrangements apparently could not be made and months passed without a trip to Wilson's hometown.[45]

SLOWLY, WILSON BEGAN TO settle into his new regimen. Drawers of neatly folded clothes faced the perfectly made bed, groceries were carefully arranged in the refrigerator, and intentionally placed chairs displayed a high level of organization in both the kitchen and living room. Wilson expressed great pride in the tidiness of his abode. Opening the refrigerator door or pulling out his sock drawers, the elderly man would point and nod, drawing visitors' attention to the near-military arrangement of his belongings. Observers concluded that years of institutional life had fostered Wilson's habits of organization.[46] Wilson and the staff collaborated in the effort to maintain tight order in the house. Perhaps staff members' diligence reflected a desire to demonstrate their affection for and good treatment of Wilson. Certainly they understood that the cottage was an extension of the hospital and that it was their duty to keep the area clean.

In time, Wilson also began to follow new social and activity regimens. Eating sausage biscuits and sweet tea at Hardee's or lunch at the K & W Cafeteria, watching episodes of *The Price is Right*, and piecing together puzzles all became regular features of his week.[47] Hospital-sponsored recreational and leisure activities were held in the Day Hospital, and Wilson was invited to attend. The institution also included Wilson in monthly deaf programs with other patients.[48] Wilson went back to the ward to visit both staff members and former hall mates in the Woodard Building. Often he joined them for a meal or wandered his old halls and sitting room.[49] Occasionally, he joined in movie viewing and various recreational activities.

Wilson probably communicated with McNeil and others, describing with signs and occasional vocalized sounds what his home and new life were like. Such interactions do not appear in Wilson's medical journal. It is unclear how much he actually shared with his former hall mates. It is impossible to know what he thought during these visits. But Wilson's numerous visits and emo-

Wilson laughing (Courtesy of Everett Parker)

tional attachment to the people and place of his earlier years at Cherry clearly mattered. Even after excursions to nearby sights, picnics in local parks, or visits with Parker, Wilson often insisted on returning to the ward. As one entry notes that spring, "He got a little upset, because he wanted to go over to Woodard." The technicians eventually complied.[50]

The treatment team sometimes felt uncomfortable with the amount of time Wilson wanted to linger on the wards. They met to discuss time limits for the visits and began to consider whether select patients could leave the ward to go see Wilson in the cottage.[51] James McNeil eventually came to visit the house.

As with all his special visitors, Wilson gave McNeil a tour of the rooms, pointing out prized possessions and directing his guest to take a seat. The two sat in the living room and conversed. Staff members did not understand their conversations. Nor did they discuss the irony of the situation. McNeil, as a *Thomas S.* plaintiff, was slated to leave the hospital but his guardians had not located an acceptable alternative.

One can only imagine how McNeil felt as staff escorted him to the cottage. The little house had been McNeil's morning destination for years when he first began wearing the policeman's uniform. Clyde Brown's family lived in the same house back in the 1940s and 1950s. "Policeman Dummie" ate breakfast with the family, helped Mrs. Brown with dishes and sweeping, and often sat on the front porch, newspaper tucked under his arm, watching cars and people pass by.[52] Although most of the current staff did not know the historic meaning of the brick building to McNeil, it is highly likely that the cottage's new inhabitant did.

Any number of emotions might have passed through and between the men. Perhaps McNeil felt surprise or delight, wistfulness, emptiness, longing, or even amusement at the prospect of returning as a guest to the cottage. Wilson clearly enjoyed showing off his possessions and expressed pleasure at McNeil's visits. But long years inside the institution had fostered a strong sense of territorial claim. Perhaps he goaded McNeil with the comparative opulence of his new setting. Perhaps McNeil was relieved he had not been removed from his residence and peers of so many years.

MCNEIL VISITED REPEATEDLY during the next few months. Sometimes the two men shared meals. Usually, they sat in the living room, watching TV or entertaining themselves with other activities. On warmer days, they went to the porch.[53] Occasionally Everett Parker would join them. The jovial Parker told stories and jokes, reminding Wilson of their trips together and of local deaf events and people. McNeil must have felt that he was an outsider during these exchanges. His more limited language skills might have hampered his participation in the conversations. His social skills with noninstitutionalized deaf people like Parker were unpracticed since he lacked hospital support for a signing deaf companion. Still, friendly gatherings on the veranda offered McNeil, who no longer had permission to wander the campus at will, and Wilson, who had limited access to the wards now, with an opportunity to enjoy moments with one another. Staff approvingly noted that both Wilson and McNeil seemed glad for the visits.

At the end of the stays, the men waved goodbye to one another as a staff member escorted McNeil back to the Woodard Building. Although the geriatric building was only about a hundred yards from the cottage, the distance seemed worlds apart.

SIX MONTHS AFTER Wilson moved into his cottage, James McNeil passed away from heart failure. He died at Dorothea Dix Hospital in Raleigh.[54] By most accounts, McNeil's death was the first major loss of a companion for Wilson. It appears that Wilson did not learn of his death immediately. A treatment team member explained that because Wilson was removed from the wards, he was more isolated from circulating news. "For example," said the staff member, "when a friend died, Wilson wouldn't know right away."[55] Even if he had been in the middle of things still, it certainly would be difficult to convey the news. Wilson apparently understood the sign for "death" and "gone" but he might not have known right away whom the staff was talking about since they used different names for McNeil. His interpreter repeatedly attempted "to explain the death before . . . [the] funeral" but Wilson "showed no reaction."[56]

On 10 August, hospital employees took Wilson to the chapel for the memorial service. Silvia Weaver described the ceremony. "I spoke at Mr. McNeil's funeral," she explained. She remembered his distinctive role at the hospital: "I know I mentioned that my first exposure to him was seeing him direct traffic. . . . I suppose that sticks with a lot of people."[57] Vernon Price Jr.'s portrait of McNeil stood near the casket. One technician described his friend's features warmly. "His face was thin, kind of relaxed. . . . He had a pouty look with his lower lip. He had a small head with a fine dark hair." These staff members knew McNeil as an amiable man, constantly seeking the company of others. "He smiled all the time," one Cherry employee said, and he "liked to kid around."[58] It is unclear whether an interpreter was present to help Wilson take in the conversations around him.

The group then drove to Wayne Memorial Park, a cemetery near the hospital. Modest gravestones dotted the grassy banks along the waters of Legion Lake, curving gently nearby. Both Wilson and Cherry Hospital employees watched the graveside ceremony solemnly. One attendant thought the ceremony "did allow [Wilson] to be able to grieve." During the funeral Wilson "was sad and almost cried." At that point the emotional display ended. The attendant felt that "on the way back to the hospital, [Wilson] showed no emotion" and did not "[speak] much about it . . . afterwards."[59]

After the funeral, one nurse made note that the deaf man "has been somewhat more agitated for the past few days when I've visited the Wilson House for 9 pm meds." His hands flashed, but the staff member could not understand their meaning. "He tries to express his concerns to me thru gesturing, pointing, and muttering," she noted. Eventually he gave up and accepted his medication.[60]

The treatment team concluded that he was coping with McNeil's death. It was time to move on. Physician Nelson Macatangay reported that Wilson attended various hospital activities in the month following the funeral. The doctor seemed satisfied that Wilson had interacted well with staff, and, when prompted, "he spelled his name."[61] Subsequent team progress notes make no mention of McNeil's death or the possible lingering effects of this loss for Wilson.

STAFF MEMBERS' ACTIONS indicate they were concerned about Wilson, even if no one said it explicitly. Linda Taylor and others sought to fill McNeil's empty shoes by fostering closer ties between Wilson and his relatives. The social worker called the Sidberrys, and they arranged a small social gathering so that Wilson could get to know his extended kin better.[62]

On 20 August, the Castle Hayne couple waved greetings as they welcomed Wilson and his caretakers into their home. Once inside, the Sidberrys showed Wilson around. A small party followed. The family's kindness pleased Taylor, who later reported that the relatives, including younger generations, "were pretty well entertaining to the patient and he was quite attentive with the occasion."[63] Others agreed that Wilson enjoyed the trip.[64]

The visit was not without awkward moments. Several staff, including a nurse, accompanied Wilson, disrupting the feeling of a family reunion. Surely the long separation between the deaf man and his original community must have been in the back of the minds of at least some relatives. Communication difficulties marked the day. Family members were generally unaccustomed to using an interpreter. In addition, Wilson's unique linguistic forms of expression made it difficult for even skilled interpreters to convey accurately what Wilson thought or felt.[65]

Staff began driving Wilson to his hometown regularly, often meeting Annie Sidberry for lunch or driving around the familiar roads of Castle Hayne. Taylor praised the cousins, exclaiming, "We had a wonderful time at your home. It was interesting to hear about various members of the family, including Junius's sister. Is there any chance she might send you (or to us), some photos of herself and her family?" But her next statement revealed the limitations of her hope for family connection: "I would like for Mr. Wilson to have a chance to see photos of her and to see if he recognized her in them."[66] The siblings had not seen one another for at least fifty years.

Although neither Wilson nor his relatives asked, Taylor still might have hoped that the family would eventually want to take him in. For various reasons, including language barriers, economic constraints, and tangled historical relations, Taylor's hopes did not materialize. It is unclear whether Wilson himself had hoped to return to the community of Castle Hayne. Although he appeared to enjoy the road trips, a Cherry employee wrote in his assessment, "When he visits there he seems only mildly pleased to be there and does not protest or seem unhappy when [it is] time to return."[67]

AROUND THE TIME Junius Wilson started to visit Castle Hayne more often, John Wasson received a phone call from André Branch, Arthur Smith Jr.'s grandson in Seattle. Wilson's cousin was upset. He found Wilson's current situation intolerable. He rejected the assumption that Wilson's transfer to the cottage represented a final resolution to the injustices the deaf man had endured and he recoiled at the prospect of a white state employee such as Wasson maintaining permanent authority over Wilson. Branch believed that by denying Wilson the opportunity to move away from the hospital that had wrongly kept him, Wasson had continued an injustice that had now spanned more than six decades. Branch and Wasson faced an impasse.

A treatment team note written shortly after the conversation suggests that Branch's call upset Wasson. "Mr. Branch was demanding that Mr. Wasson resign as guardian and that he be appointed," read the note. "Mr. Wasson refused to do this and asked the treatment team for any comments."[68] Members considered Branch's desires both to become guardian and to remove Wilson from the hospital grounds. "Mr. Marshall Smith [the hospital director] stated he was concerned that Mr. Branch would not be objective," the treatment team noted.

The hospital was taken off guard by Branch's irritation. His attitudes differed sharply with the positive exchanges they had shared with the relatives in Castle Hayne. Since meeting Wilson, the Sidberrys had visited him several times and expressed a deep concern for his welfare. Although they seemed committed to developing a relationship with their relative, they had complimented the hospital's actions and seemed satisfied with the cottage situation. Branch's objectives were unexpected.

Despite the animosity that had existed between Wasson and Cherry Hospital administrators, the institution thought that Wasson was a preferable choice to Branch. Wasson had expressed his belief that "Cherry has done a first rate job and [he] thinks Mr. Wilson is in the best possible place for the rest of his life." Staff members questioned Branch's motives as well as his reasoning. Marshall Smith suggested that "a change in the current guardian was not supported unless the consideration be either the Sidberrys and/or others who have exhibited genuine interest in Mr. Wilson."[69]

Having no direct contact with Branch over the next several months, Cherry staff members settled further into a regimen with Wilson. He visited local eateries and interacted with Everett Parker, while staff watched him and provided regular updates in his medical log. But during this time, Branch met with lawyers to consider options for removing Wilson from the hospital grounds and compensating him for the many wrongs committed against him. Because Branch lived in the state of Washington and Wilson in North Carolina, lawyers urged him to consider a federal civil suit.

In mid-November 1994, Wilson's caretakers learned that André Branch had officially filed a complaint in federal court on behalf of his cousin.[70] Using many of the same legal and medical documents Wasson and Pooley had provided in their campaign to move Wilson to the cottage, Branch sued the state of North Carolina, Cherry Hospital, Wilson's guardian and the New Hanover County Department of Social Services, and Pooley's Carolina Legal Assistance. Referring to the 1925 court case that landed his cousin at Cherry as well as to hospital documents that suggested the charges had been dropped, Branch charged that the plaintiffs were guilty of assault and battery as exemplified by Wilson's castration and subsequent loss of ability to procreate. He also charged them with false imprisonment demonstrated by keeping the deaf man in the institution for seven decades. Branch's lawyers added that the state and others "deprived [Wilson] of his liberty although he had committed no crime and was not mentally ill or developmentally disabled."[71] The lawsuit built on recent disability rights legislation. According to Branch's legal team, North Carolina had violated section 504 of the 1973 Rehabilitation Act as well as the Americans with Disabilities Act "by excluding Mr. Wilson from participation in, and denying the benefits of, public facilities and/or programs receiving financial assistance and subjecting him, a deaf-mute since birth, to discrimination on the basis of his handicap while under the care and custody of defendants at Cherry Hospital, a public facility receiving federal financial assistance and/or programs."[72]

In front of a group of reporters, Branch gave a stinging indictment of North Carolina's mental health system. Reminding citizens of the egregious wrongs perpetrated against his cousin, Branch sought retribution. His lawsuit concluded that the state's acts were "negligent, unlawful, malicious, and deliberate." The state had caused Wilson "physical and mental injuries, unlawful deprivation of liberty and freedom of association and right to counsel, violation of his civil rights under the United States Constitution and United States and North Carolina statutes and common law, pain and suffering, mental distress, loss of earnings, loss of freedom to worship, also of enjoyment of life, and loss of his ability to procreate."[73] The amount sought in the suit rang out like an siren: $150 million.

Branch's vision was a starkly different interpretation of Wilson's placement in the cottage than the celebratory reports in newspapers earlier that year. Criticizing both Wilson's guardian and the 1993 legal settlement, Branch argued that "Mr. Wilson received no monetary compensation of any kind, lost his causes of action for grievous and heinous injuries sustained over 69 years, and had no guardian ad litem or personal attorney to represent his interest when the purported 'Settlement Agreement' was entered into by Mr. Wasson, the Guardian of his person."[74] If a settlement generated a financial award, Wilson legally would have needed an advocate "ad litem," meaning a person appointed for one particular issue. Legal guardians have no authority to oversee financial matters. The federal charge critiqued the settlement:

> The state of North Carolina has no consideration, or inadequate consideration, to Mr. Wilson under the purported "settlement agreement" since everything it "obligated" itself to do it was already obligated to do: provide minimally adequate care and treatment to Mr. Wilson as an in-

mate of Cherry Hospital; and since the magnitude of Mr. Wilson's injuries are incalculably greater than anything to be done by the state of North Carolina under the agreement. The "cottage" allegedly prepared for Mr. Wilson is an existing structure renovated, not for Mr. Wilson *per se*, but as a building to be used generally as a "half way" house for inmates who might be released into the community.[75]

This vision also clashed with the view of Wilson's situation held by most North Carolinians. For people who worked for and within the state system, Wilson's transfer to the cottage was a victory over enormous bureaucratic barriers. Concerned that Wilson might die before achieving "freedom" from the locked wards, his advocates had opted for expedience, agreeing not to press for financial compensation or additional legal reinforcement in exchange for the use of the house and continued care for Wilson. Technically, however, Wilson was vulnerable to losing the house since it belonged not to him or his guardians but to the state. There was not even specific money committed to fund the elderly man's care. Cherry Hospital could have moved him into a nursing home or other facility at any point.[76]

Branch's case described the family as collateral victims of Cherry Hospital's historic racism over the decades. It asserted, "Mr. Wilson's relatives at all times did all they could to give aid and comfort to him including either visiting him or wishing they could visit him despite their financial condition and their overwhelming mistrust and fear of white men, their institutions and their control of all aspects of North Carolina life and society." Branch continued, noting specific dates when relatives purportedly sought Wilson's release but were spurned, as well as documented evidence that he himself had personally visited or attempted to visit Wilson during the winter holidays since learning about his estranged cousin.[77]

Answering reporters, Branch's lawyers concluded, "It is better for a family member to be a guardian than the state of North Carolina, which was the guardian for 67 years. We are 100 percent confident that André Branch would look out for his interest better than they did."[78]

THE FEDERAL COURT entered the complaint in mid-December. At the same moment, Linda Taylor was writing to the Sidberrys, describing holiday preparations going on at the Wilson house. A fresh pine tree glittered with ornaments "and it looks *really* pretty," she effused. In her invitation to the family she diplomatically added, "Please extend this invitation to family member, André Branch, as I do not have his address."[79]

That Christmas season, Wilson enjoyed multiple visits from family members. Willie and Annie Sidberry and their daughter Crystal lunched with him. Reciprocating their hospitality, Wilson showed his Castle Hayne family around the house, pointing at pictures on the wall and beaming with pride.[80]

Three days before Christmas, Wilson's Seattle relative moved to be appointed guardian ad litem as a step toward being appointed full legal guardian. Two days later he went to visit Wilson at the cottage. When André Branch visited on Christmas Eve, accompanied by cousin Lydell Nixon and friend Danny Wilson, employees in the cottage did not offer them the warm welcome they had offered the Sidberrys. At first they refused to admit them because the men had not been cleared through the nursing office. A phone call to the nursing manager soon clarified the situation and the guests finally joined Wilson inside the cottage. Staff members likely knew that Branch had initiated legal charges against the hospital. Perhaps they were particularly protective of Wilson and the space in which they served him. Branch, for his part, also might have been tense, trying to celebrate the holidays with a long lost relative while at the same time facing a circumstance he found intolerable.

As Wilson showed the guests around his home, a staff member saw one of the men pull out his camera. The employee later reported that "one of them took a picture of bedroom before he could be stopped." Quickly the employee told the men that there would be "no pictures without permission." André Branch argued back, saying that he wanted a picture of himself with his cousin. Surely the hospital would not stop one of Wilson's relatives from taking their picture together in the man's own home.

The staff member telephoned an administrator. They waited. The administrator finally returned the call, informing Branch that he could not in fact take the photograph. Branch argued with the nurse administrator but she refused to relent. After staying with Wilson for two hours, Branch and the others left. A witness to the visit claimed that Branch "left very angry." According to the employee's notation in the log that evening, Branch made it clear that the situation was not over, saying that "in thirty days [the nursing administrator] and Cherry would be sorry they ever heard the name André Branch."[81]

STAFF BELIEVED THAT THE tensions flaring around Wilson did not strongly affect the deaf man. After Branch left the house, Wilson placed the gifts and fruit basket from his cousin under his Christmas tree and got ready for bed.[82] The next morning, a delighted Wilson opened brightly wrapped boxes while staff looked on. Everett Parker had given him a shirt, which he proudly displayed. New Air Jordans and a Seattle Supersonics baseball cap came from Branch. He received a scarf and additional presents from other relatives and friends. After opening gifts, Wilson and staff members headed to Farmville for

Christmas dinner. Wilson spent several leisurely hours with Parker and his wife. The Parkers related news and recalled previous holidays. Wilson mostly watched the signed conversation, occasionally offering nods of approval. In contrast to their emotions during Branch's time at Wilson's house, staff relaxed and looked approvingly at the happy group. The rules were clearly different with the deaf couple at their home. Staff noted in the medical log, with no sense of irony or inconsistency, "Wilson had picture taken with Parker at Parker house."[83] That evening, like all evenings for the past seven decades, Wilson went to bed on the grounds of Cherry Hospital.

10

Judgments (1994–1997)

He was certainly not insane when he went into that institution.... He has
lived 70 years in the company of insane people. That is criminal.

ANDRÉ BRANCH, TO REPORTER TINA KELLEY, 26 JANUARY 1996

SOCIAL WORKER AND EVALUATOR Roger Williams, who worked with Junius
Wilson in the 1990s, believed that the Sidberry family "seemed to have the
feeling [of] a genuine sense of responsibility." For them, Wilson "was kin."
Because of that kinship, they wanted to establish a relationship. They had "that
kind of family value sense. . . . I think they wanted whatever was best" for
Wilson. The problem was that "they weren't sure what exactly they *should* be
doing." They trusted that Wilson's caretakers knew how to look after him in the
most effective manner. The Sidberrys generally approved of Wilson's living
situation. "I thought the house was beautiful," Annie Sidberry noted. "I
thought it was—it was well kept. He appeared to be real happy. I thought it was
real nice."[1]

Willie Sidberry felt that "staff was always hospitable to us" and "there was no
problem. As far as we could see, they had done nothing to us. So it would have
no bearing on us, on our state of mind . . . as far as us having any kind of
feelings toward the hospital." The couple's philosophical approach to the complex situation in which they found themselves and their cousin emphasized
forgiveness and tolerance. "You can't have anything harsh against anybody for
whatever reason," Willie Sidberry explained.[2] The Sidberrys viewed Cherry in a
positive light.

OPPOSED TO THE STANCE taken by the Sidberry family, André Branch considered his relative's current situation unacceptable. He blamed the hospital for past and present wrongs, including its unwillingness to let Wilson visit his sister in New York City and to move him away from the campus. He sought Wilson's complete removal from the hospital grounds, explaining that his family had attempted to retrieve Wilson multiple times in the past but were always thwarted by Cherry officials. He articulated his belief that family, not the state, should decide Wilson's fate and further proposed that relatives should be deeply involved in Wilson's daily life.

Roger Williams felt that Branch's critique was sometimes more theoretical than practical. As he said, "I always had the perception that Mr. Branch had as much a concern for the principles as the patient—that it was horrific that the state of North Carolina had done this, and he wanted the state to recompense and be punished for the transgression. I had the sense that this was perhaps more the issue than what was best for Mr. Wilson."

Cherry Hospital staff members were aware that Wilson's relatives were not united in their estimation of the man's situation. "It seems . . . at this point in time that the family is somewhat divided on their expectations and hopes for Mr. Wilson," wrote Linda Taylor in the spring of 1995. "Some family members seem to be quite happy with the arrangements that have been made for Mr. Wilson at his home on Cherry Hospital grounds," she continued, "while other family members seem to feel that these arrangements are not in the best interests of Mr. Wilson."[3]

Branch made fiery charges and accusations against not only the state but also Wilson's representatives Wasson and Pooley. He hoped that residents of North Carolina would join in his denunciation of the state's long history of Jim Crow racism and critique the specific legal, physical, and emotional violations that Wilson had experienced. Instead, Branch's proposal quickly became mired in controversy.

For many people in the state of North Carolina, his claim was not as easy to swallow as Wasson's less confrontational approach. Many people felt that justice had already been served when Wilson moved to the cottage and was provided with care and services already costing the state hundreds of thousands of dollars annually. Others questioned Branch's motives. The exorbitant monetary amount he sought made some wonder whether he was merely trying to take advantage of his already exploited relative.

When approached by reporters, Wasson criticized the lawsuit on both professional and personal grounds. In one article he postulated that the elderly deaf man likely would not live long enough to benefit from a financial windfall were one to be awarded. Branch's case could even hurt Wilson in the long run if a trial ensued and Wilson's guardian ad litem failed. The long-term Cherry resident could lose his cottage and care.[4] Wasson appealed to the belief of many that Wilson already had found a suitable home: "What I adamantly think is that Junius Wilson ought to stay in his home, which is the cottage at Cherry Hospital," he proclaimed. Suggesting that Branch would provide an inferior setting for his relation, Wilson's guardian stated, "I would hate to see him wrenched from that and placed in a rest home somewhere."

Media reporting intensified matters. Once the news of Branch's lawsuit spread, the press quickly rallied to Wasson's side. As one article proclaimed, "John Wasson [has] no business as a plaintiff. He's the best friend Junius Wilson has had in years."[5] The allegiance seemed natural. Wasson, who had called reporters' attention to the case in the first place, was well acquainted with these state reporters. Branch, a resident of Seattle, was not. To top it off, Wilson's cousin had chosen to leave North Carolina to live a life not encumbered by what he saw as the oppressive system of racial etiquette still in place in the South. Some Carolinians did not feel comfortable with Branch because he was an educated, professional, and nondeferential African American man. Other state residents, insisting that they were not responding out of racism, did not react positively to criticism by a person who had chosen to be an outsider.

Instead, many state residents, including not only reporters but Cherry staff members who had resisted Wasson's efforts before, now identified with the well-mannered white social worker's efforts to reform the state from the inside. Over the previous year, articles about Wilson's plight celebrated his eventual move to the cottage as if it were a full resolution. For many, this symbolic and literal liberation from the locked wards of Cherry represented a true example of justice. Branch's lawsuit challenged this congratulatory stance, chastising the public to understand Wilson's plight in light of racism inherent, and still present, in the mental health system. This tact generated a great deal of resistance.

André Branch's case galvanized a bond—in appearance if not in fact—between Wasson and Cherry Hospital. Now codefendants, the social worker and the hospital against which Wasson campaigned so vigorously were suddenly required to work together. They had to consider ways to protect themselves, their institutions, and, to varying degrees, Wilson himself. In his affidavit to the court, Wasson had guardedly complimented Cherry Hospital, saying, "Over time I have observed a marked and increased willingness on the part of the authorities of Cherry Hospital to comply with the provisions of the Settlement Agreement." He was sincere in his belief that despite the wrongs they had committed before, the mental institution was finally doing right by Wilson.

FROM THE ATTORNEY GENERAL's office in Raleigh, lawyer Bruce Ambrose read through Branch's suit and compiled a list of questions and potential sources for answers. There were a variety of challenges to consider: Was there a statute of limitations on the violations Wilson had experienced? If Wilson was not mentally ill, could he, as Branch's lawyers argued, qualify under the Americans with Disabilities Act? Who were the alleged family members that repeatedly had sought Wilson's release? Why had they not visited him? Ambrose also wondered how Wilson had ended up in the hospital in the first place. The North Carolina attorney started a list of individuals to depose. Near the top were not only Branch but also Cherry staff members and state officials, including caseworker Linda Taylor, guardian John Wasson, hospital doctors Macatangay and Vitols, and North Carolina state official Charles Robin Britt Sr. Also included on the list were other relatives of Junius Wilson. Ambrose began deposing them that fall.

ANDRÉ BRANCH, ACCOMPANIED by his legal team, came to Raleigh in early November 1995. Ambrose and his colleague Robert Hargett met the group in a local law office's conference room. The deposition did not proceed especially smoothly. Sharp intellect and barely concealed hostility marked the direct examination. To many questions that Ambrose posed, Branch offered either ambiguous or intensely literal answers, forcing his interrogator to rephrase queries. The deposition progressed slowly.

Branch presented an image of Wilson's story that starkly contrasted with the articles that had splashed across newspapers earlier in 1994. He saw Wilson not as an atypical figure but as a symbol of the horror of Jim Crow and its descendants still in operation in North Carolina. Branch pointed out that the residual effects of southern racism, intimidation, and violation lingered and permeated virtually all aspects of Junius Wilson's life. For Branch, race rather than special needs was the pivotal factor in the justice denied Wilson. He asserted that it was no solution to place the deaf man in a modest cottage on the grounds of the state hospital. This was no liberation; it was continued captivity, furnished with colonial style fixtures and a front porch.

When Ambrose asked Branch about his knowledge of Junius Wilson, he testified that Carrie Gill had been his primary source of information. The deaf man's sister, explained Branch, said she could communicate with her brother and that he was "well educated" at the deaf school in Raleigh.

To Ambrose's questions about the absence of family visits during Wilson's long years at the hospital, an angry Branch argued that intimidation and racism thwarted the family's efforts. According to Branch, relatives had sent packages and letters and tried to contact Wilson several times. When Gill attempted to visit her brother in the 1940s, she and her father were "not treated well; their journeys were long and arduous."

Branch reported that Gill "missed her brother a great deal and that other relatives missed him a great deal. She used words like 'sick' to describe their feelings."[6] He recounted that Wilson's niece Annie Williams had a special relationship with her deaf relative; she remembered Wilson as "very smart" and that "they played." According to Branch, Williams claimed that Mary Wilson Clark "was sick" with grief by her son's arrest. "In fact," said Branch, "her words were, 'She never was quite right after they took her baby.' "[7]

When impelled to describe other previous conversations, Branch consistently demurred, claiming that he could not recall. Frustrated by Branch's opaque responses about the family, Ambrose asked whether he would chart out a paper of the family tree. The lawyer asked, "Can you assist me in doing that?" Branch replied, "I would not." Ambrose followed up, "You decline to do that?" Branch answered smartly: "I am delighted to answer any question that you have." When asked whether there might be a family Bible that could provide the court with a genealogical tree, the witness replied, "We have many Bibles in our family. We are Christian people. We attend church regularly." He added that his grandfather Arthur Smith Jr. was "a minister of the gospel."[8] But he could not or would not offer conclusive testimony that his elders owned a Bible that outlined family relations.

Ambrose repeatedly pressed Branch to hand over contact information for the relatives. Branch continued to turn Ambrose's questions back against him, asking why a family should have to prove its relation to one another or validate their emotions. "These people want their relative out of that horrible institution," he insisted, "and they want restitution made for how he has been treated." Branch summed up, "I agree with them and I don't want them to be harassed."

Branch's frustration and hostility simmered: "I will not promise to provide you with anything. I will tell you that *my* relatives are well aware that racism is still alive and well in North Carolina—in fact, across this country—and they pray for me regularly because they think it is rather dangerous for me to be bringing a lawsuit involving white people."[9] Although he, as an educated outsider, felt that it was possible to criticize those in authority in North Carolina, Branch understood his relatives' concern: "I . . . don't want them to have to live with fear of white people doing something to them. They tell me regularly that I need to be careful because I never know what people might do to me. The fear for them is quite real."[10]

When Ambrose asked pointedly what evidence he had of intimidation and harassment of family members, Branch said, "Mr. Wasson and Mr. Pooley have not allowed Mr. Wilson to be reunited with his sister."[11] In addition, Branch added that Macatangay had told him "that I could not visit with him away from Cherry Hospital." He was forced to amend his statement; Macatangay insisted that Wilson's health would not allow travel. Although Branch was righteously angry about the racism that had so profoundly shaped the lives of his family, he was not able to provide Ambrose with adequate examples of many of the claims that he made.[12]

After repeated attempts to solicit contact information for Wilson's relatives, Ambrose read into evidence Branch's position: he "objects to providing any further information about relatives of Junius Wilson to the State of North Carolina unless all defendants agree to a protective order prohibiting harassment or intimidation of the relatives and controlling contacts with them to ensure that harassment and intimidation do not occur."[13] The deposition ended after Branch's lawyer stated they would consider the state's demand for contact information about the family.

Although many people interpreted Branch's prevarications as hostility, perhaps they were simply defensive efforts to disguise his ignorance of the case. For his entire life, Wilson's family had refrained from talking much about what had happened in 1925 or even about the details of exactly who was biologically related to whom. Although Branch had copies of the 1925 court charges against Wilson, he apparently was unaware of what seems to have actually happened.

AS THE STATE PREPARED its defense, Cherry staff members were compelled to reconsider their previous interpretations of Junius Wilson. Thomas Smith noted in a regular psychiatric evaluation in the spring of 1995 that "Mr. Wilson shows no evidence of behavior disorder. . . . There is no evidence that he is dangerous to himself or others. On the contrary, he seems quite benign in his outlooks and attitudes."[14] Treatment team members pursued communication issues more intently. "We are carrying forward with the videotaping to codify Mr. Wilson's own communication style," wrote one. "We hope to use this medium to help others to understand him as he has little patience with learning ASL."[15]

In the meantime, both sides in the lawsuit agreed to bring in outside consultants who specialized in placement for people with disabilities. John Bundor, Barry Critchfield, and Roger Williams—three specialists in deaf services and mental health from South Carolina—arrived at Cherry, where they spent several days combing through almost 4,000 pages of Wilson's records; interviewing staff, doctors, his interpreter, and his case manager; and interacting with the deaf man. Administrator Marshall Smith asked the men to consider what living condition was best suited for Wilson and to appraise his current situation.

These new evaluators possessed experience and perspectives that reflected a radically different interpretation of deaf people and deafness than Cherry historically had held. Expertly proficient in sign language, all three considered deaf people as part of a cultural community and passionately advocated for signed communication. They were also aware of the complex interactions of deafness and racial identity.

Most of the evaluators' time at Cherry was spent in and around the Wilson cottage.[16] At first Wilson apparently wondered why the strangers had come. The close attention they and Cherry representatives displayed seemed to concern him: "I recall him as being somewhat intimidated. That certainly was my impression anyway," Critchfield wrote in his report. "The interview was held in his home, but there probably were half a dozen people in the room at the time and he didn't seem very comfortable. A lot of people were obviously talking about him."[17] Unable to follow their conversations, Wilson went back to his activities. Roger Williams observed Wilson's shift, recognizing that "he didn't really care who we were."

Williams tried to communicate directly with Wilson. The fluent signer waved his hand to catch Wilson's eye. "I told him, 'Come on, let's go talk,'" recalled Williams. Wilson perked up, resuming his role as host. "He and I went out and he showed me into his bedroom and he showed me his hats and he showed me his picture frame and the balloons around it. We . . . sort of started to establish a little bit of a relationship, I think." Wilson finger spelled his name to the visitor. As they moved about the house, he also answered some of the questions the evaluator asked.

Their interaction was interrupted when another resident from the hospital came by. The three experts watched Wilson participate in a group activity with staff, the interpreter, and the other patient.[18] The South Carolinians "noticed that he again started to kind of tune out in that setting."

They intervened. "We kind of told everybody to get lost," said Williams. "He, John [Bundor], and I sat and talked for a while. Then Mr. Parker arrived."[19] The mood lightened. Wilson smiled and nodded as Parker swapped stories with him and the newcomers. Eyes and hands negotiated across different languages.

The team recognized the link between education and Wilson's linguistic identity. "Wilson had distinctive Garner-style signing," observed one evaluator, confirming Parker's claim. Roger Williams, familiar with the State School for the Colored Blind and Deaf in Raleigh from his previous work in North Carolina, distinguished between Garner dialect and American Sign Language. "The signing . . . is more 'forceful,'" said the evaluator. There is "a 'push' to it; signs are shorter," he noted, and vocabulary is not as standardized as it is in ASL. Williams offered a comparison: a vocalized version would sound like "'Hi, howyadoing.' There's a punch. Jerkier. . . . The grammar is different, [the] accent is different."[20] Despite their awareness of Garner signs, sometimes Williams or the other evaluators had trouble understanding Wilson. Parker tried to intervene, prompting the questions in new ways. Wilson occasionally answered them. Still, "communication was halting."[21]

Sparse data from Wilson's file, combined with his limited ability to communicate with the evaluators, made it difficult for them to interpret some of their client's answers. When they asked whether Wilson had enjoyed school, the deaf man nodded. Did he live in the dorms? Yes. Through gestures and signs, Wilson articulated that he had had "lots of friends there and he hadn't seen any since he left."[22] More questions followed. Why did you leave? Arthritic fingers described images that baffled them at first. "He said he ran off," Williams remembered, "that he had left the school, and he told us that he was 15 when it happened, which was not consistent with what the record had said."

The evaluators struggled to follow the picture Wilson painted. "His sign skills were not [totally clear]. . . . We had pieces that were missing." They surmised that Wilson had "joined a circus" and that he remembered "crossing a field . . . [and] saw something." Williams thought that Wilson might have been describing an elephant or some other exotic animal. The deaf man signed FAIR as he tried to clarify. Williams got the image of "a freak show, strange people like a fat woman . . . that sort of exotic part of it." Nothing in Wilson's medical file explained the vivid story.[23]

Without context, the evaluators could not understand Wilson's seemingly invented story and concluded that he was being unreasonable. Had he misunderstood their questions? Had he seen a circus on television recently? Of course, Wilson actually was conveying information, even if not in articulate signs. When the evaluators finally learned the facts of Wilson's 1924 escapade at the Negro State Fair and subsequent expulsion from the school, his message seemed not only rational but fluent. There is no evidence that he had told this story for almost seventy years.

Over the next few days, the guest evaluators learned other aspects of Wilson's case: his pleasure working at the car wash, a deep affection for some of the staff and for Parker, how much he missed riding his bicycle. When asked about his family, Wilson replied: "They're dead, they're gone. . . . I have no family." One specialist added that "Wilson didn't talk about his family really" and "at no time did he seem sad" except when describing his stroke.[24]

The evaluators, who had not been authorized specifically to ask about Wilson's perception of why he was at the hospital, did not press him. They did not ask much about his relatives. They never mentioned his castration. In spite of their expertise and Parker's help interpreting Wilson's signs, the three men from South Carolina were only able to gain limited information from the deaf man. Still, it was more than Cherry staff had garnered in all his decades at the hospital.

Although the evaluation team advanced a culturally and racially sensitive assessment of Wilson, they understood the inherent limitations of state systems: a dearth of resources, the lack of qualified support staff, and the limited understanding of deafness. The three men could not fundamentally challenge Cherry Hospital or the state. Their formal report concluded that "Mr. Wilson exhibited numerous difficulties in communicating. He is most comfortable communicating in a one-to-one situation with an individual known to him. In large group situations or with strangers, he will avoid eye contact as a way of avoiding communication but did not demonstrate any anger or frustration. Communication is limited to finger spelling (with his left hand since the 1986 [stroke]), gestures, inarticulate verbalizations, and a limited repertoire of American Sign Language in the variant singular to the school which he attended."[25]

The interviews clearly articulated that Wilson was not mentally deficient. Williams later recalled an incident during their introduction that showed Wilson's unwillingness to tolerate others' deficiencies. When they first met, the men had introduced themselves using their sign names. "Barry [Critchfield's] formal sign name is ABC." According to Williams, "Mr. Wilson looked at him signing ABC, thought that Barry doesn't sign very well if he's just signing ABC, and [basically] ignored him the rest of the weekend."[26]

Although he misjudged Critchfield, Wilson was more astute with the other evaluators. He assessed John Bundor, originally from Sierra Leone. Although Bundor was not a native signer, his status as black and deaf put Wilson at ease. Wilson also interacted well with Williams, even though he was hearing and white, perhaps because Williams "signed a little faster" and exhibited deaf cultural behavior that Wilson recognized and understood.

Their conclusion echoed previous accusations: "Mr. Junius Wilson . . . has been unnecessarily confined at the State Hospital at Goldsboro (now Cherry Hospital) for a period of seventy years."[27] Like Branch, the evaluators felt that Wilson's continued placement at Cherry was on questionable legal grounds. The mental health specialists were aware of the need to take into account the complexities of Wilson's situation. "Deafness immeasurably complicates any kind of treatment situation," said one. "Especially when you are talking about mental health treatment, 90 percent of the treatment is done through language, and without that communication between physician and patient, I believe that . . . is what caused the lack of delivery of services."[28]

A final question remained: Should Wilson stay in the cottage or be removed to a new location? Interviews with Wasson, the Sidberrys, staff, Parker, and Wilson pointed to one answer: while he enjoyed visits to Castle Hayne, Wilson often referred to the cottage and hospital as his "home." To remove him, evaluators said, could be seen as cruel and unusual.[29] Although his placement on the grounds of the hospital was not a perfect answer, it seemed to them the best option.

AS THE LAWSUIT ON Wilson's behalf proceeded, attorneys from both sides sought to find points of agreement and to craft partial resolutions. André Branch's initial suit had named not only the state but also county social worker John Wasson and Carolina Legal Assistance as defendants.

This had brought unexpected negative attention to Branch's cause. Articles throughout 1995 cast Wasson as a "Good Samaritan" unjustly treated. Newspaper headlines proclaimed, "Guardian Sued for Helping Man" and "Man Who Helped Free Patient in Mental Ward Is Sued." One *USA Today* editorial sarcastically asked, "What did Wasson get for his troubles? He, Wilson's attorneys, the county, and the state were sued for $150 million by a cousin of Wilson's who alleges they violated his rights causing suffering and mental anguish."[30]

Particularly proud of his advocacy work on behalf of Wilson, Wasson resented Branch's accusation that he ultimately oppressed and disempowered his ward. "If I sound bitter, it's because I am," Wasson told a journalist. "I'm angry at being sued for helping Mr. Wilson after he had been so wronged for so many years." Known as an advocate in social justice cases, the Wilmington administrator added, "You can bet I'll look twice before jumping into another one."[31] In a parting shot at his accuser, Wasson wryly reminded a reporter that his own highly publicized advocacy efforts were what had encouraged the "relative of Mr. Wilson's finally [to come] forward."[32] Realizing the disadvantages of attacking people seen as proponents of social justice, Branch's lawyers agreed to drop them from the suit. Legal representative Richard Ralston reasoned that dropping "marginal defendants" from the case was "essentially recognizing that the main defendant is the state, and it allows us to continue our litigation with North Carolina."[33]

Wasson wanted the settlement. He feared that a prolonged lawsuit would undermine his authority as Wilson's guardian, harming the deaf man's chances of receiving continued care. "I'm basically damaged goods," he admitted to one reporter.[34] As part of the settlement, Wasson agreed to accept the appointment of Branch or anyone else as Wilson's guardian. His agreement promoted his position that Wilson's interest remained the priority. It left the question of guardianship open to a judge or clerk. Wasson promised to share any relevant information about his ward with the new guardian. He also stated that he would testify in court if asked by Branch's lawyers to do so.[35]

In exchange for being dropped from the suit, New Hanover County agreed to pay $6,000, half of which covered fees for the plaintiff's legal team. The judge held the remaining $3,000 until the rest of the suit was resolved.[36] Wasson stated, "I am comfortable with this end result with the exception of the money. I wish the county didn't have to pay it."[37] Still, the settlement saved his district collateral damages from a protracted suit. Time and resources that had been routed to address the legal charges could be refocused on social services. In exchange for their own dismissal, Carolina Legal Assistance committed twenty hours each month of free work to Branch's legal team for one year or "until the trial ends, whichever comes first."[38]

News that John Wasson and Carolina Legal Assistance had been dismissed from the case was released at the end of 1995. The details of the settlement remained closed for almost two months while the court decided whether or not to replace Wasson with Branch as Wilson's guardian.

AS RESEARCHERS LOOKED deeper into records about Wilson's past, they unearthed new information that surprised both his guardian and caretakers. Although for decades Cherry Hospital has believed the man was born in 1898, they now found contrary evidence in his school file. Like most of the other students' files, Wilson's information was incomplete. Despite its limitations, the file clearly documented his birth date: 8 October 1908. That made him nearly eleven years younger than his caretakers had long believed he was.[39]

Would the hospital have treated him differently if they had known how young a boy he was when he was admitted? Had they known during Wilson's long incarceration that he was a much younger man, would they have presented different opportunities to him? Surely he would not have been put on the ward for geriatric patients when he was only in his mid-fifties. Perhaps they might have made greater efforts to deinstitutionalize him if they had known how many years he might have left. Would Wasson, Pooley, and the other advocates have insisted on greater remedies had they realized at the beginning that Wilson was significantly younger than they believed?

IN THE MEANTIME, Bruce Ambrose continued to depose witnesses. Carrie Gill, Wilson's sister, declined to testify, stating that her poor health prohibited her from remembering accurately. She told Branch's lawyers that "since her daddy died, she figured there wasn't much that could be done for her brother."[40]

On 19 December 1995, Wilson's niece Jennie Bowman gave her deposition in New York City. Although the seventy-two-year-old woman was just an infant at the time of Wilson's arrest, she was raised by Mary Wilson Clark after her own mother died. She intimately knew the family's history. No one anticipated the revelation that Bowman would share.

Bowman confirmed Wilson's immediate family tree and explained their relationship to the Smith family. Ambrose asked her about Wilson and why he was arrested. "Well, what I've heard and been told was that something concerning my uncle bothering with [Arthur Smith's] wife," she began. The judge tried to interpret Bowman's skeptical tone. Was Wilson guilty of attempted rape? "No, probably going around the house and acting like Peeping Tom, something like that. They was acting they was afraid of him, but he didn't act like to hurt anyone."[41] And others in the family apparently agreed, too. "What I've been told, he didn't do anything to her," concluded the elderly witness.[42]

Most of Wilson's recent advocates, as well as his caretakers throughout the years, had assumed Wilson was accused by white men of attempted rape of a white woman. But now Bowman was hinting at a much more complex truth. The information sank in slowly as the judge asked Bowman to clarify her statements. Wilson's uncle made the charges? "Yes, and had him put away," answered Bowman. "My grandmother knew they was coming to get him." Then Bowman suggested that the events of 1925 created a rift in the family. "I never thought anything about that, that she didn't care too much about [Arthur Smith Jr.]," she began. "Me being young, [I did not think about] how much [Mary Wilson Clark] disliked him for putting him away." As time went on, Bowman became more aware of their difficult relationship. "She would only speak to him—I notice that she would give him the time of day and that is it."[43] Her answer riveted those present in the courtroom. She continued, "This was widely known by the family."[44] Wilson had been "sent away" because Arthur Smith Jr. had had him arrested, apparently under false pretenses.

Other relatives from Wilson's generation confirmed the startling facts. Wilson's other niece by his sister Asynia offered an eyewitness account of the arrest. Annie Mae Williams explained that she was "four or five. I just remember the guy handcuffing him." Her interrogator was incredulous. "You really do?" She answered, "Yes." She then recounted the policemen's visit as the family gathered firewood. One officer gave her grandmother a letter, apparently a warrant.[45] Williams remembered that grandmother Mary Clark said nothing at the time but later explained the situation to her. "She said he had raped somebody, but she didn't believe it. . . . She might have said more, but I don't remember now," Junius Wilson's niece told the attorneys.[46]

Fannie Thomas, Arthur and Lizzie's daughter, testified, "I heard that it was a conflict between my mother and father. . . . I heard that he was attacking my mother, and of course, that was why he was sent away."[47] Under direct examination, Virginia Smith Branch explained that her relatives "said my father put him in jail."[48] Even Arthur Smith Jr.'s own children seemed to believe the charges were false. When Ambrose asked her whether she thought Wilson had actually attacked her mother, Virginia Branch replied that she "didn't think it was true. . . . I didn't get the sense it was true."[49]

Although Wilson's arrest and the issues surrounding it had apparently not been shared with most of the younger generations in the family, some of the deaf man's age peers were aware where he was. One cousin acknowledged, "Yeah. I heard that he was in Cherry Hospital."[50] Another, Annie Mae Williams, once had visited the Goldsboro institution for other reasons but "never went to see Junius" while she was there.[51] She explained, "I was visiting. I had taken some friends there to see their daughter."[52] The lawyer asked, "Did you know then that Junius was there?" She affirmed that she did. He followed up: "Was there some reason you didn't try to see him?" Williams answered, "No, just didn't bother."[53]

LOCAL NEWSPAPERS PICKED up the story of the family's disposal of Junius Wilson, exposing across their pages the family's long-held secret.[54] John Wasson recalled feeling "absolutely blown away" by the news. "It is a Southern gothic horror tale," he told one reporter.[55] The story also forced a reassessment of André Branch's case. For many, the family's complicit role in Wilson's plight undercut their image as victims. It particularly hurt Branch's role as spokesman for the family, partially because he was apparently unaware of what had happened. Perhaps most condemning of all was that he was the grandson of Arthur Smith Jr., the alleged perpetrator of Wilson's arrest. Even state officials used the information to discredit Branch. One bureaucrat told the press that Wilson "has been the victim of social politics that we look back on now and are deeply troubled by. . . . I think we owe Mr. Wilson a good quality of life for the rest of his life. I'm not sure we owe the relatives anything."[56]

JENNIE BOWMAN'S DECLARATION and its subsequent confirmation transformed family dynamics. That Wilson was a relative held wrongly in a mental hospital shocked relatives who had never known him. To learn that their own kin might have initiated the events that ultimately led him to Cherry was nothing short of incredulous. Most of the extended family was called to Raleigh to give testimony during the summer of 1996. Although the case was not designed to determine the complicity of relatives in the incarceration of Junius Wilson, family members felt uncomfortable facing the intrusive questions of the court.

Media attention was even more prying, and the questions of reporters often seemed like accusations. During her deposition, Annie Sidberry acknowledged that the media coverage had been hard on the family.[57] She had refused to read newspaper articles about her kin but could not escape the news that swirled around Castle Hayne and across the state. Born long after Wilson's arrest, Annie Sidberry mainly discussed the complicated branches of the family tree. When asked about Arthur Smith Jr.'s wife, whom Mrs. Sidberry had known well, the soft-spoken woman shook her head, stating that she could not believe that Lizzie would make a false accusation.[58]

Willie Sidberry shared his own anguish over the family secret during his deposition an hour after his wife's. He gently stated, "I loved my grandmother [Lizzie Smith] dearly. She was an inspiration to me." Jennie Bowman's revelation had struck him deeply. "When I heard of this and how the media was making it sound so awful, it upset me," he said.[59] Willie Sidberry had not known his grandfather Arthur Smith Jr. very well.[60]

Others focused their anger against Smith's grandson. Some, like Wilson's cousin Fannie Thomas, echoed Jennie Bowman's disapproval of Branch's lawsuit and questioned his claim that he represented the family.[61] André Branch's aunt Sarah Peoples took umbrage with her nephew's claim that the family had been too poor and too intimidated by the white establishment to visit Wilson in Goldsboro.[62]

Annie Mae Williams, Wilson's niece, hotly rejected Branch's actions. Contradicting his claims that the two had shared a long phone conversation about their relative at Cherry, Williams insisted that she had hung up on Branch shortly after he called "because I'm not with him on anything." Specifically, Williams noted, "I don't want him over my uncle. . . . Because, he doesn't know him. He doesn't know nothing about the whole thing."[63]

Williams found it unacceptable for Arthur Smith Jr.'s grandson to intervene. When Ambrose asked her what she thought of Branch's requests, she shot back, "His grandfather is the cause of him going there all these years anyways. You know that don't you?"[64] The judge asked for a precise answer. Do you approve of what he's doing? "No," she replied, "I don't."[65]

BRENDA TUCKER, THE New Hanover County clerk of superior court, ruled against André Branch, keeping John Wasson as guardian.[66] Branch expressed his disappointment in the ruling, as well as his irritation: "We would like to see regard taken for the family of Junius Wilson and what we think is best for him," Branch said. "From my perspective, what the family wants has been totally disregarded this morning.'"

John Wasson did not anticipate the court's decision. One newspaper report suggested that Wasson felt it "validated the work he'd done with Mr. Wilson."[67]

NEXT, THE COURT CONSIDERED whether Branch's larger lawsuit should go forward. The attorney general's office and Branch's Washington State legal team lobbied hard for their positions. Finally, Judge Britt issued his decision. Branch's dogged determination not to yield to state demands came back to haunt him.

Neither he nor his lawyers could proceed with a federal lawsuit on Wilson's behalf.

Federal procedures had required that Branch supply the court with information about his relatives. Attorney Helen Hinn later explained that Branch "ignored the order, so the judge ordered him to Raleigh and told him he was dismissed as to bringing the suit against the state."[68] Later, the same judge ordered Branch's lawyers to pay the state for the cost of researching that information and locating the family members.

Branch's legal representatives appealed the decision, but the ruling permanently undercut his cause as well as his message. André Branch moved into the margins of Wilson's story. He also moved into the margins of Wilson's life. According to the cottage medical logs, after that decision the elderly man received neither visits nor care packages from his Seattle relative.

Wasson and others who worked within the state system breathed a sigh of relief. "I think the ruling is definitely in Mr. Wilson's best interest," the New Hanover guardian told the press.[69] Wasson's boss at the Department of Social Services, F. Wayne Morris, was less diplomatic. "Goodbye and good riddance," he declared.[70]

AFTER HIS OWN LOSSES in court, Branch petitioned to make relative Gracie Pulliam the guardian of Wilson's estate. He hoped she would be granted the authority to supervise expenditures and investments from any money Wilson earned through settlement. These new motions made their way through the North Carolina courts.

Pulliam, a teaching assistant at the Gregory School of Science, Mathematics, and Technology, had had no interaction with Wilson or with the people at Cherry who took care of him. Rejecting Branch's proposal to give Pulliam control of Wilson's finances, Clerk of Court Brenda Tucker explained that "ordinarily, the court would automatically lean toward family members." Nevertheless, in this case, the court found that the proposed guardian was not "in a position to say she is more aware of his needs than any other person."[71]

Instead, Tucker concluded that "the person most suited to meeting his needs would be the [county's] public guardian." She picked Helen Hinn, a Long Island native who had served as an attorney in Wilmington since the early 1980s. The local attorney agreed to donate her services.[72] Hinn felt that after she was chosen, Pulliam seemed "greatly relieved when she was not appointed." Hinn continued, "She seemed like a nice, sincere lady but I did not see that she really wanted it."[73] Wilson's new advocate remembered that when Pulliam "left the courtroom, she patted me on the shoulder and said, 'Good luck, Miss Hinn.'" The lawyer reflected on her action: "That said to me, 'That was one relieved lady.'"[74]

Wilson's new guardian went to visit her ward at his cottage. Marshall Smith accompanied Hinn to the front door. As they entered, she saw that "Wilson was sitting there watching TV, looking perfectly content. His two caretakers were there and they seemed like very caring gentlemen." Her deaf client eyed the white stranger and then began his ritual. "He motioned for me to come into this room and he pointed out all his hats. And they seemed to have significance to him," she remembered. Laughing, she added that afterwards he "went back to the TV." She understood that "he'd 'finished his duty as host.' "[75]

IN THE SUMMER OF 1996, John Wasson left his position in New Hanover County for a new job. The eighteen-year veteran of the county's social work department vividly remembered, "My last day, July 19, was my last day as Mr. Wilson's guardian."[76] Although Wasson had not interacted frequently with Wilson, he had made his client's case a public cause. Many people saw Wasson as the true hero of Wilson's story because of both the 1992 lawsuit and the media blitz that Wasson had helped orchestrate. The social worker drew satisfaction from this effort but keenly felt the cost of his focused advocacy: "Mr. Wilson's case took away a lot of time from other stuff I was doing at DSS," he confessed, "but I don't regret it; I'm sorry about the other things that could have been done."[77]

The move to a new job in Stokes County was bittersweet for Wasson. As a director of social work in the more rural North Carolina county, Wasson had the opportunity to exercise more authority, a challenge to which he looked forward. His move coincided with the appointment of Hinn to Wilson's case. The two advocates knew each other well. Wasson trusted that a fair resolution would be reached for Wilson. Nevertheless, Wasson knew that his efforts in the Wilson case were perhaps the most important work he had done in his life. He was sad to be distanced from it.

AFTER JOHN WASSON CHANGED jobs, F. Wayne Morris, the director of the New Hanover County Department of Social Services, became Wilson's guardian of the person. Pat Jessup entered Wilson's life at that point, serving as case manager for Morris and the department. Wasson's former colleague participated in the monthly staff meetings and visited the Wilson house. The deaf man led this new African American visitor through the same initiation rite that all visitors and caretakers experienced: the tour of the house that highlighted his collections and pictures.[78] Jessup also checked in with the Sidberrys and considered additional ways to enhance Wilson's social circle and sense of family.

She did not pursue contact with André Branch, but she shared the same hope of reuniting Wilson with his sister, Carrie Gill. The native North Carolinian tried to contact a woman she thought was Gill's daughter but was apparently her niece "to let me have contact, even just a phone call, any way to make arrangements to meet." Jessup had hoped to retrieve "some kind of information" or have her "send photos." Repeated phone calls and letters went unanswered. "Knowing she was out there but not able to contact her was a disappointment," the energetic social worker lamented.[79]

THREE DAYS AFTER WASSON's departure, Helen Hinn presented a motion to the court to appoint her as the guardian ad litem. The next month the courts removed Branch from the position, opening the path for Hinn to pursue a modified version of the lawsuit originally presented by him.[80]

The Wilmington attorney immediately hired a Charlotte firm known for its civil rights work: Ferguson, Stein, Wallas, Adkins, Gresham & Sumter. Unlike Branch's legal team and its intense focus on race and racism, the new team of lawyers emphasized civil rights violations based on Wilson's deafness.

After the judge granted a period of discovery for all sides to gather new information, Ferguson and his colleagues looked for specialists considered significantly removed from the state's mental health agencies. They contacted deaf psychologist and university professor Barbara Brauer. Brauer and her colleague Alan Marcus were affiliated with Gallaudet University, the nation's premier institution serving deaf and hard of hearing students. Considered a hub of deaf culture, Gallaudet was known for its activist faculty and research on issues related to deaf people and deafness. Wilson's legal representatives asked the team specifically to consider whether Wilson had received different treatment at Cherry over the years because of his deafness.

Knowing that communication had been a critical issue in their client's situation, the attorneys also inquired whether Wilson would have benefited from earlier accommodation to his deafness. The psychologists had to assess what the "absolute best level of care" could be for the Cherry resident. They were also charged with examining whether North Carolina had upheld its side of the 1992 settlement.[81]

The introduction of Gallaudet specialists marked a shift in Wilson's case to a stronger deaf cultural perspective. Brauer and her colleagues held the most progressive and uncompromising view of deaf identity of the specialists consulted for the suit. With no previous relations with the plaintiff or defendants, the academic researchers had fuller reign to assess the specific ramifications of Wilson's care at Cherry. This included the first comparative study of Wilson's treatment records with those of nondeaf patients at Cherry and other North Carolina hospitals, providing greater context and overall data for the evaluators.

BY THE END OF 1996, the two sides prepared to engage one another in front of the judge. In court filings, Ferguson and his team focused on the systemic oppression Wilson experienced as a deaf black man at Cherry Hospital. From the duration of time he spent there to the delay in receiving medical care for his stroke because of language barriers, the plaintiff's representatives mapped out the power of racism and disability discrimination. Jim Crow racism led to serious and long-term damages for Wilson. Disability discrimination, particularly in regards to his deafness, further oppressed and violated his civil rights.

The filings showcased Brauer's preliminary report.[82] Wilson, according to the psychologist, had never received services comparable to those of nondeaf patients. Since staff were generally ignorant of sign language and unique features of deafness and mental health, they were "never able to genuinely 'connect' with Mr. Wilson." Her team had noted that in contrast to other patient files they had read, Wilson's file had no "treatment plan that lists criteria he would need to meet to be discharged from the hospital."[83]

Repeatedly calling Wilson's case "striking," their evaluation further trampled the image of Cherry as a benevolent institution. Scouring his medical files, their eyes were drawn to the various notes that showed Wilson trying to interact with others using sign language. In each instance, the staff did not comprehend what he was doing. Brauer called his experience "a social vacuum." As "the sole deaf patient," Wilson "had effectively been placed in a form of solitary confinement" by the utter lack of communication with those surrounding him.[84] Cherry Hospital had discriminated against Wilson because he was deaf and because he needed sign language to communicate.

The team acknowledged that the hospital began to provide sign interpreters after 1992. They hastened to note that given Wilson's stroke earlier and his many years in linguistic isolation, "these services seem to have come too late."[85] For Brauer, Wilson's plight could have been avoided had others understood deafness and sign language.[86] Simply put, the report proclaimed that "Mr. Wilson is experiencing the effects of past racial and disability discrimination at Cherry Hospital."[87]

THE ATTORNEY GENERAL's office had formulated a multipronged defense. First, North Carolina Justice Department attorneys argued that Wilson's case had exceeded the statute of limitations. The primary violations, they had argued, occurred in the 1920s and 1930s, when he entered the institution and was castrated. Second, the 1992 settlement agreement had addressed previous wrongs and precluded further litigation.

Even if North Carolina was partly to blame for wrongdoing, defense lawyers added, Wilson's relatives also contributed to his plight, alluding to Arthur Smith Jr.'s accusations that placed Wilson in jail. Because relatives did not regularly visit Wilson, they further posited, the deaf man had nowhere to go even when the hospital began searching out ways to deinstitutionalize him.[88]

Lawyers for the state agreed that Wilson was not mentally ill but used this fact in their own favor. At Cherry Hospital, Wilson's "saneness" disqualified him from disability protection provided under the mandates of the Americans with Disabilities Act. According to these lawyers, people with mental illness could invoke the ADA, but Wilson could not. State attorneys even questioned the constitutionality of the ADA and the meaning of "obligations" states must meet under its policy.

IN JANUARY 1997 Judge Britt met with representatives from each side to consider their motions. This time, the state essentially lost. "Time had not run out in the matter," Britt confirmed flatly.[89] He also dismissed the 1992 settlement, noting that Wasson technically had no authority as guardian to sign it. Therefore, the agreement could not obstruct the subsequent lawsuit.[90] The plaintiffs could seek money damages as well.

The lawyers left Britt's courtroom and began preparing for trial. As filings passed through the courthouse, Hinn's team of lawyers brought Brauer and Alan Marcus to Goldsboro to assess Wilson in person. Once again, Wilson sat with outsiders to his world, answering questions and watching them as they observed his responses.

The new group of evaluators generally confirmed what previous experts had noted: "Mr. Wilson was quite gregarious and social. He interacted with me when I initiated conversation and appeared to comprehend some of my humor," wrote Marcus. Paying close attention to cultural behavior, the Gallaudet staff member noted that Wilson "would gesture and utter non-comprehendible sounds that looked as if he was trying to say something. His mannerism was very similar to a hearing person who would talk and gesture." He considered Wilson's language use. "If I were to comment on his attempt at communication I would venture to say that he is doing what he has seen for the last 50 years. He resided in a hospital where he interacted primarily with hearing patients and staff who probably knew little if any sign language. What he most likely had was people talking and gesturing at him which is what he does now."[91]

During a break in the interview, Marcus had given Wilson a Gallaudet University baseball cap. The deaf man grinned and became more effusive. Now he accepted the visitors. They trailed behind Wilson as he gave them a formal tour of his home.[92] Their summary claimed that "Junius is basically a very personable, gregarious fellow and does not present himself as mentally ill in any way nor as mentally retarded." They also found that his difficulties interacting with others "signal[ed] an emotional impoverishment."[93]

The Gallaudet contingent proposed that Wilson have continued opportunities to socialize with deaf people and that trained instructors teach him more sign language. They explicitly demanded that experts, not caring staff like Hiram Grantham or even Everett Parker, supervise and assess ways of integrating Wilson into the broader African American deaf community in North Carolina. The psychologists likely felt that this would protect caretakers and Wilson alike from administrative pressure, latent paternalism, and parochialism.

WHILE HIS ADVOCATES battled in court, Junius Wilson's daily life changed little. One of the changes he did experience during this period was the presence of a new friend. Staff brought an African American deaf resident of the Woodard Building to the cottage for regular visits in 1996 and 1997. Perhaps the two men met during Wilson's sojourns from his cottage back to the wards.

Waving and smiling at the man's approach, every week Wilson directed his guest to a chair at the dining room table. The two elderly gentlemen, according to staff, worked on craft projects and puzzles at the same time but did not actively collaborate. Occasionally, Wilson's visitor traveled with him around town, perusing local clothing stores and eating at Hardee's. The men seemed to enjoy each other's companionship.[94]

Medical logs note the visits but do not explicitly acknowledge that the two men communicated with each other. Anecdotal evidence suggests that Wilson's friend had limited sign skills and might have used his voice rather than extensive signed communication.[95] It is possible that this other Cherry resident attended the school for black deaf students in Raleigh, but apparently he was not a pupil at the time Wilson attended. By 1998 Wilson's regular guest from the ward no longer appeared in the house logbook. The gentleman died in 1999.

AS CHRISTMAS APPROACHED each year, advocates and cottage staff tried to bring holiday cheer to Junius Wilson. In 1996 staff members took him to meet "Lady Santa" at a community event. She gave him a small gift and he thanked her. Staff viewed this visit as a way to give Wilson a sense of normalcy. At the same time, the situation reveals the abnormalcy of Wilson's existence. He was not a child, but an elderly man. His interaction with Lady Santa was partly comical because it was so unexpected. At the same time, the Christmas exchange embodied a certain generosity and paternalism that had defined much of Wilson's interaction with staff over the last few decades. Clearly, he enjoyed receiving his gift.

Helen Hinn recalled that she, Pat Jessup, and Cherry staff celebrated Christmas annually with Wilson. "Cherry Hospital provided lots of goodies and I brought up . . . smoked salmon dip, nice things. They had very elegant parties,"

Junius Wilson, Christmastime 2000 (Courtesy of Everett Parker)

Hinn remembered. "There'd be a pile of presents for him under the tree. I think I brought him a new cap or such." One gift particularly caught his attention: "a wallet with money in it." Hinn recounted, "That got the biggest smile. He had the concept of knowing what money can do. That, I'm sure, was his favorite present that year."[96]

BECAUSE OF WILSON's interest in money, his attendants helped him learn to pay for his lunches at Hardee's. The deaf man carried the wallet and handed cashiers money for items he wanted to purchase. But institutional habits were hard for him to break. Often he hoarded cash in his socks and tried to pocket food that nurses might confiscate.[97] Staff members complained about these habits but persisted in their efforts to reeducate him.

They also encouraged Wilson to make a few independent decisions in his daily activities. When he went to fast-food restaurants and cafeterias, they encouraged him to point to the items he wanted to eat and drink. At the local grocery store, according to the occupational therapist who worked with him, Wilson "usually indicate[d]" that he desired "to purchase cookies."[98] Although not everyone was pleased with the choices he made, most people recognized that Wilson now had the right to make those choices and that the staff had the responsibility to assist him in learning how to do so.

EXPOSURE TO AMERICAN SIGN Language became a primary goal and symbol of Wilson's rehabilitation. As a visual language, ASL offered access to language for Wilson that spoken and written English did not. With ASL skills, the deaf man would be more able to socialize with a broad array of people and use his professional sign language interpreters more effectively. Tutors reported some progress in the last years of Wilson's life. Brenda Aron perceived early in her work with him that his "language skills [are] not highly developed but he does understand more than he can express or show."[99] When individuals modeled signs in ASL, the deaf man often nodded and occasionally mirrored the signs. In one session, deaf tutor Paul Schreyer said that after watching a sign language videotape for a few minutes, Wilson "picked up three signs."[100]

At the same time, the decision to tutor Wilson specifically in American Sign Language presented complications. While he clearly responded positively to signers, he remained generally distant in conversations, watching more often than responding. Observers commonly described Wilson's nods and smiles and socially appropriate behavior, like shaking hands. But these responses also can represent efforts to "pass"—to appear to understand in order to get by. In some situations, these tactics did not seem to work. When trying to converse with others independently, Wilson resorted to his more limited ASL vocabulary, Raleigh signs, and homemade gestures.[101] Consequently, even fluent signers like Aron, Schreyer, and Parker could not fully comprehend him.

It appears that Wilson struggled to understand them at times, as well. Notes throughout his medical files suggest that he responded wrongly to questions posed to him, or grew frustrated and signed FINISH ("enough") when solicitors asked him to explain more abstract concepts.[102] Games like Bingo pushed Wilson to connect signs with cards, but he thwarted such efforts by refusing to look at the signer.

In time he warmed to his interpreters, but he also frequently ignored them and resisted efforts to learn how to use them more effectively through focused attention or by soliciting information from them. Prior to the 1990s, Wilson likely never had an opportunity to work with an interpreter and might not have felt comfortable with the communication dynamics they presented. Given the linguistic differences between Raleigh signs and ASL, it is possible that Wilson did not find the new sign language particularly relevant.

Although Wilson's caretakers and guardians recognized the important linguistic, cultural, and relational role Raleigh school graduate Everett Parker played in Wilson's life, there was no serious discussion about the option to train staff and interpreters in Raleigh signs. And Wilson himself proved tenacious in his refusal to incorporate much of the sign training he did receive, resorting instead to his current pigeon of Raleigh signs, basic ASL, and homemade signs.

Wilson, Parker, and Cherry Hospital staff at Wrightsville
Beach (Courtesy of Everett Parker)

Deaf advocates, hoping to provide both language and cultural connections, assumed cultural deaf community norms that did not easily fit with Wilson's experience and perhaps even his sense of self.

DURING THE LATE 1990S, trips around the county became a staple in Wilson's life. Sometimes he visited the residences of volunteers who socialized with him or the homes of some of his caretakers.[103] He attended local parades and took trips to baseball games. Sometimes, he rejected overtures to participate in hospital day programs, pointing instead at cars and nodding vigorously that he wanted to take a drive instead. Time in the car particularly pleased him. The trips to and from Parker's house regularly elicited gleeful waves and gestures at road signs and billboards.

Staff at Cherry Hospital sometimes felt uncomfortable inviting Wilson's family to visit, despite the warm relations the institution had established previously with the Sidberrys. As one treatment team member noted, "They have been reluctant to contact for visitations since the 'family' has brought action against the Division."[104] Another employee conjectured later, "I suppose it was difficult for all of us, being involved almost in the public eye at that point. And the fears of saying the wrong thing, doing the wrong thing."[105] Media attention to the lawsuit haunted staff and administrators, who felt they had never been able to convey their side of the story to news reporters and policy makers.

In an effort to prove their good faith efforts, Doug Dexter, the hospital's case manager, asked his colleagues to extend a welcoming hand to the family. He also asked that the hospital document every effort made toward this end.[106] By the close of 1997, the paper trail mostly marked failed attempts. "Ms. Linda Taylor continues to do monthly letters, calls, etc. but still no response from family members," complained a treatment team report. Although Dexter "expressed pleasure in the family involvement with Mr. Wilson during the Wilmington and Castle Hayne trips," he was "concerned about the lack of family contact at the hospital."[107]

Wilson and his team did continue to pack into a van and drive to the Wilmington area to see the family there. During one autumn lunch date, Annie Sidberry brought along her cousin Louis Dixon, a man who remembered playing with the deaf man when they were children. Wilson did not seem to recognize Dixon and showed little emotion when they were reintroduced.[108]

AFTER LUNCH, THEY caravanned back to the Sidberry residence to spend time with Willie Sidberry and André Branch's mother, Virginia Smith Branch. Wilson watched the others as they chatted, nodding or gesturing occasionally to the questions or comments directed his way. As with most social visits, Wilson was more of a bystander than an active participant, even when he was purportedly the center of attention.

As Wilson and the cottage staff prepared to leave, Willie Sidberry presented Wilson with a gift: four small watermelons. The deaf man displayed a big smile. Simple expressions of connection meant more to him than tedious efforts to communicate more explicitly. One staff member remarked that Wilson "seemed to understand that these people were family." Still, "he did not appear overly excited. He shrugged and leaned away when they attempted to hug him." Instead, Wilson cursorily "smiled and waved 'good bye' when [they] departed."[109] Although Wilson did not always appear especially moved, he took pleasure in the visits. As an observer noted, "Mr. Wilson seemed to enjoy the trip very much, pointing to different things and making sounds as we rode to and from Wilmington."[110]

LINDA TAYLOR RECORDED that Wilson continued to sign, FAR FAR, I WANT TO FAR FAR. He strenuously produced the sign for "home," fingers held together at his cheek. Everett Parker had always interpreted the signs to mean that Wilson wanted to go to Castle Hayne, but his inconsistent recognition of local sites and his lackluster responses to relatives made Taylor and other staff members question what he really intended.[111] What did seem clear to them, however, was that Junius Wilson sometimes did not consider the cottage on the grounds of the hospital as his home.

AS THE SUMMER OF 1997 turned to autumn, lawyers on both sides of the case acknowledged that they did not want the suit to drag on. They were ready to move toward settlement. Hinn was happy: "My position was Mr. Wilson doesn't have so many years to live that he'll be able to enjoy and use a very large sum of money. So we reached a reasonable settlement." She agreed to a fraction of what Branch sought: a $226,000 payment and a guarantee that Wilson would remain in the house with the same level of care.

Hinn acknowledged that Wilson's advanced age influenced her decision. "If Mr. Wilson were a much younger gentleman," she explained, "our thinking might have been different."[112] She continued, "To hold out for more than he could enjoy I felt was pointless. Getting a significant amount had some symbolism to me. It was well more than enough for Wilson to utilize. It meant caretakers could take him overnight to different places. Put a little more excitement in his life. Money could pay for hotels, meals."[113]

John Wasson praised Hinn for her advocacy and expressed satisfaction with the resolution. "I think the fact that this settlement elicited a promise that (the state) will continue the state-of-the-art care is a good thing," he told a reporter.[114] Obliquely referring to André Branch, Wilson's former guardian added that, "More than anything, I do not want to see upon his death any of his so-called family benefit."[115]

IN NOVEMBER 1997 Judge Britt closed the case of *Junius Wilson v. the State of North Carolina*. Although a small flurry of appeals followed, all were dismissed by the end of the following year. In the same year, Artie Martinez, the deaf man who had been wrongly held in an Arizona state mental hospital for four decades, received his own out-of-court settlement for more than $150,000.[116]

For Wilson, the swirling legal battles that occurred from 1994 through 1997 were all but meaningless. Staff and guardians never discussed with Wilson the issues the court addressed on his behalf. Such questions as whether Wilson actually owned the cottage or whether his care was guaranteed for his remaining years were issues debated in Raleigh rather than the man's own living room. These conversations would have been difficult even if language did not pose a barrier.

When the court cases and settlements were fully resolved, André Branch returned to his diversity consulting work in Seattle and then moved down the West Coast to pursue a university career. Most of the Branch and Smith family did not maintain strong connections with Junius Wilson. The Sidberrys continued to see him in Goldsboro and occasionally invite him to visit them in the Wilmington area. They retained fond memories of their time with him. "I thoroughly enjoyed the relationship with Mr. Wilson," remembered Annie Sidberry. "I thought he was a beautiful person and I just loved him."[117]

The Sidberrys continued to defend Branch's lawsuit, believing that he truly wanted justice served and not personal gain. At the same time, their diverging approaches to Junius Wilson and the state served to separate family members even further than the miles already did.

From before the Branch case started until years after its resolution, Junius Wilson continued to visit the local Hardee's, attend activities on the Cherry Hospital campus and around North Carolina, and sleep under a flowered bedcover in his own bedroom. Regardless of the season, he and Parker continued their gentle communing on the front porch.

11

The End? (1997–)

I'm not sure we've changed the world. But
we've changed Mr. Wilson's world.

**JOHN WASSON, QUOTED IN GARY WRIGHT,
"DENIED TRIAL, DEAF MAN CASTRATED, LOCKED UP
FOR DECADES," *BALTIMORE SUN*, 24 JUNE 1993**

What happened with him was sad and should never happen again.
He was left for so many years. But his situation was/is not the only
one. There's considerable other anecdotal evidence about people
who have been wrongly labeled, kept wrongly in institutions for years
because their behavior seemed different. It can happen.
And America is supposed to be about freedom.

ANONYMOUS, INTERVIEW BY SUSAN BURCH, 24 AUGUST 2005

JUNIUS WILSON SPENT HIS final years as a voluntary patient residing in the cottage on Cherry Hospital's campus. Smiling, he would put a hat on and walk out to an awaiting car that would take him downtown, to baseball games, or to his friend Everett Parker's home. Wilson's medical log boasts regular trips, cottage visitors, and modest shopping sprees. It also reveals continual negotiations between the deaf man, his guardian, and Cherry staff. Efforts to obtain tobacco or sausage biscuits—small but unhealthy pleasures—often met with shaking heads. Occasionally his requests resulted in knowing winks and hidden gifts.

Residents of Goldsboro recognized Wilson as a fixture. Pity coated the lens through which many citizens—black and white—observed the deaf man and his small team of caretakers as they lunched in local restaurants, shopped in local stores, or otherwise skirted the edges of social life in the town.[1]

IN THE WINTER OF 2000, Wilson's health declined markedly. Trips back and forth to a local hospital confirmed that he had pneumonia.[2] He seemed to be fading away. Cherry staff and Wilson's guardians debated how best to serve his needs. Hinn admitted, "There was talk [that] he needed to be back in the facility," meaning the nursing unit of the hospital, but the guardian of Wilson's estate wanted him to stay in his house. "I yelled and screamed," she

Wilson in front of his cottage (Courtesy of Everett Parker)

said, "but it became apparent that his needs were greater than could be met in the house." In the end she conceded that "it was clear his health was declining and he wouldn't rally."[3]

It is unknown how much, if at all, staff explained to Wilson why he was being transferred from the cottage. He had never been known for assertive questioning. His illness might have made it more difficult to communicate if he could not focus well. The move to Wayne Memorial Hospital further isolated him. Friends at Cherry, especially patients, were not able to visit him in the ward. He apparently had a room with a window, but how much he was able to appreciate the view never appeared in his medical log. Someone stayed in the room most of the time, but it was increasingly difficult—for him and his caretakers—to express what was happening and why.

A longtime aide and companion went to visit Wilson. "When I walked in the room, he smiled," remembered the Cherry employee. The elderly guest smiled back. "[Wilson] was glad to see me." The deaf man attempted to sign to his friend. He would "always do a little gesture," the man remembered, but the arms and hands were more feeble now.[4] Unversed in American Sign Language or Raleigh signs, the visitor could only talk to Wilson vocally, gesturing and perhaps patting the deaf man's arm. It was the last time they saw one another.

JUNIUS WILSON DIED of respiratory failure at Wayne Memorial Hospital on Saturday, 17 March 2001.

WHEN HELEN HINN RECEIVED the news of Wilson's passing, she and Pat Jessup went to Wayne Memorial Park to select a plot for his burial. Flowering bushes and trees dotted the trimmed grass. The waters of Legion Lake snaked lazily around the perimeter. An attendant showed them a general area that suited their needs. The women found one spot especially appealing because it reminded them of Wilson's earlier pastime. "We chose a plot near the water," Hinn explained. Wilson and coveys of patients had waded in the local rivers on hot summer days and unearthed worms to sell along their banks. Neither Hinn nor Jessup realized when they chose the location that one plot behind Wilson's future resting place was James McNeil's headstone. It read: "Julius James McNeil: 'Dummie Graham.' "

Hinn made elaborate arrangements for Wilson's funeral. His black casket gleamed with silvery metal and polished wood, many groupings of flowers were ordered, and the parlor picked a tasteful suit in which to dress him. Friends ordered additional floral arrangements, including one from staff shaped like a fish. In a nod to Wilson's old habit, onto the brightly colored petals of one arrangement, someone tacked a packet of Redman chewing tobacco.

IN THE MODEST CHAPEL at Cherry Hospital, over 100 people came to pay their respects to Wilson on Friday, 23 March.[5] Health care technicians served as pallbearers, while other staff and community members looked on.[6] John Wasson, Willie Sidberry, Marshall Smith, and other friends recounted special memories they had of this man who loved ice cream and baseball hats. To hospital administrator Marshall Smith, Wilson was a true institution. From his boyhood, Smith had known the deaf man, having purchased worms from him for his fishing trips. Smith recalled fondly, "He was industrious." In later years as a member of the Cherry community, Smith noted, "We appreciated Mr. Wilson. We loved him and we know he loved us. . . . We were like family."[7]

Other members who knew Wilson nodded in agreement.[8] Robert Kornegay, a health care technician at Cherry, sang "If I Can Help Somebody," blending the image of hospital staff's care with Wilson's own service to others. Linda Taylor stepped forward and placed her violin on her shoulder. The social worker, whose forceful persistence finally coerced the lethargic bureaucracy into treating Wilson's case in a new way, began to play "It is Well with My Soul." The hymn, composed in the 1870s by Horatio Spafford and Philip Bliss, evoked images of water, like the Cape Fear and Little Rivers that wound through all the chapters of Wilson's life. Although unspoken during Taylor's performance, the song's lyrics had great resonance:

When peace, like a river, attendeth my way,
When sorrows like sea billows roll;
Whatever my lot,
Thou has taught me to say,
It is well, it is well, with my soul.

John Wasson found the performance especially moving. Taylor "played the violin for him," he recalled, "and that was such a tribute to him. . . . It also tells me how much she cared for him."[9] From the front row of the chapel, Everett Parker watched his interpreter. He smiled gently and nodded as Taylor finished the piece, although he was unable to hear the music. Wilson's companion remained quiet and reserved throughout, paying witness to the testimony of others about his friend.

As people filtered out of the chapel, Parker reached out to Wasson. The former guardian fondly recalled, "Mr. Parker made me feel really good. . . . He squeezed my hand or something and I knew we had done the right thing."[10] Afterwards, many gathered at the riverside cemetery where Wilson's coffin was buried, facing toward his favorite fishing spot. Hinn was pleased. "It was a very dignified service."[11]

LOCAL NEWSPAPERS ACKNOWLEDGED Wilson's passing but no longer as front-page news. The headline in the obituary section of the *Raleigh News and Observer*, 21 March 2001, revealed the persistent mystery and confusion about him: "Deaf-Mute Man, Wrongly Punished, Dies: Junius Wilson Was of Unknown Age." Reporters contacted Cherry staff and Wilmington social workers. They all offered generous comments about the man as well as the institution that had kept him for so many years. One recalled fondly that Wilson "loved to laugh." Defending previous charges in the lawsuits, she continued, "He could make his needs and wants known, whether he liked it or disliked it, by his facial expression or by pulling his baseball cap down over his face." Another added that, "though he could not hear or talk, his communications using signs and gestures kept his caregivers in tune with his needs."[12] A social worker said, "People who worked with him felt like he always had a positive attitude on life."[13] The articles moved quickly through his bleak history at Cherry. One emphasized that "his last years were lived in comfort and with the opportunity to experience the association of friends and family."[14]

Some people valorized Wilson for his apparent stoic attitude in the face of stultifying oppression. "Despite his confinement and the injustice perpetrated

Pat Jessup, John Wasson, Helen Hinn, and Julia Talbutt (Photograph by Susan Burch)

upon him," one newspaper article began, "Mr. Wilson remained steadfastly optimistic and serene in his demeanor." A hospital publication read: "The beauty of Mr. Wilson's spirit is a testament to the indomitability of the human spirit."[15]

PARTICIPANTS IN WILSON'S difficult story try to express its deep meanings. Silvia Weaver, an occupational therapist, feels that Wilson's case brought "attention to the plight of the hearing impaired. Because it is a whole different culture and it's something I never thought about until his situation came to the forefront. . . . So a lot of good came from this."[16]

To advocates like Helen Hinn, the Wilson story serves as a reminder of the dangers in America's past. She is quick to point out that significant progress has also occurred: "I know today what happened to Mr. Wilson couldn't happen. Nobody calls the jailer over to the courthouse to ask, 'Is he competent?' . . . I've never come upon anything that says Mr. Wilson had an attorney for the crime, and that wouldn't happen today."[17] In this respect, Hinn is correct. Legislation since Wilson's incarceration more explicitly enforces legal representation for defendants and communication facilitation through interpreters for deaf people or others who cannot communicate in English.

As one deaf advocate stated, Wilson's example suggests even more critical analysis: "If left unchecked, those with authority can act with absurd impunity and people can lose their identity and freedom. Who gets to determine what happens to another person? People at the top levels of power had unchecked power [in the past] and that's simply dangerous. We need representation: interpreters and advocates who are determined to work with the community to protect vulnerable people like Wilson."[18] Roger Williams agrees: "It's not that this is a horrible thing that happened in the past, but that *today* deaf people are being just as isolated, and just as deprived in institutions around the country." The conclusion is "not that we should castigate North Carolina for their horrendous behavior circa 1920," he believes, "but that we need to go look at our systems today."[19]

JUNIUS WILSON'S STORY does not end with his death. According to Marshall Smith, the previous director of Cherry Hospital, policies sparked by Wilson's legal challenges and other disability class action suits promised greater protection for current and future disabled inmates across the nation. In 1994 North Carolina created a specialized treatment unit at Dix Hospital that serves deaf patients.[20] And Roger Williams, who evaluated Wilson in the 1990s, noted that a similar lawsuit in his state of South Carolina resulted the discovery of eleven patients who were deaf and who had been denied language accommodation.[21]

Reports from disability rights organizations also point to progress. In Ohio in 2005, advocates sued on behalf of a deaf client in a mental institution who had been denied an interpreter. Ultimately, the individual transferred to a facility that specifically served deaf people with mental illness.[22] Other efforts have pushed society at large to consider its treatment of those deemed "different."

IN THE YEARS SINCE Wilson's death, North Carolina has joined several other states in publicly acknowledging the long history of eugenic sterilizations. In 2001 Virginia, the state that sparked the Supreme Court case of *Buck v. Bell* when it sought to sterilize twenty-one-year-old Carrie Buck in 1927, became the first state to acknowledge publicly and then apologize for its campaign of forced sterilizations.[23] Oregon followed in early December 2002. Facing thousands of citizens sterilized under his state's program, Oregon's governor John Kitzhaber created an annual Human Rights Day to commemorate the state's "misdeeds."[24] Several days later, pressure in North Carolina escalated when the *Winston-Salem Journal* launched a five-part series titled "Against Their Will."[25] The chilling exposé, based in part on research done by historian Johanna Schoen, laid bare the systemic attempt to shape the composition and nature of the Tar Heel State's inhabitants.[26]

The reports forced a response. Governor Mike Easley issued a statement to the newspaper the following week: "This is a sad and regrettable chapter in the state's history, and it must be one that is never repeated again."[27] Activists and survivors wanted more. In the spring of 2003, the North Carolina Senate voted to remove its sterilization law. On 18 April, Easley signed off on the repeal and announced that he would establish a committee to consider ways to compensate victims of the state's eugenic program.

Since these pronouncements by Easley, the movement has stalled. Federal legislation such as the Health Insurance Protection and Portability Act, designed to protect current patients' privacy, prohibits most historical researchers from accessing any of the Eugenics Board files. Since 2005 the records from North Carolina's Eugenics Board, previously housed in the State Archives and supervised by the Department of Cultural Resources, have become the ward of the Department of Health and Human Services.[28] Repeated efforts to obtain information from these board files have not yet been successful.

Compensation also has not come to sterilized North Carolinians. Across a March 2006 *Newsweek* cover splashed the title, "A Shameful Little Secret," along with a sober picture of two African American women sterilized in the North Carolina program. The main story noted North Carolina's eugenic history and its promises made—but unfulfilled.[29]

SADLY, MANY PEOPLE CONTINUE to fall through the cracks. Six months after Junius Wilson's funeral, a news account broke in the nation's capitol that echoed Wilson's experiences. In Washington, D.C., a center of the deaf cultural community, deaf African American Joseph Heard was held in jail for nearly two years after misdemeanor charges against him had been dismissed. After his file was mistakenly labeled inactive, he was put in a solitary cell in the jail's mental health unit. Heard, who could not articulate vocally, wrote on paper to inform his jailers that he was being held wrongly. On the note he repeatedly spelled one word: "Innocent." When he was eventually freed, Heard stated in American Sign Language, "I tried to communicate and write notes and tell them that I'm innocent. The officers would look at the piece of paper and ignore it." During his incarceration, Heard's family had no idea where he was. Officials primarily blamed computer problems and case management for the gross error. Public statements by jail administrators provided conspicuously little comment on language access—much less explicit recognition of deafness or sign language— even though the jail is located about two miles from the front gates of Gallaudet University. No doubt many other deaf people remain in mental institutions and state facilities, denied signed communication and wrongly diagnosed as mentally ill or retarded or criminal primarily because of the misunderstanding of their deafness.[30]

It would be easy—though incorrect—to conclude that wrongful incarceration is merely a problem of deafness. Consider the experiences of Joe Redd, an inmate at St. Elizabeth's Hospital in Washington, D.C. Redd, who exhibited violent psychotic outbreaks as a youth, was placed in the hospital by his aunt in the summer of 1968. As deinstitutionalization spread and hundreds of patients with more severe mental illness left the wards, Redd was held in St. Elizabeth's criminal wing for twenty-three years. For eight additional years, he lived in the maximum security section. Administrators did not release the African American man even though he apparently wanted to go and was qualified for community placement. Poor and black, and lacking networks or a strong support system, many people like Redd have been lost in the system.[31] Disability lawyer Paul Pooley warns that "we still institutionalize and commit people on not very good reasons, because some people want to warehouse people today."[32]

RARELY DO WE WHO LIVE on the "outside" gain access to institutionalized people or their tales. Junius Wilson's story, while unique, is but one of many over the centuries. Attitudes and policies, as well as literal walls, keep us from knowing the details or recognizing the faces of these men, women, and children. Even this account of one such person, an account that benefited from access to private medical files as well as numerous interviews, cannot show a full portrait of Junius Wilson. He remains both real and elusive, only partly held in photographs and reports. He is a cipher in the mind's eye of each person who knew him or writes about him.

Junius Wilson's life offers powerful reminders that there are no simple answers to the thorny questions surrounding racism, poverty, policy toward people with disabilities, and institutionalization. It is not even clear how best to provide justice to those who have been wronged in the past. But Wilson's story clearly demonstrates the danger of believing that the problems of the past are behind us. As his story attests, we are inextricably bound to who we have been and what we have done as a society.

SITTING AT HOME IN HIS reclining chair with his family surrounding him, Everett Parker, Junius Wilson's deaf companion, offers perhaps the most appropriate ending to this story. "I miss him," Parker says, his eyes shining, his head nodding slowly as he looks through a scrapbook. "We were friends."

Notes

ABBREVIATIONS

AAD   *American Annals of the Deaf*

CO   *Charlotte Observer*

CRH   Clyde R. Hoey Papers, North Carolina State Archives, Raleigh

GNA   *Goldsboro News-Argus*

JCBE   J. C. B. Ehringhaus Papers, North Carolina State Archives, Raleigh

JMB   J. Melville Broughton Papers, North Carolina State Archives, Raleigh

JWMF   Junius Wilson Medical Files, Cherry Hospital, Goldsboro, N.C.

LHH   Luther H. Hodges Papers, North Carolina State Archives, Raleigh

N&O   *Raleigh News and Observer*

N&R   *Greensboro News and Record*

WMS   *Wilmington Morning Star*

WSN   *Wilmington Star-News*

INTRODUCTION

1. Anecdotal evidence of this process of socialization is so widespread in the deaf cultural community as to be considered cultural "fact." See, for example, the videotapes *Tales from a Clubroom* (Washington, D.C.: Department of Television, Film, and Photography, Gallaudet College, 1991) and *Festival of American Folklife* (Washington, D.C.: Gallaudet University Archives, S. Carmel, 1981); Susan Dell Rutherford, "A Study of American Deaf Folklore" (Ph.D. diss., University of California, Berkeley, 1987); Carol

Padden and Tom Humphries, *Deaf in America: Voices from a Culture* (Cambridge: Harvard University Press, 1988); Larry Hott (director), *Through Deaf Eyes* (PBS, 2007), documentary film; Lois Bragg, ed., *Deaf World: A Historical Reader and Primary Sourcebook* (New York: New York University Press, 2001).

2. The MindFreedom Oral History Project offers rich testimony to the experiences of individuals who have lived in mental institutions. See <http://www.mindfreedom.org/>. See also Samuel E. Wallace, ed., *Total Institutions* (Chicago: Aldine Publishing Company, 1971); and Daniel J. Levinson and Eugene B. Gallagher, *Patienthood in the Mental Hospital: An Analysis of Role, Personality, and Social Structure* (Boston: Houghton Mifflin, 1964). International studies support this, as well. See, for example, Joseph Melling and Bill Forsythe, eds., *Insanity, Institutions, and Society, 1800–1914: A Social History of Madness in Comparative Perspective* (New York: Routledge, 1999).

3. Steven Noll, *Feeble-Minded in Our Midst: Institutions for the Mentally Retarded in the South, 1900–1940* (Chapel Hill: University of North Carolina Press, 1995); Peter McCandless, *Moonlight, Magnolias, and Madness: Insanity in South Carolina from the Colonial Period to the Progressive Era* (Chapel Hill: University of North Carolina Press, 1996).

4. Erving Goffman, *Asylums: Essays on the Social Situation of Mental Patients and Other Inmates* (Garden City, N.Y.: Anchor Books, 1961); *Stigma: Notes on the Management of Spoiled Identity* (Englewood Cliffs, N.J.: Prentice-Hall, 1963).

5. Gerald N. Grob has produced numerous works in the field of institutional history. See, for example, *From Asylum to Community: Mental Health Policy in Modern America* (Princeton: Princeton University Press, 1991); *The Mad Among Us: A History of the Care of America's Mentally Ill* (New York: Free Press, 1994); *Mental Illness and American Society, 1875–1940* (Princeton: Princeton University Press, 1983); and *The State and the Mentally Ill: A History of Worcester State Hospital in Massachusetts, 1830–1920* (Chapel Hill: University of North Carolina Press, 1966).

6. See, for example, Paul Longmore and Lauri Umansky, eds., *The New Disability History* (New York: New York University Press, 2001); Steven Noll and James W. Trent Jr., eds., *Mental Retardation in America: A Historical Reader* (New York: New York University Press, 2004); Hugh Gregory Gallagher, *FDR's Splendid Deception: The Moving Story of Roosevelt's Massive Disability and the Intense Efforts to Conceal It from the Public* (Arlington, Va.: Vandamere Press, 1999); Kim Nielsen, *The Radical Lives of Helen Keller* (New York: New York University Press, 2004); Susan Burch, *Signs of Resistance: American Deaf Cultural History, 1900 to World War II* (New York: New York University Press, 2002).

7. For more on deaf culture, see Padden and Humphries, *Deaf in America*; and John Van Cleve and Barry Crouch, *A Place of Their Own* (Washington, D.C.: Gallaudet University Press, 1989).

8. For example, see Fitzhugh Brundage's *The Southern Past: A Clash of Race and Memory* (Cambridge, Mass.: Belknap Press of Harvard University Press, 2005); *Where These Memories Grow: History, Memory, and Southern Identity* (Chapel Hill: University of North Carolina Press, 2000); *Lynching in the New South: Georgia and Virginia, 1880–*

1930 (Urbana: University of Illinois Press, 1993); and his edited work, *Under Sentence of Death: Lynching in the South* (Chapel Hill: University of North Carolina Press, 1997).

9. See Glenda Elizabeth Gilmore, *Gender and Jim Crow: Women and the Politics of White Supremacy in North Carolina, 1896–1920* (Chapel Hill: University of North Carolina Press, 1996); Jane Dailey, Glenda Elizabeth Gilmore, and Bryant Simon, eds., *Jumpin' Jim Crow: Southern Politics from Civil War to Civil Rights* (Princeton: Princeton University Press, 2000); Jacquelyn Dowd Hall et al., *Like a Family: The Making of a Southern Cotton Mill World* (Chapel Hill: University of North Carolina Press, 1987); Jacquelyn Dowd Hall, *Revolt against Chivalry: Jessie Daniel Ames and the Women's Campaign against Lynching* (New York: Columbia University Press, 1979); Jennifer Ritterhouse, *Growing Up Jim Crow: How Black and White Southern Children Learned Race* (Chapel Hill: University of North Carolina Press, 2006).

10. Melton McLaurin, *Celia, a Slave* (Athens: University of Georgia Press, 1991); Suzanne Lebsock, *A Murder in Virginia: Southern Justice on Trial* (New York: W. W. Norton, 2003).

11. Katherine Castles, "Quiet Eugenics: Sterilization in North Carolina's Institutions for the Mentally Retarded, 1945–1965," *Journal of Southern History* 68 (November 2002): 849–78.

12. Johanna Schoen, *Choice and Coercion: Birth Control, Sterilization, and Abortion in Public Health and Welfare* (Chapel Hill: University of North Carolina Press, 2005).

13. See Schoen, *Choice and Coercion*; Noll, *Feeble-Minded in Our Midst*; Castles, "Quiet Eugenics"; and Edward Larson, *Sex, Race, and Science: Eugenics in the Deep South* (Baltimore: Johns Hopkins University Press, 1995).

CHAPTER ONE

1. Daniel Nixon, interview by Susan Burch, 20 March 2002; Willie and Annie Sidberry, interview by Susan Burch, 20 March 2002. A neighbor stated that her home got electricity in 1955 and running water in 1973.

2. Various documents spell her name differently. For the sake of consistency, we will refer to her as "Asynia."

3. The 1880 census suggests that Johanna Nixon Foy's first husband Edmund died in 1880, suggesting that her second husband Nathaniel was Mary's actual father. See *United States Census of Population, 1880*, North Carolina: New Hanover County, Cape Fear Township, sheet 181C, E.D. 148; Apex, Ware, E.D. 279, line 1. Mary's mother Joanne was also called Johanna in various documents. She was listed as "Johanner Nixon" in the 1870 census, along with apparent relatives Kenny, James, James B., Fannie, Jane, and Mary. See *United States Census of Population, 1870*, North Carolina: New Hanover County, Harnett Township, p. 10, lines 6–12.

4. In the 1900 U.S. Census, Johanna is listed as the head of her family. In 1910 Nathaniel had returned and was working as a carpenter.

5. *United States Census of Population, 1900*, North Carolina: New Hanover County, Cape Fear Township, S.D. 3, E.D. 61, lines 1–7; *United States Census of Population, 1900*, North Carolina: New Hanover County, Cape Fear Township, S.D. 11, E.D. 61, sheet 11,

lines 40–41. Mary Clark's death certificate lists Nathaniel Foy as her father, but neither the 1890 and 1990 census materials nor her mother's marriage certificate list Nathaniel. James and Annie Wilson can be found in *United States Census of Population, 1900*, North Carolina: New Hanover County, Craven Township, p. 17A, lines 34–41. It is suspected that the one child not listed in the family may be Sidney.

6. *United States Census of Population, 1880*, North Carolina: Pender County, Grant Township, E.D. 159, S.D. 3, sheet 33, lines 41–43. There is also a "Lucy Wilson" who was a cook, but her relationship to Sidney, if any existed, is uncertain.

7. The Wilson and extended Smith family lived along the same road. See *United States Census of Population, 1910*, North Carolina: New Hanover County, Cape Fear Township, sheet 15A, E.D. 18, S.D. 6, lines 10–33.

8. Paul D. Escott, *Many Excellent People: Power and Privilege in North Carolina, 1850– 1900* (Chapel Hill: University of North Carolina Press, 1985), 3–20.

9. William McFee Evans, *Ballots and Fence Rails: Reconstruction on the Lower Cape Fear* (Athens: University of Georgia Press, 1995), 33–50, 50–62.

10. Evans, *Ballots and Fence Rails*, 63–101.

11. Ibid., 94–102; Hugh Talmage Lefler and Albert Ray Newsome, *North Carolina: The History of a Southern State* (Chapel Hill: University of North Carolina Press, 1973), 538; Manuel Houston Crockett and Barbara Crockett Dease, *Through the Years, 1867–1977— Light out of Darkness: A History of the North Carolina School for the Negro Blind and the Deaf* (Raleigh: Barefoot Press, 1990).

12. Evans, *Ballots and Fence Rails*, 120, 137; Glenda Gilmore, *Gender and Jim Crow: Women and the Politics of White Supremacy in North Carolina, 1896–1920* (Chapel Hill: University of North Carolina Press, 1996), 21; H. Leon Prather, *We Have Taken a City: Wilmington Racial Massacre and Coup of 1898* (Cranbury, N.J.: Associated University Presses, 1984), 19–29; John L. Godwin, *Black Wilmington and the North Carolina Way: Portrait of a Community in the Era of Civil Rights Protest* (Lanham, Md.: University Press of America, 2000), 15–16.

13. Evans, *Ballots and Fence Rails*, 150–55; Godwin, *Black Wilmington and the North Carolina Way*, 15–16; Gilmore, *Gender and Jim Crow*, 21; Prather, *We Have Taken a City*, 30–33.

14. Prather, *We Have Taken a City*, 33–35. Prather states that according to "an often repeated claim," after the 1896 Fusion victory, there were more than 1,000 African American state officeholders. See also David S. Cecelski and Timothy B. Tyson, eds., *Democracy Betrayed: The Wilmington Race Riot of 1898 and Its Legacy* (Chapel Hill: University of North Carolina Press, 1998).

15. Laura F. Edwards, "Love, Hate, Rape, Lynching: Rebecca Latimer Felton and the Gender Politics of Racial Violence," in *Democracy Betrayed*, ed. David S. Cecelski and Timothy B. Tyson.

16. Cecelski and Tyson, eds., *Democracy Betrayed*, 23.

17. Ibid., 28.

18. Ibid., 34.

19. Prather, *We Have Taken a City*, 181.

20. William H. Chafe, Raymond Gavins, and Robert Korstad, eds., *Remembering Jim Crow: African Americans Tell about Life in the Segregated South* (New York: New Press, 2001), 57. See also Prather, *We Have Taken a City*; Leslie H. Hossfeld, *Narrative, Political Unconscious, and Racial Violence in Wilmington, North Carolina* (New York: Routledge, 2005).

21. James S. Hirsch, *Race and Remembrance: The Tulsa Race War and Its Legacy* (Boston: Houghton Mifflin Company, 2002), 55–56; Philip Dray, *At the Hands of Persons Unknown: The Lynching of Black America* (New York: Random House, 2002), 163. See also Alfred L. Brophy, *Reconstructing the Dreamland: The Tulsa Riot of 1921: Race, Reparations, and Reconciliation* (Oxford: Oxford University Press, 2002).

22. See Ida B. Wells, *Southern Horrors and Other Writings*, ed. Jacqueline Jones Royster (Boston: Bedford Books, 1997).

23. David Carter, "Outraged Justice: The Lynching of Postmaster Frazier Baker in Lake City, South Carolina, 1897–1899" (undergraduate history honors thesis, University of North Carolina at Chapel Hill, 1992); Bruce E. Baker, "North Carolina Lynching Ballads," in *Under Sentence of Death: Lynching in the South*, ed. W. Fitzhugh Brundage (Chapel Hill: University of North Carolina Press, 1997); Joel Williamson, *The Crucible of Race: Black-White Relations in the American South since Emancipation* (New York: Oxford University Press, 1984), 117–18, 190–91.

24. Baker, "North Carolina Lynching Ballads," 221–22.

25. Chafe, Gavins, and Korstad, eds., *Remembering Jim Crow*, 57; see also Jennifer Ritterhouse, *Growing Up Jim Crow: How Black and White Southern Children Learned Race* (Chapel Hill: University of North Carolina Press, 2006).

26. It appears that the name changed later to Holly Shelter Road. Annie Sidberry, interview by Susan Burch, 20 March 2002.

27. Junius Wilson Student File, School for the Deaf Archives, Raleigh School Files, Morganton, N.C.

28. Parents of deaf children commonly describe similar experiences.

29. *United States Census of Population, 1920*, Georgia: Ware County, Waycross Township, sheet 1A, E.D. 150, S.D. 55, lines 14–15, Sidney Wilson and Avery Wilson.

30. Thomas Dixon Jr., *The Leopard's Spots: A Romance of the White Man's Burden* (Ridgewood, N.J.: The Gregg Press, 1967), 354, 415, 417–18. An excellent analysis of the parallels between *The Leopard's Spots* and the Wilmington riot can be found in Gilmore, *Gender and Jim Crow*, 135–36.

31. Thomas Dixon Jr., *The Clansman* (Ridgewood, N.J: Gregg Press, 1967; originally published in 1905 by Doubleday, Page and Co.), 312–14.

32. Woodrow Wilson, *History of the American People* (New York, London: Harper and Brothers, 1902); Williamson, *The Crucible of Race*, 154.

33. It is also possible that educational options were not a major consideration for the family.

34. Anecdotes abound in the deaf world of children's traumatic first days and months at deaf schools. Many individuals describe a slow process of acclimating to the residential institution and eventual affection for peers there. See Larry Hott (director), *Through Deaf Eyes* (PBS, 2007).

35. North Carolina School for the Deaf and Dumb, *Ninth Biennial Record* (1907–8), 12–13; Junius Wilson School Report, North Carolina State School for the Negro Deaf and Blind Student Files, School for the Deaf Archives, Raleigh School Files, Morganton, N.C.

36. "School Items," *AAD* 63 (1918): 223; "The First State School for the Deaf," *AAD* 63, no. 2 (March 1923): 97–120.

37. "Miscellaneous," *AAD* 61 (1916): 285. See also Hannah Joyner, *From Pity to Pride: Growing Up Deaf in the Old South* (Washington, D.C.: Gallaudet University Press, 2004).

38. "Mrs. Blanche (Wilkins) Williams," *Silent Worker* 38, no. 5 (February 1926): 225. Williams's husband died suddenly in 1907. Once her children completed grammar school, she moved north. A passionate Christian missionary, Williams was an outspoken advocate for her race and her deaf peers. Some considered her "the most accomplished deaf lady of her race in America."

39. Thomas Flowers, "The Education of the Colored Deaf," in *Proceedings of the Conference of American Instructors of the Deaf, 1914* (Washington, D.C.: U.S. Government Printing Office, 1915), 100–101.

40. Joseph Lacy Sewell, "The Only Negro Deaf Mute Lawyer," *Silent Worker* 39, no. 6 (March 1927): 169–70; "Deaf Mute Made Lawyer," *Silent Worker* 2, no. 10 (July 1909): n.p.

41. Data are conflicting. Statistical data on schools in the *American Annals of the Deaf* (1918) note one deaf educator at the school. School documents, however, stop listing Flowers as a faculty member after 1916. For information on Flowers and Williams in Chicago, see *Mt. Airy World*, 30 September 1920, 7.

42. "Colored School," *Report of the State School for the Blind and the Deaf, 1916–1918* (Raleigh: Edwards & Broughton Printing Co., 1918).

43. For more on the impact of oralism, see Susan Burch, *Signs of Resistance: American Deaf Cultural History, 1900 to World War II* (New York: New York University Press, 2002); and John Van Cleve and Barry Crouch, *A Place of Their Own* (Washington, D.C.: Gallaudet University Press, 1989).

44. Lineberry, a white native of Chatham County, a graduate of Wake Forest College, and former president of Chowan College from 1914 to 1918, had served eleven years as a board member for the Raleigh school. See Otis Betts, *The North Carolina School for the Deaf at Morganton, 1894–1944* (Morganton, N.C.: North Carolina School for the Deaf, 1945), 26; "Gustavus Ernest Lineberry," in *Dictionary of North Carolina Biography*, vol. 4, ed. William S. Powell (Chapel Hill: University of North Carolina Press, 1991), 69–70; "School," *AAD* 64 (1919): 80. Before 1939, there were no courses for African American teachers of the deaf and blind. Helen Clark Thomas, "A Study of the Educational Opportunities Offered in the Negro and White Departments of the Schools for the Deaf in the Southern Region" (master's thesis, Hampton Institute, 1950), app. D.

45. Crockett and Dease, *Through the Years*, 23–25.

46. Ibid., 23.

47. See, for example, *Report of the State School for the Blind and the Deaf, 1914–1916* (Raleigh: Edwards & Brothers, 1916), 44. Subsequent reports repeat the same claims. There is reason to question even the modest assertions made in these annual publications. State reports are notoriously unmatched to the actual experience of teaching and

learning at the schools involved. Schools often boasted of a "rigorous curriculum" in bureaucratic documents, even if no such thing was provided to the average student.

48. Crockett and Dease, *Through the Years*, 21.

49. Ibid., 22; *Report of the State School for the Blind and the Deaf, 1914–1916*, 43.

50. Crockett and Dease, *Through the Years*, 25.

51. Flowers, "The Education of the Colored Deaf," 100–101.

52. North Carolina School for the Negro Deaf and Blind Student Files, School for the Deaf Archives, Raleigh School Files, Morganton, N.C.; *Report of the State School for the Blind and the Deaf, 1914–1916*, 43.

53. It appears that distinct language systems developed in many of the other segregated schools for African American deaf children. Consequently, students from one black deaf school likely would not fully understand students from any other school for the deaf—black or white. Further research is needed to verify the extent of the linguistic variation between segregated deaf schools, as well as the impact of Jim Crow on African American deaf communities. For more general information on black sign language, see James Woodward Jr., "Black Southern Signing," *Language in Society* 5 (1975): 211–18; John Lewis, Carrie Palmer, and Leandra Williams, "Existence of and Attitudes toward Black Variations of Sign Language," in *Communication Forum 1995: School of Communication Student Forum*, vol. 4, ed. Laura Byers, Jessica Chaiken, and Monica Mueller (Washington, D.C.: School of Communication, 1995); Anthony J. Aramburo, "Sociolinguistic Aspects of the Black Deaf Community," in *The Sociolinguistics of the Deaf Community*, ed. Ceil Lucas (New York: Academic Press, Inc., 1989); Ceil Lucas, Robert Bayley, and Clayton Valli, *Sociolinguistic Variation in American Sign Language* (Washington, D.C.: Gallaudet University Press, 2001).

54. Susan Burch, personal correspondence with Rachel Wright, April 2001. Paul Schreyer, a deaf linguist and interpreter trainer who assessed Wilson, supports this claim. Paul Schreyer, interview by Susan Burch, 13 December 2004.

55. Susan Burch, personal correspondence with Rachel Wright, April 2001. As Roger Williams, a social worker brought in to evaluate Wilson, explained: "The schools being segregated, [Wilson's] school did not have access to the same quality of teachers and as a result, the school kind of made up its own sign language, if you will. In part there is an American Sign Language vocabulary component, but there are also signs that sort of the school made up over the years. . . . There are one or two signs that are sort of unique to that school [other residential schools]. But because [the school] was so segregated, that was true even more so, and so the students kind of taught themselves sign and it was kind of handed down over the years." Roger Williams, deposition, 11 December 1995, 13.

56. At the school Wilson also learned to finger spell his name, enforcing the understanding that he had a distinct identity.

57. They also state explicitly that he was not mentally deficient. See Barry Critchfield, deposition, 11 December 1995, 45. Rachel Wright evaluated Wilson in 1981 and noted that he could finger spell, sign, and write, and that his "education has suffered loss due to lack of persons to communicate appropriately in his language." She continued: "He was putting a huge complex jig-saw puzzle together when the social worker and I first visited

him." Through signs he was able to communicate about his work, where he was from, that he had not seen his family in a long time, etc. Rachel Wright, Evaluation Summary, 13 May 1981, JWMF; Rachel Wright, interview by Susan Burch, 6 August 2003; Paul Schreyer, interview by Susan Burch, 13 December 2004.

58. This kind of cultural expression was common at virtually all residential deaf schools during the nineteenth and twentieth centuries. Graduates of both African American and white schools offer similar anecdotes about school life. Everett Parker, interview by Susan Burch, 21 March 2002; Jack Gannon, *Deaf Heritage* (Silver Spring, Md.: National Association of the Deaf, 1981). For more on the school Wilson attended, see Crockett and Dease, *Through the Years*. For more on American deaf culture in general, see Carol Padden and Tom Humphries, *Deaf in America: Voices from a Culture* (Cambridge: Harvard University Press, 1988); and Carol Padden and Tom Humphries, *Inside Deaf Culture* (Cambridge: Harvard University Press, 2005).

59. His student records for 1922 to 1924 do not recognize any extended absence from the school.

60. W. C. Linville letter to Mr. J. S. Tant, 6 November 1918, Governor Morehead School Principal's Office, Correspondence of Principals, 1897–1921, North Carolina State Archives, Raleigh; G. E. Lineberry, correspondence, September–December 1918, North Carolina State Archives, Raleigh.

61. Interviews with individuals who knew Wilson in the 1920s described outbursts by the deaf boy when he could not communicate with other children. Commonly, communication barriers have motivated conflict between deaf and hearing people.

62. There is anecdotal evidence that Wilson was close to his younger sister Carrie. He also was known for his love of fishing, a skill he probably gained as a young boy in Castle Hayne.

63. In later years, Wilson described his affection for the school and his friends there. Roger Williams, phone interview by Susan Burch, 22 July 2005.

64. It is possible that he returned in 1919, or never left, but the student form explicitly states that he reentered in 1920. For information about the Red Summer of 1919, see William M. Tuttle Jr., *Race Riot: Chicago in the Red Summer of 1919* (Urbana: University of Illinois Press, 1970; Illini Books edition, 1996); Arthur I. Waskow, *From Race Riot to Sit-In* (Garden City, N.Y.: Doubleday and Co., 1966); Grif Stockley, *Blood in Their Eyes: The Elaine Race Massacres of 1919* (Fayetteville: University of Arkansas Press, 2001); and Lee E. Williams and Lee E. Williams II, *Anatomy of Four Race Riots: Racial Conflict in Knoxville, Elaine (Arkansas), Tulsa, and Chicago, 1919–1921* (Hattiesburg: University and College Press of Mississippi, 1972).

65. R. W. Kilgore, "Some Results of Fair Work in North Carolina" (Raleigh: Agricultural Extension Service, 1919); "Unusual Crowds at Negro Fair," *N&O*, 24 October 1924; "Negro Fair Will Open on Tuesday," *N&O*, 19 October 1924; "Negro Fair Has Finest Exhibits," *N&O*, 22 October 1924; "Negro Fair Has a Good Opening," *N&O*, 23 October 1924. An advertisement for the Negro State Fair in Raleigh (21–24 October) claims that "All Roads Lead to the Negro State Fair"; "Horse Races: Steeple Chase, Running, and Trotting Races Daily"; "At Night: Fireworks; Brilliant, Unusual, and Costly Pyrotechnic

Display." *Norfolk (Va.) Journal and Guide*, 11 October 1924 (Duke University Archives, box S137).

66. Junius Wilson Student Record, North Carolina School for the Deaf and Blind, Negro Department, School for the Deaf Archives, Raleigh School Files, Morganton, N.C.

67. Decades later, Wilson described being drawn to the fair. One of his interviewers said that Wilson "wanted to go . . . and wasn't supposed to and got in trouble." Roger Williams, interview by Susan Burch, September 2001.

68. Roger Williams, interview by Susan Burch, September 2001 and 22 July 2005.

69. Wilson never expressed any hostility toward the school, but he showed great interest in meeting other alumni of the institution. He told interviewers that he liked the school and missed his friends there. Roger Williams, interview by Susan Burch, 22 July 2005.

70. During later interviews, Wilson postulated that he must have been sent to the insane asylum because he had stayed at the state fair. He believed that all of the different punishments he received stemmed from that act. Roger Williams, interview by Susan Burch, 22 July 2005.

71. Junius Wilson Student File no. 313, State School for the Negro Blind and Deaf, School for the Deaf Archives, Raleigh School Files, Morganton, N.C.

CHAPTER TWO

1. <http://www.filmsite.org/birt.html>. Also see Anthony Slide, *American Racist: The Life and Films of Thomas Dixon* (Lexington: University Press of Kentucky, 2004); Raymond Allen Cook, *Fire from the Flint: The Amazing Careers of Thomas Dixon* (Winston-Salem, N.C.: John F. Blair, 1968); Joel Williamson, *The Crucible of Race: Black-White Relations in the American South since Emancipation* (New York: Oxford University Press, 1977); John Hope Franklin, "*The Birth of a Nation*: Propaganda as History," in *Race and History: Selected Essays, 1938–1988*, ed. John Hope Franklin (Baton Rouge: Louisiana State University Press, 1989).

2. John L. Godwin, *Black Wilmington and the North Carolina Way: Portrait of a Community in the Era of Civil Rights Protest* (Lanham, Md.: University Press of America, 2000), 25–26. Godwin points out another reason for the popularity of rallies: "Klan rallies attended by thousands held at local beaches also provided a crude form of entertainment for those who were dazzled by the image of burning crosses shot into the nighttime sky" (26). For more information about Wilmington during this period, see H. Leon Prather, *We Have Taken a City: Wilmington Racial Massacre and Coup of 1898* (Cranbury, N.J.: Associated University Presses, 1984); David S. Cecelski and Timothy B. Tyson, eds., *Democracy Betrayed: The Wilmington Race Riot of 1893 and Its Legacy* (Chapel Hill: University of North Carolina Press, 1998); Joel Williamson, *The Crucible of Race: Black-White Relations in the American South since Emancipation* (New York: Oxford University Press, 1977); and Glenda Elizabeth Gilmore, *Gender and Jim Crow: Women and the Politics of White Supremacy in North Carolina, 1896–1920* (Chapel Hill: University of North Carolina Press, 1996). The Klan continued to have a national presence through the 1920s but it became especially powerful in the South. Some sources suggest that Klan membership was as high as 8 million by 1925.

3. Godwin, *Black Wilmington and the North Carolina Way*, 25–26.

4. Certificate of Marriage, Henry Clark and Mary Wilson, 13 March 1917, New Hanover County Courthouse, Indexed Register of Marriages, Wilmington, N.C.

5. Vital Records, New Hanover County Courthouse, Indexed Register of Marriages, Wilmington, N.C.; *United States Census of Population, 1930*, North Carolina: New Hanover County, E.D. 65–2, S.D. 12, sheet 2B, line 51.

6. *United States Census of Population, 1920*, North Carolina: New Hanover County, Cape Fear Township, S.D. 6, E.D. 89, sheet 2B, lines 1–7.

7. It was a common misconception that deaf people could be barred from marrying either deaf or hearing people. Most deaf individuals who attended residential schools during the nineteenth and twentieth centuries married classmates.

8. Daniel Nixon, interview by Susan Burch, 20 March 2002.

9. Data from census rolls frequently are unreliable in this regard. The censuses between 1910 and 1930 offer conflicting evidence for the extended Wilson and Smith families. The 1930 census showed that Lizzie Smith could read and write but Arthur Smith and Mary Clark could not.

10. Annie Sidberry, interview by Susan Burch, 20 March 2002.

11. Daniel Nixon, interview by Susan Burch, 20 March 2002.

12. Robert W. McCulloch, "Castle Hayne: A Study of an Experiment in the Colonization of Foreign-Born Farmers in North Carolina," in *Immigrant Farmers and Their Children*, ed. Edmund Des. Brunner (Garden City, N.Y.: Doubleday, Dorn & Company, 1929), 139–54.

13. Jennifer Ritterhouse, "Learning Race: Racial Etiquette and the Socialization of Children in the Jim Crow South" (Ph.D. diss., University of North Carolina–Chapel Hill, 1999); Jennifer Ritterhouse, *Growing Up Jim Crow: How Black and White Southern Children Learned Race* (Chapel Hill: University of North Carolina Press, 2006).

14. Roger Williams, interview by Susan Burch, September 2001, suggested that at most Wilson looked Lizzie Smith over. Jennie Bowman, Wilson's niece, suggests the same. Jennie Bowman, deposition, 19 December 1995, 20.

15. Annie May Williams, deposition, 24 May 1996, 17, lines 11–14. Williams also claimed that Arthur Smith was the cause of Wilson's tribulations.

16. Witnesses for the state in Wilson's arrest included Lizzie Smith (his "aunt"), Arthur Smith ("uncle"), Mary Clark (mother), Jim Smith (Arthur's brother), Estelle Riggins (a cousin), and Jim Nelson and Herbert Nixon (African American neighbors). The charge was attempt to commit rape; charged 16 November 1925. Relatives like Jennie Bowman later suggested in court depositions that the charges were false. Jennie Bowman, deposition, 19 December 1995, 20–22.

17. A relative not present at the time but who later spoke with Mary Wilson Clark about the incident suggests that Wilson's mother may have been forewarned about the warrant. See Jennie Bowman, deposition, 19 December 1995, 20.

18. Jennie Bowman, deposition, 19 December 1995; Annie Mae Williams, deposition, 24 May 1996; Fannie Thomas, deposition, 8 May 1996.

19. Deciding to send relatives away—to institutions or jail—often involves numerous

factors. There is considerable anecdotal evidence and some secondary scholarly material on families who chose to institutionalize disabled relatives. See, for example, M. Friedberger, " 'The Decision to Institutionalize': Families with Exceptional Children in 1900," *Journal of Family History* 6 (1981): 396–409. Mary Austin institutionalized her daughter, who was developmentally disabled, in 1904. Her autobiography, *Earth's Horizon* (1932), includes a discussion of this difficult decision. Other studies provide an international context, but many reveal common factors that influenced families' decisions. See, for example, L. Morrison, "Ceausescu's Legacy: Family Struggles and Institutionalization of Children in Romania," *Journal of Family History* 29, no. 2 (April 2004): 168–82.

20. Lisa Lindquist Dorr, *White Women, Rape, and the Power of Race in Virginia, 1900–1960* (Chapel Hill: University of North Carolina Press, 2004); Michael J. Pfeifer, *Rough Justice: Lynching and American Society, 1874–1947* (Urbana: University of Illinois Press, 2004).

21. *State of North Carolina v. Junius Wilson, 1925*, State Courthouse Files, Raleigh, N.C.

22. No evidence could be located that Cook had any deaf relatives or friends. Many people assume universality in gestural communication, and it is possible that Cook in fact knew no authentic signed languages.

23. It is unclear from the available information whether the family did not disclose this information or whether this information merely was not documented or acknowledged by the courts. Repeatedly, relevant information about Wilson's identity, mental status, and other personal data was lost or misreported in state institutional documents.

24. *State of North Carolina v. Junius Wilson, 1925*. The quotations "coherent," "intelligent," and "dangerous" are from the questions asked by attorney Woodus Kellum in the trial. Carl Cook responded that those words were accurate.

25. For more on Britt, see his entry in *The Lonely Road: A History of the Physicks and Physicians of the Lower Cape Fear, 1735–1976* (N.C.: Research and Romance of Medicine Committee of the Auxiliary to the Medical Society of New Hanover, Brunswick, and Pender Counties, 1977).

26. *State of North Carolina v. Junius Wilson, 1925*. All of the following information about the lunacy jury is from this document. There is no evidence in the record that Junius Wilson had a lawyer to represent his own interests.

27. Distinctions and confusions between lunacy and idiocy have a long history. See, for example, James Trent, *Inventing the Feeble Mind: A History of Mental Retardation in the United States* (Los Angeles: University of California Press, 1994); Steven Noll, *Feeble-Minded in Our Midst: Institutions for the Mentally Retarded in the South, 1900–1940* (Chapel Hill: University of North Carolina Press, 1995); Peter McCandless, *Moonlight, Magnolias, and Madness: Insanity in South Carolina from the Colonial Period to the Progressive Era* (Chapel Hill: University of North Carolina Press, 1996). For more on Kellum, see New Hanover Public Library, *Biographical Sketches of Wilmington Citizens*, "Woodus Kellam," 209.

28. *WMS*, 1 November 1925, 13.

29. For more on the judge, see William S. Powell, ed., *Dictionary of North Carolina Biography*, vol. 2 (Chapel Hill: University of North Carolina Press, 1986), 11–12.

30. *State of North Carolina v. Junius Wilson, 1925*, attachment 1. Different state documents call the institution by various names, including the Asylum for Colored Insane, Eastern North Carolina Insane Asylum, the State Hospital for Insane (Negroes), Goldsboro, the Eastern Asylum for the Colored Race at Goldsboro, and the State Hospital in Goldsboro. In 1961 it became Cherry Hospital.

31. David White, "Cherry Hospital: History Report" (Goldsboro, N.C.: Cherry Hospital Museum), 21–22.

32. As suggested by the *Biennial Report of the State Hospital at Goldsboro* (1924–26), 6.

33. "Superintendent's Report," *Biennial Report of the State Hospital at Goldsboro* (1924–26), 5.

34. *Legislative Report*, 1906–8, cited in White, "Cherry Hospital," 18.

35. The cages were not removed until 1957. Cecil Cahoon II, "Cages, Electric Shock Treatments Are History," *GNA*, 5 October 1993.

36. *Biennial Report of the State Hospital at Goldsboro* (1924–26), 17.

37. In 1927, only two years after Wilson's arrival, inspectors expressed deep concern that a wing in the dilapidated building would collapse. *A Study of Mental Health in North Carolina: Report to the North Carolina Legislature of the Governor's Commission, Appointed to Study the Care of the Insane and Mental Defectives* (Ann Arbor: Edwards Brothers, 1937), 231.

38. Descriptions of the bull pen differ. One hospital report claims that the living room area of the ward was reconfigured each day to serve as the "bull pen." Pictures of patients at Cherry Hospital's Museum show fenced-in yards that also might have been called "bull pens."

39. Ken Plummer, "Cherry Hospital: 10 Decades of Growth," *GNA*, 4 July 1976.

40. *A Study of Mental Health in North Carolina*, 232–33; White, "Cherry Hospital," 16. Between 1924 and 1926, twenty-three male patients entered the criminal insane unit, and eleven from the total male population in the criminal unit had died. "Showing Movement of Criminal Insane for Two Years Ending June 30, 1926," *Biennial Report of the State Hospital at Goldsboro* (1924–26), 9.

41. H. Jack Allen described patients in the 1950s carrying used chamber pots out of their rooms every morning. H. Jack Allen, interview by Susan Burch, 11 August 2005. Hospital employee Garde Parson recalled visiting the criminal ward—probably in the 1940s or 1950s—when she was a little girl. "It was a horrible place," she said. Cells were so small that "you could hardly turn around in them." She remembered that "people were always escaping." Frightened by the "very violent patients" and the traumatic conditions, she refused to go in the ward again. Garde Parson, interview by Susan Burch, 16 August 2004.

42. M. H. Greenhill, "Inspection of the State Hospital at Goldsboro by the North Carolina State Board of Pubic Welfare," March and November 1948, 2; Robert Whitaker notes that the influx of diverse populations generally doomed hospitals to poor treatment. Robert Whitaker, *Mad in America: Bad Science, Bad Medicine, and the Enduring Mistreatment of the Mentally Ill* (Cambridge, Mass.: Perseus Publishing, 2002).

43. *Biennial Report of the State Hospital at Goldsboro* (1924–1926), 5.

44. "Superintendent's Report," *Biennial Report of the State Hospital at Goldsboro* (1924–26), 5, 16.

45. Erving Goffman offers a cogent description of patient treatment in asylums like Goldsboro Hospital. See Erving Goffman, *Asylums: Essays on the Social Situation of Mental Patients and Other Inmates* (Garden City, N.J.: Anchor Books, 1961), 6–7.

46. Daniel Nixon, interview by Susan Burch, 20 March 2002. Goffman argues that especially in mental asylums, "statements made by inmates are often discounted as mere symptoms, with staff giving attention to non-verbal aspects of his reply." Goffman, *Asylums*, n. 45.

47. Plummer, "Cherry Hospital: 10 Decades of Growth."

48. *A Study of Mental Health in North Carolina*, 166.

49. Ibid.

50. Cahoon, "Cages, Electric Shock Treatments Are History."

51. For deeper study of attendants, see, for example, Whitaker, *Mad in America*, 35; Elizabeth Lunbeck, *The Psychiatric Persuasion: Knowledge, Gender, and Power in Modern America* (Princeton: Princeton University Press, 1995); David J. Rothman, *Conscience and Convenience: The Asylum and Its Alternatives in Progressive America* (Boston: Little, Brown and Company, 1980), 22–23.

52. Gerald N. Grob, *Mental Illness and American Society, 1875–1940* (Princeton: Princeton University Press, 1983), 15.

53. Clark R. Cahow, *People, Patients, and Politics: The History of the North Carolina Mental Hospitals, 1848–1960* (New York: Arno Press, 1980), iv.

54. The North Carolina State Board of Charities and Public Welfare in 1921 created a Bureau of Mental Health and Hygiene. "The authority of the new division, however, was minimal since the state as a whole functioned under a highly decentralized system that left authority in the hands of independent institutional boards." Grob, *Mental Illness and American Society*, 213–14.

55. For more on this dynamic, see Grob, *Mental Illness and American Society*, 22.

56. Nathan O'Berry, "Letter of Transmittal," *Biennial Report of the State Hospital at Goldsboro* (1924–26), 4.

57. O'Berry, "Letter of Transmittal," 3.

58. White, "Cherry Hospital," 6. The practice of attempting to cut per capita costs despite continual hospital population increase was maintained in order to persuade the legislature to appropriate funds for physical expansion. Cahow, *People, Patients, and Politics*, 41.

59. O'Berry, "Letter of Transmittal," 3.

60. Ibid., 4.

61. *A Study of Mental Health in North Carolina* (1937), 237; "Dr. W. C. Linville, Superintendent of State Hospital, Dies at Home," *GNA*, 20 August 1938; "States Leaders Attend Rites for Dr. Linville," *GNA*, 31 August 1938. After passage of the Civil Rights Act (1964), the number dropped to 2,000. Karinne Young, "Unknown Number of Dead Reside in Hospital Graveyards," *GNA*, 30 July 1995.

62. L. M. Blue, "Letter of Transmittal," *Biennial Report of the State Hospital at Golds-*

boro (1928–30). Ironically, even as he cut costs for the institution, his order to enlarge, alter, and furnish his office added $5,395.32 to the permanent repair cost of the hospital between 1926 and 1928. O'Berry, "Letter of Transmittal," 4.

63. "Superintendent's Report, 30 June 1928," *Biennial Report of the State Hospital at Goldsboro* (1926–28), 5.

64. "Report of Agricultural Department for Biennium, 1928–30," *Biennial Report of the State Hospital at Goldsboro* (1928–30), n.p.

65. For more on the rise of insane asylums, see Grob, *Mental Illness and American Society*, 75; Andrew Scull, "Madness and Segregative Control: The Rise of the Insane Asylum," *Social Problems* 24, no. 3 (1977): 337–51; Ian Dowbiggin, "Midnight Clerks and Daily Drudges: Hospital Psychiatry in New York State, 1890–1905," *Journal of the History of Medicine and Allied Sciences* 47, no. 2 (1992): 130–52. In the 1840s and 1850s, inspired in part by Dorothea Dix's class for humanitarian reforms, states responded with a wave of asylum building. Whitaker, *Mad in America*, 34.

66. Whitaker, *Mad in America*, 57.

67. John R. Sutton, "The Political Economy of Madness: The Expansion of the Asylum in Progressive America," *American Sociological Review* 56 (October 1991): 665–78.

68. Gerald N. Grob, *From Asylum to Community: Mental Health Policy in Modern America* (Princeton: Princeton University Press, 1991), 6.

69. Gerald N. Grob, "Illusion and Reality in American Psychiatric Thought," in *Genetics and Criminality: The Potential Misuse of Scientific Information in Court*, ed. Jeffrey R. Botkin, William M. McMahon, and Leslie Pickering Francis (Washington, D.C.: APA, 1999), 10.

70. Grob, *Mental Illness and American Society*, 143. See also Dowbiggin, "Midnight Clerks and Daily Drudges," 149.

71. Sutton, "The Political Economy of Madness," 670, citing Grob, *Mental Illness and American Society*, 74–75.

72. Grob, *Mental Illness and American Society*, 104.

73. Dowbiggin, "Midnight Clerks and Daily Drudges," 134.

74. See, for example, Grob, "Illusion and Reality in American Psychiatric Thought," 9.

75. American Eugenics Society, *A Eugenics Catechism* (New Haven: AES, 1926), 31.

76. Susan Burch, *Signs of Resistance: American Deaf Cultural History, 1900 to World War II* (New York: New York University Press, 2002), 134.

77. Kenneth M. Ludmerer, *Genetics and American Society: A Historical Appraisal* (Baltimore: The Johns Hopkins University Press, 1972), 15, 23.

78. See, for example, W. A. Hammond, cited in Elof Axel Carlson, *The Unfit: A History of a Bad Idea* (Cold Spring Harbor, N.Y.: Cold Spring Harbor Laboratory Press, 2001), 202–3; Philip Reilly, *The Surgical Solution: A History of Involuntary Sterilization in the United States* (Baltimore: The Johns Hopkins University Press, 1991), 9; Angela Gugliotta, "'Dr. Sharp with His Little Knife': Therapeutic and Punitive Origins of Eugenic Vasectomy—Indiana, 1892–1921," *Journal of the History of Medicine and Allied Sciences* 53, no. 4 (October 1998): 376.

79. Carlson, *The Unfit*, 202.

80. Moya Woodside, *Sterilization in North Carolina: A Sociological and Psychological Study* (Chapel Hill: University of North Carolina Press, 1950), 33.

81. John Hurty, cited in Gugliotta, " 'Dr. Sharp with His Little Knife,' " 406.

82. Ludmerer, *Genetics and American Society*, 93.

83. Donald K. Pickens, *Eugenics and the Progressives* (Nashville: Vanderbilt University Press, 1968), 99, n. 46; Abraham Myerson et al., *Eugenical Sterilization: A Reorientation of the Problem* (New York: Macmillan Co., 1936), 177–79.

84. Ian Dowbiggin, *Keeping America Sane: Psychiatry and Eugenics in the United States and Canada, 1880–1940* (Ithaca: Cornell University Press, 1997), 100.

85. Joel T. Braslow, "In the Name of Therapeutics: The Practice of Sterilization in a California State Hospital," *Journal of the History of Medicine and Allied Sciences* 51 (January 1996): 41.

86. *Human Sterilization*, published by Human Betterment Foundation (California) in R. Eugene Brown, *Eugenical Sterilization in North Carolina* (Raleigh: Eugenics Board of North Carolina, 1935), n.p.

87. Ellsworth Huntington, *Tomorrow's Children: The Goal of Eugenics* (New York: John Wiley and Sons, Inc., 1935), 51. For Paul Popenoe, see J. H. Landman, *Human Sterilization: The History of the Sexual Sterilization Movement* (New York: Macmillan Company, 1932), 39; citing Popenoe, "Number of Persons Needing Sterilization," *Journal of Heredity* 19 (1928): 405–10. Many believed that the sole way this protection could be extended was through sterilization. As John Hurty put it, "the knife only can reach them." John Hurty, cited in Gugliotta, " 'Dr. Sharp with His Little Knife,' " 406.

88. Nancy Ordover, *American Eugenics: Race, Queer Anatomy, and the Science of Nationalism* (Minneapolis: University of Minnesota Press, 2001), 134.

89. See, for example, Steven Noll, *Feeble-Minded in Our Midst: Institutions for the Mentally Retarded in the South, 1900–1940* (Chapel Hill: University of North Carolina Press, 1995).

90. Charles B. Davenport, *Heredity in Relation to Eugenics* (New York: Henry Holt and Co., 1911), 1.

91. Buck had been raped by one of her foster family's nephews. Claiming the pregnancy demonstrated Buck's promiscuity and questionable intellect, the family and state had the teenager committed. Ordover, *American Eugenics*, 167.

92. In Joseph B. Lehane, "The Morality of American Civil Legislation Concerning Eugenical Sterilization" (Ph.D. diss., Catholic University of America, 1944), 24; *Buck v. Bell*, 274 U.S. 200; 71 L. Ed 1000, 1002.

93. Edward J. Larson, "Criminal Determinism," in *Genetics and Criminality*, ed. Jeffrey R. Botkin, William M. McMahon, and Leslie Pickering Francis, 33; Landman, *Human Sterilization*, 105.

94. Ludmerer, *Genetics and American Society*, 3.

95. Landman, *Human Sterilization*, 113.

96. Ordover, *American Eugenics*, 134; Grob, *Mental Illness and American Society*, 173. Between 1907 and 1940, 30,038 people diagnosed as mentally retarded were sterilized.

97. Junius Wilson's hospital file from his first two decades of incarceration lacks infor-

mation from the first few years. It contains no cover sheet, admission page, commitment papers, psychiatric note in the file, or psychiatric threshold exam. There is no indication that anyone examined him to determine his psychiatric issues or appropriate treatment.

98. "Order for the Asexualization or Sterilization of Mental Defective and Feeble-Minded Inmates of Charitable and Penal Institutions of North Carolina and Certain Cases Not Inmates of Public Institutions" (Cold Spring Harbor, N.Y.: Eugenics Record Office, 19 December 1931).

99. Junius Wilson Student File, School for the Deaf Archives, Raleigh School Files, Morganton, N.C. Also exhibit no. 1, p. 313 in Wilson Court Documents, State Courthouse Files, Raleigh, N.C.

100. "Order for the Asexualization or Sterilization of Mental Defective and Feeble-Minded Inmates."

101. At that time, all cases of syphilis were treated with neoarsphenamine and other drugs such as mercury, bismuth, and iodides. There was no evidence that Wilson was ever given these medications or treated for syphilis. *A Study of Mental Health in North Carolina*, 240.

102. Junius Wilson File, Eugenics Record Office, Cold Spring Harbor, N.Y.; papers given to Susan Burch by Helen Hinn and John Wasson.

103. Orders for sterilizations required the signatures of the commissioner of Charities and Public Welfare of North Carolina, the secretary of the State Board of Health of North Carolina, and the chief medical officer of each of any two of the institutions for the feebleminded or insane of the state of North Carolina. "An Act to Provide for the Sterilization of the Mentally Defective and Feeble-Minded Inmates of Charitable and Penal Institutions of the State of North Carolina" (1929); Wilson's form was signed off on 20 December 1931. For more on North Carolina's general eugenic sterilization campaign, see Johanna Schoen, *Choice and Coercion: Birth Control, Sterilization, and Abortion in Public Health and Welfare* (Chapel Hill: University of North Carolina Press, 2005).

104. Brown, *Eugenical Sterilization in North Carolina*, 38.

105. Gugliotta, "'Dr. Sharp with His Little Knife,'" 402. As one historian put it, "Medical autonomy and authority were issues taken for granted." Grob, *Mental Illness and American Society*, 177–78. Also see Landman, *Human Sterilization*, 276.

106. Brown, *Eugenical Sterilization in North Carolina*, 5.

107. *A Study of Mental Health in North Carolina* (1937), 365.

108. Letter to R. Eugene Brown, North Carolina Eugenics Board, from H. H. Laughlin (Eugenics Record Office): *Effects of Sterilization Operations, 1936*, North Carolina State Archives, Raleigh.

109. Junius Wilson File, Eugenics Record Office, Cold Spring Harbor, N.Y.; papers given to Susan Burch by Helen Hinn and John Wasson.

110. There are many fine works on the racist nature of eugenics, but few that focus comprehensively on African Americans. See Edward J. Larson, *Sex, Race, and Science: Eugenics in the Deep South* (Baltimore: The Johns Hopkins University Press, 1995); Ordover, *American Eugenics*; Mark Haller, *Eugenics: Hereditarian Attitudes in American Thought* (New Brunswick: Rutgers University Press, 1984); and J. David Smith, *The*

Eugenic Assault on America (Fairfax, Va.: George Mason University Press, 1993). For biographies of institutionalized people, see Gary Penley, *Della Raye: A Girl Who Grew Up in Hell and Emerged Whole* (Gretna: Pelican Pub., 2002); and Michael D'Antonio, *The State Boys Rebellion* (New York: Simon & Schuster, 2004).

CHAPTER THREE

1. *Biennial Report of the State Hospital at Goldsboro* (1924–26), 7; *A Study of Mental Health in North Carolina: Report to the North Carolina Legislature of the Governor's Commission, Appointed to Study the Care of the Insane and Mental Defectives* (Ann Arbor: Edwards Brothers, 1937), 233.

2. The museum at Cherry Hospital at one time exhibited an admissions book; an entry book from several decades later notes Wilson's entrance to Goldsboro. Copies of this admissions page provided to the authors does not offer names but does show that both men and women of different ages and professions were entering the hospital at that time. Census reports from 1930 further confirm this.

3. Mintauts Vitols, deposition, 13 November 1995, 28. See also Edward E. Cales, "Inspection of the State Hospital at Goldsboro by the North Carolina State Board of Public Welfare" (March and November 1950). Exhibit S 10, *Junius Wilson v. North Carolina* (1990s), 3. Legal papers donated to author by Barbara Brauer, with permission from Helen Hinn, guardian of Junius Wilson's estate.

4. *A Study of Mental Health in North Carolina*, 236.

5. Memo to Mrs. W. T. Bost from James Watson, M.D., 1 March 1942, Agencies, Commissions, Departments, and Institutions, 1941–44, box 47, State Hospital for the Insane, Goldsboro, Folder, JMB.

6. "History of Cherry Hospital," handout (Goldsboro: Cherry Hospital Museum).

7. Memo to Mrs. W. T. Bost from James Watson, M.D.

8. *A Study of Mental Health in North Carolina* (1937), 233. On the main campus, patient revolt was more common. In the summer of 1933, a group of male patients rioted, taking control of one of the buildings. After a long standoff, the patients gave up and no one was injured. In April 1934 a patient from the criminal ward called "Sunshine Jones" sawed though the bars during a rainstorm and fled the grounds. Jones, like most of the other rebels at the institution, was captured and returned. Thomas O'Berry to Governor J. C. B. Ehringhaus, 26 June 1933, General Correspondence, 1933–37, box 11, State Hospital for the Colored Insane, Goldsboro, Correspondence 1933–35 Folder, JCBE; J. A. Phillips to Governor J. C. B. Ehringhaus, 13 April 1934, General Correspondence, box 11, State Hospital for the Colored Insane, Goldsboro, Folder, JCBE.

9. The 1930 U.S. Census shows that Mary Wilson Clark was a "widow" living with Annie Smith, who was head of household. James and Arthur, Annie's sons, had their own homes next door. *United States Census of Population, 1930*, North Carolina, New Hanover County, Cape Fear Township, sheet 2B, E.D. 65-2, S.D. 12, lines 51, 58–64. Relatives also suggested that Mary lived with Smith relatives at various times. Willie Sidberry, interview by Susan Burch, 19 November 2003. Junius Wilson's sister Carrie eventually moved to New York City.

10. A psychological evaluation of Wilson by Rose Verhoeven in 1991 suggested that Wilson was uncomfortable when he saw generic pictures of family members embracing and refused to look at pictures that expressed sadness. Rose Verhoeven, Psychological and Mental Status Evaluation, 3 June 1991, JWMF. Roger Williams, who evaluated Wilson several years later, also describes Wilson as reluctant to discuss his family. Roger Williams, deposition, 11 December 1995; Roger Williams, interview by Susan Burch, September 2001 and 22 July 2005.

11. Fannie Thomas, deposition, 8 May 1996; Jennie Bowman, deposition, 19 December 1995.

12. Annie May Williams, deposition, 24 May 1996; Jennie Bowman, deposition, 19 December 1995; André Branch, deposition, 3 November 1995.

13. Jennie Bowman, deposition, 19 December 1995; Annie Mae Williams, deposition, 24 May 1996; Charles E. Smith, deposition, 9 May 1996.

14. F. L. Whelpley to Clyde R. Hoey, 28 February 1940, CRH. James Watson, who inspected Goldsboro Hospital in 1942, notes that better salaries at Goldsboro would possibly help raise that standard of care and personnel. See Memo to Mrs. W. T. Bost from James Watson, M.D.

15. Johanna Schoen, *Choice and Coercion: Birth Control, Sterilization, and Abortion in Public Health and Welfare* (Chapel Hill: University of North Carolina Press, 2005), 10.

16. "Superintendent's Report," *Biennial Report of the State Hospital at Goldsboro* (1926–28); Karinne Young, "Unknown Number of Dead Reside in Hospital Graveyards," *GNA*, 30 July 1995. During this time, local schools apparently brought young people through the institution on field trips. It is unclear how the visitors responded to what they saw, but Superintendent Whelpley noted in his diary that "a bunch of colored students here & [it was some] trouble to show them around." F. L. Whelpley Diary, 20 October 1936, Cherry Hospital Museum, Goldsboro.

17. This situation continued well into the 1940s and 1950s. See Clark R. Cahow, *People, Patients, and Politics: The History of the North Carolina Mental Hospitals, 1848–1960* (New York: Arno Press, 1980), 134.

18. W. A. Dees to Governor J. Melville Broughton, 15 June 1943, Agencies, Commissions, Departments, and Institutions, 1941–44, box 47, State Hospital for the Insane, Goldsboro, Folder, JMB.

19. Cahow, *People, Patients, and Politics*, 106.

20. Young, "Unknown Number of Dead Reside in Hospital Graveyards"; *A Study of Mental Health in North Carolina*, 166.

21. Cahow, *People, Patients, and Politics*, 106.

22. *A Study of Mental Health in North Carolina*, 236.

23. For example, see "Superintendent's Report, 30 June 1928," *Biennial Report of the State Hospital at Goldsboro* (1926–28); F. L. Whelpley, "Report of the Superintendent," *Biennial Report of the State Hospital at Goldsboro* (1936–38), 41.

24. "Report of the Executive Committee of the North Carolina Hospitals Board of Control of the Investigation Conducted following the Truck Accident at the Hospital in Goldsboro," General Correspondence, 1956, box 95, Hospitals Board of Controls Folder,

A–G, LHH, 2. One informant noted that "not too long after I got there [to Cherry] they stopped using the farm. There was an accident and some patients got hurt. And they stopped them from working on the farm . . . by 1970 there wasn't any patients working on the farm." The accident occurred after 1965. Some patients had been riding in the back of a truck and fell out. Anonymous (A-5), interview by Susan Burch, 10 August 2005.

25. Memo to Mrs. W. T. Bost from James Watson, M.D.; General Correspondence, 1956, box 95, Hospitals Board of Controls Folder, A–G, LLH, 2.

26. Many northern states also used this system of labor but might not have had the same racial connotations as southern institutions did. George W. Dowdall, *The Eclipse of the State Mental Hospital: Policy, Stigma, and Organization* (Albany: State University of New York Press, 1996).

27. Mark Colvin, *Penitentiaries, Reformatories, and Chain Gangs: Social Theory and the History of Punishment in Nineteenth-Century America* (New York: St. Martin's Press, 1997), 246–48.

28. Convicts to Governor, 7 March 1920; and Convicts to Governor Bickett, 17 March 1919, Department of Social Services Records, State Board of Public Welfare, North Carolina State Archives, Raleigh; cited in Alex Lichtenstein, "Good Roads and Chain Gangs in the Progressive South: 'The Negro Convict Is a Slave,'" *Journal of Southern History* 59, no. 1 (February 1993): 92.

29. For more on convict labor, see, for example, Timothy Dodge, "State Convict Road Gangs in Alabama," *Alabama Review* 53, no. 4 (October 2000): 243–70; Jesse F. Steiner and Roy M. Brown, *The North Carolina Chain Gang: A Study of County Convict Road Work* (Chapel Hill: University of North Carolina Press, 1927); and Martha A. Myers and James L. Massey, "Race, Labor, and Punishment in Postbellum Georgia," *Social Problems* 38, no. 2 (May 1991): 267–86.

30. Whelpley, "Report of the Superintendent," 41.

31. Ibid.

32. The Halifax County trial records list McNeil as "Dummy Graham." Hearing people often used the pejorative term "dummy" as a nickname for deaf people. It is not fully clear why he was referred to as "Graham." Since his family was not contacted by the police or court system, perhaps the state assigned the man the name, which was common in the area, instead of "Doe" or "Smith." Census evidence most strongly suggests the scenario in which Winnie Graham played a role in McNeil's common name. For more on Winnie Graham and James Graham, see *United States Census of Population, 1930*, North Carolina, Halifax County, Faucett Township, sheet 9B, E.D. 42-11, S.D. 9, lines 67–72. For information on Patti Alston, see sheet 2B, E.D. 42-11, S.D. 3, line 77.

33. McNeil's nickname appears as "Dummie," "Dummy," or "Dummey" in various documents. For the sake of consistency, we will refer to him in this context as "Dummie."

34. *State v. Dumie Graham*, TD No. 652, PD no. 1965, Clerk of Court Office, Permanent Criminal Docket, Superior Court 1, Halifax County Courthouse; *Minutes to Halifax Superior Court*, January term, case number 652 (February 1933).

35. On 31 January 1933 Halifax Court committed McNeil (called Dummie Graham at

the time) to Goldsboro's Asylum. *State v. Dumie Graham*; Minutes to Halifax Superior Court.

36. North Carolina Eugenics Board Report, 21 March 1934. The petition to sterilize Dummie Graham was filed on 13 November 1933. "No relatives could be found . . . the social history contained in the petition indicates that the operation is expected to help the patient adjust to institutional life. The Board authorizes the operation." Dummie Graham was "asexualized by doing a castration. Dr. W. C. Linville. April 13, 1934." North Carolina Eugenics Board Reports, 20 April 1934.

37. Lulu Jolliff, interview by Susan Burch, 26 August 2004; Garde Parson, interview by Susan Burch, 16 August 2004.

38. McNeil attended the Raleigh School with Wilson. *United States Census of Population, 1920*, North Carolina, Wake County, Raleigh, sheet 20A, E.D. 134, S.D. 4, State School for the Blind and Deaf Colored, line 86 ("James McNeal"). A file for Superintendent G. E. Lineberry shows a prepaid order from Corinth for James McNeil for that time as well. Governor Morehead School Principal's Office, Correspondence of Principals, 1897–1921, G. E. Lineberry, Misc/undated Letter File, North Carolina State Archives, Raleigh.

39. Mintauts Vitols, deposition, 13 November 1995, 132.

40. Douglas Carl Abrams, *Conservative Constraints: North Carolina and the New Deal* (Jackson: University Press of Mississippi, 1992), 176–77.

41. Ibid., 255.

42. Ibid., 53.

43. *Biennial Report of the State Hospital at Goldsboro* (1938–40), 4, 7.

44. Ibid.

45. F. L. Whelpley to Clyde R. Hoey, 28 February 1940, CRH; "The National Hospital Survey and Construction Act of 1946" (also known as the Hill-Burton Act) provided federal matching funds for hospitals. Southern states exploited a clause in the law that specifically allowed funds to be used for segregated facilities, the "only phrase in federal legislation in the twentieth century that explicitly permitted federal money to be used for exclusionary services based explicitly on race." David Barton Smith, *Health Care Divided: Race and Healing a Nation* (Ann Arbor: University of Michigan Press, 2002), 47. For more on Hill-Burton and its effect on racially segregated hospitals, see Thomas J. Ward Jr., *Black Physicians in the Jim Crow South* (Fayetteville: University of Arkansas Press, 2003), 176; Cahow, *People, Patients, and Politics*, 129; Jill Quadagno and Steve McDonald, "Racial Segregation in Southern Hospitals: How Medicare 'Broke the Back' of Segregated Health Services," in *The New Deal and Beyond: Social Welfare in the South since 1930*, ed. Elna C. Green (Athens: University of Georgia Press, 2003), 119–20.

46. Goldsboro board member John Cranmer insisted on resigning, and the governor chastised Goldsboro to have more meetings. John B. Cranmer to J. C. B. Ehringhaus, 2 July 1935; J. C. B. Ehringhaus to John B. Cranmer, 5 July 1935; Letter of resignation from John B. Cranmer; Cranmer to J. C. B. Ehringhaus, 25 June 1935; all in General Correspondence, 1933–37, box 11, State Hospital for the Colored Insane, Goldsboro, Correspondence 1933–35 Folder, JCBE. Chairman F. L. Whelpley to Clyde R. Hoey, 28 February 1940, CRH.

47. Cahow, *People, Patients, and Politics*, 9.

48. Ibid., 17. Cahow also provides the citations for the Jimison article (p. 9, n. 16).

49. Cahow, *People, Patients and Politics*, 67–68.

50. Ibid., 79.

51. Ibid., 114.

52. In the 1930s and 1940s, Albert Deutsch, a prominent reporter, especially focused on the plight of mental patients. See Albert Deutsch, *The Shame of the States* (New York: Harcourt, Brace and Company, 1948); Albert Deutsch, *The Mentally Ill in America: A History of Their Care and Treatment from Colonial Times* (New York: Columbia University Press, 1967; originally published by the American Foundation for Mental Hygiene, Inc., 1937). Conscientious objectors who worked in mental hospitals during the war played a significant role in drawing attention to the issue. For an overview of this movement, see Stephen J. Taylor, "Conscientious Objectors at State Institutions," Center on Human Policy: Disability Studies for Teachers (Syracuse University, 2003), <http://www.disabilitystudiesforteachers.org/lesson.php?id=1> (18 July 2005).

53. Cahow, *People, Patients, and Politics*, 115.

54. Chaplain Ronald Coley claims that the patient leasing program ended in 1956; "Chaplain Ronald Coley gives a view in retrospect to his knowledge of Cherry hospital dating back sixty years ago," cited in David J. White, "Cherry Hospital: A History Report Presented to the Faculty of Mount Olive College," 29 November 2001, 25. Documents from Wilson's file, however, note that he was working on the farm well into the 1960s. See also *Biennial Report of the North Carolina State Board of Charities and Public Welfare* (1938–40), 9, <http://docsouth.unc.edu/nc/charities1940/charities1940.html>.

55. Edward H. Beardsley, *A History of Neglect: Health Care for Blacks and Mill Workers in the Twentieth-Century South* (Knoxville: University of Tennessee Press, 1987), 82.

56. Abrams, *Conservative Constraints*, 169. Spaulding later organized the Durham Committee on the Affairs of Black People, which played a significant role in the sit-in movement of the 1950s and 1960s.

57. Ward, *Black Physicians in the Jim Crow South*, 154.

58. Smith, *Health Care Divided*, 14.

59. Historical documents offer inconsistent dates for Leonard's formation. Some cite 1880, when a committee officially formed the school; others recognize 1882, when the school had several buildings, a larger faculty, and an enrollment of 15 students.

60. Wilbur H. Watson, *Against the Odds: Blacks in the Profession of Medicine in the United States* (New Brunswick: Transaction Publishers, 1999), 33.

61. Watson, *Against the Odds*, 33.

62. See Abraham Flexner, *Medical Education in the United States and Canada: A Report to the Carnegie Foundation for the Advancement of Teaching* (New York: Carnegie Foundation for the Advancement of Teaching, 1910), 181. By the late 1920s, associations like the Julius Rosenwald Fund and the Duke Endowment were providing some funds to North Carolina for segregated hospitals and scholarships for African Americans to attend medical and nursing school. See Edward H. Beardsley, "Making Separate Equal: Black Physicians and the Problems of Medical Segregation in the Pre–World War II

South," *Bulletin of the History of Medicine* 57 (Fall 1983): 382–96; Edward H. Beardsley, "Dedicated Servant of Errant Professional: The Southern Negro Physician before World War II," in *The Southern Enigma: Essays on Race Class, And Folk Culture*, ed. Walter J. Fraser Jr. and Winfred B. Moore Jr. (Westport, Conn.: Greenwood Press, 1983), 149. Yet even with this support, Jim Crow complicated matters. Talented black students who aspired to the health professions had to leave the state to get an education, incurring costs that exceeded the fellowships granted them. And when they returned to North Carolina, whites still ran most hospitals and blocked black staff and physicians, even as patients asked for black medical professionals. When the Great Depression hit, resources evaporated. Across the South, the number of practicing black doctors fell 12 percent during the first decade of Roosevelt's administration, from 2,295 to 2,018. This meant that there was only a single black doctor for every 4,913 African Americans. On the national level, the ratio was 1 to 3,377. During the same ten years, the total number of American physicians increased by 12 percent. See Ward, *Black Physicians in the Jim Crow South*, 39. Shut out from traditional medical societies and most hospitals, some black doctors created their own associations and networks. One of the original societies began in North Carolina, the society to which Blackman and Spaulding belonged. The Old North State Medical Society (originally named North Carolina Medical Pharmaceutical and Dental Association), founded in 1887, actively pursued integration in the American Medical Association, as well as in hospitals, clinics, and medical schools across the state.

63. C. C. Spaulding to Gov. J. C. B. Ehringhaus, 20 April 1934, General Correspondence, 1933–37, box 11, State Hospital for the Colored Insane, Goldsboro, Negro Interns, Folder (1935), JCBE.

64. Ibid.; Chairman Ex. Committee State Hospital, Goldsboro to Gov. J. C. B. Ehringhaus, 13 April 1934, General Correspondence, 1933–37, box 11, State Hospital for the Colored Insane, Goldsboro, Negro Interns, Folder (1935), JCBE.

65. W. C. Linville to J. C. B. Ehringhaus, 20 July 1934; J. C. B. Ehringhaus to Dr. W. C. Linville, 21 July 1934; W. C. Linville to J. C. B. Ehringhaus, 20 July 1934; J. C. B. Ehringhaus to Dr. Edson E. Blackman, Old North State Medical Society, 21 July 1934; all in General Correspondence, 1933–37, box 11, State Hospital for the Colored Insane, Goldsboro, Folder, JCBE.

66. Edson E. Blackman, Chairman, to J. C. B. Ehringhaus, 23 January 1935, General Correspondence, 1933–37, box 11, Appointments, 1933–35, State Hospital for the Colored Insane, Goldsboro, Folder, JCBE.

67. William F. Scholl to Gov. J. C. B. Ehringhaus, 20 May 1935, General Correspondence, 1933–37, box 11, State Hospital for the Colored Insane, Goldsboro, Folder, JCBE.

68. J. C. B. Ehringhaus to William F. Scholl, 21 May 1935, General Correspondence, 1933–37, box 11, State Hospital for the Colored Insane, Goldsboro, Negro Interns, Folder (1935), JCBE.

69. Superintendent Vitols testified that he was the first administrator to hire black professionals. Mintauts Vitols, deposition, 13 November 1995.

70. Gov. Clyde R. Hoey to W. A. Dees, 23 September 1938, Hospitals, Orphanages, Training Schools and Institutes, box 61, State Hospital for the Insane, Goldsboro, Folder, CRH.

71. Ibid.

72. W. A. Dees to Gov. Clyde R. Hoey, 28 September 1938, Hospitals, Orphanages, Training Schools and Institutes, box 61, State Hospital for the Insane, Goldsboro, Folder, CRH.

73. C. C. Spaulding to Clyde R. Hoey, 21 June 1940, Hospitals, Orphanages, Training Schools and Institutes, box 61, State Hospital for the Insane, Goldsboro, Folder, CRH. In May 1953 lawyer Leon Brassfield recommended that C. A. Hayward of Raleigh (an African American) be appointed to the board of trustees at Goldsboro. E. L. Rankin to Leon Brassfield, 15 May 1953, William B. Umstead and Luther H. Hodges Appointments 1953–60, box 28, State Hospital, Goldsboro, Folder, William B. Umstead Papers, North Carolina State Archives, Raleigh; Leon Brassfield to Gov. William B. Umstead, 9 May 1953, William B. Umstead and Luther H. Hodges Appointments 1953–60, box 28, State Hospital, Goldsboro, Folder, William B. Umstead Papers, North Carolina State Archives, Raleigh.

74. W. A. Dees to Gov. J. Melville Broughton, 15 June 1943, Agencies, Commissions, Departments and Institutions, 1941–1944, box 47, State Hospital for the Insane, Goldsboro, Folder, JMB.

75. Admittedly, most investigations were weak and palliative, but as examples from conscientious objectors during the Second World War have demonstrated, certain improvements could be achieved when the public learned about appalling institutional conditions.

76. Bureau of Vital Statistics, Standard Certificate of Death: Annie Smith (North Carolina State Board of Health, Wilmington, N.C.); Bureau of Vital Statistics, Standard Certificate of Death: Arthur Smith (North Carolina State Board of Health, Wilmington, N.C.).

77. Sidney Wilson and his new wife Avary were renting a home. Sidney, listed as forty-one years old, was working as a laborer for the "railroad shop"; Avary, age twenty-five, was a "laundress" in her "own home." *United States Census of Population, 1920,* Georgia, Ware County, Waycross Township, sheet 1A, S.D. 55, E.D. 150, lines 14–15.

78. The copy of this report shows a blurred signature. It is possible that the actual name of the social worker is Jim Johnson, but several people who have seen the document concur that "GM" is the best estimate.

79. Junius Wilson might not have understood that his sister had married, or she might not have shared this news with him. He continued to refer to her as "Carrie Wilson" rather than "Carrie Gill" (5 June 1947, JWMF).

80. For decades after, when staff asked Wilson about moving to a new location, he apparently nodded vigorously, took a piece of paper and pencil, and wrote his mother's name (Wilson), sometimes Carrie's name, and his home address in Castle Hayne.

81. Vitol's letter to Mary Wilson Clark was sent to New York City to the same address that Carrie Gill had given in 1947 (5 May 1958, JWMF).

82. H. Jack Allen, interview by Susan Burch, 11 August 2005.

83. Ibid. In a 1993 article, McNeil's younger brother Charles claims he visited him "three or four times" but did not recall when the two had last seen one another. "Cherry

Hospital Evaluating Two More Deaf Patients"; and Stan Swofford, "Not Unique: Others Lost in System," *N&R*, 31 January 1993.

84. White, "Cherry Hospital"; Superintendent Vitols attempted to end this practice. Mintauts Vitols, deposition, 13 November 1995, 121–22.

CHAPTER FOUR

1. See Gerald N. Grob, *From Asylum to Community: Mental Health Policy in Modern America* (Princeton: Princeton University Press, 1991); Gerald N. Grob, *The Mad Among Us: A History of the Care of America's Mentally Ill* (New York: Maxwell Macmillan International, 1994); Gerald N. Grob, *Mental Illness and American Society, 1875–1940* (Princeton: Princeton University Press, 1983); Albert Deutsch, *Mentally Ill in America: A History of Their Care and Treatment* (New York: Columbia University Press, 1949); Steve Noll, *Feeble-Minded in Our Midst: Institutions for the Mentally Retarded in the South, 1900–1940* (Chapel Hill: University of North Carolina Press, 1995); Peter McCandless, *Moonlight, Magnolias, and Madness: Insanity in South Carolina from the Colonial to the Progressive Era* (Chapel Hill: University of North Carolina Press, 1996).

2. "An Act Providing for Changing the Names of the Several State Hospitals and Training Schools," State of North Carolina General Assembly, H.B. 1311, Chapter 1028 *Session Laws* (Raleigh, 1959), 1054.

3. William Novasky, "The Racial Desegregation Study: First Interim Report" (North Carolina, 1965), 8. Novasky notes that the quote came from a statement by one of the business staff.

4. Ibid., 10.

5. Ibid.

6. Quoted in ibid.

7. Robert H. Barnes, *Inspection Report of the State Hospital at Goldsboro*, 27 December 1955, 6.

8. Pete Daniel, *Lost Revolutions: The South in the 1950s* (Chapel Hill: University of North Carolina Press for the Smithsonian Institution, 2000), 204.

9. Robert R. Mayer et al., *The Impact of School Desegregation in a Southern City: A Case Study in the Analysis of Educational Policy* (Lexington, Mass.: Lexington Books, 1974), xxi.

10. Mayer et al., *The Impact of School Desegregation*, xviii.

11. At the same time, Headstart programs in the area remained strongly segregated. See *Title IV: One Year Later. A Survey of Desegregation of Health and Welfare Services in the South* (United States Commission on Civil Rights, 1966), 44, <http://www.law.umary land.edu/Marshall/usccr/documents/cr12h34.pdf>.

12. Mayer et al., *The Impact of School Desegregation*, 39.

13. Ibid., 107.

14. Ibid., 20.

15. "NMHA and the History of the Mental Health Movement," <http://www.nmha .org/about/history.cfm> (15 October 2006).

16. Grob, *The Mad Among Us*, 250.

17. Norwood Davis, interview by Susan Burch, 3 October 2005.

18. Anonymous (A-5), interview by Susan Burch, 25 November 2003 and 10 August 2005.

19. Charles Gaylor, interview by Susan Burch, 10 August 2005; W. Eugene Howe, deposition, 12 December 1995; Norwood Davis, interview by Susan Burch, 3 October 2005.

20. Norwood Davis, interview by Susan Burch, 3 October 2005.

21. Chris Lancaster, interview by Susan Burch, 26 February 2002 and 13 August 2005. "Survival was key—if you could hustle, it makes things easier."

22. Clyde R. Brown Jr., interview by Susan Burch, 22 November 2005.

23. Norwood Davis, interview by Susan Burch, 3 October 2005.

24. Chris Lancaster, interview by Susan Burch, 26 February 2002 and 13 August 2005. An anonymous interview confirms that Wilson resold goods from the store. Anonymous (A-3), interview by Susan Burch, 10 October 2005.

25. Chris Lancaster, interview by Susan Burch, 26 February 2002 and 13 August 2005.

26. Ibid.

27. Timothy Paul Harvey, interview by Susan Burch, 8 August 2003.

28. Sylvia Weaver, interview by Susan Burch, 10 November 2004.

29. Charles Gaylor, interview by Susan Burch, 10 August 2005.

30. "You could see Junius all over the campus," remembered one staff member. "There never was any kind of restrictions on him. Graham was the same way." Anonymous (A-2), interview by Susan Burch, 28 September 2004.

31. Anonymous (A-4), interview by Susan Burch, 16 January 2004; Chris Lancaster, interview by Susan Burch, 26 February 2002 and 13 August 2005; H. Jack Allen, interview by Susan Burch, 11 August 2005.

32. Anonymous (B-3), interview by Susan Burch, 12 October 2005.

33. Lulu Jolliff, interview by Susan Burch, 26 August 2004.

34. H. Jack Allen, interview by Susan Burch, 11 August 2005. Sylvia Weaver recounts that her sister-in-law, who worked at Cherry Hospital and was married to a police officer, donated her husband's old uniforms to McNeil.

35. Anonymous (A-5), interview by Susan Burch, 25 November 2003 and 10 August 2005. What the nameplate said: Chris Lancaster, interview by Susan Burch, 26 February 2002 and 13 August 2005.

36. H. Jack Allen, interview by Susan Burch, 11 August 2005.

37. Norwood Davis, interview by Susan Burch, 3 October 2005.

38. Anonymous (B-1), interview by Susan Burch, 2 February 2005.

39. Chris Lancaster, interview by Susan Burch, 26 February 2002 and 13 August 2005.

40. H. Jack Allen, interview by Susan Burch, 11 August 2005.

41. Garde Parson and another anonymous staff member remember seeing McNeil direct traffic when they were children.

42. Lulu Jolliff, interview by Susan Burch, 26 August 2004.

43. Anonymous (B-3), interview by Susan Burch, 12 October 2005.

44. Chris Lancaster, interview by Susan Burch, 26 February 2002 and 13 August 2005.

45. Ibid.

46. H. Jack Allen, interview by Susan Burch, 11 August 2005.

47. James McNeil apparently left no written documents behind and his medical files have since been destroyed. As with many institutionalized people, his story remains mostly in ephemeral tales shared by others.

48. Clyde R. Brown Jr., interview by Susan Burch, 22 November 2005.

49. Ibid.

50. Ibid.

51. H. Jack Allen, interview by Susan Burch, 11 August 2005.

52. Ibid.

53. Clyde R. Brown Jr., interview by Susan Burch, 22 November 2005.

54. Ibid.

55. Ibid.

56. Ibid.

57. Ibid. An anonymous interview and Norwood Davis offer similar descriptions. Anonymous (A-5), interview with Susan Burch, 25 November 2003 and 10 August 2005; Norwood Davis, interview by Susan Burch, 3 October 2005.

58. "Captain" is a pseudonym used in order to protect the patient's privacy.

59. Clyde R. Brown Jr., interview by Susan Burch, 22 November 2005.

60. Ibid.

61. Anonymous (A-3), interview by Susan Burch, 10 October 2005.

62. Ibid.

63. Sylvia Weaver, interview by Susan Burch, 10 November 2004. An anonymous interview seconded her thought: Happy Hill was "a place between everything." Anonymous (A-3), interview by Susan Burch, 10 October 2005.

64. Clyde R. Brown Jr., interview by Susan Burch, 22 November 2005.

65. Ibid.

66. Ibid.

67. Former hospital employee Pandora Wooden recounted, "He always expressed much joy when he was remembered." Pandora Wooten to Susan Burch, 31 April 2004. There is some question whether she meant Wilson or McNeil. The general description of "Dummie's" actions most accurately reflects McNeil. An anonymous interview confirms that Pandora Wooten, now deceased, was close to James McNeil although she knew him only as Dummie. Anonymous (A-4), interview by Susan Burch, 16 January 2004.

68. Pandora Wooten to Susan Burch, 31 April 2004.

69. Clyde R. Brown Jr., interview by Susan Burch, 22 November 2005. Some patients might have had trunks in which they stored their special outfits. Anecdotal evidence suggests that the laundry also delivered outfits to the wards and patients would pick through them. For example, Anonymous (B-1), interview by Susan Burch, 2 February 2005.

70. Pandora Wooten to Susan Burch, 31 April 2004; Anonymous (A-4), interview by Susan Burch, 16 January 2004. Dancing is a popular entertainment for deaf people. Vibrations from the music enable individuals to follow songs. It is likely that Wilson and

McNeil were exposed to dancing at the Negro school in Raleigh. Everett Parker, who attended the school some years later, delighted in dancing with deaf friends and took great pride in his ability. Everett Parker Sr., interview by Susan Burch, 21 March 2002.

71. Anonymous (A-4), interview by Susan Burch, 16 January 2004.

72. H. Jack Allen, interview by Susan Burch, 11 August 2005.

73. Anonymous (A-4), interview by Susan Burch, 16 January 2004.

74. H. Jack Allen, interview by Susan Burch, 11 August 2005. He emphasized, "My name—after he'd seen it over and over, he'd recognize it."

75. Chris Lancaster, interview by Susan Burch, 26 February 2002 and 13 August 2005.

76. H. Jack Allen, interview by Susan Burch, 11 August 2005.

77. Anonymous (B-3), interview by Susan Burch, 12 October 2005.

78. Chris Lancaster, interview by Susan Burch, 26 February 2002 and 13 August 2005.

79. H. Jack Allen, interview by Susan Burch, 11 August 2005.

80. Most likely, Wilson hoarded his funds on his person or in or near his bed before the hospital began saving money in an account for him.

81. Anonymous (A-4), interview by Susan Burch, 16 January 2004.

82. Rick Mileski, interview by Susan Burch, 10 August 2005.

83. Anonymous (A-3), interview by Susan Burch, 10 October 2005.

84. Anonymous (A-5), interview by Susan Burch, 25 November 2003 and 10 August 2005; Anonymous (A-3), interview by Susan Burch, 10 October 2005.

85. Anonymous (A-3), interview by Susan Burch, 10 October 2005.

86. Ibid.

CHAPTER FIVE

1. Edward H. Beardsley, *A History of Neglect: Health Care for Blacks and Mill Workers in the Twentieth-Century South* (Knoxville: University of Tennessee Press, 1987), 266.

2. William Novasky, "The Racial Desegregation Study: First Interim Report" (North Carolina, 1965), 38.

3. Ibid., 18.

4. Lulu Jolliff, interview by Susan Burch, 26 August 2004. It is probable that she is referring to Ladislaw Peter, who served only one year at the hospital as superintendent.

5. Silvia Weaver, interview by Susan Burch, 19 November 2004. "All staff were involved in sensitivity classes through the Staff Development Department."

6. Lulu Jolliff, interview by Susan Burch, 26 August 2004. For more on deinstitutionalization, see Gerald N. Grob, "Deinstitutionalization: The Illusion of Policy," *Journal of Policy History* 9, no. 1 (1997): 48–74; and Phil Brown, *Transfer of Care: Psychiatric Deinstitutionalization and Its Aftermath* (Boston: Routledge & Kegan Paul, 1984).

7. Novasky, "The Racial Desegregation Study"; Gary L. Wright, "It Was Like Going Back to the Last Century," *CO*, 13 September 1992, <www.uncc.edu/thomass/last.htm> (5 October 2005).

8. Novasky, "The Racial Desegregation Study," 40.

9. Ibid., 7.

10. Ibid., 17.

11. Ibid., 8.

12. Ibid., 59.

13. Anonymous (A-5), interview by Susan Burch, 25 November 2003 and 10 August 2005.

14. Sylvia Weaver, interview by Susan Burch, 10 November 2004.

15. Chris Lancaster, interview by Susan Burch, 13 August 2005.

16. Anecdotal evidence suggests that the error was unintentional, a filing mistake or inaccurate estimate of his actual age by staff from an earlier period. Several individuals who worked with Wilson noted in his medical log that he seemed especially spry for the age they (wrongly) assumed he was.

17. Anonymous (A-8), interview by Susan Burch, 29 September 2006; psychiatric survivor organizations like MindFreedom offer testimony by ex-patients/psychiatric survivors. See <www.mindfreedom.org>. Richard Cohen's documentary *Hurry Tomorrow* (Halfway House Films, 1975) exposes cruel and inhumane treatment in a California mental hospital in the 1970s. Many mental health advocates describe much of patient treatment since the Second World War as punishing and dehumanizing. See, for example, Vanessa Jackson, "In Our Own Voice: African American Stories of Oppression, Survival, and Recovery in Mental Health Systems," <www.mindfreedom.org/pdf/in ourownvoice.pdf> (10 January 2005).

18. H. Jack Allen, interview by Susan Burch, 11 August 2005.

19. For more on disability civil rights and disability critiques of the body, see, for example, Joseph Shapiro, *No Pity* (New York: Three Rivers Press, 1994), 41; James I. Charlton, *Nothing About Us Without Us: Disability Oppression and Empowerment* (Berkeley: University of California Press, 2000); Paul K. Longmore, *Why I Burned My Book* (Philadelphia: Temple University Press, 2003); and Simi Linton, *Claiming Disability* (New York: New York University Press, 1998).

20. Shapiro, *No Pity*, 41, 161.

21. For more on CILs, see Paul Longmore, "The Disability Rights Movement: Activism in the 1970s and Beyond," in *Why I Burned My Book* (Philadelphia: Temple University Press, 2003), 103; and Shapiro, *No Pity*, 41–73.

22. Longmore, "The Disability Rights Movement," 113.

23. Jacqueline Vaughn Switzer, *Disabled Rights: American Disability Policy and the Fight for Equality* (Washington, D.C.: Georgetown University Press, 2003), 40.

24. Marcia Bok, *Civil Rights and the Social Programs of the 1960s: The Social Justice Functions of Social Policy* (Westport, Conn.: Praeger, 1992), 130.

25. LeLand V. Bell, *Treating the Mentally Ill: From Colonial Times to the Present* (New York: Praeger, 1980), 173.

26. Gerald N. Grob, *The Mad Among Us: A History of the Care of America's Mentally Ill* (New York: Free Press, 1994), 290.

27. Bok, *Civil Rights and the Social Programs of the 1960s*, 104–5; William A. Pearman and Philip Starr, *Medicare* (New York: Garland Publishing, Inc., 1988), 3; Grob, *The Mad Among Us*, 265–66.

28. Bok, *Civil Rights and the Social Programs of the 1960s*, 104–5, 107.

29. Beardsley, *A History of Neglect*, 307; Andrew Scull, "Historical Reflections on Asylums, Communities, and the Mentally Ill," *Mentalities* (New Zealand) 11, no. 2 (1997): 7.

30. Shapiro, *No Pity*, 41, 65; Longmore, "The Disability Rights Movement," 104.

31. 30 January 1969, JWMF. See also 31 May 1968 and 23 August 1968. The entry for 18 August 1969 shows him working on the grounds.

32. 4 April 1969, JWMF, 33; Anonymous (A-8), interview by Susan Burch, 29 September 2006.

34. Eugene Howe, deposition, 12 December 1995, 13.

35. Anonymous (A-2), interview by Susan Burch, 28 September 2004.

36. Eugene Howe, deposition, 12 December 1995, 10.

37. Anonymous (A-2), interview by Susan Burch, 28 September 2004.

38. Eugene Howe, deposition, 12 December 1995, 22.

39. Chris Lancaster, interview by Susan Burch, 26 February 2002 and 13 August 2005.

40. Anonymous (A-2), interview by Susan Burch, 28 September 2004.

41. Eugene Howe, deposition, 12 December 1995, 21.

42. A year earlier he earned $2.58 an hour. William Howe Jr., Work Therapy Carwash Form, 4 March 1986, 5 February 1986, 6 August 1985, 5 May 1985, and 5 October 1985; all in JWMF.

43. Chris Lancaster, interview by Susan Burch, 26 February 2002.

44. Ibid. Other staff members confirm that Wilson felt especially connected to the car wash. One report noted that "he has an IT assignment that he enjoys and seems to have a close attachment to the staff there." Psychological Assessment, 26 February 1982, JWMF. Wilson "readily agreed to go [to the community house] . . . as long as he would be allowed to continued [*sic*] with his regular participation in Industrial therapy where he does car washing regularly." Dr. Nelson M. Macatangay, Treatment Team Note, 22 February 1979, JWMF.

45. Chris Lancaster, interview by Susan Burch, 26 February 2002 and 13 August 2005.

46. Ibid.

47. Lulu Jolliff, interview by Susan Burch, 26 August 2004.

48. Anonymous (A-2), interview by Susan Burch, 28 September 2004.

49. Ibid.

50. Anonymous (A-3), interview by Susan Burch, 10 October 2005.

51. Everett Parker, interview by Susan Burch, 21 March 2002 and 9 August 2005.

52. Anonymous (B-1), interview by Susan Burch, 2 February 2005; Anonymous (A-3), interview by Susan Burch, 10 October 2005; Chris Lancaster, interview by Susan Burch, 26 February 2002 and 13 August 2005.

53. Clyde Brown Jr. confirms that fair trips did not happen when he was young during the preintegration period: "They might have gone later on, but I was about grown when that happened." Clyde R. Brown Jr., interview by Susan Burch, 22 November 2005. For more on the state fair see, for example, "50 Years of Cows, Concerts," *N&O*, 23 October 2002; "Burlesque Shows, Once a Staple at the Fair, Vanished Because TV Shows Today Are Just as Revealing," *N&O*, 18 October 1999; "The Great Depression,

Fires, Gypsies, and Fairs: A History of the North Carolina State Fair," in *Seeds of Success: Agricultural Fairs in North Carolina* (online booklet, 1997).

54. Chris Lancaster, interview by Susan Burch, 26 February 2002 and 13 August 2005.

55. Ibid.

56. Although she did not attend the state fair with Junius Wilson, one employee took other patients from different wards. She "took money and made sure they could do stuff." Anonymous (B-3), interview by Susan Burch, 12 October 2005. The money was often the patients' own money earned from their IT jobs.

57. Chris Lancaster, interview by Susan Burch, 26 February 2002 and 13 August 2005.

58. Bell, *Treating the Mentally Ill*, 167.

59. Dee Gamble, interview by Susan Burch, 12 October 2005.

60. John Wasson, interview by Susan Burch, 4 October 2005.

61. For more on this, see E. Fuller Torrey, *Out of the Shadows: Confronting America's Mental Illness Crisis* (New York: John Wiley & Sons, 1997).

62. Rick Mileski, interview by Susan Burch, 10 August 2005.

63. Nelson Macatangay, deposition, 2 November 1995, 39. That document could not be located later and might not have been available in his file in 1970.

64. Garde Parson, interview by Susan Burch, 16 August 2004.

65. James Burnette to Clerk of Court, James G. McKeithan, 17 September 1970, *Junius Wilson v. North Carolina*, legal file, State Courthouse Files, Raleigh, N.C.

66. This letter also can be found in court documents, exhibit 8, Attachment A, *Junius Wilson v. North Carolina*, legal file, State Courthouse Files, Raleigh, N.C.

67. Elizabeth M. George, letter to James F. Burnette, 4 November 1970, *Junius Wilson v. North Carolina*, legal file, State Courthouse Files, Raleigh, N.C.

68. James F. Burnette, social worker, to Mrs. Mary Clark 137 W. 141 St. N.Y., N.Y. It is unclear what medication Wilson was then taking. Later documents suggested that he never took—or needed—drug treatments until decades later when his health began to decline.

69. Bureau of Vital Statistics, Standard Certificate of Death: Mary Clark (North Carolina State Board of Health, Wilmington, N.C.).

70. *Junius Wilson v. North Carolina*, state defendant's memorandum in support of their motion for summary judgment, 8 July 1996, pleadings file 57-1104, 6, State Courthouse Files, Raleigh, N.C.

71. E. C. Fowler to Mrs. Carrie Gill, 2 December 1970, JWMF.

72. Lulu Jolliff and Olivia Whichard to New Hanover County Dept. of Social Services, 26 July 1972, JWMF.

73. Grace S. Hixson and Lela Moore Hall to Lulu Jolliff, 1 August 1972, JWMF.

74. Treatment Team Progress Notes, 1 November 1972, JWMF.

75. Certificate of Death, Sidney Wilson, file no. 11097, Georgia State Office of Vital Records; Certificate of Death, Avery Wilson, file no. 11104, Georgia State Office of Vital Records.

76. Lulu Jolliff, interview by Susan Burch, 26 August 2004.

77. Chris Lancaster, interview by Susan Burch, 26 February 2002 and 13 August 2005.

78. Nelson Macatangay, deposition, 2 November 1995, 21.

79. July 1975 note, JWMF, vol. 1.

80. Hernane Restar, 29 March 1977, JWMF.

81. Garde Parson, interview by Susan Burch, 16 August 2004.

82. Rick Mileski, interview by Susan Burch, 10 August 2005.

83. Lulu Jolliff, interview by Susan Burch, 26 August 2004.

84. Garde Parson, interview by Susan Burch, 16 August 2004.

85. Referral and Report, 30 October 1979, JWMF. A year earlier a nurse had suggested that Wilson's long-term goal should be "to communicate [with] others by signs, motions etc" The official "plan" for staff: "Learn his signs, motions, grunts etc. in a friendly cooperative manner. Let him write as often as he will." Mildred Croom, treatment plan, 19 March 1978, JWMF. Apparently, this approach did little to help Wilson.

86. For example, Referral and Report, 30 October 1979, JWMF, vol. 1.

87. Treatment Team Review, 19 October 1978, JWMF.

88. Donald F. Davis, M.D., Treatment Review Note, 14 March 1983, JWMF.

89. Treatment Plan Notes, 27 July 1978, JWMF.

90. Donald F. Davis, M.D., Treatment Team Review Note, 28 November 1983, JWMF.

91. Silvia Weaver, interview by Susan Burch, 19 November 2004.

92. In 1972 North Carolina Medicaid service coverage was expanded to include "Inpatient Mental Hospital Services for the Over 65, and Mental Health Centers." On 1 January 1974, Supplemental Security Income (SSI) became effective. This program administered federal assistance payments to the aged, blind, and disabled and relieved the state of this responsibility. At that time, states had the option of extending Medicaid coverage to all SSI recipients and an administrative option for the Social Security Administration to accomplish all eligibility determinations. North Carolina declined both options, choosing to administer its own program and to employ more restrictive eligibility criteria for adults, thus becoming what is termed a "209(b) state, referring to the pertinent regulatory authority." It is unclear whether a representative filed tax reports for Wilson, but the hospital did keep account of his savings. Wilson's treatment team agreed that Mrs. Griffin would cut down his money below $1,000 to buy clothing and other personal needs and to be eligible for Medicaid. (Hernane Restar, Notes, 24 April 1975, JWMF.) By the summer, Griffin reported that Wilson was already on Medicaid and that she bought him a TV, a watch, clothing, and a recliner chair. (Hernane Restar, 31 July 1975, JWMF.) Three years later, Wilson was again disqualified for Medicaid. (Treatment Team Notes, 17 October 1975, JWMF.)

93. 8 June 1983, JWMF.

94. Treatment Plan Notes, 27 July 1978: Disposition, JWMF.

95. Dr. Louis Gagliono, Report, 19 January 1976, JWMF.

96. Treatment Plan Notes, 27 July 1978, JWMF.

97. Silvia Weaver, interview by Susan Burch, 19 November 2004.

98. Rick Mileski, Social Worker, Report of Community House Screening Team, 24 April 1980, JWMF.

99. Garde Parson, interview by Susan Burch, 16 August 2004. The references suggest a

uniquely North Carolinian insult. Parson was justifying her actions as "local v. Raleigh" and implied that Raleigh's remote authority might have done otherwise.

100. Wilson, 19 February 1982, JWMF.

101. Robin Hall (PA) and Nelson Macatangay, Treatment Notes, 1 December 1982, JWMF.

102. Garde Parson, interview by Susan Burch, 16 August 2004.

103. See, for example, 19 April 1969 entry on daily assessment ("helpful on ward"), JWMF; 24 September 1974 ("helps out with the ward work"), JWMF; 22 January 1975 ("helps out with some of the ward work at night"), JWMF; 28 August 1975, JWMF; Progress Report, 12 July 1982, JWMF.

104. Dr. Donald Davis, 29 October 1984, JWMF.

105. A. Y. Elliott, N. Macatangay, Note, 12 May 1982, JWMF.

106. Lulu Jolliff, interview by Susan Burch, 26 August 2004.

107. See, for example, *Junius Wilson/ André Branch v. NC/NC Department of Human Resources*, Civil Action 594CV 878BR3, 16 November 1994, 8.

108. Garde Parson, interview by Susan Burch, 16 August 2004.

109. Anonymous (A-2), interview by Susan Burch, 28 September 2004.

110. The "Qualified Physician Examination and Evaluation to Determine Necessity for Involuntary Commitment to a Facility of the N.C. Division of Mental Health Services" noted on 29 December 1975 "Indications for Mental Illness of Inebriety."

111. *Junius Wilson v. North Carolina*, pleadings file 1–56, "Answer of Defendant Carolina Legal Assistance, Inc. 1 Feb 1995; tagged #13" (State Courthouse Files, Raleigh, N.C.).

112. Rick Mileski, Social Worker, Treatment Team Progress Notes, 20 September 1971, JWMF. Documents provide conflicting descriptions of whether Wilson actually signed the forms or whether others sign it for him. Lulu Jolliff and F. Richard Mileski to Lela Moore Hall, New Hanover Co. Dept. of Social Services, 26 September 1973, in JWMF. See *Junius Wilson v. North Carolina*, pleadings file 1–56, 5, "Answer of Defendant Carolina Legal Assistance, Inc., 1 February 1995; tagged #13" (State Courthouse Files, Raleigh, N.C.); *Junius Wilson/ André Branch v. NC/NC Department of Human Resources*, Civil Action 594CV 878BR3, 16 November 1994, 8; RAISED BY DEFENDANTS' MOTION FOR SUMMARY JUDGEMENT, 27 March 1997, tagged as 152, 6.

113. McNeil was classified as a voluntary patient from 1979 to 1990, also. David Brantley, Wayne Co. Clerk of Superior Court, cited in Stan Swofford, "Not Unique: Others Lost in System," *N&R*, 31 January 1993.

CHAPTER SIX

1. Rachel Wright, interview by Susan Burch, 6 August 2003; Rachel Wright, Evaluation Summary: Junius Wilson, 13 May 1981, JWMF.

2. The deaf Tillinghast brothers had taught at both Raleigh schools before white students were transferred to Morganton. Wright had grown up conversing in American Sign Language, but a dialect essentially frozen in time, before the 1900s.

3. Rachel Wright, interview by Susan Burch, 6 August 2003.

4. Ibid.

5. Rachel Wright, Evaluation Summary: Junius Wilson, 13 May 1981, JWMF.

6. Ibid.; Rachel Wright, interview by Susan Burch, 6 August 2003.

7. Rachel Wright, interview by Susan Burch, 6 August 2003.

8. Wilson's social worker in 1985, Dorthy Owens, also noted that "in 1983, one of the vocational rehabilitation sign language instructors came over and attempted to communicate with patient at length via sign language. . . . Patient did relate to her that he had attended the deaf and Dumb School." Dorthy Owens, Notes, 13 June 1985, JWMF.

9. Dorthy J. Owens, 21 May 1984, Psychosocial History and Assessment Update, JWMF. The information cited is the social worker's account.

10. Treatment Team Progress Notes, 19 July 1986, JWMF.

11. Treatment Team Progress Notes, 8 August 1986, JWMF.

12. Ibid.

13. Anonymous (A-6), interview by Susan Burch, 27 February 2006.

14. Sharon Moore, Referral, 19 August 1986, JWMF. It is unclear whether McNeil also received language evaluations from people like Wright, Jordan, and Moore. Social workers oversaw external evaluations and treatment teams varied in composition even for members in Woodard. Thus it is equally possible that others questioned the traditional perception of McNeil as a "dummy" as it is that no one assessed him at all. Later commentary on McNeil suggests conflicting views of his intellectual and language capacity. Some believed that he had cognitive disabilities, while others merely believed that his language skills were inferior to Wilson's. In either case, the ambiguity, complicated by language access, suggests that an evaluation of McNeil was less likely to be accurate than even those of Wilson.

15. Anonymous (A-6), interview by Susan Burch, 27 February 2006.

16. Roger Williams, interview by Susan Burch, 22 July 2005.

17. Linda Taylor, Treatment Team Notes, 12 October 1990, JWMF.

18. Donald Davis, Treatment Team Review, 10 March 1986, JWMF.

19. Roger Williams, interview by Susan Burch, 22 July 2005.

20. Treatment Team Review Notes, 11 January 1990, JWMF.

21. Progress Notes, 13 July 1992, JWMF; see also Donald Davis, Treatment Team Review, 10 December 1987, JWMF; "He at times attempts to defend his property and has been assaultive." Donald Davis, Treatment Team Note, 9 February 1989, JWMF.

22. It is unknown how Wilson's stroke effected his relationship with James McNeil. By most accounts, Wilson had enjoyed greater command of sign language previously than did McNeil. Often deaf peers are particularly sensitive to the cultural meaning of traumas like strokes and to other situations that isolate members of the deaf world. McNeil's presence in Woodard might have been both comforting and aggravating for Wilson. Later testimony suggests that Wilson had perceived himself as McNeil's superior, particularly because of his higher intellectual capability. Wilson's compromised functioning might have made him seem more like "Dummie Graham," a comparison that he apparently resented.

23. Roger Williams, interview by Susan Burch, 22 July 2005.

24. Donald Davis, Treatment Team Progress Notes, 25 August 1986, JWMF.

25. Some later medical files are even more inaccurate, overstating Wilson's age by upwards of eleven years.

26. Derek Lewis, Physical Therapy Evaluation, 18 November 1986, JWMF.

27. Donald Davis, Treatment Team Progress Note, 9 February 1987, JWMF.

28. David Hinds, 26 October 1993, JWMF. Lewis reiterated this much later when Pam King came with him to the consult in order to translate. Derek Lewis, Physical Therapy Evaluation, 10 November 1992, JWMF; also see evaluation from 10 September 1992.

29. Treatment Team Review Notes, 11 January 1990, JWMF.

30. Nelson Macatangay (director of geropsychiatry), Treatment Team Progress Notes, 11 October 1989, JWMF.

31. See, for example, Treatment Team Notes, 12 February 1987, JWMF.

32. Treatment Team Review, signed by Donald Davis, 5 July 1987, JWMF.

33. Treatment Team Notes, signed by D. Davis, 17 November 1988, JWMF.

34. Chris Lancaster, interview by Susan Burch, 26 February 2002; Chris Lancaster, interview by Susan Burch, 13 August 2005.

35. For more significant events in Disability activism in the 1980s, see "A Chronology of the Disability Rights Movements," <http://www.sfsu.edu/~hrdpu/chron.htm> (16 October 2006).

36. The original plaintiff was identified in the case by his first name and the initial of his last name: Thomas S. See James R. Dudley, Mary Lynne Calhoun, and Lynn Ahlgrim-Delzell, eds., *Lessons Learned from a Lawsuit* (Kingston, N.Y.: NADD Press, 2002), 3–4.

37. Paul Pooley, interview by Susan Burch, 8 August 2005.

38. Ibid.

39. Ibid.

40. Ibid.

41. Ibid.; Dudley, Calhoun, and Ahlgrim-Delzell, eds., *Lessons Learned from a Lawsuit*, 12, 131.

42. Anonymous (A-1), interview by Susan Burch, 24 August 2005; Paul Schreyer, interview by Susan Burch, 13 December 2004.

43. One person familiar with Wilson's case found the experience frustrating: "The hospital hadn't really changed or improved much even with . . . recommendations [given them]. . . . They weren't sincere about changing. For example, [a sign instructor] would go and teach staff sign language for a while but most staff did not apply what they learned and try to sign with Wilson nor McNeil. Apparently, the staff felt forced to take up sign language and felt it was a waste of their time. Their attitude was awful. A lot of people there don't even have a college degree and they don't value communication. It's like their attitude is one merely of just wanting to take care of patients." Anonymous (A-1), interview by Susan Burch, 24 August 2005.

44. Paul Pooley, interview by Susan Burch, 8 August 2005.

45. Linda Taylor, deposition, 3 November 1995, 12.

46. Ibid., 13.

47. Taylor might have actually seen more deaf people in her experience as an undergraduate at the Rochester Institute of Technology, which was home of the National

Technical Institute for the Deaf. Even if she did not socialize with deaf students, she might have seen them as a normal part of society. Taylor describes her academic background in her deposition, 3 November 1995, 7.

48. Linda Taylor, deposition, 3 November 1995, 24. An article by Stan Swofford says that McNeil was also diagnosed with an organic brain disorder and the hospital asked for a guardian for him in 1990—the same year as Wilson. Stan Swofford, "Not Unique: Others Lost in the System," *N&R*, 31 January 1993.

49. For example, see Donald Davis, Treatment Team Review, 6 August 1987; Donald Davis, Treatment Team Note, 10 December 1987, JWMF.

50. Linda Taylor, deposition, 3 November 1995, 25. In the deposition, Taylor did not acknowledge McNeil by name, but staff and others familiar with Wilson, McNeil, and the ward confirmed that "the deaf friend" was McNeil. Anonymous (A-1), interview by Susan Burch, 24 August 2005; Anonymous (B-1), interview by Susan Burch, 2 February 2005.

51. Hospital policy and reality precluded technicians from readily accessing medical files. Thus it would be nearly impossible for health care staff to know that others had evaluated Wilson and documented that he was sign literate.

52. Camille Costa (speech-language pathologist), Follow-up of Speech Evaluation Report to Dr. Macatangay, 13 September 1990, JWMF. A copy can also be found in *Junius Wilson v. North Carolina*, Chronological Summary of Medical Records for Junius Wilson, 1986–97.

53. Camille Costa, Follow-up of Speech Evaluation Report to Dr. Macatangay, 13 September 1990, JWMF.

54. Costa's report does not state this, but Taylor's later reference to the evaluation suggests that the idea originated with Costa. Linda Taylor, deposition, 3 November 1995, 27. It is possible she was referring to a later evaluator, Brenda Aron.

55. Linda Taylor, deposition, 3 November 1995, 27.

56. Ibid.

57. Ibid.

58. Treatment Team Notes, 26 June 1990, JWMF.

59. John Wasson to Linda Taylor, 18 December 1990, JWMF.

60. John Wasson, interview by Susan Burch, August 2003.

61. Ibid. Wasson entered social work at Chapel Hill in the 1960s on the wave of social activism. A keen interest in antipoverty work led him to specialize in community organization.

62. Donald F. Davis to John Wasson, 16 January 1991, JWMF.

63. Ibid.

64. John Wasson, interview by Susan Burch, August 2003.

65. Donald Davis to John Wasson, 16 January 1991, JWMF.

66. John Wasson, interview by Susan Burch, August 2003.

67. Linda Taylor to Louise Core, Clerk of Court, Department of Special Proceedings, Wilmington, 30 January 1991; Linda Taylor, Treatment Team Progress Notes, 12 February 1991, JWMF; John Wasson to Linda Taylor, 13 February 1991.

68. John Wasson to Linda Taylor, 13 February 1991. *Junius Wilson v. North Carolina*, legal file.

CHAPTER SEVEN

1. Letters of Appointment Guardian of the Person, 12 March 1991, file no. 91 F 143, New Hanover County, N.C..

2. John Wasson, interview by Susan Burch, August 2003.

3. Ibid.

4. Paul Pooley, interview by Susan Burch, August 2005.

5. Ibid.

6. Ibid.

7. Denise Parks, interview by Susan Burch, 10 August 2005.

8. Ibid.

9. Ibid.

10. Ibid.

11. Denise Parks, letter to Paul Pooley, 29 April 1991, JWMF.

12. Ibid.

13. Denise Parks, interview by Susan Burch, 10 August 2005; Denise Parks, letter to Paul Pooley, 29 April 1991.

14. Denise Parks, interview by Susan Burch, 10 August 2005.

15. She added, "I recommended that they use Total Communication." Denise Parks, interview by Susan Burch, 10 August 2005.

16. John Wasson to Rose Verhoeven, 2 June 1991. Files donated to author by Barbara Brauer.

17. Anonymous (B-4), interview by Susan Burch, 23 January 2006; Linda Taylor, Treatment Team Progress Notes, 12 June 1991, suggests that Paul Pooley, when contacted about Verhoeven's impending visit, informed the staff that Wilson's representatives could send whomever they wished, whenever they wanted. The treatment team note appears to express resentment over Verhoeven's planned visit.

18. Anonymous (B-4), interview by Susan Burch, 23 January 2006.

19. Rose Verhoeven, Psychological and Mental Status Evaluation: Junius Wilson, 3 June 1991, 3.

20. Ibid.

21. Ibid., 2.

22. Ibid.

23. Ibid., 3–4.

24. Ibid., 4.

25. John Wasson, interview by Susan Burch, 26 January 2006.

26. Paul Pooley, interview by Susan Burch, August 2005.

27. Ibid.

28. Wright, "Prisoner of the State," *CO*, 20 June 1993.

29. Stan Swofford, "Trapped in an Insane World," *N&R*, 31 January 1993.

30. Ibid.

31. Paul Pooley, interview by Susan Burch, August 2005.

32. Linda Taylor, deposition, 3 November 1995, 29.

33. Cathy Sweet-Windham, interview by Susan Burch, 23 January 2006.

34. Ibid.

35. Ibid.

36. Hiram Grantham was volunteering with Wilson. Treatment Team Notes, 27 August 1992, JWMF; Rick Mileski, interview by Susan Burch, 10 August 2005.

37. John Wasson, interview by Susan Burch, August 2005.

38. Swofford, "Trapped in an Insane World."

39. Settlement Agreement, State of North Carolina, Wake County (also exhibit 1).

40. Tinker Ready, "Forgotten Man's Walls of Silence Breaking Down," N&O, 10 November 1992. (Roger Manus was on the form for attorney for Wilson.) Settlement Agreement, State of North Carolina, Wake County (also exhibit 1).

41. John Wasson, interview by Susan Burch, August 2005.

42. Kirsten B. Mitchell, "67-Year Ordeal for Deaf Man Coming to End," WMS, 11 November 1992.

43. Swofford, "Trapped in an Insane World."

44. Ibid.

45. Ready, "Forgotten Man's Walls of Silence Breaking Down."

46. Mitchell, "67-Year Ordeal for Deaf Man Coming to End."

47. Ibid.

48. Gary Wright, "Denied Trial, Deaf Man Castrated, Locked Up for Decades," Baltimore Sun, 24 June 1993.

49. See, for example, "A Tragedy with No Answer," Atlanta Constitution, 13 November 1992; Mary Connor, "Sane Man Spends 67 Years in State Mental Hospital Because He's Deaf," Boca Raton Sun, 26 January 1993; "Psychiatric Hospital to Release Deaf Man after 67 Years," Topeka Capital Journal, 11 November 1992; "Deafness Kept Man in Mental Hospital," Philadelphia Inquirer, 11 November 1992; "Deaf Man to Be Freed after 67 Years in Asylum," San Francisco Chronicle, 30 November 1992.

50. John Wasson, interview by Susan Burch, August 2005.

51. Wright, "Denied Trial, Deaf Man Castrated, Locked Up for Decades."

52. Ready, "Forgotten Man's Walls of Silence Breaking Down."

53. Mitchell, "67-Year Ordeal for Deaf Man Coming to End." Looking back, Paul Pooley recalled, "We were aware . . . [and would] not fall into this powerless and victimization and internalized oppression thing where we'd throw our hands up." Paul Pooley, interview by Susan Burch, 8 August 2005.

54. Josie Douglas, "Deaf Need Services," N&O, 24 November 1992.

55. Ibid.

56. Walter Stelle, deputy director of mental health services for the state, told a reporter. "A Stranger, and Alone," N&O, 16 November 1992.

57. Kirsten B. Mitchell, "Deaf Man's Ordeal Gets National Attention," WMS, 12 November 1992.

58. J. Field Montgomery was Cherry Hospital's director. Tinker Ready, "Hospitals to Provide Interpreters for Deaf," N&O, 11 November 1992.

59. Stan Swofford, "Not Unique: Others Lost in System," N&R, 31 January 1993.

60. Ready, "Hospitals to Provide Interpreters for Deaf"; "A Stranger, and Alone."

61. Paul Pooley, interview by Susan Burch, 8 August 2005.

62. Ibid.

63. Swofford, "Trapped in an Insane World."

64. Ibid.

65. Chris Lancaster, interview by Susan Burch, 13 August 2005.

66. Ibid.

67. Lulu Jolliff, interview by Susan Burch, 26 August 2004.

68. Annie and Willie Sidberry, interview by Susan Burch, 20 March 2002; see also Annie L. Nixon-Sidberry, deposition, 10 May 1006, 11.

69. Kirsten Mitchell, "Life Emerges from a World of Silence," *WMS*, 30 September 1996.

70. The news of Wilson family members coming forward startled Wasson: "I had actually sent people who were African American who worked for DSS into Castle Hayne . . . to see whether there was any family. They couldn't find anybody." John Wasson, interview by Susan Burch, August 2003.

CHAPTER EIGHT

1. This trip followed a brief visit to Wilmington, where Wilson met Annie Sidberry at the city's Department of Social Services. Wasson told the press to stay away and allow Wilson a private experience with family. Sallie Woodard, Progress Notes, 30 March 1993, JWMF. There they discussed potential future trips to Castle Hayne. John Wasson, interview by Susan Burch, 26 January 2006; Linda Taylor, deposition, 3 November 1995, 40. Linda Taylor, Pam King, a nurse, and a tech (possibly Willie Mewborn) escorted Wilson on the first trip. Linda Taylor, deposition, 3 November 1995, 41.

2. Anonymous (A-1), interview by Susan Burch, 24 August 2005.

3. Linda Taylor, deposition, 3 November 1995, 41.

4. Kirsten B. Mitchell, "Junius Wilson Makes Trip to Castle Hayne," *WMS*, 1 April 1993.

5. Willie Mewborn, Progress Notes, 2 April 1993, JWMF. "Then, a veil of sadness briefly shadowed Mr. Wilson's face." It had been thirteen years since he wrote "Castle Hayne" on paper when hospital staff asked where he wanted to go. He had been signing "far away." "On Wednesday, the 95-year-old deaf man was accompanied on the 2½ hour visit by an interpreter, a nurse, an occupational therapist, a deaf elderly friend and Mr. Wasson. . . . Though Mr. Wilson has no contact with his family, an old friend of the Wilson family contacted Mr. Wasson several weeks ago and gave him a rough idea where the Wilsons lived." Mitchell, "Junius Wilson Makes Trip to Castle Hayne."

6. Willie Mewborn, Progress Notes, 2 April 1993, JWMF.

7. Anonymous (A-1), interview by Susan Burch, 24 August 2005.

8. Willie Mewborn, Progress Notes, 2 April 1993, JWMF.

9. Ibid.

10. Nelson Macatangay, Progress Notes, 5 April 1993, JWMF.

11. Mitchell, "Junius Wilson Makes Trip to Castle Hayne."

12. Sarah Peoples, deposition, 9 May 1996, 14–15.

13. André Branch, deposition, 3 November 1995, 37. Apparently Gill had not spoken to other relatives about her brother during the news blitz or in prior years. See, for example, Annie L. Nixon-Sidberry, deposition, 10 May 1996, 11; Sarah Peoples, deposition, 9 May 1996, 14–15.

14. André Branch, deposition, 3 November 1995, 57.

15. John Wasson, interview by Susan Burch, 26 January 2006.

16. Paul Pooley, interview by Susan Burch, 8 August 2005.

17. Ibid.

18. André Branch to John Wasson, 24 April 1993, Junius Wilson Court Files (State Courthouse Files, Raleigh, N.C.), 2.

19. Ibid.

20. Ibid.

21. Ibid.

22. Ibid.

23. Ibid.

24. John Wasson to André Branch, 22 June 1993, Junius Wilson Court Files (State Courthouse Files, Raleigh, N.C.).

25. André Branch to John Wasson, 29 June 1993, Junius Wilson Court Files (State Courthouse Files, Raleigh, N.C.).

26. John Wasson to André Branch, 22 July 1993, Junius Wilson Court Files (State Courthouse Files, Raleigh, N.C.).

27. Ibid.

28. Jack Gannon, *Deaf Heritage* (Silver Spring, Md.: NAD, 1980); Leo Jacobs, *A Deaf Adult Speaks Out* (Washington, D.C.: Gallaudet University Press, 1980). Others, like Ernest Hairston and Linwood Smith, produced books that reflected the increased awareness of racial differences in the deaf world. See *Black and Deaf in America: Are We That Different?* (Silver Spring, Md.: TJ Publishers, Inc, 1983).

29. See, for example, Harlan Lane, *When the Mind Hears* (New York: Random House, 1980).

30. "Introduction to the ADA," <http://www.ada.gov/adaintro.htm> (1 March 2006).

31. Paul Pooley, interview by Susan Burch, 8 August 2005.

32. Reporter Tinker Ready noted later that Wilson interacted well with Aron and seemed to communicate comparatively well with her. Tinker Ready, interview by Susan Burch, 17 February 2006.

33. Brenda Aron, Assessment: Junius Wilson, 10 January 1993, JWMF.

34. Ibid., 8.

35. Ibid., 4.

36. Ibid., 2.

37. Paul Schreyer, interview by Susan Burch, 13 December 2004.

38. Brenda Aron, Assessment: Junius Wilson, 10 January 1993, JWMF, 12.

39. Ibid., 6.

40. Paul Pooley, interview by Susan Burch, 8 August 2005.

41. Ibid.

42. Brenda Aron, Assessment: Junius Wilson, 10 January 1993, JWMF, 6; Paul Schreyer, interview by Susan Burch, 13 December 2004.

43. Brenda Aron, Assessment: Junius Wilson, 10 January 1993, JWMF, 9.

44. Paul Schreyer, interview by Susan Burch, 13 December 2004.

45. Everett Parker, interview by Susan Burch, 21 March 2002.

46. Paul Schreyer, interview by Susan Burch, 13 December 2004.

47. Ibid.

48. Everett Parker, interview by Susan Burch, 21 March 2002.

49. Linda Taylor, deposition, 3 November 1995, 36–7.

50. Anonymous (B-5), interview by Susan Burch, 24 August 2005.

51. Paul Schreyer, interview by Susan Burch, 13 December 2004.

52. Everett Parker, interview by Susan Burch, 21 March 2002. This might not have been factually accurate, as other sign language instructors had previously worked with Wilson. Still, by most accounts, Everett Parker was Wilson's closest companion and the person with whom he most readily communicated.

53. Progress Note, 7 July 1993, JWMF; Nelson Macatangay, Progress Notes, 7 July 1993, JWMF.

54. Anonymous (A-1), interview by Susan Burch, 24 August 2005.

55. Gary Wright, "Prisoner of the State," *CO*, 20 June 1993.

56. Brenda Aron, Assessment: Junius Wilson, 10 January 1993, JWMF, 9.

57. Ibid., 10.

58. Paul Pooley, referring to Julie Hayes. Paul Pooley, interview by Susan Burch, 8 August 2005.

59. Linda Taylor, deposition, 3 November 1995, 42. She is referring to conversations that seem to occur after Wilson has already moved to the cottage.

60. John Wasson, interview by Susan Burch, August 2005; John Wasson to André Branch, 22 July 1993, Junius Wilson Court Files (State Courthouse Files, Raleigh, N.C.).

61. John Wasson, interview by Susan Burch, August 2005.

62. Anonymous (B-5), interview by Susan Burch, 24 August 2005.

63. John Wasson, interview by Susan Burch, 26 January 2006.

64. Wright, "Prisoner of the State."

65. John Wasson to André Branch, 22 July 1993, Junius Wilson Court Files (State Courthouse Files, Raleigh, N.C.).

66. Ibid.

67. Kirsten Mitchell, "Deaf Man Still Held at State Psychiatric Hospital," *WMS*, 1 December 1993.

68. John Wasson, interview by Susan Burch, 26 January 2006.

69. Mitchell, "Deaf Man Still Held at State Psychiatric Hospital."

70. Ibid.

71. Ibid.

72. See Kirsten Mitchell, "Deaf Man Caught Up in Red Tape," *WMS*, 2 December 1993; Stan Swofford, "State Still Lagging on Home for Wrongly Confined Man," *N&R*, 13 December 1993.

73. Tim Simmons, "State Offers Temporary Home for Deaf Man," *N&O*, 4 December 1993.

74. See also *WMS*, 7 December 1993.

75. "Red Tape Still Ensnares 96-Year-Old Man," *All Things Considered*, National Public Radio, 4 December 1993, T.E. transcript no. 1321-6.

76. Ibid.

77. Kirsten Mitchell, "N.C. Makes an Offer to Help Man in Asylum," *WMS*, 4 December 1993.

78. Annie Sidberry, interview by Susan Burch, 20 March 2002. André Branch offered a similar description in his deposition. André Branch, deposition, 3 November 1995, 78–79.

79. Annie Sidberry, interview by Susan Burch, 20 March 2002.

80. Branch also perceived that the interpreter did not fully understand Wilson. André Branch, deposition, 3 November 1995, 80.

81. Annie Sidberry, interview by Susan Burch, 20 March 2002; Progress Notes, 23 December 1993, JWMF.

82. Progress Notes, 23 December 1993, JWMF: "Wilson family members came to visit; Mrs. Sidberry and André Branch spent a couple of hours—shown the dining room and Wilson's bedroom."

CHAPTER NINE

1. Junius Wilson Treatment Team Meeting Minutes, 20 January 1994, JWMF, 2; Progress Notes, 27 January 1994, JWMF. The team decided to wait to travel to the school until Wilson was ensconced in the cottage.

2. Progress Notes, 27 January 1994, JWMF; Junius Wilson Treatment Team Meeting Minutes, 20 January 1994, JWMF, 2.

3. Junius Wilson Treatment Team Meeting Minutes, 20 January 1994, JWMF, 3.

4. Kirsten B. Mitchell, "Deaf Man to Move off Ward to Cottage," *WMS*, 4 February 1994.

5. Progress Notes, 27 January 1994, JWMF. She acknowledges that she "cannot use sign at present" so it is not impossible that there was a miscommunication here.

6. Dudley Price, "Freedom Begins for Deaf Man Jailed 69 Years Ago," *N&O*, 5 February 1994.

7. John Wasson, interview by Susan Burch, August 2003.

8. "Free at Last," *Eugene (Ore.) Register-Guard*, 5 February 1994, 3A.

9. John Wasson, interview by Susan Burch, 26 January 2006.

10. Kirsten B. Mitchell, "After 68 Years in Mental Ward, Junius Wilson Moves into Cottage," *WMS*, 5 February 1994; Price, "Freedom Begins for Deaf Man Jailed 69 Years Ago."

11. "After 68 Years, Innocent Man Finally Sent Home," *Washington (N.C.) Daily News*, 5 February 1994.

12. Anonymous (B-5), interview by Susan Burch, 24 August 2005; Kirsten Mitchell, "Life Emerges from a World of Silence," *WMS*, 30 September 1996; "State Makes Amends

for False Commitment; After 69 Years, Man Has New Life," *Chicago Tribune*, 4 February 1996.

13. Price, "Freedom Begins for Deaf Man Jailed 69 Years Ago."

14. Ibid.; Estes Thompson, "Deaf Man Gets Some Freedom after 68-Year Wrongful Confinement," *Greenville (N.C.) Daily Reflector*, 5 February 1994. Wilson was checked regularly while living in the Woodard Building but he might have received increased attention once he was placed in the cottage.

15. Health Care Technician Progress Notes, 15 June 1994, JWMF.

16. "Keys for the Wilson House are being made and will be available by November 3. Mr. Wilson will receive a house key for his own possession" (one year after moving in). Junius Wilson Treatment Team Meeting Minutes, 26 October 1995, JWMF, 2.

17. "Free at Last," *Montreal Gazette*, 5 February 1994; "Free at Last," *Eugene (Ore.) Register-Guard*, 5 February 1994.

18. John Wasson, interview by Susan Burch, August 2003.

19. "Free at Last," *Montreal Gazette*.

20. Thompson, "Deaf Man Gets Some Freedom after 68-Year Wrongful Confinement."

21. "Free at Last," *Montreal Gazette*.

22. Paul Pooley, cited in Price, "Freedom Begins for Deaf Man Jailed 69 Years Ago."

23. This is more complicated: Martinez was found wandering the street naked in 1955 (apparently he thought it felt good), and he got out briefly once or twice, but he then landed back in the hospital when he could not communicate with outsiders and behaved poorly. Evaluators, however, insisted that the kind of illness he had was mild and controllable with medication. Ultimately, he was kept primarily because he was deaf. In the 1990s he gave his interview apparently without any difficulty using an ASL interpreter.

24. Paul Rubin, "Deaf and Damned," *Phoenix New Times*, 2 October 1997, <www.pho enixnewtimes.com/issues/1997-10-02/news/feature_print.htlm> (10 April 2006).

25. Linda Taylor, Comprehensive Psychosocial History/Assessment, 6 April 1995, JWMF.

26. Mitchell, "Life Emerges from a World of Silence."

27. Stan Swofford, "Not Unique: Others Lost in System," *N&R*, 31 January 1993.

28. Roger Williams, interview by Susan Burch, 22 July 2005.

29. Notes, 11 March 1994, JWMF.

30. Linda Taylor, Progress Notes, 3 March 1994, JWMF. This was about one month after Wilson moved into the cottage.

31. As a *Thomas S.* plaintiff, James McNeil was slated to leave the hospital completely at an indefinite time in the future. Consequently, he could not be removed from the ward merely to be placed in a hospital cottage.

32. Anonymous (A-1), interview by Susan Burch, 24 August 2005.

33. Linda Taylor, Comprehensive Psychosocial History/Assessment, 6 April 1995, JWMF.

34. John Bundor, deposition, 11 December 1995, 44.

35. Ibid., 44. The cottage did have a TTY because the hospital moved Hiram Grantham's device to the Wilson house. It is unclear whether the deaf health care technician received a replacement. Minutes: Junius Wilson Treatment Team Meeting, 20 January 1994, JWMF, 4. TDD and TTY refer to the same device.

36. John Bundor, deposition, 11 December 1995, 35.

37. Ibid., 35.

38. Linda Taylor, Progress Notes, 5 April 1994, JWMF. Other staff complained that neighbors did not respect Wilson's space. For example, one staff member angrily asked why Wilson's garage was taken over by the neighboring family: "He lives in this house on this property. This is not what a person gets when they are renting property. These are things that will give him what [he] has not had in life [or] the respect as a rental or owner. There are also trouble with the T.V." Notes, 15 March 1994, JWMF.

39. John Wasson, interview by Susan Burch, August 2003.

40. See, for example, Progress Notes, 3 March 1994, JWMF. Wilson received a new "velour robe, a pair tan bedroom shoes, a pair black gloves, two bottles aftershave lotion and one container of body powder." He also "received a letter and Blue Cap from Gary Gould" in Michigan. Grantham read him the letter in sign language. Progress Notes, 10 June 1994, JWMF. Reporter Kirsten Mitchell noted when she visited Wilson's house that "he was almost childlike. He was just delighted to have company. He seemed genuinely pleased that we were visiting. . . . He opened the refrigerator door and was showing me the contents, showing me quite specifically [what he had]. . . . When we went into the bedroom, everything was very tidy. . . . He opened the drawers and showed off his possessions." Kirsten Mitchell, interview by Susan Burch, 23 March 2006.

41. One team member, describing Carnell Mewborn. Anonymous (B-5), interview by Susan Burch, 24 August 2005.

42. When Wilson went to a church service in Dudley he would "sit quiet for about an hour then got up ready to go. Left church and ate lunch @ Kentucky Fried Chicken." Medical Log, 12 June 1994, JWMF; see also Progress Note, Minutes, Junius Wilson Treatment Team Meeting, 26 October 1995, JWMF, 2.)

43. "State Makes Amends for False Commitment." See also M. Taswell, LPN, Notes, 25 June 1975, JWMF.

44. Linda Taylor, 15 June 1994, JWMF.

45. Ibid.

46. See Mitchell, "Life Emerges from a World of Silence."

47. Ibid.

48. "He is involved in recreational activities and leisure activities and goes to deaf program once a month." H. N. Nataraja, M.D. (staff psychiatrist), 31 May 1994, JWMF.

49. "Once a week he returns to the psychiatric ward where he eats a meal and visits with old friends." Mitchell, "Life Emerges from a World of Silence."

50. Health Care Technician (HCT), Progress Notes, 4 April 1994, JWMF. See also Progress Notes, 5 April 1994, JWMF. Wilson visited Woodard later that day. HCT note, 2 June 1994, JWMF. Since 28 April 1994, his medical file notes that Wilson had attended movies on the ward, taken bus rides, and participated in spring festival activities. D.

McNair, Progress Notes, 2 June 1994, JWMF. He also visited "peers @ Woodard" (G. Forte, HCT, Progress Notes, 18 June 1994, JWMF) and "attended a cookout" with a health care technician and his children at a local park. Later that day he went to the Woodard Building and saw peers at 1-West; Vernon H . . . HCT, Progress Notes, 19 June 1994, JWMF. Wilson repeatedly visited the wards. See, for example, Progress Notes, 20 June 1994, and Progress Notes, 21 June 1994, both in JWMF.

51. Junius Wilson Treatment Team Meeting Notes, 7 April 1994, JWMF, 2. It appears McNeil was already visiting Wilson. A note in Wilson's medical log one month earlier claimed that "another deaf patient from the ward has been visiting him and apparently has been enjoying the visit." 11 March 1994, JWMF. The treatment team considered how long Junius Wilson could visit on 1-West in the Woodard Building. Doug Dexter asked whether "Mr. McNeil and other patients could visit Mr. Wilson at the house. Ms. Martin, RN, stated staff will work on this." Junius Wilson Treatment Team Meeting Notes, 7 April 1994, JWMF, 2.

52. Anonymous (A-9), interview by Susan Burch, 6 March 2006. "Mr. Parker and his pt. friend from Woodard ate with him" at the house. Progress Notes, 16 March 1994, JWMF. "Another deaf patient from the ward has been visiting him and apparently has been enjoying the visit." Progress Notes, 11 March 1994, JWMF.

53. Anonymous (A-9), interview by Susan Burch, 6 March 2006. "McNeil visited sometimes. He'd [Junius Wilson] be glad to see him. They'd stayed inside some—they'd sit on the porch. . . . Mr. Parker joined in, too. . . . Mr. McNeil seemed glad to go visit." Progress Notes, 16 June 1994, JWMF: "Mr. Parker and his pt. friend from Woodard ate with him" at the house.

54. Note: the "informant's name" on his death certificate is Linda Taylor. Bureau of Vital Statistics, Standard Certificate of Death: Julian James McNeil, (North Carolina State Board of Health, Wilmington, N.C.), registration district no. 092-95, local no. 1661.

55. Anonymous (A-1), interview by Susan Burch, 24 August 2005.

56. Junius Wilson Treatment Team Meeting Notes, 25 August 1994, JWMF; Wayne Memorial Park, Chapel, "Memorial service and graveside service for James McNeil." J. Hope HCT, Activities Log Book, 10 August 1994, JWMF.

57. Silvia Weaver, interview by Susan Burch, 19 November 2004.

58. Anonymous (B-1), interview by Susan Burch, 2 February 2005.

59. Treatment Team Notes, 24 August 1994, JWMF; Treatment Team Meeting Notes, 25 August 1994, JWMF.

60. Visiting RN, Progress Notes, 25 August 1994, JWMF.

61. Dr. Macatangay, Treatment Team Notes, 24 August 1994, JWMF.

62. Linda Taylor to Ann Sidberry, letter, 12 August 1994, JWMF. "We are looking forward to seeing you again and to meeting some of the other members of Mr. Wilson's family."

63. Dr. Macatangay, Treatment Team Notes, 24 August 1994, JWMF.

64. Wilson "enjoyed visit w/ family." J. Langston, Activities Log Book, 20 August 1994, JWMF.

65. Staff brought along a video camera to film the event. This might have been done

to remind him of happy events after they returned, to entertain him, and to reinforce a sense of community. Treatment Team Meeting Notes, 25 August 1994, JWMF.

66. Linda Taylor letter to Mr. and Mrs. Sidberry, 12 September 1994, JWMF.

67. Linda Taylor, Progress Notes, 1 March 1995, JWMF.

68. Junius Wilson Treatment Team Meeting Notes, 25 August 1994, JWMF.

69. Ibid.

70. The suit was filed 17 November 1994; its entry date in federal court was 7 December 1994.

71. *Junius Wilson, by His Next Friend, André Branch v. State of North Carolina et al.* Complaint Civil Action No. 5: 94-CV-878-BR; complaint: 15–16.

72. Ibid., 15.

73. Ibid., 20.

74. Ibid., 10.

75. Ibid., 11.

76. Confirmed by Helen Hinn. Helen Hinn, interview by Susan Burch, 1 February 2006.

77. "In 1972, two years after the criminal case was nol prossequied [*sic*] in New Hanover County, Mr. Wilson's sister and his father sought his release but did not succeed. André Branch, his cousin, visited or attempted to visit him each Christmas in the 1990s." Plaintiff's Answers to defendant North Carolina's first set of interrogatories, Junius Wilson by his Guardian ad litem André Branch, the State of North Carolina et al., no. 5:94-CV-878-Br-3, 7.

78. "Cousin Seeks Custody of Falsely Accused Deaf Man," *Durham Herald-Sun*, 16 January 1996.

79. Linda Taylor to Willie and Annie Sidberry, 13 December 1994, JWMF.

80. "Mr. Wilson had three of his family members visit him this P.M. Mr. Willie Sidberry (cousin) Mrs. Annie Sidberry and Crystal Sidberry (cousin)." He enjoyed the visit, showed them his rooms and pictures on the wall and had lunch with them. Progress Notes, 23 December 1994, JWMF.

81. HCT Progress Notes, 24 December 1994 (10:25 P.M.), JWMF.

82. "Mr. Branch cousin of Mr. Wilson left a present and a fruit basket. Mr. Wilson wanted to put under Christmas tree." Health Care Technician Progress Note, 24 December 1994 (11:00 P.M.), JWMF.

83. Wilson House Log, HCT Progress Note, 25 December 1994 and 25 December 1994 (8:20 P.M.), JWMF.

CHAPTER TEN

1. Annie L. Nixon-Sidberry, deposition, 10 May 1996, 18.

2. Willie Sidberry, interview by Susan Burch, 20 March 2002.

3. Linda Taylor, Assessment, 6 April 1995.

4. Stan Swofford, "Guardian Sued for Helping Man," *N&R*, 28 December 1995.

5. "Public Should Know What It Settled For," *WMS*, 2 December 1995. See also Tricia Vance, "Suit Drops Guardian of Castrated Man," *WMS*, 30 November 1995.

6. André Branch, deposition, 3 November 1995, 51.

7. Ibid., 68. There were other clashes. Ambrose wanted clarification about the events surrounding Wilson's arrest. "You have alleged in some document or other in this lawsuit that Mr. Junius Wilson was working in a field at the time that he was arrested; is that correct? Do you recall making that allegation?" Branch retorted, "Your word choice amuses me, 'some document or other.' He was working in a field with his mother. That is correct."

8. André Branch, deposition, 3 November 1995, 65.

9. Ibid., 68–69.

10. Ibid., 69.

11. Ibid.

12. Branch also claimed that Wilson experienced intimidation and harassment. André Branch, deposition, 3 November 1995, 73.

13. Submitted by Branch's lawyers, read aloud by Ambrose during deposition. André Branch, deposition, 3 November 1995, 71.

14. Thomas Smith, Psychological Evaluation, 25 April 1995, JWMF.

15. Treatment Team Notes, 28 April 1995, JWMF.

16. Bunder et al. were asked to address three objectives: "evaluate [Wilson's] living conditions, observe his living conditions; consider whether his living situation was appropriate; recommend specific thing that would improve his living conditions." Included in this charge was the questions of whether Wilson should be discharged. John Bundor, deposition, 11 December 1995, 22; Bundor et al., Evaluation of Junius Wilson, 4 September 1995, JWMF. The three evaluators apparently conducted interviews on 24, 25, 28, and 30 August 1995. See also Roger Williams, interview by Susan Burch, 22 July 2005; Roger Williams, deposition, 11 December 1995, 18.

17. A. Barry Critchfield, deposition, 11 December 1995, 17.

18. They are referring to a patient known as "Mr. AM." Roger Williams, deposition, 11 December 1995, 66.

19. Ibid., 65–66.

20. Roger Williams, interview by Susan Burch, 22 July 2005.

21. Ibid.

22. Ibid.

23. Ibid.

24. Ibid.

25. Critchfield et al., "Consultant Recommendations: Junius Wilson," JWMF, 6.

26. Roger Williams, interview by Susan Burch, 22 July 2005.

27. Critchfield et al., "Consultant Recommendations: Junius Wilson."

28. A. Barry Critchfield, deposition, 11 December 1995, 57.

29. Offering a different perspective on the benefit of the lawsuit, they suggested that funds from a settlement be used to create a private nonprofit foundation to administer to Wilson's needs. Closing loopholes from the 1991 settlement, the men proposed that the foundation receive the title of the cottage so that if "Wilson must leave the cottage due to health reason, the foundation would ensure his healthcare was covered." In an

effort to promote a positive legacy, they added that "his property after death would remain with the foundation and would help deaf African Americans in North Carolina."

30. "Misguided Missiles," *USA Today*, 29 December 1995.

31. Swofford, "Guardian Sued for Helping Man"; "Guardian Who Helped Deaf Man Settles Lawsuit," *Vancouver (Wash.) Columbian*, 29 December 1995.

32. Swofford, "Guardian Sued for Helping Man."

33. Kirsten B. Mitchell, "Judge Reveals County's Settlement in Junius Wilson Case," *WSN*, 23 January 1996.

34. Scott Whisnant, "Court Won't Change Deaf Man's Guardian," *WMS*, 17 January 1996.

35. Kirsten B. Mitchell, "Judge Reveals County's Settlement in Junius Wilson Case," *WSN*, 23 January 1996.

36. Ibid.

37. Ibid.

38. Ibid. See also Tina Kelley, "After 70 Years, Where Is His Home? Deaf Cousin Is Seattleite's Cause," *Seattle Post-Intelligencer*, 26 January 1996.

39. Vance, "Suit Drops Guardian of Castrated Man." Earlier hospital documents suggest that staff overestimated Wilson's age by six or ten years. It is unclear why the margin of error varied, but shifts in personnel and limited time spent confirming details in medical charts may account for some of this.

40. Extant documents offer different variations of this statement. See, for example, *Junius Wilson, by His Next Friend, André Branch v. State of North Carolina et al*, memorandum in support of attorney Jumper's motion to withdraw (filed under seal), pleadings file 1–56, 20 December 1995 (State Courthouse Files, Raleigh, N.C.). This version appears to be a statement by attorney Sharon Jumper.

41. Jennie Bowman, deposition, 19 December 1995, 20.

42. Ibid.

43. Ibid., 20–21.

44. See, for example, *Junius Wilson, by His Next Friend, André Branch v. State of North Carolina et al*, memorandum in support of attorney Jumper's motion to withdraw (filed under seal), pleadings file 1–56, 20 December 1995 (State Courthouse Files, Raleigh, N.C.); Jennie Bowman, deposition, 19 December 1995.

45. Annie Mae Williams, deposition, 24 May 1996, 17.

46. Ibid., 55.

47. Fannie Thomas, deposition, 8 May 1996, 14–15.

48. Virginia Smith Branch, deposition, 10 May 1996, 11.

49. Ibid., 12.

50. Fannie Thomas, deposition, 8 May 1996, 14.

51. Annie Mae Williams, deposition, 24 May 1996, 14.

52. Ibid., 15.

53. It was the only time she visited the hospital. Annie Mae Williams, deposition, 24 May 1996, 15.

54. See, for example, Kirsten B. Mitchell, "Suit Claims Deaf Man Was Framed by His Uncle," *WMS*, 13 January 1996.

55. Ibid.

56. John Bagett, quoted in "State Makes Amends for False Commitment; After 69 Years, Man Has New Life," *Chicago Tribune*, 4 February 1996.

57. Annie L. Nixon-Sidberry, deposition, 10 May 1996, 12–13.

58. Ibid., 14.

59. Willie Sidberry, deposition, 10 May 1996, 20.

60. In an interview, Mr. Sidberry added to his description of Lizzie Smith: "Lizzie Smith was a darling, the sweetest person. Everybody called her Aunt Lizzie. Everybody respected her, too. She was a doll. So kind." Willie Sidberry, interview by Susan Burch, 20 March 2002.

61. Fannie Thomas, deposition, 8 May 1996, 21.

62. Sarah Peoples, deposition, 9 May 1996, 15–17.

63. Annie Mae Williams, deposition, 24 May 1996, 10.

64. Ibid., 37.

65. Ibid., 38.

66. Scott Whisnant, "Court Won't Change Deaf Man's Guardian," *WMS*, 17 January 1996.

67. Ibid.

68. Ibid. The details of Wilson's case—motions, summary judgments, etc.—had been kept sealed until representatives of the *Wilmington Morning Star* sued for access. The judge granted this in January 1996.

69. Helen Hinn, interview by Susan Burch, 1 February 2006. Later that year, Judge Britt ordered Branch's lawyers to pay the state $9,621—the amount it cost the state to find names through interviews, courthouse records, and research. Kirsten Mitchell, "Life Emerges from a World of Silence," *WMS*, 30 September 1996.

70. Junius Wilson Court Files, 28 October 1996 (State Courthouse Files, Raleigh, N.C.).

71. Chris Davis, "Cousin of Deaf Man out of Lawsuit," *WSN*, 17 August 1996.

72. Ibid.

73. Amy Turnbull, "Junius Wilson Dies," *WMS*, 29 March 2001. Tricia Vance, "Lawyer Is Made Guardian of Junius Wilson's Estate," *WMS*, 20 February 1996.

74. Turnbull, "Junius Wilson Dies."

75. Helen Hinn, interview by Susan Burch, 1 February 2006.

76. Ibid.

77. Ibid.

78. John Wasson, interview by Susan Burch, 9 August 2003.

79. John Wasson, interview by Susan Burch, 21 January 2001.

80. Observation by Anonymous (A-7), interview by Susan Burch, 19 November 2001.

81. Ibid.

82. The case took an unexpected turn. Within days, Branch's former lawyer, Sharon Jumper, motioned for the court to appoint her as guardian ad litem instead. The Charlotte attorney had served on Branch's legal team in 1995 but the Washington lawyers fired her after bitter disagreements that December. Afterwards, Jumper filed a complaint against her former colleagues, accusing them of dishonesty, inappropriate conduct, and

incompetency. Ultimately, the judge acknowledged part of her assessment but approved of her removal as a matter based mostly on professional differences.

Jumper had spoken with reporters, fueling suspicions that greed primarily motivated Branch and his legal team. After Branch and Pulliam failed to gain authority over Wilson's person and estate, Jumper had also disappeared from the spotlight. Her motion to take such a central role in Wilson's life surprised everyone. Most dismissed her, believing a desire for publicity and greed motivated her own actions this time. In early September the court handed down its decision, denying Jumper's request and granting the role of guardian ad litem to Helen Hinn. Hinn describing Sharon Jumper: "He had an attorney in Charlotte: Sharon Jumper . . . [who was] very unprofessionally attired. She has subsequently lost her license for embezzlement or such, but she has lost her license. She wanted reimbursement for trips to Seattle that she was not asked to make." Helen Hinn, interview by Susan Burch, 1 February 2006.

83. Anita S. Hodgkiss, letter to Dr. Barbara Brauer, 27 November 1996, JWMF. Gift from Barbara Brauer to Susan Burch. Hodgkiss wrote on behalf of Ferguson, Stein, Wallas, Adkins, Gresham & Sumter.

84. They also worked from other sources. Critchfield claimed that, "assuming Mr. Wilson were not deaf, I doubt that he would have been retained in the hospital for as long as he was. . . . My opinion is that if he weren't deaf, he probably would not have had to stay in the hospital as long as he did." *Junius Wilson by his Guardian Ad Litem, Helen Hinn v. the State of North Carolina et al.* (1997), no. 5: 94-CV-878-BR3, 5, State Courthouse Files, Raleigh, N.C.

85. E-mail from Alan Marcus to Barbara Brauer, 15 July 1997. Gift to author from Barbara Brauer.

86. Barbara Brauer, Preliminary Report on Junius Wilson, Brauer files given to Susan Burch.

87. Ibid., 12.

88. Barbara Brauer and Jo Ann Mackinson, Preliminary Report on Junius Wilson, *Junius Wilson v. the State of North Carolina*, 10 March 1997; Brauer to Anita Hodgkiss, gift to author from Barbara Brauer.

89. Brauer, Corbett, and Marcus, Psychological Evaluation Report, 16 July 1997, JWMF, 12.

90. "State Makes Amends for False Commitment."

91. "Judge Allows Suit Filed by Deaf Man's Relative," *WMS*, 17 January 1997.

92. Ibid.

93. E-mail from Alan Marcus to Barbara Brauer, 2 July 1997, gift to author from Barbara Brauer. See also notes from Marcus to Carolyn Corbett and Brauer from North Carolina trip, faxed 8 July 1997, gift to author from Barbara Brauer.

94. Brauer, Corbett, and Marcus, Psychological Evaluation Report, 16 July 1997, JWMF, 4.

95. Ibid., 11.

96. In order to protect the privacy of this patient, no names or initials are provided in this book. The treatment team discussed including this patient (with whom Wilson

seemed to have an established relationship) as early as October 1995. Minutes, Junius Wilson Treatment Team Meeting, 26 October 1995, JWMF, 2; Progress Notes, 9 October 1996, JWMF; Progress Note, 26 June 1997, JWMF; OT Therapy Service Notes, 23 July 1997, JWMF; Occupation Therapy Report, 24 October 1996, and OT Report, 18 December 1996, JWMF; OT Report for Junius Wilson, 14 February 1996, JWMF; W. C. Mewborn, Progress Notes, 21 March 1996, JWMF; Progress Notes, 10 October 1996, JWMF; OT Report for Junius Wilson, 27 February 1997 to 25 March 1997, JWMF; OT Report, 17 April 1997 to 21 May 1997, JWMF.

97. Evidence suggests that Roger Williams might have met this gentleman, although they were not formally introduced. Another hospital employee remembered that the man could speak vocally. Roger Williams, interview by Susan Burch, 11 September 2001; Anonymous (A-9), interview by Susan Burch, 6 March 2006.

98. Helen Hinn, interview by Susan Burch, 1 February 2006. Other observers also recalled the Christmas parties as highlights for Wilson. Anonymous (A-7), interview by Susan Burch, 19 November 2001.

99. Junius Wilson Treatment Team Meeting Notes, 19 May 1994, JWMF, 1; see also anonymous (B-5), interview by Susan Burch, 24 August 2005.

100. Occupational Therapist Report, 18 December 1996, JWMF.

101. Brenda Aron to Douglas Dexter, Language Planning Report & Sundry, 18 January 1994, JWMF, 13.

102. Junius Wilson Treatment Team Meeting Notes, 16 June 1994, JWMF.

103. Sylvia Weaver to Douglas Dexter, Occupational Therapy Report on Junius Wilson, 8 June 1994, JWMF.

104. See also Sylvia Weaver to Douglas Dexter, Occupational Therapy Report on Junius Wilson, 18 August 1994, JWMF.

105. Sylvia Weaver to Douglas Dexter, Occupational Therapy Report, 6 May 1994, JWMF; Sylvia Weaver to Douglas Dexter, 15 December 1995, JWMF.

106. Douglas Dexter, Treatment Team Notes, 28 April 1995, JWMF.

107. Silvia Weaver, interview by Susan Burch, 19 November 2004.

108. "I have instructed Ms. Taylor, social worker, to document her efforts to encourage visitation and family resistance." Douglas Dexter, Treatment Team Notes, 28 April 1995, JWMF.

109. Junius Wilson, Treatment Team Meeting Notes, 21 December 1995, JWMF.

110. James Langston Jr. HCT, Activities Log Book: Wilmington, N.C., Trip, 31 August 1996, JWMF.

111. Silvia Weaver and Carnell Mewborn, Report to Douglas Dexter, 15 December 1995, JWMF.

112. James Langston Jr. HCT, Activities Log Book: Wilmington, N.C., Trip, 31 August 1996, JWMF.

113. Linda Taylor, Progress Notes, 18 November 1996, JWMF.

114. Helen Hinn, interview by Susan Burch, 1 February 2006.

115. Cory Reiss and Kirsten B. Mitchell, "Junius Wilson: Deaf Man Settles Incarceration Suit," WMS, 22 October 1997.

116. Helen Hinn, interview by Susan Burch, 1 February 2006.

117. Reiss and Mitchell, "Junius Wilson: Deaf Man Settles Incarceration Suit."

118. Ibid.

119. Artie Martinez, who was freed in 1994 from the hospital that had wrongly kept him. <http://members.tripod.com/~deafwatch/pr1399.txt> (3 January 1999).

120. Annie Sidberry, interview by Susan Burch, 20 March 2002.

CHAPTER ELEVEN

1. See, for example, Silvia Weaver, interview by Susan Burch, 19 November 2004; Anonymous (A-7), interview by Susan Burch, 19 November 2001.

2. "Mr. Wilson had been sick since Christmas, said Pat Jessup, his caseworker from the New Hanover County department of Social services. He had been in and out of the hospital with pneumonia and never fully recovered, she said." Amy Turnbull, "Junius Wilson Dies," *WMS*, 29 March 2001.

3. Helen Hinn, interview by Susan Burch, 1 February 2006.

4. Anonymous (A-9), interview by Susan Burch, 6 March 2006.

5. "Funeral held 2:00 P.M. on Friday, March 23 at Cherry Hospital Chapel. Internment followed at Wayne Memorial Park. Shumate Faulk Funeral Home arranged." Several articles noted this. See *GNA*, 22 March 2001; and *WMS*, 22 March 2001.

6. Pallbearers were Donnie Grant, Hiram Grantham, Vernon Kornegay, Gray Autry, Greg Forte, and Larry Reid. Honorary pallbearers were Parker, Carnell Mewborn, James Langston, and Doug Dexter.

7. <http://www.dhhs.state.nc.us/newsletter/april01page2.htm> and Susan Burch, Witness Notes, 23 March 2001, Goldsboro.

8. One observer remarked, "They got up and some people made remarks at his funeral. The eulogy was done—[by] the pastor from the hospital. I think it was a nice funeral." Anonymous (A-9), interview by Susan Burch, 6 March 2006.

9. John Wasson, interview by Susan Burch, August 2003.

10. Ibid.; the congregation sang "When We All Get to Heaven" by Eliza E. Hewitt (1898):

When we all get to Heaven,
What a day of rejoicing that will be!
When we all see Jesus,
We'll sing and shout the victory!

. . . .

Let us then be true and faithful,
Trusting, serving every day;
Just one glimpse of Him in glory
Will the toils of life repay.

11. Wilson's headstone and death certificate show an inaccurate date of birth: 2 July 1902. Both the 1910 census and Wilson's school reports confirm that his actual date of birth was 8 October 1908. The death certificate also surprisingly claims that Wilson's

father's name was "Unknown" and his mother's name as "Mary Smith." Sidney and Mary Foy Wilson Clark were his parents. Certificate of Death vol. 88, p. 1049, North Carolina Department of Health and Human Services, Vital Records: Junius Wilson.

12. "Announcement: Death Notice," *WMS*, 22 March 2001.

13. Amy E. Turnbull, "Tumultuous Life of Castle Hayne Man Ends," *WMS*, 20 March 2001.

14. "Announcement: Death Notice," *WMS*, 22 March 2001.

15. Other obituaries of Wilson can be found at <http://www.dhhs.state.nc.us/news letter/april01page2.htm> (10 January 2006); *GNA*, 22 March 2001; and *WMS*, 22 March 2001.

16. Silvia Weaver, interview by Susan Burch, 19 November 2004.

17. Helen Hinn, interview by Susan Burch, 1 February 2006.

18. Anonymous (B-5), interview by Susan Burch, 24 August 2005.

19. Roger Williams, interview by Susan Burch, 11 September 2001.

20. The state began closing down Dix Hospital in 2006 and the deaf unit has been transferred to Broughton Hospital in Morganton, North Carolina. It is unknown how many deaf patients are now being served at this facility or to what extent other state facilities provide accommodation for resident deaf patients.

21. Dave Bakke's *God Knows His Name*, published in 2000, details the story of John Doe #24, a black deaf man who was found wandering the streets in Illinois in the 1940s and was then institutionalized in various settings for almost half a century. After losing his sight, he eventually was sent to a training institute and then transferred to a group home. He died in 1993.

22. <http://olrs.ohio.gov/asp/AnnualReportPart3.asp> (10 January 2006).

23. Dave Reynolds, "State Refuses to Apologize for Sterilizations," *Inclusion Daily Express*, 15 February 2001, <http://www.inclusiondaily.com/news/advocacy/vaeugenics .htm#021501> (12 January 2006); Dave Reynolds, "Virginia Governor Apologizes for Eugenics," *Inclusion Daily Express*, 6 May 2002, <http://www.inclusiondaily.com/news/ advocacy/vaeugenics.htm#050602> (12 January 2006); "Virginia Governor Apologizes for Eugenics Law," *USA Today*, 2 May 2002, <http://www.usatoday.com/news/nation/ 2002/05/02/virginia-eugenics.htm> (10 June 2006).

24. Dave Reynolds, "Oregon Governor Apologizes for Eugenics 'Misdeeds,'" *Inclusion Daily Express*, 2 December 2002, <http://www.inclusiondaily.com/news/institutio ns/ore/oreugenics.htm#120202> (10 January 2006); Dave Reynolds, "Sterilization Survivors to Get Apology from Oregon Governor," *Inclusion Daily Express*, 15 November 2002, <http://www.inclusiondaily.com/news/ institutions/ore/oreugenics.htm#111502> (12 January 2006).

25. "Against Their Will: North Carolina's Sterilization Program," *Winston-Salem Journal*, 8–12 December 2002, 16 February 2003. See also "Davis' Apology Sheds No Light on Sterilizations in California," *Los Angeles Times*, 16 March 2003, <http://hnn.us/ comments/9561.html> (12 June 2006).

26. Johanna Schoen was a pivotal force in the interpretation and dissemination of this information to the media. See also Schoen's book, *Choice and Coercion: Birth*

Control, Sterilization, and Abortion in Public Health and Welfare (Chapel Hill: University of North Carolina Press, 2005).

27. Dave Reynolds, "N.C. Gov. Issues Sterilization Apology," *Inclusion Daily Express*, 16 December 2002, <http://www.ragged-edge-mag.com/drn/12_02.shtml> (12 January 2006).

28. Effective 1 August 2005, the records of the Eugenics Board have been transferred from the Department of Cultural Resources to the custody of the Department of Health and Human Services. Individuals who are seeking confidential medical records, maintained by the board from 1924 to 1974, should contact the Office of Citizens Services of the Department of Health and Human Services. Federal and state laws prohibit access to these medical records by anyone but the individual patients, their legal guardians, or the custodial agency.

29. Many people with disabilities were affected by state laws allowing and encouraging sterilization. We have faced some difficulty obtaining information about the state's history of sterilization because North Carolina officials refused to admit to a historic record of eugenic sterilization. Thanks to the efforts of a historian of eugenics who released her own records to a newspaper reporter, the governor has recently acknowledged this past campaign and apologized to those affected. North Carolina has promised to make a great number of hidden records public. But at the same time, the result of federal policies has stymied many disability-related research endeavors. Perhaps the most obvious example is the Health Insurance Portability and Accountability Act (or HIPAA), passed in 1996. HIPAA was intended to protect the privacy of patients in the age of internet hackers and computerized medical files. Although initially it merely required researchers to provide a brief explanation of intent, requirements extended to an expansive list of regulations. In the past, privacy laws and rules applied generally to specific documents like a patient's medical chart. Now, HIPAA regulations apply to all records and documents that contain health information, regardless of the content. As one author has written, "unlike most privacy laws, HIPAA applies into perpetuity, covering forever every person, dead or alive."

The broad interpretation of this vast corpus of rules has meant that casual correspondence between, say, superintendents and doctors may be blocked from scholarly view if the records mention even minor personal medical conditions, such as a cold or a broken arm. Some archives now demand that scholars obtain permission from subjects before accessing information about them. If the subject is deceased, the scholar must obtain permission from a legal representative for the subject. Privacy boards may be petitioned to garner access if direct permission cannot be granted, but in many cases the boards will not grant permission to publish material from its archive without direct permission granted from the subjects studied or their legal representatives. While judges may intervene to allow scholars to publish their findings, the entire process strongly discourages research in the field.

30. See, for example, Lennard Davis, "The Prisoners of Silence; Deaf Prisoners," *Nation* 257, no. 10 (4 October 1993): 354. As reported in 1993, Davis notes that in prisons there are "no facilities to teach deaf inmates sign language." Davis quoted Richard

Herring, who said that "due process cannot take place in the absence of language." He goes on to describe deaf people either being left in isolation awaiting trials until they learn language or held in legal purgatory. As one study by European scholar L. Timmermans in 1989 claims, hearing patients had remained in psychiatric hospitals for an average of 148 days, while deaf patients' average stay was 19.5 years: "There is no evidence to suggest that there is any greater occurrence of mental illness in the Deaf population. But, poor diagnosis, miscommunication, and misguided treatment programmes have resulted in the gross over-representation of Deaf people in mental hospitals." <http://members.tripod.com/~deafwatch/pr1399.txt>, 3 January 1999 (12 January 2006); L. Timmermans, "Research Project for the European Society for Mental Health and Deafness," in *Proceedings of the European Congress on Mental Health and Deafness* (Utrecht, 1989), 87–91.

31. Susan Levine, "Committed to a New Life," *Washington Post*, 8 April 2001.

32. Paul Pooley, interview by Susan Burch, 8 August 2005.

Selected Bibliography

ARCHIVES, SPECIAL COLLECTIONS, AND MUSEUMS
Goldsboro, N.C.
    Cherry Hospital Museum
        Admissions Reports (1880–1900)
        F. L. Whelpley Diary
        "History of Cherry Hospital" (file)
        Ida Mae Lucas, "Let's Look at Cherry Hospital, N.C." (unpublished paper)
        M. M. Vitols, "Negro in the Changing North Carolina Mental Health Program"
            (unpublished paper)
    Goldsboro Public Library, North Carolina Room Cherry Hospital File
    Wayne County Historical Association and Museum "Goldsboro" (exhibit)
Kirksville, Mo.
    Truman State University
        Harry H. Laughlin Papers (online)
Morganton, N.C.
    North Carolina State School for the Deaf Archives
        Wilson, Junius, School Reports
Raleigh, N.C.
    North Carolina State Archives
        Clyde R. Hoey Papers
        Dan Moore Papers

Eugenics Board of North Carolina Manual, section 10, vol. 1–2. (March 1960)

J. C. B. Ehringhaus Papers

J. Melville Broughton Papers

Luther H. Hodges Papers

Proceedings of Eugenics Board of North Carolina, 1934–1940

R. Gregg Cherry Papers

State School for the Blind and Deaf, General Records; Superintendent's Reports, 1916–1945. "Proceedings by the Board of Trustees of the North Carolina State Blind Institution of the 28th of May 1920 for the Purpose of Investigating Certain Charges Preferred in Writing"

W. Kerr Scott Papers

William B. Umstead Papers

North Carolina State Library

Bost, Mrs. W. T. (biographical file)

Washington, D.C.

Gallaudet University Archives

African Americans File

Collection: Segregation of Black Deaf Children in the United States, 1867–1987

Junius Wilson (biographical file)

Smithsonian National Museum of American History

"Disability Civil Rights Movement" (exhibit)

Wilmington, N.C.

New Hanover County Public Library, North Carolina Room

Alberti, Jane. "Police in Wilmington, North Carolina" (manuscript)

Fisher, R. H. *Biographical Sketches of Wilmington Citizens* (Lower Cape Fear Historical Society, 1929)

Research and Romance of Medicine Committee of the Auxiliary to the Medical Society of New Hanover, Brunswick, and Pender Counties. *The Lonely Road: A History of the Physicks and Physicians of the Lower Cape Fear, 1735–1976* (1977)

VITAL RECORDS AND CENSUS MATERIALS

Benevolent Institutions, 1904. Washington, D.C.: U.S. Government Printing Office, 1905.

The Blind and Deaf-Mutes in the United States, 1930. Washington, D.C.: U.S. Bureau of the Census, 1931.

Clark, Henry. Certificate of Death. Registration District No. 65–2464. North Carolina State Board of Health, Bureau of Vital Records.

Clark, Henry, and Mary Wilson. Certificate of Marriage, 3 March 1917. New Hanover County Office of Vital Records, Indexed Register of Marriages.

Clark, Mary. Certificate of Death. Registration District No. 65–00. North Carolina State Board of Health, Bureau of Vital Records.

The Deaf-Mute Population of the United States: 1920, a Statistical Analysis of the Data Obtained at the Fourteenth Decennial Census. Washington, D.C.: U.S. Government Printing Office, 1928.

Deaf-Mutes in the United States: Analysis of the Census of 1910. Washington, D.C.: U.S. Government Printing Office, 1918.

Deaf-Mutes in the United States: 1920. Washington, D.C.: U.S. Government Printing Office, 1923.

Foy, Edmund, and Joan Nixon. Certificate of Marriage, 30 July 1875. New Hanover County Office of Vital Records, Indexed Register of Marriages.

McNeil, Julian James. Certificate of Death. Registration District No. 092–95, Local No. 1661. North Carolina Department of Health and Human Services, N.C. Vital Records.

Smith, Annie. Certificate of Death. Registration District No. 65–00, Certificate No. 29. North Carolina State Board of Health, Bureau of Vital Records.

Smith, Arthur, Jr. Certificate of Death. Registration District No. 65–90, Certificate No. 619. North Carolina State Board of Health, Bureau of Vital Records.

U.S. Bureau of the Census, *United States Census of Population, 1880*

U.S. Bureau of the Census, *United States Census of Population, 1890*

U.S. Bureau of the Census, *United States Census of Population, 1900*

U.S. Bureau of the Census, *United States Census of Population, 1910*

U.S. Bureau of the Census, *United States Census of Population, 1920*

U.S. Bureau of the Census, *United States Census of Population, 1930*

Wilson, Avery. Certificate of Death. State File No. 11104. Georgia State Office of Vital Records.

Wilson, Junius. Certificate of Death. Registration District No. 09690. Vol. 88, p. 1049. North Carolina Department of Health and Human Services, N.C. Vital Records.

Wilson, Sidney. Certificate of Death. Custodian's No. 15462. Ware County Health Department, Georgia Vital Records Service.

PERSONAL INTERVIEWS AND CORRESPONDENCE

Allen, H. Jack. Interview by Susan Burch, 11 August 2005.

Anonymous (A-1). Interview by Susan Burch, 24 August 2005.

Anonymous (A-2). Interview by Susan Burch, 28 September 2004.

Anonymous (A-3). Interview by Susan Burch, 10 October 2005.

Anonymous (A-4). Interview by Susan Burch, 16 January 2004.

Anonymous (A-5). Interview by Susan Burch, 25 November 2003 and 10 August 2005.

Anonymous (A-6). Interview by Susan Burch, 27 February 2006.

Anonymous (A-7). Interview by Susan Burch, 19 November 2001.

Anonymous (A-8). Interview by Susan Burch, 29 September 2006.

Anonymous (A-9). Interview by Susan Burch, 6 March 2006.

Anonymous (B-1). Interview by Susan Burch, 2 February 2005.

Anonymous (B-2). Interview by Susan Burch, 2 September 2005.

Anonymous (B-3). Interview by Susan Burch, 12 October 2005.

Anonymous (B-4). Interview by Susan Burch, 23 January 2006.

Anonymous (B-5). Interview by Susan Burch, 24 August 2005.

Branch, André. E-mail to Susan Burch, November–December 2006.

Brown, Clyde R., Jr. Interview by Susan Burch, 22 November 2005.

Davis, Norwood. Interview by Susan Burch, 3 October 2005.

Gamble, Dee. Interview by Susan Burch, 12 October 2005.

Gaylor, Charles. Interview by Susan Burch, 10 August 2005.

Harvey, Timothy Paul. Interview by Susan Burch, 8 August 2003.

Hinn, Helen. Interview by Susan Burch, 1 February 2006.

Hodgkiss, Anita S. Letter to Dr. Barbara Brauer, 27 November 1996 (gift to Susan Burch).

Jolliff, Lulu. Interview by Susan Burch, 26 August 2004.

King, Pam. Interview by Alan Marcus, Carolyn Corbett, and Barbara Brauer, 25 June 1997.

Lancaster, Chris. Interview by Susan Burch, 26 February 2002 and 13 August 2005.

Mileski, Rick. Interview by Susan Burch, 10 August 2005.

Mitchell, Kirsten B. Interview by Susan Burch, 23 March 2006.

Nixon, Daniel. Interview by Susan Burch, 20 March 2002.

Parker, Everett. Interview by Susan Burch, 21 March 2002 and 9 August 2005.

Parks, Denise. Interview by Susan Burch, 10 August 2005.

Parson, Garde. Interview by Susan Burch, 16 August 2004.

Pooley, Paul. Interview by Susan Burch, 5 September 2001 and 8 August 2005.

Ready, Tinker. Interview by Susan Burch, 17 February 2006.

Schreyer, Paul. Interview by Susan Burch, 13 December 2004.

Sidberry, Annie. Interview by Susan Burch, 20 March 2002.

Sidberry, Willie. Interview by Susan Burch, 20 March 2002.

Sweet-Windham, Catherine. Interview by Susan Burch, 23 January 2006.

Thurman, Rita. Interview by Susan Burch, 15 May 2006.

Vitols, Mintauts. Interview by Susan Burch, 15 November 2005.

Volkan, Vamik D. Interview by Susan Burch, 23 January 2006.

Wasson, John. E-mail to Susan Burch, September 2000–December 2006.

———. Interview by Susan Burch, August 2003.

———. Interview by Susan Burch, 26 January 2006.

Weaver, Silvia. Interview by Susan Burch, 19 November 2004.

Williams, Roger. Interview by Susan Burch, 11 September 2001 and 22 July 2005.

Wooten, Pandora. Letter to Susan Burch, 31 April 2004.

Wright, Mary. Interview by Susan Burch, 3 April 2001.

———. Letter to Susan Burch, April 2001.

Wright, Rachel. Interview by Susan Burch, 6 August 2003.

DEPOSITIONS AND AFFIDAVITS

Bonds, Ernestine. Deposition, 9 May 1996 (Wilmington, N.C.).

Branch, André. Deposition, 3 November 1995 (Raleigh, N.C.).

Branch, Veronica Necole. Deposition, 10 May 1996 (Wilmington, N.C.).

Branch, Virginia Smith. Deposition, 10 May 1996 (Wilmington, N.C.).

Britt, Charles Robin. Deposition, 13 December 1995 (Raleigh, N.C.).

Bowman, Jennie. Deposition, 19 December 1995 (New York, N.Y.).

Bundor, John. Deposition, 11 December 1995 (Raleigh, N.C.).

Critchfield, A. Barry. Deposition, 11 December 1995 (Raleigh, N.C.).

Howe, William Eugene. Deposition, 12 December 1995 (Raleigh, N.C.).

Lawrence, Ruth M. Peoples. Deposition, 9 May 1996 (Wilmington, N.C.).

Macatangay, Nelson. Deposition, 2 November 1995 (Raleigh, N.C.).

Nixon-Sidberry, Annie L. Deposition, 10 May 1996 (Wilmington, N.C.).

Peoples, Jeffrey. Deposition, 8 May 1996 (Wilmington, N.C.).

Peoples, Leroy. Deposition, 9 May 1996 (Wilmington, N.C.).

Peoples, Sarah. Deposition, 9 May 1996 (Wilmington, N.C.).

Sidberry, Willie James, Jr. Deposition, 10 May 1996 (Wilmington, N.C.).

Smith, Charles. Deposition, 9 May 1996 (Wilmington, N.C.).

Smith, Deames. Deposition, 9 May 1996 (Wilmington, N.C.).

Smith, Thomas Allen. Deposition, 12 December 1995 (Raleigh, N.C.).

Stelle, Walter William. Deposition, 13 December 1995 (Raleigh, N.C.).

Taylor, Linda. Deposition, 3 November 1995 (Raleigh, N.C.).

Thomas, Fannie. Deposition, 8 May 1996 (Wilmington, N.C.).

Vitols, Mintauts. Deposition, 13 November 1995 (Seattle, Wash.).

Wasson, John M. *Junius Wilson v. the State of North Carolina et al.* Affidavit No. 5: 94CV-878-Br-3.

Williams, Annie Mae. Deposition, 24 May 1996 (Macomb, Mich.).

Williams, Roger. Deposition, 11 December 1995 (Raleigh, N.C.).

STATE DOCUMENTS

"An Act Providing for Changing the Names of the Several State Hospitals and Training Schools." *Session Laws* (Raleigh, 1959).

"An Act to Amend Chapter 34 of the Public Laws of 1929 of North Carolina Relating to the Sterilization of Persons Mentally Defective." N.C. State Law, Chapter 224, H.B. 1013 (1933).

"An Act to Amend Chapter 35, Article 7, of the General Statues Relating to the Sterilization of Epileptics." N.C. State Law, Chapter 138, H.B. 192 (1967).

"An Act to Amend Chapter 35 of the General Statues to Allow the Parent of a Mentally Ill or Mentally Retarded Person to Petition the Court for the Sterilization Operation of the Mentally Ill or Mentally Retarded Person." N.C. State Law, Chapter 102, H.B. 158. (1981).

"An Act to Amend Various Sections of the General Statues to Change the Title of the County Superintendent of Public Welfare to that of County Director of Public Welfare." N.C. State Law, Session Laws, Chapter 186, H.B. 303 (1961).

"An Act to Benefit the Moral, Mental, or Physical Conditions of Inmates of Penal and Charitable Institutions." N.C. State Law, Chapter 280–81 (1919).

"An Act to Provide for the Sterilization of the Mentally Defective and Feeble-Minded Inmates of Charitable and Penal Institutions of the State of North Carolina." P. L. 1929, Chapter 34.

"An Act to Rewrite Chapter 35, Article 7, of the General Statutes Entitled 'Persons with Mental Disease and Incompetents.'" N.C. State Law, Chapter 1281, H.B. 1611 (1973).

"Hospital Authorities to Review and Treat Such Patients." N.C. State Law, Section 73, C.S. 6242 (1928).

Junius Wilson, by His Next Friend, André Branch v. State of North Carolina et al. U.S. District Court for the Eastern District of North Carolina, Raleigh Division, Complaint Civil Action No 5: 94-CV-878-BR, 1994–97.

Laws Relating to State Hospitals and Correctional Institutions of the State of North Carolina. New Bern, N.C.: Paul G. Dunn, 1928.

"Letters of Appointment Guardian of the Person." New Hanover County, N.C., File No. 91 F 143 (12 March 1991).

"Order for the Asexualization or Sterilization of Mental Defective and Feeble-Minded Inmates of Charitable and Penal Institutions of North Carolina and Certain Cases Not Inmates of Public Institutions." Cold Spring Harbor, N.Y.: Eugenics Record Office, 19 December 1931.

"Persons Acquitted of Certain Crimes or Incapable of Being Tried on Account of Insanity, Committed to Hospital." N.C. State Law Section 68, C.S. 6237 (1928).

"Rehabilitation Services, State Plans. (1) State agency for plan administration, designation, separate agencies for services to the blind and for other services, joint program; political subdivision participation waiver; qualification of State Agency." N.C. State Law Chapter 16, §721.

Settlement Agreement, State of North Carolina, Wake County. Raleigh: Junius Wilson Court File.

State of North Carolina v. Junius Wilson, 1925. Raleigh, N.C.: State Courthouse Files.

State v. Dumie Graham. Halifax, N.C.: Halifax County Courthouse, Clerk of Court Office: Permanent Criminal Docket, Superior Court 1: TD No. 652; PD no. 1965; *Minutes to Halifax Superior Court* (January Term, February 1933; Case no. 652).

Sterilization of Mentally Retarded in State Institutions. N.C. State Law §35–36, Article 7 (1919).

Sterilization of Mentally Retarded Not in State Institutions. N.C. State Law §35–37 (1919).

Title IV: One Year Later. Survey of Desegregation of Health and Welfare Services in the South. U.S. Commission on Civil Rights, 1966.

STATE INSTITUTIONAL REPORTS

Annual Report of the Board of Public Charities of North Carolina. Raleigh (1908–).

Barnes, Robert H. *Inspection Report of the State Hospital at Goldsboro, 27 Dec. 1955.*

Biennial Report of the State Hospital at Goldsboro (1889–92, 1898–1916, 1920–40).

Brown, F. Eugene. *Biennial Report of the Eugenics Board of North Carolina* (1933–42).

Cales, Edward E. "Inspection of the State Hospital at Goldsboro by the North Carolina State Board of Public Welfare" (March and November, 1950).

Greenhill, M. H. "Inspection of the State Hospital at Goldsboro by the North Carolina State Board of Public Welfare" (March and November, 1948).

Minutes to Halifax Superior Court. Case number 652: *State v. Dumie Graham.* January Term, February 1933.

North Carolina School for the Deaf. *Biennial Report* (1907–1926).

Novasky, William. "The Racial Desegregation Study: First Interim Report." North Carolina, 1965.

Petition to Sterilize Dummie Graham, 13 November 1933. North Carolina Eugenics Board Report, 21 March 1934.

Report of the Executive Committee of the North Carolina Hospitals Board of Control of the Investigation Conducted Following the Truck Accident at the Hospital in Goldsboro. Raleigh: State Archives.

Report of the State School for the Blind and the Deaf. (Raleigh) (1898–1918, 1934–36).

A Study of Mental Health in North Carolina: Report to the North Carolina Legislature of the Governor's Commission, Appointed to Study the Care of the Insane and Mental Defectives. Ann Arbor: Edwards Brothers, 1937.

Wilson, Junius. Medical Records. Goldsboro, N.C.: Cherry Hospital.

DIRECTORIES

Goldsboro, N.C. *Directory* (1920–70).

Raleigh, N.C. *Directory* (1906–40).

Wilmington, N.C. *Directory* (1900–1940).

FILMS AND TELEVISION PROGRAMS

"California/Valdez Case." *ABC Evening News*, Friday, 23 December 1983. Vanderbilt University: Vanderbilt Television News.

Cherry Hospital Historic Films. Goldsboro, N.C.: Cherry Hospital Museum.

Cohen, Richard. *Hurry Tomorrow*. Hound Dog Films, 1975. Film.

A Day in the Life of Junius Wilson. Alpha Video, Inc. 9–10 January 1996. Videotape.

Tales from a Clubroom. Washington, D.C.: Department of Television, Film, and Photography, Gallaudet College, 1991. Videotape.

PHOTOGRAPHS

Burch, Susan. Personal collection.

Cherry Hospital Museum. Superintendents. Goldsboro, N.C.

Cherry Hospital Museum. Hospital collection.

Edwards, Donald. Family collection, 1940–2002. Goldsboro, N.C.

Parker, Everett. Scrapbook, 1990–2001. Farmville, N.C.

Wasson, John. Scrapbook, 1990–2004. Shelby, N.C.

INTERNET SOURCES

Anthony, Robert G., Jr. *A Long and Continuing Tradition: African Americana in the North Carolina Collection*. University of North Carolina at Chapel Hill Libraries, Documenting the American South. <http://www.upress.virginia.edu/epub/pyatt/chap02 .html>. 15 July 2006.

"Davis' Apology Sheds No Light on Sterilizations in California." *Los Angeles Times*, 16 March 2003. <http://hnn.us/comments/9561.html>. 12 June 2006.

Jackson, Vanessa. "In Our Own Voice: African-American Stories of Oppression, Survival, and Recovery in Mental Health Systems" (2001). <http://www.findarticles.com/p/articles/mi_qa3693/is_200307/ai_n9241130>. 20 August 2006.

Mindfreedom Oral History Project. <http://www.mindfreedom.org/>. 15 January 2006.

Morris, E. C. "Prof. A. W. Pegues." Sermons, Addresses, and Reminiscences, University of North Carolina at Chapel Hill Libraries, Documenting the American South. <http://www.Docsouth.unc.edu/church/morris/ill303.html>.

Reynolds, Dave. "Oregon Governor Apologizes for Eugenics 'Misdeeds.'" *Inclusion Daily Express*, 2 December 2002. <http://www.inclusiondaily.com/news/institutions/ore/oreugenics.htm#120202>. 10 January 2006.

———. "State Refuses to Apologize for Sterilizations." *Inclusion Daily Express*, 15 February 2001. <http://www.inclusiondaily.com/news/advocacy/vaeugenics.htm#021501>. 12 January 2006.

———. "Sterilization Survivors to Get Apology from Oregon Governor." *Inclusion Daily Express*, 15 November 2002. <http://www.inclusiondaily.com/news/institutions/ore/oreugenics.htm#111502>. 12 January 2006.

———. "Virginia Governor Apologizes for Eugenics." *Inclusion Daily Express*, 6 May 2002. <http://www.inclusiondaily.com/news/advocacy/vaeugenics.htm#050602>. 12 January 2006.

Rubin, Paul. "Deaf and Damned." *Phoenix New Times*, 2 October 1997. <http://www.phoenixnewtimes.com/Issues/1997-10-02/news/feature_print.html>. 10 June 2006.

Rubinow, S. G. "Some Results of Fair Work in North Carolina." <http//:Docsouth.unc.edu/nc/fairresults/fairresults.html>. 25 August 2005.

Taylor, Stephen J. "Conscientious Objectors at State Institutions." Center on Human Policy: Disability Studies for Teachers (Syracuse University, 2003). <http://www.disabilitystudiesforteachers.org/lesson.php?id=1>. 10 April 2006.

"Virginia Governor Apologizes for Eugenics Law." *USA Today*, 2 May 2002. <http://www.usatoday.com/news/nation/2002/05/02/virginia-eugenics.htm>. 10 June 2006.

Whitted, J. A. *A History of the Negro Baptists of North Carolina*. Raleigh: Edwards & Broughton Publishing Co., 1908. <http//:Docsouth.unc.edu/church/morris/ill303.html>. 25 August 2005.

JOURNAL ARTICLES

Adamson, Christopher R. "Punishment after Slavery: Southern State Penal Systems, 1865–1890." *Social Problems* 30, no. 5 (June 1983): 555–69.

Auman, Charles, et al. "A State Mental Hospital and Public Welfare Team Up." *Public Welfare* (January 1969): 59–65.

Beardsley, Edward H. "Making Separate Equal: Black Physicians and the Problems of Medical Segregation in the Pre–World War II South." *Bulletin of the History of Medicine* 57 (Fall 1983): 382–96.

Berkowitz, Edward D. "A Historical Preface to the Americans with Disabilities Act." *Journal of Policy History* 6, no. 1 (1994): 96–114.

Bowe, Frank. "Nonwhite Deaf Persons: Educational, Psychological, and Occupational Considerations: A Review of the Literature." *AAD* 116, no. 3 (June 1971): 357–61.

Braslow, Joel T. "In the Name of Therapeutics: The Practice of Sterilization in a California State Hospital." *Journal of the History of Medicine and Allied Sciences* 51 (January 1996): 41.

Castles, Katherine. "Quiet Eugenics: Sterilization in North Carolina's Institutions for the Mentally Retarded, 1945–1965." *Journal of Southern History* 68 (November 2002): 849–78.

Chermak, Gail D. "Review of Issues in Black Dialect: A Proposed Two-Way Bilingual Educational Approach and Considerations for the Congenitally Deaf Child." *Psychology in the Schools* 13, no. 1 (January 1976): 101–10.

Cockrell, David L. " 'A Blessing in Disguise': The Influenza Pandemic of 1918 and North Carolina's Medical and Public Health Communities." *North Carolina Historical Review* 73, no 3 (July 1996): 309–27.

Crane, R. Newton. "Recent Eugenic and Social Legislation in America." *Eugenic Review* 10, no. 1 (April 1918): 24–29.

Cripps, Thomas R. "The Reaction of the Negro to the Motion Picture 'Birth of a Nation.' " *Historian* 25, no. 3 (1962–63): 344–62.

Davis, Lennard. "The Prisoners of Silence; Deaf Prisoners." *Nation* 257, no. 10 (4 October 1993): 354.

"The Deaf in the Thirteenth Census of the United States." *AAD* 66 (1921): 385–91.

Dodge, Timothy. "State Convict Road Gangs in Alabama." *Alabama Review* 53, no. 4 (October 2000): 243–70.

Dowbiggin, Ian. "Midnight Clerks and Daily Drudges: Hospital Psychiatry in New York State, 1890–1905." *Journal of the History of Medicine and Allied Sciences* 47, no. 2 (1992): 130–52.

Ewell, Jesse. "A Plea for Castration to Prevent Criminal Assault." *Virginia Medical Semi-Monthly* 11 (11 January 1907): 464.

Flood, Everett. "The Advantages of Castration in the Defective." *Journal of the American Medicinal Association* 29 (1897): 833.

Friedberger, M. " 'The Decision to Institutionalize': Families with Exceptional Children in 1900." *Journal of Family History* 6 (December 1981): 396–409.

Goodlet, Carlton B., and Vivian R. Greene. "The Mental Abilities of Twenty-Nine Deaf and Partially Deaf Negro Children." *West Virginia State College Bulletin* 4 (June 1940): 3–23.

Greene, J. E. "Analysis of Racial Differences within Seven Clinical Categories of White and Negro Mental Patients in the Georgia State Hospital, 1923–32." *Social Forces* 17 (December 1938): 201–11.

Greene, J. E., and W. S. Phillips. "Racial and Regional Differences among White and Negro Mental Patients." *Human Biology* 11 (1939): 514–28.

Grob, Gerald N. "Deinstitutionalization: The Illusion of Policy." *Journal of Policy History* 9, no. 1 (1997): 48–74.

——. "Public Policy and Mental Illnesses: Jimmy Carter's Presidential Commission on Mental Health." *Millbank Quarterly* 83, no. 3 (2005): 425–56.

Gugliotta, Angela. " 'Dr. Sharp with His Little Knife': Therapeutic and Punitive Origins of Eugenic Vasectomy—Indiana, 1892–1921." *Journal of the History of Medicine and Allied Sciences* 53, no. 4 (October 1998): 376.

Haller, Mark H. "Heredity in Progressive Thought." *Social Service Review* 37, no. 2 (1963): 166–76.

Hughes, John S. "Labeling and Treating Black Mental Illness in Alabama, 1861–1910." *Journal of Southern History* 58 (1992): 435–60.

"The Intelligence of the Negro." *Journal of Heredity* 11, no. 1 (January 1920): 45.

Justesen, Benjamin R., II. "George Henry White, Josephus Daniels, and the Showdown over Disenfranchisement, 1900." *North Carolina Historical Review* 77, no. 1 (January 2000): 1–33.

Levine, Carl. "Communication Disjunction and Mental Patient Rehabilitation." *Journal of Human Relations* 16, no. 4 (1968): 532–46.

Lichtenstein, Alex. "Good Roads and Chain Gangs in the Progressive South: 'The Negro Convict is a Slave.' " *Journal of Southern History* 59, no. 1 (February 1993): 85–110.

McClure, George M. "The First State School for the Deaf." *AAD* 68 (1923): 97–120.

Miller, Vivien M. L. "Reinventing the Penitentiary: Punishment in Florida, 1868–1923." *American Nineteenth Century History* 1, no. 1 (Spring 2000): 82–106.

"Miscellaneous: North Carolina School (Morganton)." *AAD* 61 (1916): 285.

Morrison, Joseph L. "Illegitimacy, Sterilization, and Racism: A North Carolina Case History." *Social Science Review* 39, no. 1 (1965): 1–10.

Myers, Martha A., and James L. Massey. "Race, Labor, and Punishment in Postbellum Georgia." *Social Problems* 38, no. 2 (May 1991): 267–86.

Noll, Steve. "Patient Records as Historical Stories: The Case of the Caswell Training School." *Bulletin of the History of Medicine* 68 (Fall 1994): 411–28.

"Number of Criminals, Defectives, Delinquents, and Dependents in Institutions in the United States." *Public Health Report* 1 (January 1923).

Oberndorf, Clarence P. "The Sterilization of Defectives." *New York State Hospital Bulletin* 5 (1912): 106–12.

Popenoe, Paul B. "The Progress of Eugenic Sterilization." *Journal of Heredity* 25 (January 1934): 19–26.

Radford, John P. "Eugenics and the Asylum." *Journal of Historical Sociology* 7 (1994): 462–476.

Rollins, Robert L., and Ann Wolfe. "Eugenic Sterilization in North Carolina." *North Carolina Medical Journal* 34, no. 12 (December 1973): 944–47.

Rubington, Earl. "Race Relations in a Psychiatric Hospital." *Human Organization* 28, no. 2 (Summer 1969): 128–32.

Savitt, Todd L. "Entering a White Profession: Black Physicians in the New South, 1880–1920." *Bulletin of the History of Medicine* 61, no. 4 (1987): 507–40.

——. "Training the 'Consecrated, Skillful, Christian Physician': Documents Illustrating Student Life at Leonard Medical School, 1882–1918." *North Carolina Historical Review* 75, no. 3 (July 1998): 251–76.

"School Items: North Carolina (Raleigh) School." *AAD* 63 (1918): 223.

"School Items: North Carolina (Raleigh) School." *AAD* 64 (1919): 80.

"Schools for the Deaf in the United States." *AAD* 61 (1916): 61–65.

"Schools for the Deaf in the United States." *AAD* 63 (1918): 50–53.

"Schools for the Deaf in the United States." *AAD* 65 (1920): 5–9.

"Schools for the Deaf in the United States." *AAD* 66 (1921): 36–41.

"Schools for the Deaf in the United States." *AAD* 67 (1922): 16–21.

"Schools for the Deaf in the United States." *AAD* 68 (1923): 17–21.

"Schools for the Deaf in the United States." *AAD* 69 (1924): 5–9.

Scull, Andrew. "Historical Reflections on Asylums, Communities, and the Mentally Ill." *Mentalities* (New Zealand) 11, no. 2 (1997): 1–19.

———. "Madness and Segregative Control: The Rise of the Insane Asylum." *Social Problems* 24, no 3 (1977): 337–51.

Scull, Andrew, and Diane Favreau. "A Chance to Cut Is a Chance to Cure." *Research in Law, Deviance, and Social Control* 8 (1986): 3–39.

Selden, Steve. "Eugenics and the Social Construction of Merit, Race, and Disability." *Journal of Curriculum Studies* 32, no. 2 (2000): 235–52.

Stewart, David A., and Gwendolyn Benson. "Dual Cultural Negligence: The Education of Black Deaf Children." *Journal of Multicultural Counseling and Development* 16 (July 1988): 98–109.

"Survey of Schools for the Deaf." *AAD* 73 (1928): 290–292.

Sutton, John R. "The Political Economy of Madness: The Expansion of the Asylum in Progressive America." *American Sociological Review* 56 (October 1991): 665–78.

Trent, James W. "To Cut and Control: Institutional Preservation and the Sterilization of Mentally Retarded People in the United States, 1892–1947." *Journal of Historical Sociology* (Great Britain) 6, no. 1 (1993): 56–73.

Ward, R. D. "Eugenics Immigration: The American Race of the Future and the Responsibility of the Southern States for Its Formation: The 'Survival of the Fittest.'" *American Breeders Magazine* 4, no. 2 (1913): 96–102.

Williams, E. Y. "The Incidence of Mental Diseases in the Negro." *Journal of Negro Education* 6 (July 1937): 377–92.

Woodside, Moya. "Sterilization and Social Welfare: A Survey of Current Developments in North Carolina." *Eugenics Review* 40 (January 1949): n.p. Institute for Research in Social Science, University of North Carolina (Chapel Hill).

Woodward, James J. "Black Southern Signing." *Language in Society* (Great Britain) 5 (1975): 211–18.

Wright, Gavin. "Convict Labor after Emancipation: Old South or New South?" *Georgia Historical Quarterly* 81, no. 2 (Summer 1997): 452–64.

NEWSPAPER AND MAGAZINE ARTICLES

"After 68 Years, Innocent Man Finally Sent Home." *Washington (N.C.) Daily News*, 5 February 1994.

"After 70 Years, Where Is His Home? Deaf Cousin Is Seattleite's Cause." *Seattle Post-Intelligencer*, 26 January 1996.

"Against Their Will: North Carolina's Sterilization Program." *Winston-Salem Journal*, 8–12 December 2002.

"All Deaf-Mutes Are Imbeciles." *Silent Worker*, January 1927.

"An Innocent Man Suffers." *N&O*, 3 December 1993.

"Appointment Comes as Surprise to Mrs. Bost." *N&O*, 21 February 1926.

Cahoon, Cecil, II. "Cages, Electric Shock Treatments Are History." *Goldsboro News-Argus*, 5 October 1993.

"Caring For Mr. Wilson." *CO*, 27 November 1994.

Cobb, W. Montague. "Progress and Portents for the Negro in Medicine." *Crisis*, April 1948.

"Cousin of Deaf Man Sues N.C. over Kin's Wrongful Confinement." *The State* (Columbia, S.C.), 19 November 1994.

Davis, Chris. "Cousin of Deaf Man out of Lawsuit." *WSN*, 17 August 1996.

"Deaf Man May Get Freedom at Last." *Winston-Salem Journal*, 11 November 1992.

"Deaf Man Might Stay in Mental Hospital." *CO*, 12 November 1992.

"Deaf Man Mistakenly Confined for 67 Years." *CO*, 11 November 1992.

"Deaf Man's Ordeal Gets National Attention." *WMS*, 12 November 1992.

"Deaf-Mute Man, Wrongly Punished, Dies: Junius Wilson Was of Unknown Age." *N&O*, 21 March 2001.

"Deaf Victim of Old South Is Freed after 68 Years." *Boston Globe*, 6 February 1994.

"Deaf 96-Year-Old Wrongfully Held 68 Years Is Free." *San Antonio Express-News*, 5 February 1994.

"Dr. W. C. Linville, Superintendent of State Hospital, Dies at Home." *Goldsboro News-Argus*, 30 August 1938.

"Forgotten Deaf Man Ventures Outside." *The State* (Columbia S.C.), 22 March 1993.

"For 69 Years, Man Lived 'Southern Gothic Tale.'" *Tulsa World*, 1 February 1996.

"Free at Last." *Gazette* (Montreal), 5 February 1994.

"Free at Last." *Register-Guard* (Eugene, Ore.) 5 February 1994.

"Freedom Finally Arrives for 96-Year-Old Wrongly Accused of Rape; A Deaf Man Has Been Confined to a Mental Hospital for Blacks since 1925." *Fort Worth Star-Telegram*, 7 February 1994.

"Guardian Who Helped Deaf Man Settles Lawsuit." *Columbian* (Vancouver, Wash.), 29 December 1995.

"Guardian Who Helped Imprisoned Deaf Man Settles Suit." *Durham Herald-Sun*, 29 December 1995.

Hartnett, Alice Gregory. "N.C. to Change Discharge Policy for Mentally Ill." *CO*, 4 December 2004.

"Hospitalized 67 years—Because He Is Deaf." *N&R*, 11 November 1992.

Kelley, Tina. "After 70 Years, Where Is His Home? Deaf Cousin Is Seattleite's Cause." *Seattle Post-Intelligencer*, 26 Jan. 1996, B1

"Man Claims to Be Kin of Castrated Patient; State: Throw Out Wilson Suit." *WSN*, 5 January 1995.

"Man May Remain in State Hospital." *Winston-Salem Journal*, 12 November 1992, 16.

"Man, 96, Enjoying New-Found Freedom and New Residence." *N&R*, 7 March 1994.

"Man Sues for Cousin's Confinement in Mental Ward; Suit Claims North Carolina Held Deaf Man in Hospital for 68 Years." *Spokesman-Review* (Spokane, Wash.), 20 November 1994.

"Man Suing for Deaf Cousin's Unjust Confinement in '25; 97-Year-Old Who Was Sent to Insane Asylum in N.C. Now Receives Care from State." *Dallas Morning News*, 25 November 1994.

"Man Who Helped Free Patient in Mental Ward Is Sued." Associated Press, 29 December 1995.

McMillan, Mary Lee. "Former Club President Becomes Real Legend." *Raleigh Times*, 13 February 1959.

"Misguided Missiles." *USA Today*, 29 December 1995.

Mitchell, Kirsten B. "Judge Reveals County's Settlement in Junius Wilson Case." *WSN*, 23 January 1996.

——. "After 68 Years in Mental Ward, Junius Wilson Moves into Cottage." *WMS*, 5 February 1994.

——. "Suit Claims Deaf Man Was Framed by His Uncle." *WMS*, 13 January 1996.

——. "Deaf Man Caught Up in Red Tape." *WMS*, 2 December 1993.

——. "Gap between Deaf Man, Rest of World Finally Is Being Closed." *WSN*, 14 February 1993.

——. "Deaf Man Still Held at State Psychiatric Hospital." *WMS*, 1 December 1993.

——. "Deaf Man Won't Move until Cottage Fixed." *WMS*, 10 December 1993.

——. "Deaf Man to Move off Ward to Cottage." *WMS*, 4 February 1994.

——. "67-Year Ordeal for Deaf Man Coming to End." *WMS*, 11 November 1992.

——. "Life Emerges from a World of Silence." *WMS*, 30 September 1996.

"Moving the Poor Man Would Be Cruel." *WSN*, 16 January 1996.

"N.C. State Negro Fair Comes to End in Festive Dance." *Norfolk (Va.) Journal and Guide*, 18 October 1924.

"N.C. Sued by Kin of Man Wrongly Held for 68 Years." *CO*, 18 November 1994.

"Negro Fair Has Finest Exhibits." *N&O*, 22 October 1924.

"Negro Fair Has Good Opening." *N&O*, 23 October 1924.

"Negro Fair Will Open on Tuesday." *N&O*, 19 October 1924.

"Negro State Fair" (advertisement). *Norfolk Journal and Guide*, 25 August 1923.

"New Hanover: Deaf Man's Guardian Resigning for New Job." *WSN*, June 27, 1996.

"Now Let Mr. Wilson Have a Nice Dog." *WSN*, 27 October 1997.

Price, Dudley. "96-Year-Old Ready for His Own Cottage—and Maybe a Dance." *N&O*, 5 February 1994.

"Proper Care Shouldn't Take a 67-Year Wait." *WMS*, 12 November 1992.

"Public Should Know What It Settled For." *WMS*, 2 December 1995.

Ready, Tinker. "Hard-Working Lawyers Are Making Strides for the Mentally Ill." *N&O*, 15 November 1992.

——. "Forgotten Man's Walls of Silence Breaking Down." *N&O*, 10 November 1992.

——. "Hospitals to Provide Interpreters for Deaf." *N&O*, 11 November 1992.

"Red Tape Still Ensnares 96-Year-Old Man." *All Things Considered*, National Public Radio, 4 December 1993. Transcript no. 1321-6.

"Relative Suing for Wrongly Held Man." *Record* (New Jersey), 20 November 1994.

"Righting a Wrong." Editorial. *CO*, 6 February 1994.

Robinson, K. G. "Deaf Victim Needs Help Now." *WMS*, 8 December 1993.

Schoen, Johanna. "Confronting N.C.'s Eugenics Legacy." *Durham Herald-Sun*, 23 February 2003.

"Seattle Relative Sues over Man's False Confinement." *Seattle Times*, 18 November 1994.

Simmons, Tim. "State Offers Temporary Home for Deaf Man." *N&O*, 4 December 1993.

Sinderbrand, Rebecca. "A Shameful Little Secret." *Newsweek*, 28 March 2005.

"Sister Sues California for Misplacing Brother." *New York Times*, 5 November 1983.

"Sometimes a Lawsuit Makes You Want to Scream." *N&R*, 2 January 1996.

"State Leaders Attend Rites for Dr. Linville." *Goldsboro News-Argus*, 31 August 1938.

"State Makes Amends for False Commitment; After 69 Years, Man Has New Life." *Chicago Tribune*, 4 February 1996.

"State Owes Deaf Man a Decent Home." Editorial. *WMS*, 7 December 1993.

"A Stranger, and Alone." *N&O*, 16 November 1992.

Swofford, Stan. "Guardian Sued for Helping Man." *N&R*, 28 December 1995.

——. "Most of Those Sterilized Were Black." *N&R*, 31 January 1993.

——. "Not Unique: Others Lost in System." *N&R*, 31 January 1993.

——. "State Still Lagging on Home for Wrongly Confined Man." *N&R*, 13 December 1993.

——. "Trapped in an Insane World." *N&R*, 31 January 1993.

Thompson, Estes. "Deaf Man Gets Some Freedom after 68-Year Wrongful Confinement." *Daily Reflector* (Greenville N.C.), 5 February 1994.

——. "Man Gets Justice 69 Years Late." *Tampa Tribune*, 5 February 1994.

——. "Man Released after 68-year Lockup." *News-Journal* (Daytona Beach, Fla.), 5 February 1994.

Turnbull, Amy. "Junius Wilson Dies." *WMS*, 29 March 2001.

"Under the Dome." *N&O*, 14 December 1940.

"Unusual Crowds at Negro Fair." *N&O*, 24 October 1924.

Vance, Tricia. "Lawyer Is Made Guardian of Junius Wilson's Estate." *WMS*, 20 February 1996.

——. "Suit Drops Guardian of Castrated Man." *WMS*, 30 November 1995.

"Victim of the State Deserves Action Today." *WMS*, 2 December 1993.

"Wasson, County Settle; State Still Defendant in $150 Million Action; Suit Drops Guardian of Castrated Man." *WSN*, 30 November 1995.

Whisnant, Scott. "Court Won't Change Deaf Man's Guardian." *WMS*, 17 January 1996.

"Why Was Junius Wilson Locked Up Another Year?" Editorial. *N&R*, 14 December 1993.

Wright, Gary L. "Prisoner of the State." *CO*, 20 June 1993.

——. "Deaf Man, 96, Leaves Mental Hospital Locked Ward." *CO*, 4 February 1994.

——. "It was Like Going Back to the Last Century." *CO*, 13 September 1992.

——. "In Asylum since 1925, N.C. Deaf Man Is Free." *Sun News* (Myrtle Beach, S.C.).

——. "The Shame of Cherry Hospital." *CO*, 13 September 1992.

——. "Denied Trial, Deaf Man Castrated, Locked Up for Decades." *Baltimore Sun*, 24 June 1993.

——. "Free at Last." *Houston Chronicle*, 5 February 1994.

"Wrongly Condemned in Shackles of Silence Deaf Black Man, 96, Free at Last of Lifetime as a Mental Patient." *Seattle Times*, 5 February 1994.

"Wrongly Confined Deaf Man, 97, Is Subject of Suit; He Was Held in Mental Hospital 68 Years." *St. Louis Post-Dispatch*, 20 November 1994.

BOOKS

Abrams, Douglas Carl. *Conservative Constraints: North Carolina and the New Deal*. Jackson: University Press of Mississippi, 1992.

Anderson, Glenn B. "The Impact of Sign Language Research on Black Deaf Communities in America." In *The Study of Signed Languages: Essays in Honor of William C. Stokoe*, edited by David F. Armstrong, Michael A. Karchmer, and John Vickrey Van Cleve. Washington, D.C.: Gallaudet University Press, 2002.

Ashe, Samuel A. *Biographical History of North Carolina: From Colonial Times to the Present*. Greensboro N.C.: C. L. Van Noppen, 1905.

Badger, Anthony J. *Prosperity Road: The New Deal, Tobacco, and North Carolina*. Chapel Hill: University of North Carolina Press, 1980.

Bakke, Dave. *God Knows His Name: The True Story of John Doe No. 24*. Urbana: Southern Illinois University Press, 2000.

Barnartt, Sharon, and Richard Scotch. *Disability Protests: Contentious Politics, 1970–1999*. Washington, D.C.: Gallaudet University Press, 2001.

Beardsley, Edward H. *A History of Neglect: Health Care for Blacks and Mill Workers in the Twentieth-Century South*. Knoxville: University of Tennessee Press, 1987.

——. "Dedicated Servant or Errant Professional: The Southern Negro Physician before World War II." In *The Southern Enigma: Essays on Race, Class, and Folk Culture*, edited by Walter J. Fraser Jr. and Winfred B. Moore Jr. Westport Conn.: Greenwood Press, 1983.

Beers, Clifford. *A Mind That Found Itself: An Autobiography*. Pittsburgh: University of Pittsburgh Press, 1981.

Bell, LeLand V. *Treating the Mentally Ill: From Colonial Times to the Present*. New York: Praeger, 1980.

Berkowitz, Edward D. *America's Welfare State, from Roosevelt to Reagan*. Baltimore: The Johns Hopkins University Press, 1991.

——. *Disabled Policy: America's Programs for the Handicapped*. New York: Cambridge University Press, 1987.

——. *Mr. Social Security: The Life of Wilbur J. Cohen*. Lawrence: University Press of Kansas, 1995.

Bloom, Bernard L. *Community Mental Health: A General Introduction*. Monterey, Calif.: Brooks/Cole, 1984.

Bogdan, Robert, and Steven J. Taylor. *Inside Out: The Social Meaning of Mental Retardation*. Toronto: University of Toronto Press, 1982.

Bok, Marcia. *Civil Rights and the Social Programs of the 1960s: The Social Justice Functions of Social Policy*. Westport, Conn.: Praeger, 1992.

Bond, Horane Mann. *The Education of the Negro in the American Social Order*. New York: Octagon Books, 1934, 1966.

Botkin, Jeffrey R., William M. McMahon, and Leslie Pickering Francis. *Genetics and Criminality: The Potential Misuse of Scientific Information in Court*. Washington, D.C.: American Psychological Association, 1999.

Brophy, Alfred L. *Reconstructing the Dreamland: The Tulsa Riot of 1921: Race, Reparations, and Reconciliation*. New York: Oxford University Press, 2002.

Brown, R. Eugene. *Eugenical Sterilization in North Carolina*. Raleigh: Eugenics Board of North Carolina, 1935.

Brown, Phil. *Transfer of Care: Psychiatric Deinstitutionalization and Its Aftermath*. Boston: Routledge & Kegan Paul, 1984.

Brundage, W. Fitzhugh. *Under Sentence of Death: Lynching in the South*. Chapel Hill: University of North Carolina Press, 1997.

——. *Lynching in the New South: Georgia and Virginia, 1880–1930*. Urbana: University of Illinois Press, 1993.

——. *The Southern Past: A Clash of Race and Memory*. Cambridge, Mass.: Belknap Press of Harvard University Press, 2005.

——. *Where These Memories Grow: History, Memory, and Southern Identity*. Chapel Hill: University of North Carolina Press, 2000.

Bullock, Henry Allen. *A History of Negro Education in the South from 1619 to the Present*. Cambridge, Mass.: Harvard University Press, 1967.

Burch, Susan. *Signs of Resistance: American Deaf Cultural History, 1900 to World War II*. New York: New York University Press, 2002.

Cahow, Clark R. *People, Patients, and Politics: The History of the North Carolina Mental Hospitals, 1848–1960*. New York: Arno Press, 1980.

Cameron, Davis, and Fraser Valentine, eds. *Disability and Federalism: Comparing Different Approaches to Full Participation*. Montreal: McGill-Queen's University Press, 2001.

Campion, Frank D. *The AMA and U.S. Health Policy since 1940*. Chicago: Chicago Review Press, 1984.

Carlson, Elof Axel. *The Unfit: A History of a Bad Idea*. Cold Spring Harbor, N.Y.: Cold Spring Harbor Laboratory Press, 2001.

Cecelski, David S. *The Waterman's Song: Slavery and Freedom in Maritime North Carolina*. Chapel Hill: University of North Carolina Press, 2001.

Cecelski, David S., and Timothy B. Tyson, eds. *Democracy Betrayed: The Wilmington Race Riot of 1893 and Its Legacy*. Chapel Hill: University of North Carolina Press, 1998.

Chafe, William H. *Civilities and Civil Rights: Greensboro, North Carolina, and the Black Struggle for Freedom*. New York: Oxford University Press, 1980.

Chafe, William H., Raymond Gavins, and Robert Korstad, eds. *Remembering Jim Crow: African Americans Tell about Life in the Segregated South*. New York: The New Press, 2001.

Chalmers, David. *Hooded Americans: The History of the Ku Klux Klan*. Durham: Duke University Press, 1987.

Charlton, James I. *Nothing About Us Without Us: Disability Oppression and Empowerment*. Berkeley: University of California Press, 2000.

Cole, J. Timothy. *The Forest City Lynching of 1900: Populism, Racism, and White Supremacy in Rutherford County, North Carolina*. London: McFarland & Company, 2005.

Colvin, Mark. *Penitentiaries, Reformatories, and Chain Gangs: Social Theory and the History of Punishment in Nineteenth-Century America*. New York: St. Martin's Press, 1997.

Cook, Dennis H. *The White Superintendent and the Negro Schools of North Carolina*. Nashville, Tenn.: George Peabody College for Teachers, 1930.

Cook, Raymond Allen. *Fire from the Flint: The Amazing Careers of Thomas Dixon*. Winston-Salem, N.C.: John F. Blair, 1968.

Crockett, Manuel H., and Barbara Crockett Dease. *Through the Years, 1867–1977—Light out of Darkness: A History of the North Carolina School for the Negro Blind and the Deaf*. Raleigh, N.C.: Barefoot Press, 1990.

Crow, Jeffrey J., Paul D. Escott, and Flora J. Hatley. *A History of African Americans in North Carolina*. Raleigh, N.C.: Division of Archives and History, 1992.

Dailey, Jane, Glenda Gilmore, and Bryant Simon. *Jumpin' Jim Crow: Southern Politics from Civil War to Civil Rights*. Princeton: Princeton University Press, 2000.

Daniel, Pete. *Lost Revolutions: The South in the 1950s*. Chapel Hill: University of North Carolina Press for the Smithsonian Institution, 2000.

D'Antonio, Michael. *The State Boys Rebellion*. New York: Simon & Schuster, 2004.

Davenport, Charles B. *Heredity in Relation to Eugenics*. New York: Henry Holt and Co., 1911.

David, Sheri I. *With Dignity: The Search for Medicare and Medicaid*. Westport, Conn.: Greenwood Press, 1985.

Dee, Ivan R. *Lyndon Johnson and the Great Society*. Chicago: The American Way Series, 1998.

DeParrel, G., and Mrs. Georges Lamarque. *The Deaf Mutes: As a Medical, Pedagogical, and Social Study*. 1933.

Deutsch, Albert. *Mentally Ill in America: A History of Their Care and Treatment*. New York: Columbia University Press, 1949.

——. *The Shame of the States*. New York: Harcourt, Brace and Company, 1948.

Dixon, Thomas, Jr. *The Clansman: An Historical Romance of the Ku Klux Klan*. New York: Doubleday, Page & Company, 1905.

——. *The Leopard's Spots: A Romance of the White Man's Burden—1865–1900*. Ridgewood, N.J.: The Gregg Press, 1967.

Donaldson, Kenneth. *Insanity Inside Out*. New York: Crown Publishers, Inc., 1997.

Dorr, Lisa Lindquist. *White Women, Rape, and the Power of Race in Virginia, 1900–1960*. Chapel Hill: University of North Carolina Press, 2004.

Dowbiggin, Ian. *Keeping America Sane*. Ithaca: Cornell University Press, 1997.

Dowdall, George W. *The Eclipse of the State Mental Hospital: Policy, Stigma, and Organization*. Albany: State University of New York Press, 1996.

Dozier, Howard D. *A History of the Atlantic Coast Line Railroad*. New York: Augustus M. Kelley Publishers, 1971.

Dray, Philip. *At the Hands of Persons Unknown: The Lynching of Black America*. New York: Random House, 2002.

Dudley, James R., Mary Lynne Calhoun, and Lynn Ahlgrim-Delzell, eds. *Lessons Learned from a Lawsuit*. Kingston, N.Y.: NADD Press, 2002.

Egerton, John. *Speak Now against the Day: The Generation before the Civil Rights Movement in the South*. New York: Alfred A. Knoff, 1994.

Ehrenreich, John H. *The Altruistic Imagination: A History of Social Work and Social Policy in the United States*. Ithaca: Cornell University Press, 1985.

Evans, William McKee. *Ballots and Fence Rails: Reconstruction on the Lower Cape Fear*. Athens: University of Georgia Press, 1995.

Flexner, Abraham. *Medical Education in the United States and Canada: A Report to the Carnegie Foundation for the Advancement of Teaching*. New York: Carnegie Foundation for the Advancement of Teaching, 1910.

Flowers, Linda. *Throwed Away: Failures of Progress in Eastern North Carolina*. Knoxville: University of Tennessee Press, 1990.

Franklin, John Hope. "*The Birth of a Nation*: Propaganda as History." In *Race and History: Selected Essays, 1938–1988*, edited by John Hope Franklin. Baton Rouge: Louisiana State University Press, 1989.

Fraser, Walter J., Jr., and Winfred B. Moore Jr., eds., *The Southern Enigma: Essays on Race, Class, and Folk Culture*. Westport, Conn.: Greenwood Press, 1983.

Fuller, Jennifer, et al. *Black Perspectives on the Deaf Community*. Washington, D.C.: Gallaudet University, RSA Interpreter Training Project, 2005.

Gilmore, Glenda Elizabeth. *Gender and Jim Crow: Women and the Politics of White Supremacy in North Carolina, 1896–1920*. Chapel Hill: University of North Carolina Press, 1996.

Gish, Lowell. *Reform at Osawatomie State Hospital: Treatment of the Mentally Ill, 1866–1970*. Lawrence: University Press of Kansas, 1972.

Godwin, John L. *Black Wilmington and the North Carolina Way: Portrait of a Community in the Era of Civil Rights Protest*. Lanham, Md.: University Press of America, 2000.

Goffman, Erving. *Asylums: Essays on the Social Situation of Mental Patients and Other Inmates*. Garden City, N.J.: Anchor Books, 1961.

Goldfield, David. *Black, White, and Southern: Race Relations and Southern Culture, 1940 to the Present*. Baton Rouge: Louisiana State University Press, 1990.

Grob, Gerald N. *From Asylum to Community: Mental Health Policy in Modern America*. Princeton: Princeton University Press, 1991.

———. *The Mad Among Us: A History of the Care of America's Mentally Ill*. New York: Free Press, 1994.

———. *Mental Illness and American Society, 1875–1940*. Princeton: Princeton University Press, 1983.

——. *The State and the Mentally Ill: A History of Worcester State Hospital in Massachusetts, 1830–1920*. Chapel Hill: University of North Carolina Press, 1966.

Guggenheim, Laurie. "Ethnic Variation in ASL: The Signing of African Americans and How It Is Influenced by Conversational Topic." In *Communication Forum 1993*. Vol. 2. Edited by Elizabeth A. Winston. Washington, D.C.: Gallaudet University School of Communication, 1993.

Hairston, Ernest, and Linwood Smith. *Black and Deaf in America: Are We That Different?* Silver Spring, Md.: TJ Publishers, Inc., 1983.

Hale, Grace E. *Making Whiteness: The Culture of Segregation in the South, 1890–1940*. New York: Pantheon Books, 1998.

Hall, Jacquelyn Dowd, et al. *Like a Family: The Making of a Southern Cotton Mill World*. Chapel Hill: University of North Carolina Press, 1987.

——. *Revolt against Chivalry: Jessie Daniel Ames and the Women's Campaign against Lynching*. New York: Columbia University Press, 1979.

Haller, Mark. *Eugenics: Hereditarian Attitudes in American Thought*. New Brunswick: Rutgers University Press, 1984.

Hirsch, James S. *Riot and Remembrance: The Tulsa Race War and Its Legacy*. Boston: Houghton Mifflin Company, 2002.

Holmes, S. J. *The Eugenic Predicament*. New York: Harcourt, Brace and Company, 1933.

Horwitz, Elinor Lander. *Madness, Magic, and Medicine: The Treatment and Mistreatment of the Mentally Ill*. Philadelphia: Lippincott, 1977.

Jones, Kathleen. *Asylums and After: A Revised History of the Mental Health Services: From the Early 18th Century to the 1990s*. London: The Athlone Press, 1993.

Jones, Philip R., and Ailsa Cregan. *Sign and Symbol Communication for Mentally Handicapped People*. London: Croom Helm, 1986.

Joyner, Hannah. *From Pity to Pride: Growing Up Deaf in the Old South*. Washington, D.C.: Gallaudet University Press, 2004.

Kevles, Daniel J. *In the Name of Eugenics: Genetics and the Uses of Human Heredity*. New York: Knopf, 1985.

Landman, J. H. *Human Sterilization*. New York: Macmillan, 1932.

Larson, Edward J. *Sex, Race, and Science: Eugenics in the Deep South*. Baltimore: The Johns Hopkins University Press, 1995.

Laughlin, Harry H. *Eugenical Sterilization: 1926, Historical, Legal, and Statistical Review of Eugenical Sterilization in the United States*. New Haven: The American Eugenics Society, 1926.

Lebsock, Suzanne. *A Murder in Virginia: Southern Justice on Trial*. New York: W. W. Norton, 2003.

Leiby, James. *A History of Social Welfare and Social Work in the United States*. New York: Columbia University Press, 1978.

Levine, Murray. *The History and Politics of Community Health*. New York: Oxford University Press, 1981.

Lewis, George. *The White South and the Red Menace: Segregationists, Anticommunism, and Massive Resistance, 1945–1965*. Gainesville: University Press of Florida, 2004.

Lewis, John, Carrie Palmer, and Leandra Williams. "Existence of and Attitudes toward Black Variation of Sign Language." In *Communication Forum 1995: School of Communication Student Forum*. Vol. 4. Edited by Laura Byers, Jessica Chaiken, and Monica Mueller. Washington, D.C.: Gallaudet University School of Communication, 1995.

Longmore, Paul K. *Why I Burned My Book*. Philadelphia: Temple University Press, 2003.

Lucas, Ceil, ed. *The Sociolinguistics of the Deaf Community*. New York: Academic Press, Inc., 1989.

Lucas, Ceil, Robert Bayley, and Clayton Valli. *Sociolinguistic Variation in American Sign Language*. Washington, D.C.: Gallaudet University Press, 2001.

Ludmerer, Kenneth M. *Genetics and American Society: A Historical Appraisal*. Baltimore: The Johns Hopkins University Press, 1972.

Lunbeck, Elizabeth. *The Psychiatric Persuasion: Knowledge, Gender, and Power in Modern America*. Princeton: Princeton University Press, 1995.

Mama, Amina. *Beyond the Masks: Race, Gender, and Subjectivity*. London: Routledge, 1995.

Margo, Robert A. *Race and Schooling in the South, 1880–1950: An Economic History*. Chicago: University of Chicago Press, 1990.

Marmor, Theodore R. *The Politics of Medicare*. New York: Aldine de Gruyter, 2000.

Martindale, Don, and Edith Martindale. *Mental Disability in America since World War II*. New York: Philosophical Library, 1985.

Mayer, Robert R., et al. *The Impact of School Desegregation in a Southern City: A Case Study in the Analysis of Educational Policy*. Lexington, Mass.: Lexington Books, 1974.

McCandless, Peter. *Moonlight, Magnolias, and Madness: Insanity in South Carolina from the Colonial Period to the Progressive Era*. Chapel Hill: University of North Carolina Press, 1996.

McCord, Charles. *The American Negro as a Dependent, Defective, and Delinquent—Calls for Unsexing of Unfit Blacks*. Nashville: Benson Printing, 1914.

McCulloch, Robert W. "Castle Hayne: A Study of an Experiment in the Colonization of Foreign-Born Farmers in North Carolina." In *Immigrant Farmers and Their Children*, edited by Edmund Des. Brunner (Garden City: Doubleday, Dorn & Company, 1929).

McLaurin, Melton. *Celia, a Slave*. Athens: University of Georgia Press, 1991.

Melling, Joseph, and Bill Forsythe. *Insanity, Institutions, and Society, 1800–1914: A Social History of Madness in Comparative Perspective*. London: Routledge, 1999.

Meyerson, Abraham. *Eugenical Sterilization*. New York: Macmillan, 1936.

Miller-Hall, Mary. *Deaf, Dumb, and Black: An Account of the Life of a Family*. New York: A Hearthstone Book, 1994.

Mitchell, David T. M., and Sharon L. Snyder, eds. *The Body and Physical Difference: Discourses of Disability*. Ann Arbor: University of Michigan Press, 1997.

Newby, Idus A. *Jim Crow's Defense: Anti-Negro Thought in America, 1900–1930*. Baton Rouge: Louisiana State University Press, 1965.

Nieman, Donald G., ed. *Black Southerners and the Law, 1865–1900*. New York: Garland Publishing, 1994.

Noll, Steven. *Feeble-Minded in Our Midst: Institutions for the Mentally Retarded in the South, 1900–1940*. Chapel Hill: University of North Carolina Press, 1995.

———. "Under a Double Burden: Florida's Black Feebleminded, 1920–1957." In *The African American Heritage of Florida*, edited by David R. Colburn and Jane L. Landers. Gainesville: University Press of Florida, 1995.

Noll, Steven, and James W. Trent Jr., eds. *Mental Retardation in America: A Historical Reader*. New York: New York University Press, 2004.

O'Brien, Ruth. *Crippled Justice: The History of Modern Disability Policy in the Workplace*. Chicago: University of Chicago Press, 2001.

Odum, Howard. *Social and Mental Traits of the Negro*. New York: Columbia University Press, 1910.

Ordover, Nancy. *American Eugenics: Race, Queer Anatomy, and the Science of Nationalism*. Minneapolis: University of Minnesota Press, 2001.

Padden, Carol, and Tom Humphries. *Deaf in America: Voices from a Culture*. Cambridge: Harvard University Press, 1988.

Parasnis, Ila. *Cultural and Language Diversity and the Deaf Experience*. Cambridge: Cambridge University Press, 1996.

Pearman, William A., and Philip Starr. *Medicare*. New York: Garland Publishing, Inc., 1988.

Pearson, Hugh. *Under the Knife: How a Wealthy Negro Surgeon Wielded Power in the Jim Crow South*. New York: Free Press, 2000.

Penley, Gary. *Della Raye: A Girl Who Grew Up in Hell and Emerged Whole*. Gretna: Pelican Pub., 2002.

Pernick, Martin S. *The Black Stork: Eugenics and the Death of "Defective" Babies in American Medicine and Motion Pictures since 1915*. New York: Oxford University Press, 1996.

Pickens, Donald K. *Eugenics and the Progressives*. Nashville: Vanderbilt University Press, 1968.

Powell, William S., ed. *Dictionary of North Carolina Biography*. Vols. 2–4. Chapel Hill: University of North Carolina Press, 1986–91.

Prather, H. Leon. *We Have Taken a City: Wilmington Racial Massacre and Coup of 1898*. Cranbury, N.J.: Associated University Presses, 1984.

Quadagno, Jill, and Steve McDonald. "Racial Segregation in Southern Hospitals: How Medicare 'Broke the Back' of Segregated Health Services." In *The New Deal and Beyond: Social Welfare in the South since 1930*, edited by Elna C. Green. Athens: University of Georgia Press, 2003.

Rabinowitz, Howard N. *Race Relations in the Urban South, 1865–1890*. Chicago: University of Illinois Press, 1978.

Raper, Arthur F. *Mass Violence in America: The Tragedy of Lynching*. New York: Arno Press, 1969.

Reilly, Philip. *The Surgical Solution: A History of Involuntary Sterilization in the United States*. Baltimore: Johns Hopkins University Press, 1991.

Reisch, Michael, and Janice Andrews. *The Road Not Taken: A History of Radical Social Work in the United States*. Philadelphia: Routledge, 2001.

Rice, Thurman. *Racial Hygiene; A Practical Discussion of Eugenics and Race Culture*. New York: Macmillan, 1929.

Richardson, Theresa R. *The Century of the Child: The Mental Hygiene Movement and Social Policy in the United States and Canada*. Albany: State University of New York Press, 1989.

Ritterhouse, Jennifer. *Growing Up Jim Crow: How Black and White Southern Children Learned Race*. Chapel Hill: University of North Carolina, 2006.

Robitscher, Jonas, ed. *Eugenic Sterilization*. Springfield, Ill.: Charles C. Thomas, 1973.

Ross, Malcolm. *The Cape Fear*. New York: Holt, Rinehart and Winston, 1965.

Rothman, David J. *Conscience and Convenience: The Asylum and Its Alternatives in Progressive America*. Boston: Little, Brown and Company, 1980.

Salvaggio, John. *New Orleans' Charity Hospital: A Story of Physicians, Politics, and Poverty*. Baton Rouge: Louisiana State University Press, 1992.

Sareyan, Alex. *The Turning Point: How Men of Conscience Brought About Major Change in the Care of America's Mentally Ill*. Washington, D.C.: American Psychiatric Press, Inc., 1994.

Schoen, Johanna. *Choice and Coercion: Birth Control, Sterilization, and Abortion in Public Health and Welfare*. Chapel Hill: University of North Carolina Press, 2004.

Schulman, Bruce J. *From Cotton Belt to Sunbelt: Federal Policy, Economic Development, and the Transformation of the South, 1938–1980*. New York: Oxford University Press, 1991.

Shapiro, Joseph. *No Pity*. New York: Three Rivers Press, 1994.

Shorter, Edward. *A History of Psychiatry: From the Era of Asylum to the Age of Prozac*. New York: John Wiley & Sons, 1997.

Shroyer, Edgar H., and Susan P. Shroyer. *Signs across America: A Look at Regional Differences in American Sign Language*. Washington, D.C.: Gallaudet University Press, 1984.

Silvers, Anita, David Wasserman, and Mary B. Mahowald. *Disability, Difference, Discrimination: Perspectives on Justice in Bioethics and Public Policy*. Lanham, Md.: Rowman & Littlefield Publishers, 1998.

Slide, Anthony. *American Racist: The Life and Films of Thomas Dixon*. Lexington: University Press of Kentucky, 2004.

Smith, David Barton. *Health Care Divided: Race and Healing a Nation*. Ann Arbor: University of Michigan Press, 2002.

Smith, J. David. *The Eugenic Assault on America*. Fairfax, Va.: George Mason University Press, 1993.

——. *Minds Made Feeble: The Myth and Legacy of the Kallikaks*. Rockville, Md.: Aspen Systems Corp., 1985.

——. *The Sterilization of Carrie Buck*. Far Hills, N.J.: New Horizon Press, 1989.

Sprunt, James. *Chronicles of the Cape Fear River, 1660–1916*. Raleigh: Edwards & Broughton Printing Co., 1916.

Stanton, William. *The Leopard's Spots: Scientific Attitudes toward Race in America, 1815–59*. Chicago: University of Chicago Press, 1960.

Switzer, Jacqueline Vaughn. *Disabled Rights: American Disability Policy and the Fight for Equality*. Washington, D.C.: Georgetown University Press, 2003.

Szasz, Thomas S. *The Manufacture of Madness: A Comparative Study of the Inquisition and the Mental Health Movement*. New York: Harper & Row, 1970.

Trent, James. *Inventing the Feeble Mind: A History of Mental Retardation in the United States*. Los Angeles: University of California Press, 1994.

Tuttle, William M., Jr. *Race Riot: Chicago in the Red Summer of 1919*. Urbana: University of Illinois Press, 1996.

Unsworth, Clive. *The Politics of Mental Health Legislation*. Oxford: Clarendon Press, 1987.

Van Cleve, John, and Barry Crouch. *A Place of Their Own*. Washington, D.C.: Gallaudet University Press, 1989.

Van Wagenen, B. "Preliminary Report of the Committee of the Eugenic Section." In *Problems in Eugenics: First International Eugenics Congress*. London: Knight, 1912.

Waddell, Alfred Moore. *A History of New Hanover County and the Lower Cape Fear Region*. Wilmington, N.C.: 1909.

Ward, Thomas J., Jr. *Black Physicians in the Jim Crow South*. Fayetteville: University of Arkansas Press, 2003.

Watson, Wilbur H. *Against the Odds: Blacks in the Profession of Medicine in the United States*. New Brunswick: Transaction Publishers, 1999.

Whitaker, Robert. *Mad in America: Bad Science, Bad Medicine, and the Enduring Mistreatment of the Mentally Ill*. Cambridge, Mass.: Perseus Publishing, 2002.

Who's Who of the Colored Race: A General Biographical Dictionary of Men and Women of African Descent. Vol. 1. Chicago: F. L. Mather, 1915.

Williams, Juan. *Eyes on the Prize: America's Civil Rights Years, 1954–1965*. New York: Viking, 1987.

Williams, Lee E., II. *Post-War Riots in America, 1919 and 1946*. Lewiston: The Edwin Mellon Press, 1991.

Williamson, Joel. *The Crucible of Race: Black-White Relations in the American South since Emancipation*. New York: Oxford University Press, 1977.

Wilson, Woodrow. *A History of the American People*. Vol. 5. New York: Wm. H. Wise & Co., 1911.

——. *Epochs of American History: Division and Reunion, 1829–1909*. London: Longmans, Green, and Co., 1912.

Woodside, Moya. *Sterilization in North Carolina: A Sociological and Psychological Study*. Chapel Hill: University of North Carolina Press, 1950.

Wright, Mary Herring. *Far from Home: Memories of World War II and Afterward*. Washington, D.C.: Gallaudet University Press, 2005.

——. *Sounds Like Home: Growing Up Black and Deaf in the South*. Washington, D.C.: Gallaudet University Press, 1999.

DISSERTATIONS AND THESES

Alderson, Adeline Cheryl. "A Study of the Variable of Black Dialect as It Affects the Performance of Black Children on a Speech-Sound Discrimination Test." Master's thesis, University of Northern Iowa, 1971.

Gillespie, Tracy J. "The Effects of Sign Language on Sight Word Acquisition and Retention in Retarded Individuals of Normal Hearing." Master's thesis, St. Cloud University, 1988.

Jones, Ronald Count. "A Survey of Parents of Black Hearing Impaired Children and Their Attitudes Regarding the Educational and Personal Effects of Deafness in Their Children." Ph.D. diss., University of Cincinnati, 1981.

Lehane, Joseph B. "The Morality of American Civil Legislation Concerning Eugenical Sterilization." Ph.D. diss., Catholic University of America, 1944.

McKellar, Margaret. "The Colored Deaf in School and After." Master's thesis, Gallaudet College, n.d.

Palumbo, Delores V. "An Investigation into the Educational, Social, and Legal Status of the Deaf in the Nineteenth and Twentieth Centuries." Master's thesis, Southern Connecticut State College, 1966.

Ritterhouse, Jennifer. "Learning Race: Racial Etiquette and the Socialization of Children in the Jim Crow South." Ph.D. diss., University of North Carolina–Chapel Hill, 1999.

Rutherford, Susan Dell. "A Study of American Deaf Folklore." Ph.D. diss., University of California, Berkeley, 1987.

Thomas, Helen Clark. "Study of the Educational Opportunities Offered in the Negro and White Departments of the Schools for the Deaf in the Southern Region." Master's thesis, Hampton Institute, 1950.

White, David J. "Cherry Hospital: A History Report Presented to the Faculty of Mount Olive College." 29 November 2001.

Acknowledgments

When Junius Wilson died in March 2001, Susan drove from Northern Virginia to Goldsboro, North Carolina, to attend his funeral. Immediately upon her arrival in the town, the transmission in her car gave out. Thus began an unanticipated adventure and, ultimately, unexpected friendships. We would like to thank the good people of Goldsboro for their generosity, including everything from help with tow trucks and directions to rich local stories and a willingness to participate in our research project.

Without the generous support and vast knowledge of several people, this book simply could not have been completed. Our deep thanks go to John Wasson, who provided essential information and introductions to others as well as answers to our many questions. By granting us permission to access medical and legal information, Helen Hinn (the guardian of Mr. Wilson's estate) enabled us to access a life story that otherwise would have remained locked in boxes and filing cabinets. Everett Parker regaled us with personal stories, showing us a deeply human side to this tale. His children Doris Bowden and Everett Parker Jr. provided meals, assistance in translating Raleigh sign language, and additional insight into African American deaf culture in North Carolina. We also wish to thank Rachel Wright and Paul Pooley for extensive help with many details in our research. Attorney Julia Talbutt provided tasty meals and clarified legal questions. Don Edwards became our walking encyclopedia for local Goldsboro information. Warm hospitality and sincere love for their relative Junius Wilson infused the many visits to Willie and Annie Sidberry's home.

Because medical and legal files hold only narrow insights into the lives of people like

Junius Wilson, we relied heavily on oral history interviews. For various reasons some of the people we talked to chose to remain anonymous or only to offer information off the record. Others sent us documents and contact information to further our research. For the many people—named and unnamed—who were willing to trust us with their memories and their artifacts, we offer our sincere and deep thanks.

Other kind folks helped us with the minutiae of historical research. Gifted and dependable, our research assistant Jessica Lee gathered numerous primary sources and shared in our excitement as we pieced this puzzle together. The late psychologist Barbara Brauer donated her files from the Junius Wilson case and offered both her memories of work with him and her passionate interest in mental health treatment for deaf Americans. Bill and Micki Simpson helped us locate vital school information and provided a tour of Morganton. The Lower Cape Fear Historical Society found biographical information and sent it to us, as did Joy Heitman at the Wake County Genealogy Society. We also owe a great debt to Public Services Branch supervisor Debbi Blake and others from the North Carolina State Archives and the state library for their commitment to research and vast knowledge of the history of North Carolina. Teri Carpenter, Carol Morgan, Weebie Berryhill, and Becky Bowen at the State Courthouse in Raleigh helped us navigate the copious pages of Wilson's lawsuits.

Legislative librarian Cathy Martin supplied relevant North Carolina statutes and bills. The staff at Gallaudet University's archives and library have been immensely helpful to us in this project as well as others. We thank Ulf Hedberg, Michael Olson, Sara Robinson, and the others who work there. Researchers who visit the Cherry Hospital Museum are always welcomed by its kind staff. We are grateful to Tanya Rollins and her colleagues for their interest in and support of our project. We also thank Raleigh transcriber Kay McGovern for providing copies of depositions.

This project forced us to examine topics that neither of us had previously studied in depth. We have benefited greatly from the expertise of scholars like Gerry Grob, Kathy Castles, Michael Stein, Johanna Schoen, and Todd Savitt. Special thanks also go to activists of psychiatric survivor networks, especially Vanessa Jackson and members of the organization Mindfreedom. Their insights significantly enhanced our discussion of "life on the inside."

We are fortunate that many gifted and helpful scholars went through our work and offered suggestions. Katherine Ott and Penny Richards have our eternal gratitude for reading and editing multiple drafts of the entire book, enthusiastically supporting the project, and expanding our understanding of lives in the margins of history. Bobby Buchanan, Steven Noll, J. David Smith, and Kim Nielsen also provided essential feedback. We also thank the University of North Carolina Press's anonymous reviewers, whose thoughtful and enthusiastic comments sparked new ideas and improved the manuscript. Charles Joyner and Brenda Jo Brueggemann, masterful wordsmiths both, helped us envision better ways of telling the story. Superb editors Nicole Klungle and Jeannette Redmond made our early chapters shine. We thank them all.

We are privileged to have collaborated with the amazing staff at UNC Press. Sian Hunter assisted us as we went from a few early pages to a full manuscript. Her insights and convictions energized this project and clarified its goal. Our copyeditor Jay Mazzocchi worked magic on our manuscript. Nicole Hayward provided us with the cover design. We appreciate their hard work.

Colleagues in the Department of History and Government at Gallaudet University deserve recognition. Special thanks to Russ Olson, Donna Ryan, Dave Penna, and Barry Bergen for their patience, good humor, and unflagging support.

Multiple trips to North Carolina were necessary to obtain interviews and other vital materials. Dear friends Susie Ehrlich and Jeff Engel, as well as Steve and Liza Hardy-Braz, opened their doors, their refrigerators, and their hearts to us and this project. They have our heartfelt gratitude.

For Ian, David, and Abraham, we owe more than words can capture. They gave us thoughtful suggestions about racism in America, the value of friendships, the intersection of language and identity, and the hope of social justice activism. In words and deeds, they deserve special recognition for helping us bring this story to light. We thank them for their patience, their brilliance, and their love.

Index

Wilmington, N.C., 9, 10–14; and Ku Klux Klan, 32–32
Wilmington Race Riot (1898), 12–14, 17–18. *See also* Race Riots
Wilson, Asynia, 9, 32
Wilson, Junius: and Castle Hayne, 9, 10, 17, 26–27, 32–34, 149; early years, 16–17; perceived as dangerous, 17, 30, 33–34, 37, 38, 40–41, 47–48, 91, 103, 111, 134; at deaf school, 18–20, 24–25, 26, 27–30; legal status of, 38, 59–60, 70, 108, 110–12, 127, 167, 209; enters North Carolina State Hospital for the Colored Insane, 38–41; perceived as not dangerous, 49, 52–53, 60, 111, 112, 188, 259 (n. 40); family seeks return of (1947), 68–71; and age issues, 87, 94–95, 109, 129, 136, 193, 207, 244 (n. 16); and activities, 87–88, 171, 172, 205, 209; experiences stroke, 118–22, 126, 191, 249 (n. 22); during Christmas, 160–61, 179–81, 202–3; death and funeral of, 211–12, 267–68 (nn. 10–11).

Wilson, Mary. *See* Clark, Mary Wilson
Wilson, Sidney, 9–10, 14, 17, 68–70, 105, 239 (n. 77)
Wilson's extended family, 7, 8, 143–44, 146–48, 186–88, 193–96, 206–8, 211, 219 (n. 3); visits with Wilson, 145–46, 160–61, 176, 179–80, 254 (n. 1); and Cherry Hospital, 183–85, 195, 205–6. *See also* individual members; Legal challenges and court cases
Woodard Building, 107, 113, 124, 134, 160–61, 172, 173, 174, 260–61 (n. 50)
Wooten, Pandora, 85, 242 (n. 67)
Work: and institutionalized people, 42, 43, 51–52, 56–58, 63–64, 68, 83–84; and forced labor, 57; as therapy, 57, 98, 113; Wilson and patients selling goods, 76–77, 86, 109; and McNeil, 59, 80–81, 83, 86–88; Wilson and car wash, 97–99, 114, 245 (n. 44). *See also* Desegregation; Farm Colony
Wright, Mary, 24
Wright, Rachel, 113–18, 223–24 (n. 57)